STRANGE DUETS

STUDIES IN

THEATRE HISTORY

AND CULTURE

Edited by Thomas Postlewait

KIM MARRA

Strange Duets

Impresarios and Actresses in the American Theatre, 1865–1914

UNIVERSITY OF IOWA PRESS, IOWA CITY

University of Iowa Press, Iowa City 52242

Copyright © 2006 by the University of Iowa Press

www.uiowapress.org

Printed in the United States of America

Design by Richard Hendel

The University of Iowa Press is a member of Green Press Initiative
and is committed to preserving natural resources.

Printed on acid-free paper

Library of Congress Cataloging-in-Publication Data

Marra, Kim, 1957–.

Strange duets: impresarios and actresses in the American theatre,
1865–1914 / by Kim Marra.

p.   cm.—(Studies in theatre history and culture)

Includes bibliographical references and index.

ISBN-10: 0-87745-993-2 (cloth)

ISBN-13: 978-0-87745-993-4 (cloth)

1. Actresses—United States—Biography.

2. Impresarios—United States—Biography.   I. Title.   II. Series.

PN2286.8.M37 2006

792.02'8092273—dc22   2006044524

[B]

06   07   08   09   10   C   5   4   3   2   1

For my mother and father,

Diane de Nancrede Marra

and

Ronald Anthony Marra

CONTENTS

ACKNOWLEDGMENTS

This book has been fourteen years in the making. Many individuals and organizations helped me along the way. First, I must thank Thomas Postlewait, editor of the Studies in Theatre History and Culture Series. After contracting the project in 1999, Tom responded to various drafts with extraordinary thoroughness, rigor, and insight. He is truly the type of editor who helps one discover what one's subject really is and how best to present it. I also benefited greatly from his choice of John Frick as an outside reader whose enthusiastic and careful review of the manuscript spurred my efforts on the final revision. This is a much sharper, better-written book because of Tom's strong editorial hand and John's detailed comments. I am deeply grateful to Holly Carver, director of the University of Iowa Press, for her friendship and for all the care and sagacious guidance she has given this project. Thanks also to her dedicated and gracious staff, whom I have been able to meet and work with on a personal basis: Karen Copp, Joseph Parsons, Allison Thomas, Rhonda Wetjen, Deidre Woods, and Charlotte Wright. It has been a special pleasure to see the book go through the production process on my home campus. I extend gratitude as well to my meticulous and congenial copy editor, Michael Levine, of New York City.

Research in archives provided the lifeblood of this project. I received generous assistance from Marty Jacobs in the Theatre Collection of the Museum of the City of New York; Robert Taylor and the Reading Room staff of the Billy Rose Theatre Collection at the New York Public Library for the Performing Arts; Bernard Crystal at the Rare Book and Manuscript Library of Columbia University; Jeanne Newlin at the Harvard Theatre Collection; Bernard McTigue at the University of Oregon Special Collections; Kath Pennavaria at the Kinsey Institute for Sex, Gender, and Reproduction; Sidney Huttner and Kathryn Hodson in the University of Iowa Special Collections; and the University of Iowa reference librarians Helen Ryan and Kathy Magarrell. While ensconced in the Billy Rose Theatre Collection, I met Mary Ellen Kelly, Belascophile extraordinaire. She has my great gratitude for all the camaraderie, help, and insight she has given me over the years, and for her illuminating interview with erotica historian Dr. Clifford Scheiner. Conversations with fellow archival travelers Craig Clinton about Mrs. Leslie Carter and Aileen Hendricks-Wenck about Ada Rehan also enlivened my research. Thanks to Cindy Rosenthal for gathering some initial *Chantecler* material for me from the Billy Rose, including the photograph of the two "chics" on the cover, and to Marlis Schweitzer for sharing the *Chantecler* hats.

For help with illustrations, I would like to thank Marguerite Lavin in Rights and Reproductions of the Museum of the City of New York; Bettina Smith of the Folger Shakespeare Library; Nancy Shawcross and John Pollack of the Rare Book and Manuscript Library of the University of Pennsylvania; and Nicolette Bromberg of the University of Washington Special Collections Department. Kathleen Kleugel and Dawn Schmitz heroically unearthed a photograph for me from among some five thousand items in the as yet uncatalogued Theodore Leavitt Collection of theatre prints at the University of Illinois at Urbana-Champaign Library. Thanks to Peter Davis in the Illinois Department of Theatre for helping to facilitate that search.

My archival research was funded with a travel grant from the National Endowment for the Humanities and numerous awards from the University of Iowa: two Old Gold Summer Fellowships, a College of Liberal Arts and Sciences Dean's Scholar Award, two grants from the Arts and Humanities Initiative, and a book subvention from the Office of the Vice President for Research. In the final phases of revision, I was in residence at the Obermann Center for Advanced Studies at the University of Iowa, where I benefited from the generous support of Jay Semel, Carolyn Frisbie, and Karla Tonella.

Work on this project coincided with work on three books on gays and lesbians in American theatre history that I co-edited with Robert Schanke. His fellowship and wise counsel have been mainstays of support all along the way. I also cherish the ongoing friendship of my college mentor, Nancy Kindelan, who first encouraged me to specialize in American theatre history, and to do so within the framework of American Studies. Numerous other colleagues have lent assistance by reading and commenting on various parts of this book, joining forces on related panels, engaging in formative conversations, and inspiring me with their own scholarship in American theatre studies. In particular, I would like to acknowledge Rosemarie Bank, Jill Dolan, Harley Erdman, Barbara Grossman, Alison Kibler, Margaret Knapp, Bruce McConachie, Elizabeth Mullenix, Renée Sentilles, Don Wilmeth, and Stacy Wolf. Many thanks to Ellen Gainor and Jeffrey Mason, editors of *Performing America* (1999), for their helpful comments on my essay, parts of which are incorporated in revised form in chapter 2. I am also grateful for the inspiration and insights of the Feminist Historiography Working Group of the

American Society for Theatre Research, and especially for the scholarly models offered by its founders, Gay Cima and Tracy Davis.

At the University of Iowa, my Americanist reading group—Kathleen Diffley, Laura Rigal, and Leslie Schwalm—cheerfully read multiple drafts of every chapter and continually enriched this work with their astute comments and encouragement. Many other colleagues cheered me on by reading various parts of the manuscript, attending talks drawn from the material, and helpfully responding to my constant stories of these strange duets. They are Bluford Adams, Loyce Arthur, Florence Babb, Susan Birrell, Art Borreca, John Cameron, Dare Clubb, Corey Creekmur, Eric Forsythe, Richard Horwitz, Kevin Kopelson, Judy Leigh-Johnson, Teresa Mangum, William Moser, Judith Pascoe, John Raeburn, Victoria Rovine, David Schaal, Claire Sponsler, and Nicholas Yablon. A special word of thanks goes to Jane Desmond, who has made team teaching a rich pleasure and taught me much about doing cultural studies and reading the body queerly. I am very grateful as well to my two department chairs, Alan MacVey in Theatre Arts and Lauren Rabinovitz in American Studies, for their unflagging understanding and support over the long journey. Their planning enabled me to have research assistance from several graduate students: Kirsten Greenidge, Suzanne Hauser, Eriko Ogihara, Danielle Rich, Matthew Thomas, and Charles Williams.

My partner, Meredith Alexander, has lived with this project for more than half of our marriage. Her motivation to see it completed has often exceeded my own. I thank her for listening, sometimes to points beyond endurance; for reading countless drafts of papers and chapters over the years and then finding the fortitude to review the whole manuscript in the crunch of final revisions; for keeping me company and assisting me on long research trips, even helping me pore over some of the titles at the Kinsey that were in Belasco's pornography collection; for lending her insights as a professionally trained actor, director, and acting teacher; for allowing me inordinate amounts of time to work; and for sustaining me in ways I can't enumerate. My stepchildren and grandchildren, Ashley, Karl, Maile, and Henry Smith Souza, Jessica Smith, M.D., and Zachary and Page Smith, also generously gave gifts of time, understanding, and joyful company, as did their father and grandfather, Bradford Hansen-Smith. In the last two years, new joy has arrived with the miraculous births of Dilen and Ronly Marra to my brother, Kendall Marra, and sister-in-law, Susan McCormack. Maybe someday my nieces and grandchildren will read this book and understand more about the odd and consuming passion for theatre history that has become part of their heritage.

My mother, Diane Marra, and father, Ronald Marra, never graduated from college, but they furthered my education in every way they could, and in ways they might not have planned or anticipated. It was they who first made me wonder about the dynamics of strange duets. My mother was a beautiful, venturesome woman of many talents, including professional acting, singing, and rodeo riding. Research trips East always included stops to visit her and exchange stories at her home in Pennsylvania. I wish she had lived to savor this book's publication with me. I am blessed that my father and stepmother, Adair Marra, both avid theatergoers, are very much here to do so.

Introduction

In the spring of 1888, Daly's Theatre company set sail for a momentous English tour. The repertoire featured impresario Augustin Daly's adaptation of *The Taming of the Shrew*, starring his leading lady, Ada Rehan, as the eponymous Katharine. *Shrew*'s London premier would mark the first production of a Shakespearean comedy by an American company on the bard's home turf.[1] The performance pressures bearing on Daly and his players were enormous. Additional tensions flared within the company when Daly aroused Rehan's jealousy by starting a flirtation with her cabin mate, Phoebe Russell, who played the supporting role of Bianca. Daly continued such taunts during the early weeks of the tour, and they culminated in near disaster the night of *Shrew*'s much-anticipated opening. While preparing for the performance, Rehan discovered a note backstage in Daly's handwriting containing the message: "Enclosed you will find $200. There is more where this comes from." Because of the ongoing flirtation, Rehan assumed the money was intended for Russell, though it was actually for Daly's paid puff, William Winter, the dean of American theatre critics, who had accompanied the troupe to England. In a rage, Rehan refused to perform. Daly had to implore her on bended knee, whereupon, according to a witness, she took his hand to her mouth and bit his flesh "to the bone." With Daly's blood fresh on her lips, Rehan commanded the play to begin a half hour late. Still seething with fury when she entered as Katharine, her performance reportedly "took the audience's breath away."[2] The London *Era* exclaimed:

> If a better Katharine has been seen on the boards than Ada Rehan, we have not seen her. From the moment this lady swept on to the stage in a whirlwind of 'temper'... boxing her sister's ears [Russell as Bianca], jousting at flouts and jeers with Petruchio, and breaking the flute over the musician's head, to the final scene of all, when tamed and transformed, she lectures her fellow wives upon their duties and makes sweet submission to her lord, Miss Rehan held the audience firmly in her grip.[3]

As well as marking the zenith of Rehan's acting career, the transformation of Katharine from raging virago into supplicant helpmate perfectly played out on stage the sexually charged game of power and acquiescence that Daly regularly played backstage with his leading lady.

Such stagings of sexual conquest were part of a broader web of social and economic aspirations that impresario and actress pursued together.[4] To audiences on both sides of the Atlantic, the performance signaled a major victory for emergent American "high culture" and its self-proclaimed apostle, Augustin Daly (1838–1899).[5] A theatrical autocrat, Daly controlled all aspects of his domain, from box office and marketing to the minutest details of staging the plays. Along with choosing and often writing or doctoring the scripts, he cast and rehearsed the players and even attempted to dictate their conduct offstage as well as on. He gave as much attention to the decor and architecture of his theatre buildings as he did to designing settings and costumes. With such impresarial control, he aimed to achieve unprecedented levels of artistic unity and civility in American theatrical production.[6] Ada Rehan (1860–1916) proved to be the most famous and enduring member of his company. During the two decades of their involvement (1879–1899), Daly's Theatre became the preeminent "drawing-room home of the drama," and Rehan, with Katharine as her signature role, a widely worshipped national icon.[7] In making her a star, Daly also made himself a success. Through their stormy partnership, he and his actress, both from impoverished Irish Catholic immigrant roots, rose to the heights of Anglo-American society. Commentators compared them in status to British theatre royalty, the soon-to-be knighted actor-manager, Henry Irving, and his leading lady, Ellen Terry. Fashionable women sought to emulate Rehan's dress and mannerisms. Daly became a governor of the Shakespeare Memorial in Stratford and a founding member of New York's exclusive men's club, the Players, which commingled respectable theatrical leaders, powerful businessmen, and noted literati.[8]

Daly's and Rehan's ascent heralded a major post–Civil War development in which the managerial role, traditionally fulfilled by the leading actor or actress who organized the staging (usually to his or her benefit), evolved into a separate occupation. Company management was assumed either by the producer who oversaw all the elements of the commercial enterprise or the director, a new figure who took responsibility for unifying the elements of acting and design according to his interpretation of the play. An impresario like Daly, functioning as both producer and director, claimed managerial omnipotence. As the occupation of manager separated from that of actor or actress and gained executive power, it also became an increasingly male preserve. Audiences seeking both pleasure and respectability favored male over female managers because they believed men were more suited to positions of authority and could better control the theatre's potentially dangerous and seductive entertainments.[9]

While men took over theatrical management, actresses increasingly outstripped actors in popularity and profitability. In 1891, Benjamin Orange Flower, the editor of *Arena* magazine, proclaimed: "The era of Woman has dawned, bearing the unmistakable prophecy of a far higher civilization than humanity has ever known."[10] Woman triumphed on stage as well as in society. Writing in the *New York Times* in 1905, the critic "Pendennis" explained why:

> It is the woman who confirms most vividly in the theatre the illusion of power and passion. It is the woman who fastens upon us the heart-tones and all the bantering witchcraft of undiscovered sources of feeling across the footlights. . . .
>
> In the bigger dream we call life they are the same, it is women who make its real surprise, it is women who give it heart and comfort, or darkness and confusion, and so it is in the theatre, where all that is seemingly poetic in the actor is but the movement of a woman's plot.
>
> The essential ingredient in a play is the woman.[11]

Given the greater drawing power of the woman on stage, numerous managers, following Daly's example, launched performers of both genders to stardom but achieved the greatest success with female stars. The Pygmalion or, more particularly, the racially marked Svengali mode of star making became a key theme of the era.

Daly's two most successful followers in this managerial line were Charles Frohman (1860–1915), for whom the career-making actress was Maude Adams (1872–1953), and David Belasco (1854–1931), for whom it was Mrs. Leslie Carter (1862–1937).[12] Like Daly, Frohman and Belasco came from poor immigrant roots; both were Jewish at a time when Jews, as well as Irish (and Italians and many others), were classified among nonwhite "races."[13] Frohman was of more assimilable German extraction, Belasco of Sephardic Portugese descent yet "Oriental" in appearance. Each sought upward mobility by turning a struggling or outcast Gentile woman into a luminous star. Other entertainment entrepreneurs also came from poor immigrant backgrounds and advanced their careers with female stars, including Frohman's brother Daniel; their rivals Lee, Sam, and J. J. Shubert; the musical comedy team of Edward Harrigan and Tony Hart; the early vaudevillian Tony Pastor;

the burlesque wizards Joe Weber and Lew Fields; and the follies impresario Florenz Ziegfeld. In most of these cases, as with the Anglo-American vaudeville magnates B. F. Keith and Edward Albee, the relationship with any single female star was relatively short because the impresarios promoted a changing roster of talent. Part of what set the partnerships of Daly and Rehan, Frohman and Adams, and Belasco and Carter apart from other impresario and actress pairings was their remarkable duration. Daly and Rehan were together twenty years, Frohman and Adams twenty-five, and Belasco and Carter seventeen. While Daly, Frohman, and Belasco managed other female stars for shorter periods during these years, Rehan, Adams, and Carter remained their respective primary leading ladies. Because they were together for such a long time, the identities of the two individuals within each couple became bound up with one another to an extraordinary degree. Unlike other highly successful theatrical entrepreneurs, Daly, Frohman, and Belasco each moved up the socioeconomic hierarchy to the top of their profession chiefly with one particular actress.

Along with the duration of their relationships, these three impresario and actress couples were also distinguished by the venue and genre in which they specialized. Rather than vaudeville, circus, or burlesque, they worked in the "legitimate" theatre.[14] Even though managers of other venues were instituting reforms to draw respectable audiences, the legitimate theatre was still the venue of greatest social cachet and thus the one in which the expectations for impressing the richest and most powerful classes were the greatest. Based in the legitimate theatre, these couples primarily produced spoken drama, as opposed to musical comedy, variety, or short farcical sketches. Their relationships involved the special rigors of training to sustain a believable, lifelike character through a live performance of a full-length play. That credibility hinged not only on highly skilled outward physicality but also on the ability to convey an inner emotional truth at a time when both expert medical opinion and popular belief held that female emotions sprang primarily from the reproductive organs and hence were fundamentally sexual in nature. Accordingly, through their long-term star-making relationships, Daly, Frohman, and Belasco could profess to exert greater control than managers in other theatrical venues and genres over actresses and their sexuality.

Within the realm of legitimate theatre, there were other famous duos, but none that rivaled these three status-seeking Svengalis and their protégées in attaining both commercial clout and social prestige. For example, the Canadian born half-Indian McKee Rankin purportedly wielded a "Svengali-like influence" for more than a decade over the beautiful Nance O'Neil whom *The Critic* described as "thoroughly American."[15] However, Rankin's erratic temper and record in business prevented the pair from achieving sustained financial reward and a high degree of social respectability. E. H. Sothern and Julia Marlowe and Harrison Grey Fiske and Minnie Maddern Fiske had more egalitarian but less sensational relationships, at least partly because of their more genteel Anglo-American personas and the fact that they were legally married. Primarily an actor, Sothern played opposite his wife when the two toured as a celebrated Shakespearean combination. They prospered from their fame but had to rely on other producers and thus could not acquire fortune and power equivalent to that of the leading impresario-actress couples. The Fiskes operated in defiance of the commerical power structure and alternated established, popular fare with more artistic, socially challenging dramas, such as the plays of Ibsen. While managing the industry's primary trade paper, *The Dramatic Mirror*, Harrison wrote and produced some of the works in which his wife appeared. Yet she also wrote, produced, and directed plays as well as acted. Occasionally the Fiskes profited financially from their productions, but by 1911 Harrison had to sell the paper and by 1914 had declared bankruptcy.[16] They and others achieved greater artistic and critical distinction than the three couples at the center of this study; however, without sustaining commercial success, they could not command as great a hold on public attention.

Amassing wealth and fame through long records of profitable plays, Daly and Rehan, Frohman and Adams, and Belasco and Carter reigned over the commercial production of spoken drama. Moreover, they did so during the American theatre's most culturally and socially prominent era. In the decades between the Civil War and World War I, before cinema usurped its position, the commercial theatre, centered in New York City, was the nation's leading entertainment medium. With its higher prestige and generally more lifelike production values than vaudeville or burlesque, the legitimate theatre most directly promulgated the fashions, manners, and beliefs of the upper classes. In cities and towns across the country, as the old resident stock companies gave way first to touring stars and then whole productions touring from New York City on the rapidly expanding railway system, Broadway theatre became national theatre.[17] Nationally circulating magazines and newspapers featuring photographic reproductions made possible by newly invented halftone engraving kept the names and faces of theatrical luminaries before a transcontinental audience. These technologies fueled a burgeoning culture of celebrity focused on image and personality in which readers avidly followed the on- and offstage lives of stars and their makers.[18] In this era, theatrical personalities gained a level of media attention comparable to that lavished on Hollywood stars today.

But more than individual celebrity, Daly and Rehan, Frohman and Adams, and Belasco and Carter drew keen public interest as long-term, "legitimate" couples at a time of historic challenges to white, Anglo-Saxon Protestant male dominance and traditional gender roles. The period from 1865 to 1914 was one of enormous cultural transformation. Major changes included a shift from a predominately rural to a predominately urban industrial economy, rapid imperial expansion across the frontier and beyond U.S. borders, a massive influx of immigrants from southern and eastern Europe into northeastern cities, a series of chaotic economic panics and labor disputes, advancements in women's rights and the breakdown of Victorian gender roles, and the formation of the modern categories of hetero- and homosexuality.[19] Amid these changes, self-made titans of industry like John D. Rockefeller and Andrew Carnegie became cultural heroes by creating monopolies and attaining new levels of male power, even as increasing numbers of women defied tradition and claimed male prerogatives. Leading authorities in science, medicine, politics, and journalism, informed by Darwinian theories of evolution, linked unruly women and racial and sexual Others to savages and perverts or "inverts" in need of taming and containment. Rising up together from lowly "racial" and class origins, impresarios and actresses compelled intense fascination because of how, as highly visible celebrities, they played out these cultural tensions, both onstage in performance and, often most intensively and intriguingly, behind the scenes in the process of training and rehearsal. Indeed, to a large degree, institutionalized actor training in the United States came into being in the sexually and racially charged context of these impresario and actress relationships.

With spectacular élan, the impresarios emulated the consolidation of power that industrial titans enacted in the business world, while their star actresses embodied various aspects of the newly emergent American "Womanhood" that B. O. Flower and many others heralded. Of the three men, only Frohman became part of an actual monopoly, the Theatrical Syndicate, which formed in 1896, but Daly and Belasco were no less monopolistic of authority within their organizations. Like Rockefeller, Carnegie, and other contemporary paragons of entrepreneurial success, all three adopted an imperial, conquering style in their management practices and in the architecture and decor of their theatres. Daly's Fifth Avenue Theatre (1873) and Daly's Theatre at 30th and Broadway (1879), Frohman's Empire Theatre (1893), and Belasco's Republic (1901) and Stuyvesant (1907) Theatres each echoed elements of the classical revival architecture and decor that connoted the absolute power of the French Bourbon kings and the self-made Emperor Napoleon. Trappings of great wealth—fine upholstery, lush carpeting, velvet drapery, gilt carvings, ornate domed ceilings, and artworks—adorned the interiors. Although graduated ticket prices allowed middle- and some lower-middle-class patrons to attend performances at these theatres, the impresarios wanted most to impress high society, the members of Ward McAllister's Four Hundred, and celebrated military and political leaders. Increasingly, women—the wives and daughters of this aristocracy as well as middle-class matrons and "matinee girls"—dominated theatrical attendance, but Daly, Frohman, and Belasco still sought above all to gain the admiration and respect of America's most powerful men.[20] That quest became most pointedly evident at premieres, when the fruits of the struggles in rehearsal were triumphantly revealed for high society approval. For these occasions, the impresario would prepare playbills and often expensively bound souvenir programs with a heading built around the key verb "presents," as in "Charles Frohman Presents Maude Adams in *Peter Pan*." Thus, whatever the particular play was about, the production was also about a presumed model of male managerial achievement and control.

As the centerpiece of her impresario's presentation, the star protégée embodied a luminous yet potentially volatile combination of feminine forces. If the "era of Woman" had dawned, the so-called "New Woman" was perhaps its most talked about representative. A multifaceted type, she was supposedly more modern, more energetic, far less deferential and modest, and, in the era's increasingly visual culture, more beautiful and robust than her Victorian forebears. As such, she was a figure of enormous marketability and sex appeal. But potentially more threatening to the social order, she also embodied feminist independence and political aspirations and growing influence in the new industrial, consumer-driven economy. Rehan, Adams, and Carter did not explicitly identify with the label "New Woman," nor did they publicly advocate for her main political cause of woman suffrage (as did Olive Logan, Ethel Barrymore, and other actresses of the period), nor pursue her demand of higher education.[21] Nevertheless, as highly successful, unmarried working women, they represented other key aspects of New Womanhood. With their long professional history, actresses, as Simone de Beauvoir would point out in *The Second Sex*, were pioneers in the area of women's employment and economic achievement.[22] Historically, their public professionalism and independence carried the stigma of sexual licentiousness, which turn-of-the-century moralists feared would be the result of the New Woman's push for greater power and freedom. These particular actresses—Rehan, Adams, and Carter—were also highly athletic, an attribute of the New Woman that the popular illustrator Charles Dana Gibson, for example, celebrated in his widely reproduced images of the Gibson Girl.[23] Their physical prowess, seemingly unquenchable appetite for gorgeous sets and costumes, and unruly sexuality that was the legacy of their profession made control of these actresses' bodies a special challenge and a social necessity. In appearing to meet that challenge, Daly, Frohman, and Belasco reassured audiences that the exhilarating but anxiety-producing New Woman could be simultaneously bridled and enjoyed.

Although the balance of power in these relationships was ostensibly tipped heavily in favor of the impresarios, the couples, in fact, functioned as highly symbiotic duets with each party linked to the other in a dynamic of mutual dependency in pursuit of complementary personal and professional goals. Daly lorded his authority over *Taming of the Shrew*, but Rehan reduced him to a bleeding, kneeling beggar by refusing to go on. He needed her performance to publicly realize his power as much as she needed him to promote her career. As the London *Era* noted, it was she who "held the audience firmly in her grip"; he could only do so through her. This intertwining of fortunes was true of all three couples, but their duets were composed of very different personalities and passions and thus contained distinctive leitmotifs. Tall, lithe, blue-eyed, and handsome, Daly "tamed" the fiery, statuesque Rehan while actively subscribing to the double standard of sexual morality. With the cleverly nunlike Adams, who hailed from the Mormon West, the squat, balding Frohman danced a colorfully coded, highly witty pas de deux founded on shared understandings about each other's secret homosexual lifestyles. In marked contrast, the diminutive, Mandarin-collared Belasco staged a torrid opera of carnal expiation with the infamously lapsed convent girl, Mrs. Leslie Carter, through which she pursued social restoration as a mother and he a pseudo-priestly mission to heave the bosoms of the power elite.

These were "strange" duets, partly because of the impresarios' and actresses' marginalized "racial" and religious roots, but also because of how they crisscrossed the borders of tradition and propriety. Each couple operated within an accepted professional framework of manager-employee relations, yet their bond also invoked more personal connections. As the principal occupants of theatres configured as palatial "homes," they could stand in the public imagination for husband and wife, even though all but Rehan and Carter were married or domestically partnered with others. More titillatingly, their relationships suggested a long-term liaison—in the cases of Frohman and Adams and Belasco and Carter, a cross-"racial" liaison—between man and mistress or, given their immense wealth, emperor and consort. Rumors to that effect, however well or ill founded, helped sell tickets, served the impression of male potency and female allure, and sometimes usefully distracted attention from other dealings behind the scenes. Whether the imagined relation was marital or extramarital, audiences saw the impresario proffer lavish *mise-en-scènes* filled with expensive, often exotic costumes, sets, and props, to display his leading lady, whose star turn manifested his self-made manhood as well as her professional success. Avidly consuming press coverage of these celebrity couples, fans looked not only for confirmation of these outward shows of power and respectability but also for humanizing or scintillating cracks in the facade. Impresarios and actresses well understood and played to these ambivalent needs through play choices and media manipulation. Public on a vast scale yet also intriguingly private, their relationships inspired visions of both idealized and forbidden conduct in a climate of increasing turmoil between men and women, management and labor, and white and nonwhite "races."

To explore the distinctive interactions these theatrical potentates developed with their leading ladies, this study looks at the three impresarios in turn, with two chapters devoted to Daly, two to Frohman, and three to Belasco. In each case, the first of the chapters examines the impresario's early dealings with women and other associates that shaped his later relationship with his primary leading lady. The second (and third in Belasco's case) of the chapters then turns to that primary relationship and to how the on- and offstage performances of impresario and actress tapped into the tastes and social preoccupations of audiences. Sexuality is central to this investigation because demonstrable management of carnal appetites was the key to the upward mobility sought by both impresario and actress. Private habits of these celebrities—notably, pornography collecting, extramarital affairs, and intimate same-sex liaisons—informed perceptions and behavior that entered the rehearsal hall and the stage as well as the bedroom and thus had public consequence. Moreover, sexuality—its control or lack thereof—mobilized prevailing assumptions about gender, "race," and class. Taking all these interlocking forces and facets of identity into account, the analysis makes extensive use of primary sources such as letters, diaries, memoirs, scrapbooks, clipping files, promptbooks, programs, and production photographs and illustrations (forty of which are reproduced in the book) in major archives on each of the six principal figures. Their relationships and the performances they produced richly illuminate the culturally formative era at the turn of the last century, when the whitest "races" claimed the greatest sexual control and the theatre dominated the cultural landscape.

STRANGE DUETS

1

Pioneering on the Theatrical Frontier

AUGUSTIN DALY'S EARLY VENTURES

*No apology is needed for giving an account of
the man who lifted the American stage from a
very low estate to a position of great dignity,
and gave the dramatic art of his own country
a first place in two continents; and who did
all his life work with such courage in the face
of obstacles and such steadfastness in pursuit
of a single purpose, that the history of his
career must give heart to every self-reliant,
intelligent striver in every business of life.*

—Joseph Francis Daly, preface to
The Life of Augustin Daly, 1917

In the annals of theatre history, Augustin Daly (1838–1899) holds the status of first American *régisseur*, or autocratic producer-director. Employing methods analogous to those of the seminal European *régisseurs* Richard Wagner and Georg II, Duke of Saxe-Meiningen, Daly made each stage presentation a realization of his own, singular vision. Like Wagner, he believed his vision would edify both theatre and society, and like Saxe-Meiningen, he invoked the posture of a state authority figure to enforce its realization. Company members addressed him as governor, while less flattering commentators compared his regime to that of a Napoleonic dictator, Roman emperor, military commander, martinet, and mounted despot driving his company with whip and spur. With his authoritarian methods, Daly exceeded earlier managers in his attempts to control the anarchy and disrepute associated with the unruly audiences and itinerant stars who had dominated much antebellum theatrical activity. In so doing, he achieved an unprecedented level of civility and artistic unity in stage production in the United States, set the mold for later autocratic impresarios, and thereby contributed instrumentally to the modernization of American theatre.

Stanley Kauffmann, in one of the most recent published studies of Daly, finds the American *régisseur*'s contributions all the more remarkable because he accomplished them in a relative cultural vacuum; that is, unlike Wagner and Saxe-Meiningen, Daly lacked the support of a well-established system of state-sponsored theatre and orchestra whose increasingly romantic repertoires necessitated an omnipotent interpretive conductor. To account for how Daly achieved his innovations without such benefits, Kauffmann concludes: "Daly . . . seems to have summoned from within his own being the equivalent of the large cultural forces that had caused change in Europe."[1]

Kauffmann's assertion is both problematic and illuminating—problematic because there was significant cultural context, including some direct American theatrical antecedents, for Daly's innovations, but illuminating because the production of "his own being" was central to his enterprise. Where Wagner's and Saxe-Meiningen's autocracies were linked to German unification and the nationalizing myth of a collective *volk*, Daly's was tied to post–Civil War U.S. expansion and the American nationalizing myth of bourgeois individualism. The absence of government sponsorship for his efforts, rather than a disadvantage, as Kauffmann implies, was precisely the condition that enabled them. Instead of state-sponsored artistic institutions, venture capitalism and private business provided the primary cultural as well as economic framework for his career. In the 1850s and 1860s several entrepreneurs, including his own father-in-law, demonstrated the viability of theatre companies as respectable business ventures. Daly expressed his admiration of the self-made business tycoon when he compared himself to a "foreman in Carnegie's steelworks." After he opened his first theatre in 1869, Daly invoked the image of a captain of industry: "I went upon the stage and felt as one who treads the deck of a ship as its master."[2]

This is not to argue that Daly's enterprise was driven more by profit than artistic motives but rather to suggest that the two impulses were conjoined in his pursuit of success. For Daly, making theatre and making money were primarily means of making himself or achieving selfhood in dominant cultural terms. That is, under increasingly urban and xenophobic circumstances, the production of respectable, profitable theatre provided a way of overcoming the disadvantages of his relatively impoverished Irish Catholic origins and gaining acceptance into Anglo-Saxon-Protestant, bourgeois society. An arriviste, Daly sought upward mobility not only socioeconomically and culturally, but also in terms of gender; he aspired to a standard of proper and accomplished manhood sanctioned by the ruling class.[3] Helping to set that standard, Civil War generals provided the models for executive—including presidential—leadership amid the northern industrial and westward expansion of the Gilded Age.[4] Daly echoed the aggressive rhetoric of military and capitalist heroes when he wrote to his closest confidant and first biographer, his brother Joseph Francis Daly, in 1865: "I have the will and disposition to ride over every puny obstacle."[5] Like Andrew Carnegie, he advanced through conquest in the business sphere. Rather than land and ore, the theatre, and especially its putatively wayward and seductive leading ladies, became the raw matter he cultivated for profit. As Daly ventured into theatre, first as a curious youth and then professionally as a journalist, playwright, tour manager, and publicist, encounters with various actresses prompted his major career transitions and shaped his emerging social and artistic aims.

Beginning the Battle of Life

As Joseph Daly, Augustin's younger brother, close collaborator, and biographer, notes: "It was owing to the impression made upon my brother's mind by the conditions existing in his youth that he instituted reforms in every direction when he opened his first theatre."[6] Joseph and Augustin spent that youth with their mother, Elizabeth Daly, the daughter of Irish Catholic immigrants, on the Southeast Coast. Their father, the Irish-born Captain Denis

Daly, had staked his fortune on the trading ship *Victor* in the West Indies before settling in Plymouth, North Carolina, to start his family. He died of fever contracted at sea in 1841 when Augustin was just three years old and Joseph still a toddler. After settling her husband's affairs, Elizabeth moved with her boys to Norfolk, Virginia, where she enrolled them in school and took up sewing to support them. In 1849, when Augustin was eleven and Joseph nine, the family moved North and made New York its permanent home. By his early teenage years, Augustin was eager to make his own way; according to Joseph, he had "inherited to the full" the "adventurous disposition and fearlessness" of his father.[7]

"Much to the distress of our dear mother," continues Joseph, young Augustin determined to wage his "battle of life" in the theatre, a future the family regarded with fear and suspicion:

> The dread of contamination from too close association with things theatrical, which my mother in common with many other people felt in that day, was excusable for more than one reason. Theatrical management was then precarious, and places of amusement were open to grave objections. The playhouse deserved the hard things that were said about it. In every theatre there was an upper tier with a bar where strong drinks were supplied and (in some houses) where the profligate of both sexes resorted. To be sure there was no necessity for the patrons of the family circle or the boxes to come in contact with such visitors, as the bad company was confined to the upper and cheaper parts of the house — the "shilling gallery," admission to which was twelve and a half cents (there was a coin of that value in those days); but it was natural to fear that to that part of the house young men bent upon seeing life would be tempted, for access to it was open.[8]

This description aligns Mrs. Daly's opinions with familiar strains of nineteenth-century Protestant bourgeois moralizing that set the theatre in opposition to the civilizing influence of home. Besides evoking lust, the theatre incited anarchy and violence. As Joseph notes, when he and his family moved to the city, New York was still reeling from the Astor Place Riot, the violent class conflict that erupted in the Astor Place Opera House on 10 May 1849 over the rivalry between the native-born star Edwin Forrest and the touring English actor William Charles Macready.[9] A reputation for degeneracy and danger placed the theatre, in the words of the actress playwright Anna Cora Mowatt, "on the outer side of a certain conventional pale of society."[10]

To young Augustin, this urban theatrical frontier, like the mythologized Western frontier, offered both temptation and opportunity. Joseph tells of the delight the two teenaged brothers took in the mixed bills offered at Niblo's, the Bowery, the National, the Metropolitan, Wallack's, and Burton's, where for twenty-five cents they could see "a five-act tragedy, then a *pas seul* by a favorite *danseuse*, perhaps a comic song, and the whole to conclude with a rattling farce or a gorgeous extravaganza."[11] In the spring of 1853, Gertrude Dawes thrilled the boys at the Bowery with her Cowboy *pas seul* in *The Robbers of the Rhine* and *The Writing on the Wall* and another dance in *The Serious Family* at Niblo's.[12] At Wallack's, they savored the musical performances of Miss Malvina Pray, "who was soon to become Mrs. W. J. Florence and to dance through a hundred parts, from Yankee Gal to Mrs. Gilflory." These were comic roles in which she appeared opposite her husband, who pursued her as "Irish Boy."[13] The brothers also followed the scandalous career of Lola Montez, although Joseph later disparaged her as a "freak of ambition" for parlaying her past as the mistress of Franz Liszt and King Ludwig I of Bavaria into star billing in spite of a lack of real dancing or acting talent.[14]

Besides simply enjoying the feminine allurements of the stage, Augustin was motivated even as a teenager to seek opportunities to work upon and shape them. When he saw the "child of nature" Julia Dean in *Tortesa the Usurer*, probably soon after her November 1854 opening at the Metropolitan, Augustin declared: "Some day I shall write a play for her!"[15] Along with his playwriting aspirations, he was driven by what his brother calls "a haunting desire to become familiar with management."[16] A portrait photograph (fig. 1) shows a sixteen-year-old Daly already suited up in adult managerial garb looking like a budding venture capitalist ready to seek his fortune. The managerial occupation was "then precarious," as Joseph notes, because predominately male audiences overindulged in liquor, consorted with prostitutes, and disruptively expressed their opinions of performances. Moreover, traveling stars demanded that stock players and personnel give them center stage and the lion's share of receipts.[17] Daly's primary models for countering these challenges to managerial authority were W. E. Burton and James William Wallack and his son Lester, who were also star players but maintained their own theatres and ran viable stock companies known for ensemble playing. They instituted reforms that eliminated prostitution and disorderly conduct in order to make the theatre more appealing to the respectable classes.[18]

Inspired by their example, Daly, at the age of eighteen, "conceived the incredible idea of hiring a real theatre for one night and giving a genuine public

1. *The budding impresario Augustin Daly at age sixteen, in Joseph Daly,* The Life of Augustin Daly, *op. p. 19.*

performance." He found an affordable venue in Brooklyn, which was the only theatre in that borough at the time: a stage on the third floor of a building on the corner of Fulton and Orange Streets.[19] There he was able to gather the personnel and materials necessary to mount a colorful bill. The evening's entertainment consisted of a farce, *Poor Pillicoddy*; the second act of *Macbeth*, involving Lady Macbeth's goading of her husband; a comic song; and the two-act comedy, *Toodles*, about a husband's struggles with his spendthrift wife.[20] Assessing the likely intake at the box office, he determined that "none of the boy associates was to receive a penny—the glory of acting was to be ample compensation." The "female stars" needed for the featured roles of Lady Macbeth and Mrs. Toodles, however, warranted special selection through advertising and compensation "at a small salary." They might have been inspired by the "vanity of figuring on the stage," but their devotion to the project "was all hearty and womanly and good." This meant that, above all, they accepted young Daly's authority.[21] The venture made only $11.25, incurring a $64.75 loss on expenses of $76.00. Nevertheless, Augustin went home with Joseph "triumphant, to act over again in our talks with the boys for many a day the varied incidents of what must go down in history as his first public attempt at management."[22]

According to Joseph, Augustin's managerial destiny would ultimately surpass that of Burton and Wallack because, unlike them, "he was absolutely without ambition to act."[23] Eschewing acting, he did not have to make himself emotionally vulnerable or publicly put himself in the compromising or demeaning positions of characters such as Macbeth and Mr. Toodles, who were bested by women in the form of their manipulating wives. By remaining on the other side of the footlights, he could sustain greater authority in image as well as fact and constantly monitor the whole *mise-en-scène*. In separating the traditionally joint roles of the actor-manager, Daly described himself as a theatrical "pioneer."[24]

Significantly, Joseph's biography does not identify the actress-manager Laura Keene, Burton's and Wallack's notable contemporary, as a model for young Augustin in these early years. She, too, ran a well disciplined stock company in a settled establishment that outlawed prostitution and alcohol and catered to the respectable classes. Her case illustrates some of the attitudes toward women that helped shape Daly's ambitions. Actors who worked with her said she was "unsurpassed" in directorial skill, then termed "stage management," especially her understanding of the play and detailed attention to character impersonation.[25] But rather than a worthy rival in the spirit of individual enterprise and competition, male managers and journalists perceived her as a dangerous threat. She had been a featured actress for two seasons with Wallack before leaving his employ in 1853 to start a company in Baltimore and tour in California. When she returned to New York in 1855 and hired performers from Burton's to establish her own resident company, a virulent letter appeared in the *New York Express*. The letter warned that she would encourage other players to desert their companies and possibly drive "worthy and experienced managers"—i.e., men like Burton and Wallack—out of business. Because Keene's management would bring the stage into "vilest disgrace and disrepute," the public should reject her "Amazonian onslaught" and "proposed extension of woman's rights in a female managerial experiment." While renting to Keene, the letter suggested, the building's owner might want to "finish off the other portions of his premises for free love purposes."[26] Even after Keene had demonstrated her managerial competence for several seasons, a critic for the *Spirit of the Times* (10 September 1859) disparaged her efforts: "Miss Keene is a brave, energetic manager, full of ambitious courage and love of adventurous enterprise, but she is also a woman and an actress; in other words, she is mentally unstable and professionally vain."[27] This gynophobia, as Faye E. Dudden argues, contributed significantly to Keene's managerial decline by prejudicing financial and legal institutions against her. She was denied access to capital and lost crucial lawsuits that might have sustained her interests. After being pressed by financial necessity into producing "leg shows" in 1862–1863, which only exacerbated the moral stigma against her, she gave up trying to maintain a resident company and left New York to tour. Although Daly admired the ensemble playing of Keene's stock company, he also absorbed contemporary attitudes that deemed women temperamentally ill-suited to authority and in need of male control.[28]

Dramatic Moves on Feminine Nature

Having determined that his ultimate aim was to manage his own theatre but lacking the necessary resources, Daly entered the profession through a variety of other nonacting positions. He turned first to journalism, writes Joseph, "with an undefined sense that it led the way he was to go."[29] In 1859 he began as a "general writer" for the *Sunday Courier*, whose offices were located in Printing House Square, the media hub for New York City's 160 newspapers.[30] Reporters for the *Courier*, a working-class paper, frequently covered the plight of poor people, immigrants, and criminals. Among his early assignments, Daly wrote a sympathetic series on working girls.[31] In another piece, entitled "Socials and Sociables," he addressed how members of the working class might present themselves in society.[32] In addition to heightening his awareness of class differences, these assignments gave him insight into the condition of working women and the challenge of raising their social esteem, concerns that would carry over into his management of actresses.

Within a few months of joining the *Courier* staff, Daly added "drama critic" to his roster of journalistic duties. The hundreds of theatre columns he contributed to the *Courier* and four other papers—the *Times*, *Sun*, *Express*, and *Citizen*—over the next decade provided a venue for expressing his emerging cultural values. Throughout this body of work, Daly argued that the stage should represent "nature," or, more precisely, "make counterfeits of nature appear like the reality." In his view, "faithfulness to nature," as opposed to stilted tradition, was "the true standard of art."[33] While he admired the naturalistic playing of actors such as Edwin Booth and Joseph Jefferson, he deemed the primary theatrical exponents of nature, like nature herself, to be female. Defending the venerable Charlotte Cushman against an accusation that her Lady Macbeth was "too animal . . . too true, painful, fearfully natural, dreadfully intense," Daly asserted: "nature cries today from the stage, as she never cried before."[34] He praised Matilda Heron, whose 1857 debut as Camille reproduced the ardors of the boudoir and torments of the sickroom with such intensity and graphic detail that she both appalled and fascinated spectators.[35] But he found Rose Eytinge's emotional performance in *Love's Sacrifice* even more admirable:

> Miss Eytinge's capacity as an actress, and the best actress in New York, is now so fully recognized that it is hardly necessary to say that she is singularly good in these phases of deep feeling. Her best characteristic is that she is intensely womanly, whether in her devotion, her sacrifice, or her hatred. To find anyone natural in these days—largely, humanely, sobbingly, even violently natural, is a rare thing. . . . Miss Eytinge, with the art which conceals art, and does not brag about it, responds to a mood and interprets it with the intensity of the feminine nature, without effort, and consequently without exaggeration.[36]

Daly was drawn to Eytinge's ability to play emotional roles with such apparent ease, simply, he believed, by letting her "intensely womanly" self emerge. That womanliness was grounded in an essentialized notion of "the feminine nature."

These ideas of the "natural" at work in Daly's reviews differed from modernist notions of realism and naturalism that emphasize environmental determinism. Nor did Daly anticipate the more nuanced, psychologically based realism of Stanislavsky. Rather, his ideas echoed scientific and popular discourses that reinforced archetypal correlations between nature and women's bodies. The male-dominated science of obstetrics and gynecology perpetuated theories that "naturalized" the female sex by linking women more closely than men to the elemental forces of the earth and animal kingdom.[37] Women's essence was reproductive. The leading gynecologist Charles D. Meigs wrote in 1847 that woman is "a moral, a sexual, a germiferous, gestative, and parturient creature."[38] A force of nature in the family, women were deemed capable of protecting their young with the ferocity of a wild animal.[39]

Because of their closer ties to nature, women were widely believed to be more emotional than men. Darwinian theory held that expressive acts of emotion were the products of organic reflexes, habits, and actions dating back to primordial times.[40] In women, those organic reflexes stemmed chiefly from the reproductive organs, hence the ubiquitous diagnosis of "hysteria," meaning literally "that which proceeds from the uterus," for a host of emotional problems.[41] Supposedly less evolved than men, women had less force of will and intellect to control their emotions and thus were more susceptible to being overwhelmed by them. Emotional performances that purportedly revealed the force of nature in women were what Daly and his contemporaries understood as "natural."

In praising Eytinge's naturalness, Daly also applauds the apparent genuineness of her performance. He found her ability to reveal nature without effort or exaggeration to be refreshing and praiseworthy because it contrasted markedly with women's daily deportment. Women in respectable society were expected to practice strict containment of their emotions and bodily functions. As the surge of etiquette manuals published between 1830 and 1870 powerfully attests, this mandate intensified with increasing urbanization.[42] However, as Karen Halttunen explains, acceptance of this mode of social conduct "was neither complete nor permanent. . . . Middle-class Americans have continued to express grave anxieties about the hypocrisy of fashion and of ritualistic social forms" and to harbor an "underlying concern about the sincerity of culture." "The problem," Halttunen says, "is endemic to a society of men and women on the make, of geographical and social movers, of men and women who are constantly assuming new identities and struggling to be convincing in new social roles."[43] While the respectable of both sexes practiced repression and concealment, women presumably did so to a greater extent than men because of their greater proximity to nature. Moreover, the prospect of women's resulting lack of sincerity was more troubling than men's to bourgeois values because home, family, society, and nation rested on a bedrock of feminine virtue.

To critics and audiences anxious about female sincerity, actresses could be profoundly compelling figures, at once threatening and appealing. Flagrantly defying bourgeois canons of feminine purity, piety, dependency, and modesty, they more vividly realized the correlations between femininity and nature presumed to exist in all women but which respectable women kept more shrouded beneath the censoring mechanisms of civility. The linkages to nature were especially seamless in actresses such as Heron and Eytinge who appeared to relinquish control and surrender to the underlying passions. Precisely the kinds of involuntary impulses and emotional excesses polite society women were required to constrain were those that these actresses embodied with seeming abandon. Such displays, while shocking, could also be considered noble and even admirable for their seeming lack of guile. Thus, the critic William Winter, who came to New York just as Daly entered journalism, praised Heron for her extraordinary ability to render authentic passion visible: "The eye followed her with delight at absolute newness and indubitable sincerity." Even though she had made her greatest fame playing a tubercular courtesan of dubious moral character, he described her as "profound, passionate, virtuous."[44] Winter earned a reputation as a strict moralist, but he, like Daly and so many of their contemporaries, was irresistibly drawn to these performances. As societal injunctions against emotional display reached a peak in daily life, what theatre historian Garff Wilson has called the "Emotionalistic School" of acting, comprised exclusively of women with Heronesque expressive powers, rose to thrilling popularity on stage.[45]

In his theatre columns, Daly favored productions that enabled the spectator to engage with potentially ennobling "tableaus of nature." Hence, he defended contemporary local color melodramas against "the stilted and impossible declamations and allegories, fates, furies, and divine machinery of the classic tragedies."[46] Most vehemently he decried the star system that, along with lack of discipline and moral laxity, fostered hackneyed traditions like "lines of business" and vocal and physical technique displayed for its own sake. These shopworn conventions broke the illusion by serving the vanity of the star more than the credibility of the character or the play world.[47] In a 1861 *Courier* column, Daly held up the actress Jane Coombes as an object lesson in the deleterious effects of starring:

Some while ago, when she played under Burton's management, she was an immense favorite in her way; for then she was seen to advantage in parts which, in the judgment of her manager, she could only play properly. By a two-year's starring tour, she has half destroyed a rather pleasant voice which she possessed before....

She also indulges in many of the traditionary mannerisms of the past, not the least of which is the selection of some unfortunate and helpless individual in the audience to whom she speaks all her asides, pours out all her sorrows in soliloquy, and addresses generally, instead of her vis-a-vis on stage.

Miss Coombes can correct none of these faults until she resigns the "star" and enters the "stock."[48]

In Daly's view, starring negatively impacted Coombes's career because she abdicated the managerial control and discipline of a stock company. He presumes that, being a woman, she lacks the ability to judge her most advantageous parts and playing style. His developing credo: An actress needs a strong male manager to keep her performances "natural" and meet his own spectatorial needs.

Despite his condemnation of the star system, Daly was not above exploiting it when he turned to playwriting. Initially, he tried to write scripts for leading players affiliated with the stock companies he admired, beginning with Burton and Wallack.[49] He also had the temerity to approach players in Laura Keene's company, first her leading man Joseph Jefferson and then Keene herself. The men, according to Joseph Daly, sent polite rejections and some words of encouragement, but Keene lost Daly's manuscript of *Napoleon III* (1858), which included the part of Empress Eugenie, written specially for her. This seemingly careless dismissal of his overture caused Daly to despair of writing plays for the next three years. Having suffered such painful rejection by stock company players, Daly resorted to touring stars when he resumed playwriting. His particular ambition to write for "emotionalistic" actresses forcefully resurged in his breakthrough success, *Leah the Forsaken* (1862), written for Kate Bateman. Thereafter, he wrote primarily for female stars. *Andre* (1864) was written for Maggie Mitchell; *Taming a Butterfly* (1864) for Mrs. John Wood; *Lorlie's Wedding* (1864) for Marie Methua-Scheller; *Come Here!* (1870) for Fanny Janauschek; and *Judith, the Daughter of Merari* (1864), *The Sorceress* (1864), and *Garcia* (1864) for Avonia Jones.[50] These plays were adaptations from French and German originals, but *Under the Gaslight* (1867), featuring

Rose Eytinge, and its close successor, *A Flash of Lightning* (1868), starring Blanche Grey, were original melodramas of the type he advocated in his columns.[51] The money he earned from these latter two scripts, especially *Gaslight*, enabled him to open his first theatre in 1869.[52] Thus, while pandering to the star system with these plays, Daly moved closer to his managerial goals.

The scripts themselves also reflect aspects of his developing agenda. His most successful works of this early period—*Leah, Gaslight*, and *Lightning*—display naturalized female emotion that inspires male protagonists to undergo heroic transformation and move up the social ladder. The plots of these plays map Daly's own negotiations of cultural values as he strove to overcome his impoverished Catholic and Irish origins and enter the predominately WASP ranks of American businessmen.

Leah, which Daly adapted from the German *Deborah* by S. H. Mosenthal, is set in a romantic Austrian landscape in the early eighteenth century, when the country was still under strongly Catholic Hapsburg rule. The play's hero, Rudolf (namesake of the Holy Roman Emperor), ventures away from his proper religious life in the civilized village into the forest where he encounters and pursues a romance with Leah, a darkly sensual "wandering Jewess." She embodies a pre-Christian and thus, in Daly's evolutionary terms, a more "natural" or primordial state of femininity. Reflecting on their first meeting, Rudolf tells her of the disturbing hold she has on him: "since that night a strange bond draws me to thee—thou givest / me no rest nor peace—in my sleep thy image is ever present— / thy dark eyes are ever gazing in my soul— thy gleaming hair / ever twining round my hands draws me to thy heart."[53] In the course of the action, Madalena, a virginal inhabitant of the Christian village, inspires him to salvation, and he forsakes Leah to marry her. Leah seeks bloody vengeance, but she undergoes a change of heart—an implied conversion to more Christian values of forgiveness—when she realizes Rudolf and Madalena have named their daughter after her. She leaves the couple to their marital bliss and goes off to die, still an outcast but spiritually elevated. Her range of emotional expression has run the gamut from fervid love to vengeful rage, maternal sympathy, and mortal grief. Although Madalena and Rudolf defend Jews against Christian persecution, Rudolf's rejection of the torrid Leah in favor of the more continent, sentimental Madalena signifies a move from a "lower" to "higher" state of manhood.[54]

For the struggling Daly, *Leah* far exceeded his hopes of success. At a time when a month's run meant a hit, the play ran for five weeks following its 19 January 1863 New York premiere at Niblo's Garden. It moved to Philadelphia, returned to New York for another month, and then went overseas for an extended engagement at London's Adelphi Theatre, where it entertained British royalty.[55] More than heralding Daly's commercial breakthrough, *Leah* also epitomized how the theatre offered him a venue for imagining and realizing in the flesh the type of woman he aspired to conquer. The "Jewess" living in the forest outside the pale of civilization became an allegory as well as vehicle for the thrilling actress who, regardless of her actual religious affiliation, was morally unchristian by dint of her profession and thus in need of conversion to respectability. In Kate Bateman, Daly's original Leah, the figures of the actress and the Jewess literally came together, as they would more famously later in Sarah Bernhardt; however, a number of Gentile stars, including Adelaide Ristori, Fanny Janauschek, Marie Methua-Scheller, Lucille Western, Fanny Davenport, and Nance O'Neil, also vivified the allegorical connections between actress and Jewess in playing the role.[56] The wide appeal of the piece lay not only in the excitement aroused by Leah's sensual emotional displays but also in the reassurances provided by her implied conversion and death. Her fate demonstrated the power of Christianity to subdue savage threats in and beyond the borders of white settlement. Adapting Mosenthal's text peopled with markedly Catholic characters, Daly wrote fellow members of his own religion into the WASP American frontier myth. If in the play Leah's death removed the threat to Rudolf's bourgeois family, in life both the Jewess and the actress would remain tempting, destabilizing, and transformative figures for the aspiring manager.

Unlike Leah, the heroines of *Gaslight* and *Lightning* are contemporary urban bourgeois maidens, but circumstances drive them outside the bounds of respectability into lawless spaces where their Christian virtue and social status are imperiled. These sensation melodramas gave their respective stars, Rose Eytinge and Blanche Gray, ample opportunity for demonstrating raw physical as well as moral courage in the face of terror. The most compelling instance occurred when Eytinge as Laura Courtland axed her way out of a locked tool shed to rescue the one-armed Civil War veteran, Snorkey, from the path of a speeding locomotive.[57] This is one of a handful of scenes that have come to exemplify nineteenth-century melodrama, yet the enduring popular impression has been one of a woman, not a man, tied to the railroad tracks. This gender reversal belies Daly's need for violently "natural" female emotional display that inspired the original image.

In both *Gaslight* and *Lightning*, leading male characters follow imperiled ingenues into dangerous urban spaces where they are called to heroism. Drawing on his personal circumstances and journalistic experience, Daly lays out a variegated "racial" and class topography within which the heroes' transformations occur. In *Gaslight*, Laura's beloved, Ray Trafford, "one of the New York 'Bloods,'" nearly abandons her to marry her cousin Pearl, a pretentious society belle, until Laura's emotional displays of courage and loyalty convince him that the more natural girl is the worthier wife. Betrothed to Ray, Laura is restored to respectability. Meanwhile, her dramatic rescue of Snorkey compels him to relinquish his ties to an urban underworld where his companions include the Dickensian grifter, Byke; the "drunk and disorderly" Sam, "a colored citizen ready for suffrage when suffrage is ready for him"; and Rafferdi, "née Rafferty, an Irish organist from Cork," whose aping of an Italian further lowers him in the cultural hierarchy.[58] With Laura's inspiration, Snorkey moves from this base social stratum toward the morally superior white middle class.

In *Lightning*, Daly makes Irish identity central to the main plot. His heroine, Bessie Fallon, comes from an assimilating Irish immigrant family seeking to solidify its arrival into the middle class. Through Bessie, Daly explicitly voices his expectations of women when she resolves to bear the responsibility for constructing the hero's manhood. The wellborn yet ne'er-do-well Jack has always loved her, but he loses hope for a better life when he mistakenly assumes she has been faithless. Blaming her for his descent, he tells her: "Good-bye! And if you wish to think of me, remember what I might have been—an honest man! What I shall be is your work." Bessie proclaims: "I will show him the way of reparation—I will save him." To do so, she follows him into the urban underworld, risking her own physical safety and reputation. Inspired by Bessie, Jack eventually lives up to the implied promise of his class status by making himself over as a responsible engineer.[59]

Along the way, Bessie also transforms her father, Mr. Garry Fallon, "American by choice, Irish by birth, and the master in his own house."[60] His progress up the social ladder is marked in the play's opening scene with the appearance on their doorstep of the Dowderry family, disheveled new arrivals with thick Irish accents. Denying his own roots but still beset with Irish temper, Fallon spurns them. He also rashly rejects Bessie on the mistaken belief that she has jealously stolen a gold necklace he purchased for her sister Rose. Down-and-out, both Bessie and the Dowderrys end up at "Jacob's Ladder, a resort for sailors, and immigrants of the poorer class, and thieves."[61] Although poor, the Dowderrys show that they are better than other "races" of immigrants by helping the imperiled Bessie and her lover, Jack Ryver, escape the evil Benedetti and his predatory band of "Italian monkey boys." Bessie shares the Dowderry's Irish "racial" superiority over the Italians in Daly's representational scheme. She also demonstrates superior virtues in her unwavering loyalty to her family and loved ones even under extreme duress. Ultimately, her innocence is vindicated when Jack explains how the necklace disappeared in "a flash of lightning." Realizing his daughter's true character, Fallon disavows his Irish temper, asks her forgiveness, and evolves from a self-described "brute" into a more self-controlled citizen of the American bourgeoisie. Echoing Laura Courtland's inspirational powers in *Gaslight*, Bessie demonstrates that an Irish heroine can be just as virtuous and civilization-building as her more generically Anglo counterpart.

In realizing many of his personal aspirations in these plays, Daly also reached urban bourgeois audiences who were themselves "on the make," as Halttunen puts it, and anxious about their social status. The wide appeal of his dramaturgical parsing of the cultural hierarchy is evident in growing commercial success. *Gaslight* opened 12 August 1867 and surpassed *Leah*'s record, tallying over one hundred performances in New York in its first season and many more through almost yearly revivals into the 1880s and popular runs in Boston and London. *Lightning* followed suit with an initial New York run from 10 June to 1 August 1868 and subsequent engagements in Boston, Brooklyn, London, and Leeds.[62]

Even as he enjoyed the first flush of commercial success, Daly continued to develop and articulate his higher motives for theatrical production. In an 1867 editorial written for the *New York Times*, he attributes the same moral values and inspirational force to actresses as to heroines in his plays. Just as Leah, Laura, and Bessie gain moral stature through their transgressive displays of passion, so should the women who impersonate them. Paradoxically, certain leading ladies can embody "natural" forces tied to lower stages of evolution and yet rise above the social stigmas generally associated with actresses. Daly takes to task fellow journalists who fail to grant this distinction to such performers:

> the habit of calling every female in the profession "an actress"—whether she belong to the supernumerary corps or to the leading rank of her art, is an injustice and needs correction. In a measure it is like that frequent unfairness which is done another profession, when the Police happens to commit some street haranguer for disturbing the peace, or lock up some petty preacher for a misdemeanor, and the incident is printed as "A Clergyman in Trouble." . . . It is but a matter of justice, therefore, that the little outlaws and small fry of the stage be not confounded under such a general

term as that of "actress" with the honorable members of a profession made noble by Charlotte Cushman, Miss Bateman, Mrs. [John] Hoey, and other ladies of eminence who have not formally retired from it, or who still remain its active ornaments.[63]

The analogy the editorial makes between "ladies of eminence" and members of the priesthood pushes the paradox further. By acting uncivilized and unchristian, great female emotional stars, whether Gentile or Jewish, can nevertheless be civilizing and Christianizing because the "naturalness" they demonstrate inspires heroic transformation. The logic reflects the circularity of the frontier myth. Conquest of savagery is essential for civilization, but too much civilization leads to emasculating weakness and decadence, which necessitates regenerative engagements with savagery and proving of manhood through conquest.[64] Enthralled by the saving powers of their "natural" emotional performances, Daly asserts the need to protect "*ladies* of the stage from the promiscuous classification" applied to "any girl of the ballet or female of less creditable character who connects herself with a concert saloon or a varieties hall." As his rhetoric indicates, Daly strove to associate with this higher class of actress in his own climb up the cultural hierarchy.

Pursuing the Actress as Jewess

Daly's projections of salvation onto spectacularly "natural" female stars did not, however, dispel the specter of danger and dissolution his family and the dominant culture had historically imposed on these women. Like the heroes of his early plays, Daly risked his reputation and even his physical well-being by following some of these actresses into marginal social and moral territory. The most dangerous and formative of these episodes involved his personal as well as professional relations with the traveling star actresses Adah Isaacs Menken, Avonia Jones, and Kate Bateman.

In spite of his family morality and professed standards of respectability, Daly developed a decade-long friendship with Menken, one of the most infamous female figures of the nineteenth-century American stage. She attained commercial success largely through notoriety and scandal rather than the artistic stature of the "ladies of eminence" Daly praised in his editorial. Yet she won his admiration and compelled him to use his journalistic connections to advance her career. An avid theatergoer, Daly may have witnessed Menken's first performances in New York in 1857 as Pauline in *The Lady of*

Lyons and as the cross-dressed hero of *The French Spy*. The latter role, a breeches part in which she appeared corsetless and sported short, dark curls, showed off her alluring athletic physique to particular advantage and became a regular feature of her early repertoire. The *New York Clipper* proclaimed her "one of the most beautiful women now upon the boards."[65] Menken had certainly captured Daly's attention by February 1860, when widespread media coverage of her messy affair with famed pugilist John Carmel Heenan made her a national celebrity. Scandal erupted because while Menken claimed to be married to Heenan, the boxer denied she was his wife. In a scathing letter printed in Wilkes's *Spirit of the Times*, her estranged husband Alexander Isaac Menken branded her an "adventuress" and accused her of bigamy, since, to his knowledge, they had not been divorced. Defending herself in letters, essays, and poems that were published in several newspapers, Adah Menken played the martyr wronged by cruel men and prejudice against her profession and her Jewishness. Her most recent biographer, Renée M. Sentilles, finds no evidence that Menken was either born Jewish or ever officially converted to Judaism. She simply claimed to be Jewish when she sought to impress the Reform Jewish community of Cincinnati, Ohio, where she had lived in the early years of her marriage to Alexander Menken.[66] Nonetheless, the religious identification became a lasting part of her persona, so much so that Joseph Daly refers to Menken as a "singular Hebrew star."[67]

There was much to compel Augustin in the drama surrounding this performer. Menken combined the attributes of actress and Jewess that inspired his *Leah*. She seemed to be profoundly driven by "natural" emotion despite her clear propensity for manipulating the media and lack of great talent for emotional performance. If her stage acting was limited, she successfully created a self-image as a deeply passionate woman in print. She had begun publishing her writing in the 1850s when living in Cincinnati. After her move to New York, the *Sunday Mercury* published several of her essays and poetry so gut-wrenching it appeared to reveal her innermost feelings. In her most critically acclaimed poem, "The End," which appeared a few months after the Heenan scandal broke, she identifies with the biblical Judith holding the head she has just severed from Holofernes. As Judith, she anticipates the bloody flow from the fresh wound

> . . . that will thrill me with wild unspeakable joy as it courses down my
>   bare body and dabbles my cold feet!
> My sensuous soul will quake with the burden of so much bliss.

Oh, what wild passionate kisses will I draw up from that bleeding
    mouth!
I will strangle this pallid throat of mine on the sweet blood!
I will revel in my passion.[68]

Two months later, in "Passion," which readers would have more directly connected to the Heenan affair, she writes of being moved first by romantic love
and now, even after all his cruel treatment, by lust:

But, though, since all thy ways I know,
    Thy heart is worthless in my eyes;
Yet warmer still my passions glow,
    I love thee more than I despise.[69]

Menken's continuing desire for the man whom circumstances should have
driven her to hate gives the impression of a woman in the grip of "natural"
passion that exceeds rational control. Moving in journalistic circles, struck by
Menken's beauty, and attuned to her suffering through the scandal, Daly followed her literary as well as acting career. The virtue he attributed to female
"naturalness" prompted him to take up her cause in his *Sunday Courier*
columns. He enjoined other critics to act as gentlemen and respectable citizens and not besmirch a victimized woman's name.[70]

When Menken adopted her most famous role, that of Cassimer in
Mazeppa, in 1861, she thrilled Daly and throngs of other spectators with an
audacious display of woman *au naturale*. This was a breeches part in which
the hero, stripped naked and tied to his horse, was sent on a wild ride into the
hills. While the play had been in the repertoire for decades, and other
actresses had played Cassimer, none had agreed to the stripping or the main
stunt.[71] Menken ventured to do both. In the climactic scene, soldiers stripped
her down to flesh-colored tights and a white shirt that ended at mid-thigh,
lashed her spread-legged on her back across a black horse, and slapped the
steed into a canter up a forty-foot wood and canvas mountain at the back of
the stage. As the Tartary prince, she not only appeared unclad and male, but
exotic within an Orientalized *mise-en-scène*. The visual thrills did not end
when she disappeared over the mountain. Bemoaning his suffering, Cassimer
remained strapped to the horse for the entire second act as a moving pan-
orama created the illusion of a gallop through miles of wild country. However
limited Menken may have been in expressing torrents of inner passion on
stage, the evident danger of these stunts suggested she was feeling real pain

and exhibiting real courage in a role that took her spectacularly beyond the bounds of respectable American womanhood.

After Daly praised her performance in the *Courier* against the disparagements of other critics such as Winter of the *Tribune* and "Bayard" of Wilkes's *Spirit of the Times*, Menken sent him a thank you note.[72] This exchange led to a deepening of their relationship. While she was playing in New York, Menken allowed him to escort her to theatre and opera. She later referred to these outings as "charming flights of vagabondism."[73] When she went on national tour, she had Daly handle some publicity for her and sent him self-promotional copy.[74] In one letter, she instructed him to publish the following explanation of her poetic inspiration: "I have written these wild soul-poems in the stillness of midnight. . . . I know that the soul that prompted every word and line is somewhere within me, but not to be called at my bidding—only to wait the inspiration of God."[75] Although Menken employed a high level of self-conscious calculation in cultivating her persona of wildness and genuineness, her admirers accepted her emotional expressions, both performed and written, as, in Daly's words, "an honest revelation of her own feelings."[76] Menken's reputation for rebellious impulsiveness eventually took its toll. By 1865, reports were circulating about her overindulgence in alcohol and cigarettes and increasingly volatile fits of temper. Also in that year, according to her biographer, Sentilles, she and Daly had a "mysterious quarrel."[77] The conflict may have resulted from her behavior or the turn of Daly's attention to another actress, Avonia Jones, and his failure to furnish Menken with a play to resuscitate her career.[78] Nonetheless, Menken entrusted him to be the custodian and editor of her autobiographical "Notes." After her death in 1868, he published them in the *New York Times* with an introduction claiming he was doing so as "an act of justice for a poor mistaken woman." He paid tribute to her "originality" and "authenticity," even as he recognized her "innocent and allowable romancing" of her own story.[79] He also insisted on stating for the record that her real name was Adelaide McCord, not Ada Bertha Theodore, which Menken had invoked to advance her "Hebrew" identity.[80] Since that identity had been a crucial element of the actress's allure, Daly's denial of her Jewishness as part of a final defense of her character echoes some of the same ambivalence toward the Jewess that drove his portrayal of Leah.

Joseph Daly takes pains in his biography to minimize Augustin's relationship with Menken. He mentions her only twice, once just as an example of the "strange meteors" that flashed briefly in front of audiences during his and

Augustin's youth.[81] Later he refers to a letter that she wrote Augustin to refute a report of her marriage to the writer Artemis Ward. Joseph quickly downplays the significance of this correspondence by noting that "Miss Menken was a steady correspondent of the dramatic editors, who were all enrolled as 'chums.'" He then insists: "Among the Bohemians Daly was never classed. He could neither smoke nor drink."[82] Given that Menken was a notorious Bohemian and a public female smoker, the specificity of the disclaimers seems a pointed attempt to disentangle Daly from Menken and her ilk in order to bolster his brother's reputation for posterity.

While Menken's star was beginning to fade, Avonia Jones (1839–1867) captured Daly's ardent attention with her venturesome spirit and special talent for incarnating "natural" passion. Born into a theatrical family in Virginia, she was the adopted daughter of George Jones, a.k.a. Count Joannes, who built Norfolk's Avon Theatre before embarking on the long and colorful touring career that made him a national laughingstock for his terrible acting and delusions of royal grandeur. Using the mechanism of adoption, Count Joannes repeatedly went to court to maintain control over his attractive young ward and pupil. Avonia made her stage debut in 1856 at age seventeen as Parthenia in *Ingomar* at the People's Theatre in Cincinnati. When she was still a teenager, her father subjected them both to cruel ridicule by playing Romeo to her Juliet, though he was in his sixties.[83] At twenty, perhaps in part to escape her father, she embarked on a two-year tour of Australia with a repertoire that included the roles of Medea, Camille, Evadne, and Lucretia Borgia. According to a report of her performance at Lamplough, "Miss Avonia Jones took amazingly, as that sort of actress must do with such audiences as usually assemble in unsettled localities."[84] After her Australian tour, she played for two years (1861–1863) in London, where she won special acclaim for her Medea and Lady Isabel in *East Lynne*. Noting her "slight and by no means commanding form," the *London Times* reviewer for her first performance of Medea was initially concerned that "the passions of hatred and revenge [would] not receive adequate expression." But, he hastened to add, "This opinion she dissipates as soon as opportunity presents itself, and in the famous 'leopard speech,' as well as in other passages where Medea's native savagery is brought forward, she shows an intensity and an abandonment to passion which compensate in a great measure for a deficiency in physical strength."[85]

Reports from overseas of Jones's talents and accomplishments must have made her an appealing prospect when she first contacted Daly in November

1863. Kate Bateman's London triumph as Leah the preceding month prompted Jones to solicit vehicles from him for an American tour.[86] Daly quickly began adapting several plays for her from French and German originals. In the course of preparing *The Sorceress*, a play about maternal suffering under a regime of *droit de Seigneur*, he proposed making the daughter rather than the mother the play's heroine. In her letter back to him, Jones strongly objected to the idea: "I can't make out how you intend transforming Jeanne into a *'daughter'* and yet keep the powerful interest which in the original is centered in the *'mother.'* I always think the latter phase of life the most powerful and am most fond of portraying such emotions." Probably thinking of her unhappy relationship with her adoptive father, she adds: " Daughters I care little about, especially if it means love for father; I have never felt it, and cannot act it." She continues in another paragraph:

> I don't mind playing middle-aged women, for I have so long been accustomed to it in "Lady Macbeth," "Lady Constance," &c. As you have never seen me act, I must tell you that my style is passionate. When I love it must be madly; not the tender gentle love that shrinks from observation, but the love that would sweep all before it and if thwarted would end in despair, madness and death. In fact in acting I am more fond of being bad than good. Hate, revenge, despair, sarcasm and resistless love I glory in; charity, gentleness and the meeker virtues I do not care for.[87]

This missive swept away any hesitancies Daly may have harbored about creating mature, violent, viscerally passionate characters for this still young performer. He reverted to keeping the character as the mother. Jones had thrown open the door for him to create the type of female characters that most compelled him.

Joseph Daly quotes Jones's statement, but he immediately tries to prevent readers from thinking his brother was getting involved with a dangerous woman. He asserts that "This desperate character was as far from the good Miss Jones's natural disposition as from her power of portrayal. She was already the wife of the eminent English tragedian, G. V. Brooke, was devoted to her mother and her sister, and was without a particle of the stormy passion and fire in dramatic impersonations which she had evidently set up as her ideal."[88] Augustin, however, saw considerable "stormy passion and fire" in Jones, both onstage and offstage. He did not learn that she was married until many months after their association began. Her husband, whom she met in Australia, may have been an accomplished actor, but he was also twenty years older than she and an abusive alcoholic. Like Menken, she had much passion to express through her characters, some of it provoked by the cruelties of men such as Brooke and Joannes. By the time Daly met Jones, life and theatrical experience had made her considerably more complicated than the image Joseph evokes of the good woman from a stable family who cannot embody the fierce passions to which she aspires.

When Daly saw her act, Jones realized his vision of a powerful performer of "natural" emotion, especially in roles such as Judith and the Sorceress. Daly's *Judith, the Daughter of Merari* premiered at New York's Winter Garden Theatre on 4 April 1864. A *carte de visite* photograph (fig. 2) shows Jones in the role of the heroically violent and seductive biblical Jewess whom Menken had impersonated in poetry. She is wearing a heavy, richly embroidered royal robe draped to expose the smooth flesh of her neck and bare right shoulder and arm. The costume adds size, power, exoticism, and sexual allure to her form. In *The Sorceress*, which followed at the Winter Garden on 26 April, Jones played the medieval Black Janet, whom Winter likened to Cushman's Meg Merriles. He described the part as that of "a woman half crazed by terrible outrage, pursuing the vanishing shadow of her lost child, and aiming at the deadly purpose of revenge." The *Sunday Times* found Jones too youthful in appearance but nevertheless effective in realizing the character's ferocity.[89] Her performances aggrandized her in Daly's eyes. Where the *London Times* reviewer had seen a "slight figure" three years before, Daly saw a much more commanding presence: "her chief excellence was the force and fire of her personations; the representation of delicacy and girlishness was not so agreeable to her as that of a hardy and vehement nature. She was tall and robust in frame, with piercing black eyes and agreeable features."[90]

Following her spring run at the Winter Garden and a summer engagement at Wallack's, Jones enlisted Daly to accompany her as manager of a starring tour of Union-held areas in the South during the fall and winter of 1864–1865. The trip posed considerable risk, not only because of the obvious dangers of the surrounding military conflict, but also because Daly had no prior tour managing experience. A veteran of harsh conditions in Australia, Jones was evidently not daunted by the prospect of traveling long distances and encountering gunfire. Because Daly had won her confidence as a playwright, she was willing to offer him this opportunity. Enticed by the adventure and the prospect of further collaboration with her, he eagerly accepted. His job entailed coordinating and directing rehearsals with the local companies

2. *Avonia Jones as Judith, 1864. From C. D. Fredericks and Co. Nineteenth-Century Actors Photographs, UW 25987, courtesy of Special Collections, University of Washington Libraries, Seattle.*

enlisted to support the star during her various engagements. She toured a repertoire of Jewish and otherwise unchristian heroines, notably Leah, Judith, Gamea, the Jewish Mother, and the eponymous character in Matilda Heron's version of *Medea*. Seeing her embody these characters night after night on the road and keeping close quarters with her while traveling, Daly became increasingly infatuated with Jones even as conditions indeed proved harshly challenging. He wrote home frequently to his brother in letters that reflect both the fire of his youthful ambition and a loss of innocence. Not surprisingly, Joseph is highly selective in the letters he quotes in his brother's biography. He leaves out those that reveal Augustin's deepening attraction to Jones, although compelling evidence remains in the archival collection. He includes those letters for publication that "give some glimpses of local conditions seen through the smoke of battle," by which he means both the battle of the war and Augustin's developing "battle of life." While Augustin was gone, Joseph not only kept up the correspondence but covered for his brother by ghostwriting his columns for the New York papers.[91]

The five-month tour began in Norfolk on 12 September and then moved by train and riverboat to Nashville, St. Louis, Memphis, Rochester, Washington, and Baltimore.[92] Arriving in Norfolk must have been special for Daly and Jones because both had spent years of their youth there and had memories to share that perhaps brought them closer. Augustin wrote to Joseph of visiting old haunts: "I have walked again in the queer, curling, old, ridiculous old streets and the little lanes and short cuts our boy feet toddled over." He revels in eating fresh figs again from the market. "At the sight of them—at the taste— visions of our little pilferings in the back gardens of Johnson's house held me in a retrospective trance! I was a little rapscallion again up among the branches and you were the conscience-touched but overruled little brother under them catching the fruit."[93] But the town has also changed in ways that Daly finds disturbing: "our old house in Dodd's Lane . . . is now occupied by Darkies; indeed there are few places in town not filled with the black."[94] A few days later he writes of discovering in his perambulations that "the spot where the old Avon Theatre stood is now covered by the town jail. Think of it!" He does not mention Jones accompanying him on this particular walk (she may have been resting or rehearsing), but she, too, would have been struck by the fate of the theatre her father once ran. Happily for both, these changes in demographics did not prevent Jones's performances from taking Norfolk "by storm," as Augustin proudly proclaimed to his brother.[95]

Conditions worsened, however, as they moved South. Daly writes of the "horrid" railway journey to Nashville on which he and Jones suffered "low, narrow seats, dirty floors, no ventilation, brutes and blackguards in the so-called ladies' car!" He recounts trying to sterilize bad water by adding drops of whiskey.[96] Five days later he has succumbed to a bad cold through which Jones is nursing him: "[My throat] is as full of rocks now as Broadway when Russ or Belgian is being laid. I have a mountain on the outside (under my right ear) about as big as a baby's head, as hard as the heart of a melodramatic cruel uncle and as painful as love's parting."[97] By the time they got to Nashville, love was not parting but arriving and raising Daly's spirits. An anxious Joseph wrote his brother of having to deny rumors already circulating in New York that Augustin Daly and Avonia Jones were to marry.[98]

En route down the Mississippi to Memphis, the couple experienced their first taste of Civil War combat in the form of guerrilla gunfire. They counted a dozen shots as the boat sped away, but fortunately no one on board was hit. Shortly thereafter, they found themselves stranded in Cairo, which Daly describes as "the dirt box of this globe," for sixty hours after the boat ran onto a sandbar. When they finally reached Memphis, they faced audiences much less tractable than the "magnificent" houses the lovesick Daly had described in Nashville. He exclaims to Joseph:

> Such wild devils, such drinkers, such smokers, chewers, such gamblers, and uproarious fellows generally I never saw—
>
> I was whirled into the maelstrom immediately. Of course, you understand that I look, listen, but partake not. All these people—the wildest are the influential ones that I must get interested in the theatre. I am on the warpath—to conquer, or die![99]

The "influential ones" presumably refer to the military personnel, local officials, and businessmen whom Daly wanted to impress throughout the tour. Such men in Memphis apparently lacked the decorousness he associated with the respectable classes. In addition to this unruly behavior, he and Jones had to contend with further intrusions of war as alarms sounded the approach of Confederate forces. Daly tried to capture the excitement for his brother: "Friday evening about 9½ o'clock, and while the performance was going on to the biggest and most fashionable audience ever in the theatre since it was built, the four cannon were heard and the bells commenced to ring. Lord! You never saw such a lot of scared people in your life as the men were."[100] His characterization of the audience as the "biggest and most fashionable" ever in that theatre suggests success in winning their manners as well as appreciation.

Daly could not boast conquest, however, in his relationship with Jones. He had problems asserting his managerial authority on the tour, as she insisted on running some rehearsals herself, and local personnel and facilities often limited what he could do.[101] On a more personal level, they had grown closer through sharing so many adventures, but Jones could not bring herself to reciprocate Daly's amorous feelings. While she apparently cared for him and nursed him when he was ill, she viewed him as a "dear brother" rather than a lover.[102] Daly expressed his tortured feelings in such graphic and compromising terms that Joseph saw fit to destroy two of his letters and tried to get him to disentangle himself from his involvement with the actress. Joseph also relayed their mother's stern admonition: "If you get sick or anything happens to you, mother desires me to say she will blame Miss Avonia for it and wishes you to say to Miss Jones that she is to consider herself held accountable for your safe delivery home again."[103] Like bourgeois antitheatrical tracts, the warning set mother and home against actress and theatre in the struggle for the wayward son's fate.

In the last letter Augustin sent to Joseph before returning to New York (dated 15 January 1865), he reflected on his experience and hopes for the future. He wrote that his unrequited love had led him to "a very dark place, where doubts, disappointments, and retaliatory feelings have taken up their abode." However, he asserted that life would be different when he got home:

> I feel that in returning to New York I shall be ready for stupendous efforts. I shall be tied to no likes outside our own charmed ties [family] and with strength, experience, and the will and disposition to ride over every puny obstacle that our kind literary friends [critics who favored the classical repertoire over contemporary melodrama] may oppose to our progress.

Daly also indicated that in overcoming his despair, he would use the experience with Jones as material for his writing:

> I want to tell the story of a woman, self-willed—beautiful—passionate—dependent—careless of conventionalities—selfish—vain—thoughtless of others' feelings—one who is innately good—but whose pride of Virtue has made mad—to cap all she is a baby—she is a woman, too, who *would not* when Cupid *would*, and *could not* when *she* would.

Some months after his return, Daly learned for the first time that Jones was married, which helped explain her reticence toward him. He further discovered that her history of relationships with men had been deeply troubled, beginning with her unstable father. In *Under the Gaslight*, aspects of Count Joannes and Gustavus Brooke can be seen in the villainous character Byke, who makes false paternal claims in an attempt sexually to possess Laura. The complexities and fickleness Daly perceived in Jones play out in the contrasting characterizations of the passionate, innately virtuous Laura and her selfish and vain cousin Pearl.[104]

Although Daly acquired some useful dramatic material from his experience with Jones, that benefit did not eradicate the trauma of rejection. On the tour, the profound frustration and lack of control he suffered as a lover merged with his frustrations as an aspiring manager. His declaration of readiness for "stupendous efforts" on his return involved a determination to overcome obstacles and gain control on both managerial and amorous fronts.

In the months following the tour, however, another episode with an actress demonstrated his continuing personal and professional vulnerability. He sold his adaptation of *Leah* to Kate Bateman but was dissatisfied with the compensation he received and so sued her father, Hezekiah. Prosecuting attorney A. Oakley Hall won the case with a highly prejudicial argument portraying Daly as a hardworking capitalist and Bateman as "Shylock." In spite of the legal victory, Daly feared that Bateman's defense, which included a charge that he had seduced Kate, had damaged his reputation. He wrote to his "old chum," Adah Isaacs Menken for solace. She responded: "I cannot fancy you, Gus, being so frightfully 'thin-skinned' as to feel yourself the injured party in this late affair. The Don Quixotic defender of his daughter's virtue [Bateman] has got decidedly the worst of it. Oakley Hall quite settled that."[105] Whatever the truth of Bateman's claims, the lawsuit seems to have exacerbated Daly's anxieties about his managerial and sexual fortunes, which were becoming more deeply intertwined.

For the fiercely ambitious Daly, these experiences of his first decade in the theatrical profession revealed the extent to which he was disadvantaged in an industry still driven largely by the popularity of stars. The star system had repeatedly allowed actresses to gain the upper hand in his dealings with them. Even as he earned authority as a critic, the activities by which he more directly pursued a career in management—those of playwright, publicist, and tour manager—subordinated him to female stars' wishes. He worked primarily at their behest, his professional and sexual advances subject to their acceptance or rejection. As his work became better known, especially after the success of *Leah*, stars requested plays from him, but he was still working to their orders. He likewise played a subordinate role when doing publicity and managing tours for Jones, Menken, the Batemans, and Rose Eytinge. The legal dispute with Bateman's father highlighted Daly's tenuous grip on his own artistic, financial, and moral fortunes.

In 1869, two major developments occurred with significant implications for Daly's personal and professional status: his marriage, which endured for the rest of his life, and the opening of his first theatre, where he inaugurated most of the policies he would employ throughout his thirty-year career in management. Through both of these developments, Daly not only fulfilled career goals but sought to reverse the power dynamics that had rendered him vulnerable in preceding years.

Given prevailing bourgeois morality and his own family's values, Daly's marriage to Mary Duff constituted an upwardly mobile move.[106] She was the daughter of John Duff, the respected theatre capitalist who, among other investments, had gained ownership of Laura Keene's Theatre when she went out of business. On a mercenary level, Daly married into the career to which he aspired. His father-in-law's money and connections provided assistance in ensuing ventures for the next decade, though financial and policy disputes eventually alienated the two men.[107] But there were other, more lasting, advantages to the marriage. Echoing his own *Leah* plot, Daly, like Rudolf, appeared to have overcome his near-ruinous passion for the Jewish-identified actress when he took a chaste Christian maiden for his bride.[108] Not only was Mary Duff a Christian, but she embodied attributes diametrically opposed to those associated with actresses. She rarely appeared in public, was seldom photographed, did not give interviews, and left no revelatory personal papers. The only known recollection of her appears in *Stage Reminiscences*, by Mrs. G. H. Gilbert, a longtime member of Daly's company: "She was a good wife to him and a great helper in every way. She knew her husband's business thoroughly and never told a word of it, and that is saying a great deal, for curious people would often ask her questions about affairs when they would not dare ask her husband."[109] As Daly benefited from her father's wealth and connections, Mary graced his life with the comforts of home and an aura of bourgeois respectability.

Unlike the fictional Rudolf, however, Daly did not forego his passion for the forbidden seductress after marriage. He repeatedly indulged the double standard of sexual morality. Cornelia Otis Skinner, the daughter of actor Otis

Skinner who worked for Daly, called him "woman crazy" because he flirted with "women he thought might be capturable in his company. Occasionally he succeeded."[110] Home and theatre and their respective female scions served complementary functions in Daly's quest to achieve American manhood. His marriage provided a respectable shield and soothing refuge from the rigors of continued theatrical conquests, while relationships with actresses provided regenerative engagements with "natural" forces to counter the stifling threat of domestic civilization.

2

A Troubled Republic

*The great power of Augustin Daly in his chosen
field of work was his own individuality. He
stood by himself, outlined his own plans and
carried them through to a successful issue with
help from nobody. The theater which bears his
name, and whose reputation is world wide, is a
simple monument to his own individuality. He
was a stage manager and business manager
combined, and not a single detail in either line
was carried into execution until it had been
passed on and decided by himself.*
—W. W. Austin and Matthew White Jr.,
"A Famous American Manager,"
Munsey's Magazine, 1899

Beginning at New York's Fifth Avenue Theatre in 1869, Daly established an institutional structure through which he could gain and maintain control of his theatrical destiny. He resigned his various newspaper posts to devote himself to the venture full time. If in the previous decade he was obliged to work chiefly at others' behest, he now attempted to govern all aspects of production, dictating when, where, and how others would work for him. Since female stars had played leading roles in his most formative experiences and were potent audience draws, they became the main focus of his autocracy. Most centrally, he strove to control actresses' embodiments of naturalized passion to ensure that they fulfilled his own agenda for heroic conquest and upward mobility. These aims are discernible in the organizational structure, rules of conduct, and directorial methods Daly implemented throughout his thirty-year managerial career. After struggles with a series of leading ladies that prompted development of his policies, Daly most fully realized his personal and professional goals through his relationship with Ada Rehan and their definitive production, *The Taming of the Shrew* (1887).

Instituting Theatrical Dictatorship

Like his models William Burton and James Wallack, Daly organized his operation as a resident stock company, which managers believed provided a more settled, "homelike" structure for theatrical production in contradistinction to the itinerant star system.[1] As a nonactor who did not have to make himself emotionally vulnerable or lose sight of the whole *mise-en-scène* while moving in and out of character, Daly strove to assert a more absolute managerial authority over company members than his actor-manager mentors. His theatre more closely realized the household or, more precisely, home-as-castle model instituted in the business world in which the chief executive functioned as undisputed ruler, owner, and patriarch. Lea VanderVelde has analyzed the Victorian family roles inscribed in the household model of business organization and the inherent gender biases informing employment relations during the period.[2] In this feudal domestic model, all employees were positioned as vassals and serfs, but male employers related to male employees as subservient brothers and sons, whereas they related to female employees as subservient wives and daughters.

The male dominance of the home-as-castle model was extended by the military mode of operation validated during the Civil War. For many northern U.S. business and political leaders of Daly's generation, the war experience had served as a management "school" whose lessons were emblematized in the election of Ulysses S. Grant to the presidency in 1868.[3] Hailed by the *New York Times* as the leader of "that great national conquest," Grant himself, in his inaugural address, projected militaristic rhetoric onto a range of political, economic, and cultural forces, including those of frontier savagery, that might impede the expansion of northern industrial interests.[4] In the business world, the mantle of conqueror went to the industrial capitalist, in whom the ethos of militaristic paternalism vested the combined authority of father, husband, owner, and commander in chief. Identifying as a business manager as well as a theatre manager, Daly seized this power. When actor Richard Mansfield questioned him about why he disallowed opinions other than his own, the impresario replied: "I cannot afford to be less than Commander in Chief of all my forces from the highest officer under me to the humblest. Only in this way can I lead you on to victory—the victory which we both would desire."[5]

The views Daly and his brother shared of *a priori* differences between actors and actresses reinforced the gender biases inherent in these combined military and patriarchal family ideologies. Actors, Joseph asserted in chronicling Daly's management, were potential "conservative and prosperous capitalist[s]"; but actresses, in Augustin's words, were the stage's "active ornaments," goods to be "worked upon" and displayed.[6] Such constructs empowered Daly to exercise more proprietary claims over the female than the male members of his company. Moreover, he had a cultural mandate to implement his militaristic paternalism with particular force because the theatre, especially its dangerously sexual actresses, needed special control. Hence George Parson Lathrop's rationalization of the Daly regime in *Century Magazine*: "This manager is a general; his ability is nothing less than that of a great commander, when you reflect that he is managing and directing every day some two hundred people on his actual list—people by the very nature of their artistic gift most sensitive and susceptible."[7]

Most of the notorious rules by which Daly implemented his autocracy ostensibly applied to all members of his company, but given the cultural biases and his personal agenda of conquest and assimilation, the ramifications often proved more severe for women than men. When a performer entered Daly's employ, she or he signed a contract to

act and represent, to the best of [her or his] ability in the performances aforesaid, during said season, all such parts and characters as [Augustin Daly] shall direct, and to conform to and faithfully obey the RULES endorsed on this agreement, and all the rules established for such Theatre, and all alterations of and additions to such rules posted in the Green Room of such Theatre, which rules, alterations and additions are made a part of this agreement.[8]

The "RULES endorsed on this agreement" were contained in a list of twelve articles printed on the back of the contract. Many of these echoed rules imposed by earlier managers who, like Daly, attempted to increase theatrical civility. Most typical were articles prescribing behavior in the Green Room, conduct onstage and backstage during rehearsals and performances, and performers' responsibilities in obtaining and maintaining costumes. Daly's rules also included an injunction to address the manager on business only in his office, with varying amounts of salary forfeiture denoted as penalty for infractions.[9] Numerous published articles and memoirs of former Daly employees attest that what distinguished his regime was the extremity of his control. He insisted on dictating every detail of the running of his operation; he was absolutely unwilling to countenance opinions other than his own; he upheld obsessively stringent standards for what constituted an infraction of rules; and he frequently supplemented the contract regulations with posted dicta that extended to governing company members' personal as well as professional conduct.[10]

Women bore the brunt of many of the more extreme manifestations of Daly's authority. For example, his contract contained a rule enjoining performers from addressing the audience without the manager's express consent. Neither the rule nor the stiff penalty imposed for its infraction was unique to Daly's operation. But Daly was extraordinarily vigilant in ensuring its enforcement. He would spy on performers from the paint frame and backstage closets and would employ others to spy for him.[11] He was most fanatical about women's observance of this rule. Actress Dora Knowlton Ranous recounts Daly's response when some of the female performers on stage smiled at the enthusiastic applause of Colonel James Mapleson, impresario at the New York Academy of Music, seated in the audience: "my gracious, what a wigging we got from 'the Governor' the minute the curtain was down on that act! . . . no young ladies under his tutelage, he said, ever did that; and he intimated that the next young lady who should commit a similar indiscretion would shortly be conspicuous by her absence."[12] Although the rule about not acknowledging the audience as written in the contract was not gender specific, Daly's admonition reveals his particular concern that ladies in his employ not acknowledge the favors of other men, especially rival managers. This made the edict a gesture of sexual as well as aesthetic control. He would sometimes trick actresses into thinking he had left the theatre for the evening only to secrete himself in the back row of the gallery and scrutinize their behavior with opera glasses. Perceiving that they responded to male audience members, he summarily dismissed them from the company.[13] Some of the posted rules with which Daly supplemented the contract were explicitly gendered and again reflect his need to control female sexuality. Ranous recalled a stipulation that "the young women of the company shall not walk on Broadway in the afternoons" where they might have displayed themselves outside their manager's possessive gaze.[14]

Daly also exceeded other managers' rule lists with an injunction forbidding the disclosure of "the *name or nature*, or any particulars of the *plays* or entertainments in preparation at the theatre, or the giving of any *information* about the *business* or *concerns* of said theatre, until the same is publicly advertised by the manager." This was reinforced by the following sweeping dictum, which in effect superceded all the other rules: "The *directions of the Manager concerning* the *performance* and *business* of the theatre must be *obeyed*, under penalty of forfeit of *fifty dollars*, or of being discharged, or both."[15] Employees were bound by these rules without recourse or appeal to any outside agency to do whatever Daly directed in order to realize his vision. "There could be but one method of accomplishing anything; that was the method of Augustin Daly," wrote Otis Skinner.[16]

For performers, Daly's methods entailed an arduous rehearsal schedule that often included rehearsing a new play all day, performing an established piece in the evenings, and resuming work on the new piece afterward until the early morning hours.[17] Given that actresses were usually the featured attractions in Daly's productions, the workload often proved more arduous for them than their male counterparts. Concerns about placing undue stress on the "weaker sex" did not weigh heavily on Daly. Contemporary gynecologic and social discourse constructed women as "weaker" than men in the sense of greater susceptibility to animal impulses and temptations, which mandated greater discipline and training. Moreover, prevailing evolutionary theory held that women were less sensate than men and therefore inherently more tolerant of the pain and suffering an arduous work schedule could cause.[18]

In addition to endurance of long, hard hours, obedience to Daly's rules meant performers had to submit to all of his directorial ministrations. Closed to outside observers, rehearsals involved physical as well as verbal manipulations of performers.[19] Daly brooked no protest or questioning of his methods. As he sharply informed one of his workers, "When I am on stage, I permit no one to interfere with me!"[20] Male employees report being angered by Daly's more abusive exertions of authority, while actresses report being reduced to tears.[21] Daly's physical manipulations of actresses could become overtly sexualized. According to Isadora Duncan, Daly took the opportunity, while supposedly comforting her during a production, to slide his hand down the back of her dress. In anger, she resigned from the company.[22] Daly's strict veil of secrecy mystified his authority and masked the often unrespectable ways he pursued respectability. Yet Daly's reputation for womanizing and extreme authoritarianism was not entirely unknown to outsiders. His ultimate protection, along with the Victorian double standard, was the feudal domestic model of business management that at least tacitly justified his sexualized, dictatorial methods of control.

Under these circumstances, it was difficult for performers, especially actresses, to resist Daly's authority with impunity. In a precarious and largely unregulated industry, the incentive to endure his methods was considerable. Daly strove to maintain a viable stock company, which promised performers sustained employment. He also prided himself on keeping a fine facility and aimed to produce profitable theatre catering to more respectable audiences, which promised performers higher social status. In contrast, actors in combination companies often faced grueling travel schedules, endless hours on or waiting for trains, and illness from lack of sleep, regular meals, adequate dressing rooms, and clean running water. Enduring such hardships and staying in unfamiliar, frequently seedy hotels put actresses at particular risk.[23] Thus, while critical of his extreme authoritarianism, most performers far preferred the working conditions Daly offered. Company members also credited him with launching their careers and teaching them how to act. In addition, employees testified that he had a forceful, magnetic personality that made people seek his approval. Dora Ranous writes of the company's interactions with Daly after a successful opening night:

> Then Mr. Daly came on the stage, smiling his sweetest, shook hands with us, said we have done splendidly, and that he was proud of us. Never have I seen a more fascinating man when he chooses to be. His eyes have a wonderful, compelling power—they influence men and women alike. When he smiles in that way one feels ready to do anything to please him. But his smile of sarcasm is another thing.[24]

Daly's charm as well as his impresarial couture are well illustrated in a photograph taken during these early years of his career in theatre management (fig. 3).

3. *Augustin Daly, manager of his own theatre, ca. 1869, in Charles H. Shattuck,* Shakespeare on the American Stage, *vol. 2, 55. Courtesy of the Folger Shakespeare Library, Washington, D.C.*

If men and women were similarly compelled by Daly to perform, they challenged him on distinctly unequal footing. Occasionally, Daly would allow himself to be bested by actors who, as men, were his potential equals. In one instance, he upbraided E. L. Davenport for not taking his stage work seriously enough. The actor appeared in the next performance clad entirely in black and much amused the audience with feigned solemnity. Such a costume and character change was a flagrant violation of managerial policy, but Daly, in what Rose Eytinge called a rare "magnanimous action," let the actor have his way and exacted no punishment.[25] By contrast, women's resistance to Daly's directives did not prompt greater recognition of actresses as equals, but contributed to the "natural" savagery he already projected onto them. Their resistance further ripened actresses for taming and ennobled Daly when he prevailed. When May Irwin dared to contradict Daly's views of her character in rehearsal, Daly publicly humiliated her. She later recounted the incident to biographer Lewis Strang: "I had never been spoken to like that in my life. And before all the company! . . . I broke down and blubbered. [He was] inexorable."[26] Having won, Daly wished her a pleasant good morning the following day. She responded: "Mr. Daly, we are *not* on speaking terms." With the tamer's smug appreciation of his conquest's show of spirit, Daly added, laughing: "I do like a fearless, independent character!"[27]

Ironically for Daly, there was room for actresses' resistance to his regime in the construction of "naturalized" femininity itself. While controlling actresses through rigid rules and extreme vigilance, Daly still needed to display their sexuality for public consumption in order to impress ever more respectable audiences with his conquest of feminine nature in all its savage beauty. In cahoots with Augustin on his upwardly mobile quest, Joseph wrote him while he was on tour with his company in Cincinnati in the fall of 1873: "I suppose the ladies of the company were the objects of much attention and observation at the Hotel. Did Fanny [Davenport] crush 'em with her queenly presence? Did [Clara] Morris spring on their susceptibility with a 'panther-like spring'?" Two days later, Augustin replied in the affirmative, adding "the audiences grow in quality also."[28] The melodramas that dominated Daly's repertoire in the 1870s required actresses to engage in lavish, transgressive displays of primordial passion. Because Daly and his contemporaries construed such behavior as essentially feminine, there were limits to how much a male director could dictate the representation. He was obliged to rely on actresses to achieve an effect that by definition defied rational control and exceeded what he could mark in rehearsal. When these actresses were on their own onstage in performance, they held the power, in spite of Daly's much vaunted omnipotence, to determine the success of the production.

An episode involving his most famous emotionalistic player of the decade, Clara Morris, illustrates this necessary, but for Daly extremely discomfiting, shift in the power dynamic. The play in production was *L'Article 47*, a sensational vehicle Daly was fashioning to showcase Morris's virtuosic emotionalism and, more importantly, the male prowess his managing such savagery implied. Success hinged on the play's climactic "mad scene," whose enactment called for full-throttle physical and emotional pyrotechnics. In her memoir, Morris reported being unable to pull out all the stops in rehearsal: "I read my lines with intelligence, but gave no sign of what I intended to do at night. Of course that made Mr. Daly suffer great anxiety, but he said nothing, only looked at me with such troubled, anxious eyes that I felt sorry for him." She described the suffering that ensued:

> Oh, what a time of misery it was, the preparation of that play! Poor Mr. Daly—and poor, poor Miss Morris!
>
> You see everything hung upon the mad scene. Yet when we came to that, I simply stood still and spoke the broken, disjointed words.
>
> "But what are you going to do at night?" Mr. Daly cried. "Act your scene Miss Morris."
>
> Act it, in cold blood, there, in the gray, lifeless daylight? with a circle of grinning, sardonic faces, ready to be vastly amused over my efforts? He might better have asked me to deliver a polished address in beautiful, pellucid Greek, to compose at command a charming little *rondeau* in sparkling French, or a prayer in sonorous Latin—they would have been easier for me to do, than to gibber, to laugh, to screech, to whisper, whimper, rave, to crouch, crawl, stride, fall to order in street-clothes, and always with those fiendish "guyers" ready to assist in my undoing. Yet poor Mr. Daly, too! I was sorry for him, he had so much at stake. It *was* asking a good deal of him to trust his fate entirely, blindly to me.
>
> "Oh!," I said, "I would if I could—do please believe me! I want to do as you wish me to, but, dear Mr. Daly, I can't, my blood is cold in daylight, I am ashamed, constrained! I cannot act then!"
>
> "Well, give me some *faint* idea of what you are going to do," he cried, impatiently.

"Dear goodness!" I groaned, "I am going to try to do all sorts of things—loud and quiet, fast and slow, close-eyed cunning, wide-eyed terror! There, that's all I can tell about it!" and I burst into harassed tears.

He said never another word, but I used to feel dreadfully when, at rehearsals, he would rise and leave the stage as soon as we reached the mad-scene.[29]

Morris's account of the episode reveals her keen awareness of Daly's disadvantage in the situation and suggests opportunities for manipulation. How much she actually needed the mysterious nightly inspiration is debatable given other evidence of how she deliberately fostered her stage persona as "Queen of Spasms." She went so far in a subsequent production as to chew soap in order to froth at the mouth and effect a rabid excess of passion.[30] By self-consciously playing to dominant cultural beliefs in naturalized femininity, she was able to assert otherwise elusive control over her own artistic process.

Joseph Daly offers quite a different account of the production of *L'Article* 47:

In this play Miss Morris reached the height of her achievement. The scene in which, baffled of her vengeance, which had become a monomania, her overwrought emotion unseats her reason and she passes through the stages of fear, cunning, and loss of control to raving madness was electrifying; and when the curtain fell, she was the mistress of the American stage. This triumph had not been effected without extreme preparation. Long rehearsals with her ambitious and painstaking manager had shaped every movement and guided every inflection. Their joy was mutual.[31]

This narrative gives Augustin the control over female savagery he aspired to but that, in practice, his own ideology could prevent him from attaining.

If managing the most passionate actresses was supposed to augment Daly's potency, lavish emotional performances also increased actresses' popularity and risked empowering them as stars. Daly's experience with another leading lady, Agnes Ethel, impressed upon him the pitfalls of this power shift. A scion of the Matilda Heron school of emotionalism, Ethel's repertoire under Daly included his frontier melodrama, *Horizon* (1871). As Med, "white flower of the plains," Ethel incarnated mythic naturalized femininity. The part is that of a chaste but passionate bourgeois maiden susceptible to capture by the Indians. Living among them, she shows herself capable of surviving in the wilderness and guarding her virtue, when necessary, with a musket.[32] Because of the popularity gained through this and other roles, Ethel was able to leave Daly and seek a more advantageous position with rival managers Sheridan Shook and A. M. Palmer at the Union Square Theatre.[33]

Compounding his long-harbored antipathy toward the star system, this experience fueled the anger Daly discharged upon a reporter who praised Clara Morris shortly after she joined the company. The actress reported the incident in her memoir:

> One day a certain newspaper man looked in at his office, and said: "Oh, I have something here about the play, and I've given a few pretty good lines to your *find* (Clara Morris): do you want to look at them?"
>
> "I want them cut out!" sharply ordered Mr. Daly.
>
> "Cut out?" repeated the surprised man. "Why, she's the play—or mighty near it. I thought you'd want her spoken of most particularly?"
>
> And then Mr. Daly made his famous speech: "I don't want individual successes, sir, in my theatre! I want my company kept at a level. I put them all in a line, and then I watch, and if one head begins to bob up above the others, I give it a crack and send it down again!"[34]

Throughout his managerial career, Daly struggled with mixed success to ensure that his actresses' popularity primarily served his theatre's—and, by extension, his own—ascent and not their star egos and independent market-ability.

For many actresses, the ultimate resistance to Daly's methods, after they garnered the notoriety obtainable through his productions, was to follow Ethel's lead and quit the company of their own accord, often in advance of their contract terms. Between Ethel's departure in 1872 and that of Blanche Bates in 1899, twenty players precipitously left Daly's employ. Of these, four-teen were women.[35] Their complaints usually revolved around his extreme stringency, personally intrusive rules, disavowal of traditional lines of business, and denial of star status. Players would no sooner be established in lead-ing roles than they would find themselves abruptly demoted to supporting parts while a less experienced player took the lead. That more than twice as many women as men departed Daly's company suggests not only that actresses endured greater difficulties under his regime, but also that they gained more popular appeal and were more sought after by rival theatres.

Beyond their greater numbers, actresses' departures posed a greater threat to Daly's manhood than actors'. When actresses left him to star with rival male managers, such as Palmer, Wallack, or the Frohmans, their highly public desertions constituted a sexual as well as professional affront. Analogizing actresses and their previously "unsuspected talent" to available "free" or "virgin" land, Daly believed that because he had "discovered" and cultivated them, these performers were his as of right; no one else, including the performer herself, should "reap the whole harvest of the seeds he had sowed."[36]

To protect himself, Daly drew heavily on the professional as well as personal support of his brother, who had become an influential jurist. In 1871, Judge Joseph Daly rendered an opinion in *Hayes v. Willio* that did not directly involve Daly's Theatre but served its interests. Invoking Britain's *Lumley* rule in an American context, Judge Daly's opinion upheld the principle that a performer who left one manager's company could be enjoined from playing elsewhere for the duration of the contract.[37] Although the decision was overturned on appeal, the concept remained part of the agreement performers signed upon entering Daly's company. The operative clause in the contract read:

> and the party of the second part [actress] covenants that she will not act at any other Theatre or place in the City of New York, from the day of the date hereof, until the termination of this contract, without the written consent of the party of the first part [manager]. If the party of the second part shall refuse to fulfill this agreement, and shall attempt to perform at any other Theatre before the termination of this agreement, the party of the first part may, by legal process or otherwise, restrain her from so performing, on payment to her during such restraint of a sum equal to one-quarter of the aforesaid salary in lieu of the aforesaid or any other salary under this agreement during that period.[38]

The pronouns in the printed text of the contract are all feminine, which suggests that the enjoinder was used primarily for actresses. By the 1880s, the language in Daly's Theatre contract became more gender neutral, with blanks left in the text for writing in appropriate pronouns as well as names.[39] But the earlier language reveals how the policy evolved out of Daly's struggles with women.

In spite of this contractual protection, Daly's own ideology and aspirations still left him vulnerable to actresses who chose to leave. The ultimate aim of the conquest agenda in which actresses played so central a role was to bring respectability both to himself and his operation. To enforce the contract required a public lawsuit that risked breaking his veil of secrecy and besmirching his reputation. Thus, when Clara Morris left in 1873 to star at the Union Square Theatre, Joseph counseled his brother: "If she will break her contract, what can you do? Not sue her because she would only get immense popular sympathy as a 'victim.' In fact the only thing is to 'let her go.'" Insinuating that her unleashed wildness would ruin her career and prove too much for a lesser man to handle, Joseph added: "Her time will be short because she needs so much management."[40]

In one notable instance, however, Augustin, with Joseph's support, pressed ahead with legal action. At the end of the 1873–1874 season, the first of three for which she was contracted, Fanny Morant [Mrs. Smith] notified Daly that she did not see sufficient opportunities for playing major roles in his company. Daly enlisted his friend and business partner, A. Oakley Hall (the same attorney who had defended him against Hezekiah Bateman in 1865), to file an injunction with the Superior Court to block Morant's reemployment.[41] Apparently a ruling was slow in coming. When the new season began in late summer 1874, Morant appeared with the Union Square company. Lamenting Hall's apparent inaction, Augustin wrote to Joseph on 5 September: "He has done nothing in the Morant matter; there is no decision; and she plays and laughs at me!" Judge Daly was not assigned to the case, but as Lea VanderVelde has shown, his earlier opinion heavily influenced the presiding Judge Freedman.[42] In addition, Joseph may well have known Freedman personally and may even have interceded after Augustin's letter of 5 September because the ruling came just a few days later. The suit was settled in the manager's favor, with Daly needing only to continue paying Morant one-quarter of her salary to keep her inactive for the remaining two years of her contract.[43] The proceedings were made public in the *New York Daily Register* on 11 September.

VanderVelde has analyzed *Daly v. Smith* as a landmark case that, in actualizing Joseph Daly's earlier argument, canonized *Lumley* in American law. She shows how Freedman borrowed Judge Daly's language from *Hayes v. Willio* to reiterate the view that "performers, by carrying their services to other establishments, deprive [the manager] of the fruits of his diligence and enterprise, increase the rivalry against him, and cause him irreparable injury."[44] Judge Freedman's sympathies, she contends, favored Daly's capital interest and male prerogatives. Asserting that "persons should be held to a true and *faithful* performance of their engagements," Freedman portrayed Morant's departure as untrue and unfaithful.[45] His rhetoric injected the gender politics of monogamous marriage into the employment relationship and invoked the legal model of divorce proceedings that often barred remarriage in the case of female infidelity. "Just as nineteenth-century judges tended to be far harsher on women charged with marital infidelity than on men," VanderVelde writes, "so too, they appear to have been more harsh on women whose actions were perceived as employment infidelity." She adds in a footnote that Judge Freedman, in fact, ruled on a divorce case the same day he ruled on *Daly v. Smith*.[46] Attesting to the gender biases inscribed in the law, VanderVelde observes that all of the prominent cases in the *Lumley* line involved women's employment, and that only female performers were subjected to permanent injunctions against performing elsewhere for the duration of the contract.[47] As she puts it, the essence of these rulings was: "If the lady's employer could not have her services, no one could."[48]

Even with the harsh ruling against Fanny Morant in *Daly v. Smith*, however, Daly's power over her was not secure. Four days after the account of the proceedings appeared in the *Daily Register*, Augustin wrote to Joseph:

> I have nothing from Morant but a threat: if I don't let her play at the U. S. [Union Square Theatre] this week, she will take Steinway Hall and lecture on me and my injunction. I have told Mr. Hall to fix the affair at once: so as to enforce respect for my authority. I do not care to force her to return to me, however, and so long as she don't play in New York City I don't care for her at all.[49]

Omitting this development in his account of the conflict with Morant in Daly's biography, Joseph reports that after Augustin obtained the injunction, he immediately waived it and permitted the actress to play in the rival establishment. After a year with his company, Fanny Morant was no doubt well aware of Daly's obsession with secrecy and the discrepancies between the respectability he sought and many of the methods he employed to gain it. Her threat of a public lecture struck at his Achilles heel. At the time, Daly was showing considerable favoritism to the young, beautiful leading lady, Fanny Davenport. In a personal letter to Davenport written on 16 May 1874, he refers to their "years of intimate association," praises the devotion and generosity she has shown him, and promises to repay her salary, which he has been keeping on loan in order to survive the terrible losses incurred in the Panic of 1873. The possible revelation of his intimacy with Davenport and the fact that he needed to borrow money from an actress in his company were likely among the reasons why Daly suddenly dropped his landmark injunction against Morant. By portraying his granting of the waiver as a magnanimous choice rather than something he may have been forced to do against his will, Daly's brother once again secured through narrative the conquest Augustin aspired to but could not always achieve or maintain in actual practice.[50]

There was another situation complicating Daly's deliberations in the Morant case that also intensified his anxieties about maintaining control over his operation and preserving the appearance of respectability. Along with possibly providing additional motivation to drop the injunction, this situation is significant because it contributed to an important shift in managerial policy. In a letter to Joseph dated 12 September 1874, Augustin reported that when his longtime friend and attorney, A. Oakley Hall, had called on him three days before to tell him about the positive outcome in the Morant case, he also had a second matter to discuss. Hall informed Daly that he was desperately in love with another leading lady in the company, Ada Dyas. Even more shockingly, he wanted to pay Daly to release her from her contract. Augustin gave Joseph a verbatim recollection of Hall's impassioned plea:

> "I want to buy Miss Dyas from you! . . . I love her more than I have ever loved anybody and I want to make her happy. . . . You don't like her . . . Mrs. Daly doesn't like her . . . She doesn't like the *Republic* which you have organized and enforce here! . . . If I was a widower to-morrow I would marry her in spite of the prejudice against actresses. I know Nancy will call me a fool; perhaps I am but I would make any sacrifice in the world for her. . . . I have advanced you, since my partnership began, certain sums from time to time and in all (counting the $25,000 for partnership monies) amounting to about $35,000;—now I propose to make you a present of this whole sum, my right and tithe in all, and surrender my interests in the theatre on one condition—that you surrender Miss Dyas to me!"

To make his beloved happy, Hall was offering to purchase her release so that she would be "free" to join a rival company—in this case Wallack's—where she, like Morant, Morris, Ethel, and others, hoped to find a more advantageous situation. Daly confided his horror to Joseph "at the thought that this woman, like Morris, but in this instance with the convenience(?) [*sic*] of a friend of mine, had never expressed any discontent to me, but had gone on quietly planning this desertion to the enemy, and at the very opening of my season leaves me."[51] At the same time that Hall was advocating on Daly's behalf to prevent one actress from playing elsewhere, he was assisting another actress in making that very move. This distracting conflict may have accounted for his sluggishness in getting a ruling on the injunction. Whatever security Daly derived from the news of his court victory was immediately undermined by this revelation of his friend and lawyer's double-dealing.

As for the money proposition itself, Daly told Joseph it "meant nothing more than the subjugation of my manhood if I accepted (which I never for an instant thought of doing)—and placing myself under an eternal obligation to a man who could not possibly be my friend while he kept this thing from me." Daly could neither take Hall's money nor keep Dyas; "if Miss Dyas was dissatisfied I could only retain her by making sacrifices of discipline and business to her (as was demanded in Miss Morris's case)." The "sacrifices" involved granting Dyas star status to keep her happy. For Daly, this was an intolerable concession, given his established policies and well-known antipathy to the star system. But threatened by potential public scandal, he could not force her to stay without such a promise or enjoin her from performing elsewhere. His solution was to "release" Dyas as Hall asked and to extricate himself from any obligation to Hall by buying him out of the partnership.[52]

In his response to Augustin's shocking tale, Joseph offered a telling diagnosis and an influential remedy. On 15 September 1874, he wrote to his brother:

> I thought it the plot of a new drama ... Dyas the Deceiver or the Fifth Female Sloper [he counted Morant as the sixth to defect] is a thrilling play. . . . I have no doubt that Dyas came over here to win professional distinction but that her head was turned by the pride of an immediate conquest over a brilliant man. Well, your experience is this: the Enemy of the Manager is the Lover! So went Ethel and Morris. And so will go all the creatures who can inspire wild passions by their "emotional" acting. All glory to comic actresses. They gather in no noodles, milksops and fools to advise them against their better interests. . . . Try and play comedy as much as you can this season.

So compelling and dangerous are emotionalistic actresses, argued Joseph, that Hall should be absolved of fault:

> Hall, then, fought all he could for you. The depth of his feeling may be concerned when he offered $35,000 for Dyas's freedom.
>
> Such a man has not acted meanly or treacherously. He has tried to pacify Dyas until he yielded too much. Then she has commanded him in the name of the affection which he has no doubt expressed and he has had to obey against his will. Hall is a good friend to you. Shake hands with him and tell him so.

In response to Dyas's disapproval of the "'*Republic*'" Daly instituted behind the scenes, Joseph affirmed Augustin's methods and indicated that he must rule even more stringently to maintain his managerial authority.

To this end, Joseph proposed the remedy of emphasizing comedy and comic actresses. Unlike the melodramas Daly heretofore had favored, comedies did not require the torrid displays of "wild" passion that in Joseph's view had induced the recent catastrophes. Comedy traditionally appealed more to the intellect than the emotions and relied more on wit and situational and physical humor for effect. Insofar as emotions were part of comedy's appeal, they tended to be more sentimental and restrained than those in melodrama. Joseph proposed the switch in emphasis as an immediate solution to managing the rest of the 1874–1875 season after the departures of Morant and Dyas. However, his proposition portended a larger shift in aesthetic preferences and managerial policy. A trip to London in the fall of 1878 affirmed the wisdom of the shift for Augustin. He wrote to Joseph:

> I believe thoroughly in the comedy vaudeville style of entertainment; occasionally varied with the old comedy or the modern emotional pieces such as the Gaiety Theatre, the Haymarket, or even the vaudeville given here. But above all the theater ought to be a little gem of a place. Not an inch larger than the old 5th Ave., and even ten feet ought to be spared from the auditorium of that for an elegant drawing room sort of lobby. Some of the vestibules of the theatres here are parlors. Nothing that I ever did equalled them—so you see luxury pays. For these luxurious places are the ones which are crowded nightly.[53]

As a response to the dangerous passions allegedly aroused through the overproduction of melodrama, the emphasis on contemporary comedy, only occasionally varied with old comedy (chiefly Shakespearean, Restoration, and eighteenth-century) and emotional pieces, constituted a civilizing move. Daly linked the production of comedy with the production of bourgeois domestic luxury to further his pursuit of respectability.

Soon after launching Daly's Theatre at Thirtieth and Broadway in 1879, his third permanent theatre in New York, Daly formally instituted the change in emphasis. He opened the season with a comedy, *Our First Families*, by Edgar Fawcett, which began with a prologue announced as a composition of "a distinguished author," likely Augustin or Joseph Daly:

> For truth to tell, our art alone would please
> By mirthful methods, nor depart from these,
> We bid farewell to melodrama's wiles. . . .
> To ceaseless fun we dedicate our stage

Through every utterance, though we speak or sing,
The allegros of glad comedy shall ring.[54]

In what must have been a satisfying irony for the Daly brothers, the prologue was delivered by none other than Fanny Morant, who had defected in search of leading roles in melodrama; from her mouth, the line about bidding "farewell to melodrama's wiles" became all the more meaningful. At the rival Union Square Theatre, she had ended up making her name in the same kinds of character roles Daly had wanted her to play. Now at the age of fifty-nine, with her professional options even more limited to what George Odell called "her grand old ladies of comedy and drama," she came back to Daly on his terms as a character actress. Morant's position in the reorganized company emblematized the Daly strategy not just to produce comedy but to do so specifically as a means of containing unruly femininity.

Comic Triumphs and Tribulations

For the first two seasons at the new theatre, Daly's comic emphasis included both musicals and "straight" plays, but the success of *Needles and Pins* in the winter of 1880–1881 proved the greater viability of the latter.[55] With this production, Daly also established the popularity of the core group of actors that became his most famous ensemble, the so-called Big Four: character actors James Lewis and Mrs. [Anne Hartley] Gilbert; leading man John Drew; and most luminous of all, leading lady Ada Rehan. When Daly designed the baroque masthead for the theatre, it was Rehan's face he enshrined in the center as the Spirit of Comedy (fig. 4). She became the very embodiment of his enterprise. The costume designer W. Graham Robertson, who worked closely with Daly and Rehan, said this about the star's value to her impresario:

> Daly must have been a great actor who could not act. He was rough and uncouth, with harsh utterance and uncultured accent; a singer without a voice, a musician without an instrument. But in Ada Rehan he found his means of self expression; Ada Rehan with her quaint charm, her voice of music, her splendid presence and her gentle good nature which he could mould to his will.[56]

Onto Rehan, Daly projected his highest ambitions for theatrical conquest and self-transformation, along with the correspondingly high anxieties about failure and exposure that continued to haunt his quest.

*4. Ada Rehan as Comedy on the baroque masthead for Daly's Theatre
Schedule in the 1880s. Courtesy of the Museum of the City of New York.*

Daly's bond with Rehan was distinguished from those he had had with previous leading ladies by its longevity—she remained with him for the next twenty years until his death—and intensity. Robertson viewed their relationship as a "real-life Trilby-Svengali drama."[57] Like Trilby, Rehan was Irish and relatively young and obscure before coming under her Svengali's influence. Born in Limerick in 1857, she immigrated to New York as a young child with her family. Following her older sisters onto the stage to supplement the family income, she debuted in a production of *Across the Continent* in Newark in 1873. She made her first New York appearance later that year in *Thoroughbred* at Wood's Museum. Thereafter, she played a variety of Shakespearean and contemporary roles with several different companies in engagements in Philadelphia, Louisville, Albany, and Baltimore. Daly first saw her perform in Albany in 1877 when she played Bianca in David Garrick's *Katharine and Petruchio*, a portentous circumstance given her later fame as Katharine in *Taming of the Shrew*. But it was when he saw her acting with Fanny Davenport in his own play, *Pique*, staged by another company at New York's Grand Opera House in April 1879, that he was moved to hire her. She debuted under his management the next month at his father-in-law's Olympic Theatre in New York in his adaptation of *L'Assomoir*. The following September, she first appeared at Daly's company's new permanent home at Thirtieth and Broadway as Nelly Beers in Daly's *Love's Young Dream*.[58] She was twenty-two, Daly forty-one. By that time, enough prominent actresses had left and gained star billing at other theatres that, in spite of his own antipathy to starring, Daly became known as a "star maker." Rehan came to him seeking professional advancement. His greater age, experience, and managerial position vested him with considerable authority over her life.

Rehan's youthful talent and Irish charm powerfully attracted Daly. In his biography of the Dublin-born eighteenth-century comedienne, Peg Woffington, a thinly veiled tribute to Rehan, he wrote: "she was possessed of the tempting beauty of eye and mouth, the glowing health, the flashing wit, the sprightly humor and the quick intelligence of the native-born Irish girl."[59] Verbal and pictorial evidence attests that Rehan was a striking figure—tall in stature, big-boned, with classical facial features, and long, thick reddish blond hair. In addition to her ebullient wit and vivacity, she possessed superb athletic and vocal abilities. In the few heavily emotional roles she essayed, critics found her credible but limited. But to Daly she embodied a greater animal force even than his accomplished melodramatic actresses. Where he called Clara Morris a "pantheress let loose" and other actresses merely "Cats," he dubbed Rehan a "Lioness."[60]

Endowing her with more potent levels of naturalized femininity, Daly was more enamored and doting but also more rigorous in his efforts, as Graham Robertson put it, "to mould [Rehan] to his will." In her memoir, Cornelia Otis Skinner, daughter of the Daly company member Otis Skinner, explicitly divulges that the two were lovers, though both were Catholic and Daly remained married to his wife. "Ada Rehan, besides being leading lady," writes Skinner, "enjoyed the off-stage role of *grande-maitresse*—although *enjoyed* is a debatable word."[61] Daly made Rehan the chief object not only of his affections but also of the dictum Joseph had written in the wake of the disastrous conflicts with Dyas and Morant: "The actors don't get lazy nor saucy nor treacherous if you keep them well at work."[62] Whereas Daly had demoted previous leading ladies to supporting roles in an attempt to contain their individual egos, he was compelled to keep Rehan in the female leads once the Big Four gained popularity. The rigors of rehearsing a new play all the day before and well into the night after an evening performance of an established piece became more routine. The schedule became especially taxing for Rehan, whom Daly singled out for special attention in group rehearsals and additional private sessions lasting into the early morning hours.[63] According to George Parson Lathrop, Daly came to rehearsal "with the text at his tongue's end" and precise pictorial compositions already formed.[64] To stage these

compositions, he would perfect "the smallest gesture and subtlest modula-
tion of voice," wrote Otis Skinner. Skinner said he had known the maestro "to
be dissatisfied with the crook of his leading lady's forefinger and to straighten
it out, to adjust the pose of her head and the turn of her foot."[65] If his praise
was all the more gratifying to her because of their intimacy, his reprimands
were correspondingly devastating. The *Graphic* reported that his personal
insults in rehearsal could cut her to "a mere tear besoaked pulp."[66] These rigors took such a toll that some journalists reported her being gray and drawn
from overwork and expressed concern about her health. Indeed, Rehan
missed occasional performances from illness brought on by exhaustion.[67]

Although Daly did not demote Rehan from leading lady status, he used his
sexual as well as managerial power over her to "keep her in her place." In Cornelia Otis Skinner's judgment, he treated Rehan "very much as his personal
chattel. If they appeared together on the street, Daly walked ahead of her, like
an Indian, never speaking to her. Offstage, she lived alone, on his insistence."
While she remained his primary love interest, he still pursued other women
in the company, according to Skinner, and would "parade his conquests in
front of her, driving her into hysterical rages." When these pecadillos were
over, he returned to Rehan "who, wounded and morose, always took him
back." "To hold the whip handle by keeping a woman of her beauty and
prominence in the compromising position an extramarital liaison involved in
those cautious times was a sop to his will to power," opined Skinner. "It gave
him a feeling of prestige." She viewed these sexual power manipulations as
part of a purposeful agenda: "he set about making her over, deliberately
destroying her happy-go-lucky spirit, turning her into a conventional fin-de-
siècle woman of the world—poised, high-strung, witty and neurotic."[68]

Daly's simultaneous attraction to the spirit of "the native-born Irish girl" and
compulsion to change her into a more "conventional"—that is, a more WASP,
upper-class, and urbane—type reflect a complex identification with her. Rehan
not only embodied the upwardly mobile aspirations of Daly's Theatre but the
refinement of the impresario's own "lower" attributes or personal "roughness"
as well. In the era's Darwinian cultural framework, the stakes for Daly to prove
both sexual and directorial control over his leading lady went beyond power
and gratification of desire. According to the principle of recapitulation, a since
discredited but then central and popularly understood tenet of evolutionary
theory, ontogeny recapitulated phylogeny, or, the development of the individual
recapitulated that of the species. Both developments were thought to proceed
hierarchically toward an apex of adult Anglo-Saxon maleness. Lower down,

and more preserving of primate and infantile characteristics, white and, to progressively greater degrees, "darker" women were equated with savage racial Others. Following the logic of recapitulation, the upwardly aspiring male had to overcome traits not only embodied in women but also, by implication, inscribed in his own organism.[69] His conquest of an actual woman, which the impresario appeared spectacularly to enact on the actress's body, metonymically signified conquest of the feminine traits within himself. Moreover, because the logic of recapitulation meant the "higher" races featured the greatest sexual differentiation (absence of femininity in men and masculinity in women), Daly's seeming eradication of Rehan's Irishness also furthered his own ascent. "Whitening" and feminizing her according to WASP bourgeois standards, he "whitened" and masculinized himself.

The dynamics of civilizing the savagery and femininity Daly projected onto Rehan played out onstage as well as off in a series of vehicles he adapted for the Big Four. Working largely from contemporary German and French farces, he devised light social comedies whose titles suggest a preoccupation with passion and its taming: *The Railroad of Love*, *The Lottery of Love*, *Love in Tandem*, *Love in Harness*, and *Love on Crutches*. In the mounting of this repertoire, titles and character names changed, but the Big Four played slight variations of the same roles and plots.[70] Rehan, according to the *New York Tribune*, typically impersonated "a compound of the hoyden, the coquette, and the ingenue" whose youthful free spiritedness impelled her to indulge interests outside the confines of home and marriage. John Drew played the urbane lover who pursued her, either as a neglected suitor before marriage or a neglected husband afterward, anxious that her interests were inappropriately keeping her from him. The conflicting activities of hero and heroine resulted in a series of comic misunderstandings and witty quarrels that were finally resolved. In the end, the heroine joined the hero in a pledge of lasting mutual devotion.

Throughout, the farcical antics of James Lewis and Mrs. Gilbert, who enacted a rendition of the henpecked husband and domineering wife, enhanced the comedy. This older duo provided stark physical and behavioral contrast to highlight the young lovers' more desirable attributes. Bemoaning his own domestic plight, Lewis's character often expressed great admiration for Rehan's because she was so adorable by comparison to his wife. His stage relationship with Mrs. Gilbert offered an amusing but nonetheless pointed object lesson in the perils of female dominance and misdirected female passion that reinforced the heroine's conversion.[71]

Similar character types and plot motifs applied to the rendering of Old English comedies as well. Daly adapted standards like *The Merry Wives of Windsor*, *School for Scandal*, and *The Country Girl* (Garrick's version of Wycherley's *The Country Wife*) to fit the Big Four configuration. The performers donned period costumes, but the characters' basic relationships and playing styles were little altered. As the *Herald* quipped: "They have one way of playing comedy at Daly's and only one. Whether the piece be Sheridan's or Shakespeare's or Schonthan's or Jerome's, the actors are always good, bright, middle-class Americans."[72] As improbable as the situations could become in some of these Old English and contemporary vehicles, critics and audiences praised the productions for their realism.[73] Daly and his company successfully made his vision of desirable gender and class relations credible to bourgeois patrons.

All members of the Big Four became famous in their respective parts—"stars in all but the billing," write Wilmeth and Cullen—but Rehan soon surpassed the other three.[74] While others' characters sometimes came to new realizations about themselves in the course of the plays, the transformation of Rehan's character comprised the center of the action. It was on her full acceptance of the appropriate male lover and subordination of her interests to his that the fate of the social order rested. Along with the plot, Daly arranged the staging to give the leading lady primary focus. He devised business and blocking to draw audience attention to her even when the primary action of the moment lay elsewhere. He also had her deliver act-ending speeches and platitudinous epilogues on the blessings of womanly love and devotion.[75] Rehan's popularity and Daly's propensity for featuring her became so pronounced that when the company embarked on a European tour in the spring of 1886, the press heralded them as "Mr. Daly's Ada Rehan Company."[76]

Showcasing Rehan, Daly used the resources of his production apparatus to magnify the display of his managerial prowess. One strategy involved surrounding her in lavish material splendor that often exceeded the scenic requirements of the plays. Citing another of Daly's adaptations from the German, Edward A. Dithmar commented:

These German comedies were always made a bit too magnificent pictorially at Daly's. Obviously, in this case, the German playwright had treated of lower middle class life, a humble servant's *ménage* with one maid in all work. The scenic picture in the adaptation was a splendid room in a mansion in which a veritable retinue of servants would have been needed.[77]

This scenic excess aesthetically tied the world of the stage representation to that of the 1,051-seat auditorium and lobby, spaces where Daly's physical presence predominated during performances. Suffused in an atmosphere of bourgeois comfort and luxury, these areas, like the *mise-en-scène*, were appointed with lush, expensive draperies, wall hangings, upholstery, antique furnishings and artifacts, and baroque trim. The impresario reportedly spent $20,000 (about $390,000 today) on renovations to the interior that the *New York Times* pronounced "conspicuous for its elegance."[78] All these improvements bespoke Daly's triumph over adversity and attainment of wealth and success. Daly personally greeted his patrons when they entered his theatre lobby. During the performance, he remained visible at the back of the auditorium as he kept watch over the quality of the audience and the stage presentation. Omnipresent, Daly linked himself semiotically to his theatre's featured attraction, leading lady Rehan. The domestic scene on stage melded seamlessly into Daly's house, and the heroine's ultimate devotion to the leading man melded into her devotion to Daly, in life as well as theatre.

In this scheme, leading man John Drew functioned as a surrogate for the manager. Both men were tall, lithe, and vitally energetic, and each characteristically sported a full moustache. But where Daly was "rough and uncouth, with harsh utterance and uncultured accent," Drew was the epitome of polished, urbane WASP masculinity, known for his impeccable manners and flawless speech.[79] Rather than Daly himself, Drew more aptly personified the respectable sophisticate Daly aspired to become. During the performance, the heroine's conversion to womanly devotion replicated Rehan's larger conversion under Daly's management, while the leading man telegraphed an image of the self-transformation the impresario effected through that conquest.

A photograph entitled "Reading the Play" (fig. 5), which Daly had taken for public consumption in 1882 just after the Big Four attained popularity, offers a striking visual summary of the gender dynamics informing Daly's enterprise. The scene could be set either on- or offstage in the lush, homelike atmosphere of Daly's Theatre. Enthroned in an ornate armchair, the patriarch impresario sits reading the text to the company gathered attentively around him, an activity emblematizing his dictatorial control over all aspects of the production. Positioned in the same picture plane and forming almost a mirror image of his boss, John Drew sits directly opposite Daly on one end of a divan. The symbolic connection between the two is further connoted through the crossing of their lower legs in the center of the composition.

5. *Daly reading a play to his company, with Ada Rehan seated on the floor at his feet, 1882. Left to right, standing: William Gilbert, John Moore, W. J. Le Moyne, May Fielding. Left to right, sitting in chairs: James Lewis, George Parkes, Mrs. G. H. Gilbert, John Drew, Augustin Daly, Charles Fisher, Virginia Dreher. In Joseph Francis Daly,* The Life of Augustin Daly, *357.*

The only figure seated on the floor is Ada Rehan. A fur carpet cushioning her lower body fittingly signals her underlying animal nature. Resting on one hip with her elbow propped on the divan and her legs bent underneath her, she reclines at the feet of both her leading man and her manager, a picture of submissiveness and domesticity. Her torso, however, is oriented toward Daly's, and the two figures exclusively share the primary diagonal line in the composition which registers Daly's specific dominance over his leading lady. Mrs. Gilbert sits directly behind Rehan on the divan to set off Rehan's more youthful and classically beautiful features by contrast. Daly's sexual as well as managerial power is reinforced by the two young supporting actresses, May Fielding and Virginia Dreher, who flank him. They are accompanied on Daly's side of the picture only by a grandfatherly actor who, in the Darwinian value system of the period, poses little sexual competition. One seated and one standing, the two young actresses are positioned above Rehan, available for Daly to use to keep her in her place. The apparent casualness with which these artfully composed figures effect their respective postures works to naturalize the power relations portrayed.

How Rehan herself may have viewed and coped with Daly's regime is difficult to determine. Her testimony was muted by the illicit nature of their personal relationship and the impresario's edict prohibiting company members to talk to outsiders about the mechanics of his operation. Perhaps aware that her letters might be kept for posterity, she remained very circumspect in her personal correspondence regarding both Daly himself and the activities of his theatre.[80] After Daly died, she confided some of her feelings in a letter to her longtime supporter, William Winter: "I was fully alive to all he ever did for me & he knew my devotion to him & his ambitions. It was all so well understood between us that we had really grown into being One. we [sic] both worked with heart & soul—for one end. My loss. No one can ever understand."[81] As many aspiring performers had before her, Rehan came to Daly seeking professional training and advancement, but to an extent matched by none of her predecessors, she had fallen in love with and devoted herself to him. Thus, she may have been more tolerant of practices that drove others away. According to Georgie Drew, who expressed concern to Rehan about the changes in her health and temperament since joining Daly's company, Rehan confided that Daly "ruled her with almost hypnotic power."[82] Although she played the subordinate role of Trilby to Daly's Svengali, the relationship clearly served Rehan's interests as well as her manager's. Like Daly, she was marked by social stigmas, including being Irish Catholic, an actress, and a married man's mistress. She harbored her own upwardly mobile ambitions that melded with Daly's and that his directorial methods helped her fulfill. No doubt the material rewards that accrued to her through the relationship likely helped make the difficulties she suffered worthwhile. A *Theatre Magazine* account estimated her assets as of 1891, after twelve years with Daly, at $300,000 (about $6.45 million today), including "a $30,000 house in New York, various mortgages, and enough stock in a New Jersey railroad to have made her a director."[83]

Whatever the reasons for Rehan's complicity, she attained an unprecedented level of social and professional prestige for an American actress by playing the part of Daly's leading lady and protégée. Through his management, she became a dominant cultural icon of eminently desirable and emulable femininity. Papers lavished praise on her. The *New York Sun* declared her first in its 1885–1886 series "Celebrities of New York" and offered the following paean:

Ada Rehan is a thing of naturalness, kindness and light, a girl sensible, gracious, charming; less concerned to inspire the enthusiasm of Sarah Bernhardt than to diffuse around her an atmosphere peculiarly her own and of happiness. Light and airy as is her nature, it is full of harmony. You go from the theatre after seeing her with pleasant feelings and content. Her eyes are like those of the women of Limerick, singularly soft, yet laughing and sparkling with bright intelligence and good feeling. Her movements are elastic and graceful. The whole woman is essentially womanly, blending much of gentle bright tenderness with visible energy and élan.[84]

With Rehan the main attraction, Daly's Theatre, according to the *New York Dramatic News*, surpassed its rivals to win the status of "the Comedy House of New York and his company . . . the best comedy organization New York ever saw."[85] The *New York Telegram* reported that first nights attracted "the elite of the city 'upper crust.'"[86] Notable personages who favored Daly and Rehan with their attendance and applause included General William Tecumseh Sherman, General Horace Potter, Mark Twain, H. C. Bunner, George William Curtis, Charles Dudley Warner, Frank R. Stockton, Edmund Clarence Stedman, Stanford White, F. D. Millet, Edwin A. Abbey, and many others.[87]

As Rehan garnered this tremendous public adoration, she received many lucrative offers to leave Daly. One New York producer reportedly offered her $50,000 and star billing, which Daly persisted in denying her.[88] Rehan turned all these offers down, gestures which fed Daly's acute need for female fidelity after the earlier embarrassing defections from his company. If previous actresses had found their ultimate resistance to Daly's authority in leaving, Rehan may have found hers in staying. As the embodiment of his enterprise, she became its indispensable feature.

With Rehan's growing popularity and Daly's increasing identification with and need for his leading lady, her relationship with her audience became a vexing site of resistance to his authority. The plaudits of male critics in the mainstream press as well as the applause of generals, businessmen, and literati registered men's considerable admiration of her. However, her greatest following consisted of white middle- and upper-middle-class women who since the 1870s had increasingly comprised Daly's audiences. The second Daly's Theatre, at Broadway and Fourteenth Street, had been located in the fashionable shopping district known as "Ladies' Mile," and he had instituted Wednesday and Saturday matinees to cater to female shoppers.[89] This audience followed him when he moved into the third Daly's Theatre at Broadway and Thirtieth Street, where the Big Four rose to prominence in the 1880s. As Rehan earned more and more praise as an ideal female idol, women flocked to Daly's specifically to emulate her. Ladies of fashion hired couturiers to copy her costumes, while so-called Delsarte girls, female practitioners of Delsarte-based physical culture exercises, imitated her stage bearing and movement. These women consumed her image and the lush *mise-en-scènes* in which she was showcased like the goods they purchased before and after the performances.

The phenomenon continued when Daly's company played in other cities. The *Chicago Evening Mail* reported:

> The Rehan roll, a sort of Henry Irving stride between three short steps relieved by lateral twists and casual whirls has long raged as an epidemic among Delsarte girls east and west. The Rehan drawl has worried more than a few followers of this ingenious actress and it is not possible to enter an assembly of swelldom or move twenty feet on the promenade without encountering some girl trying to keep her chin tilted à la Rehan.[90]

Chicago women sported hats styled and named in Rehan's honor.[91] The *Philadelphia Republican* reported that dressmakers offered Rehan her stage clothes free in exchange for advertising their names in the program.[92]

While a testament to the height of respectability Daly's Theatre had achieved and a force for the expansion of American economic and cultural empire, audiences of female consumers also proved destabilizing to managerial autocracy. Tracing the "regenderization" of nineteenth-century American theatre audiences, Richard Butsch relates the increasing presence of women in middle-class theatres to a decline in audience sovereignty. In the male-dominated, working-class theatres of the early nineteenth century, audiences boisterously voiced their opinions and demands, forcing managers and performers to cater to their will. After the Civil War, Butsch reports, court rulings gave managers greater control and empowered them to enlist police to enforce audience decorum. The new female-dominated audience, in keeping with women's prescribed domestic roles, was expected to be a "quiet observer" of whatever stage spectacle the manager saw fit to proffer. Thus, according to Butsch, though women became the predominant presence in middle-class theatre houses, female audiences ceded greater power to management.[93]

However, this power shift was not absolute. Managers' demands for greater audience quietude and decorum constituted at least a partial appropriation of the moral reform agenda advanced chiefly by white middle-class women since the antebellum period. Respectable female audiences, then, were not simply complying with managers' dictates but were also following their own beliefs and imparting to the theatre some of the same refining influence they purportedly had over the home. Moreover, with women gaining increasing economic clout as consumers, their tastes imposed significant market pressure on theatre producers. Daly may have introduced matinees and lush contemporary costumes and sets to court these audiences, but, especially during Rehan's career, female spectators began to expect and demand these displays and thus informed—if not dictated—the terms and content of the representations.

The interchange that occurred between Rehan and her female fans within and without the theatre also troubled Daly's authoritarian regime. He was fanatical about his company members not acknowledging anyone in the audience during performances. This concern stemmed not only from his realistic aesthetics but also from his compulsion to control female sexuality and keep his actresses from responding to the desires of other men. Female consumer desire presented some different problems. All the while Rehan played her parts as directed and stayed dutifully behind the fourth wall, her female fans were scrutinizing and dissecting her image and appropriating it for their own purposes. They then left the theatre to reassemble and reenact her image in whole or in part in venues outside Daly's carefully crafted representational scheme. These reenactments, in turn, informed their expectations and demands when they returned to the theatre to see another production. In addition to investing Rehan with enormous star power of the kind Daly had spent his career combatting, these audiences took possession of his leading lady through female transactions in which he had little means of intervening.

By turning into the very idol Daly had so assiduously forged, Rehan became part of an interchange destabilizing not only to Daly's personal authority but also to the powerful men whose respect he sought. To copy Rehan, her white middle- and upper-class female fans were spending more of the money their husbands and fathers earned and were gaining influence over consumer markets. This activity undercut one of the express ideological messages of many of the Big Four comedies, the debunking of the acquisitive, henpecking matrons Mrs. Gilbert typically impersonated. Ironically, Daly's civilizing efforts had become too successful by the late 1880s. If his enterprise began as a means of proving his manhood, it now fed into a growing concern about emasculating "overcivilization." While echoing American culture's recurring fear of the deleterious effects of too much civilization, the term's coinage in the late nineteenth century reflected an intensification of that anxiety amid the increasing pressures of urbanization and the disappearance of the frontier "safety valve." In particular, the cosmopolitan, pleasure-seeking economy that fostered more luxurious lifestyles, empowered women as consumers, and supported institutions such as Daly's Theatre portended the degeneracy of bourgeois society and culture.[94]

Taming of the Shrew

In the context of these developments, Daly's adaptation of *Taming of the Shrew*, which opened on 18 January 1887 with Rehan as the eponymous Katharine, may be read as a regenerative project, one fueling American economic and cultural expansion but reasserting male control of the territory. As such, the play partook of the widespread fascination with physical force that T. J. Jackson Lears finds expressed in other literary forms of the period as "a return to pre-modern tales of adventure . . . when 'men sang a manlier way.' "[95] Through manipulation of dramatic and theatrical elements, Daly made this step backward in mythic time a potent thrust forward for his own and Anglo-Saxon manhood's conquering ambitions.

Although he cut close to one-third of Shakespeare's words, including most all of the linguistic bawdry, Daly billed his *Shrew* as the first staging of the complete play in America.[96] Unlike earlier versions, his included the Induction, featuring Sly the Tinker, who, after being kicked out of a tavern by the tyrannical Hostess, falls asleep and frames the play within a dream. In an American cultural context, this device invoked the henpecked Rip Van Winkle, thereby setting up Daly's adaptation as a flight from feminized overcivilization. Stylistically, Sly and the servant characters carried almost all of the play's farcical elements, while the major characters were played more naturalistically in the vein of romantic comedy.[97] Rather than suppressing the play's brutality, however, these manipulations of language, plot, and playing style allowed the play's archaic justice to be integrated into modern bourgeois consciousness.[98]

Most potently, Daly visually superimposed the mythos of frontier conquest onto Shakespeare's text by consolidating scenes transpiring in the same locale to facilitate changes of lavishly realistic sets and rearranging key events to create iconic tableaux. The production's signal iconic moment was Katharine's first entrance, which was forestalled until the opening of the second act to maximize anticipation (fig. 6). Daly directed Rehan to incarnate all

6. Ada Rehan as Katharine, in Taming of the Shrew.
Courtesy of the Folger Shakespeare Library, Washington, D.C.

the primordial femininity he had her so assiduously repress in the drawing-room comedies to create a spectacle that awed fashionable audiences from New York to London to Paris. Clad in a flaming crimson gown, she made Katharine "a magnificent animal. Her rage was devastating, like some great convulsion of nature," wrote A. B. Walkley of the *Times*.[99] Playing the savage offstage as well as on, as when she bit Daly and drew blood in anger over his infidelity before the high stakes London premiere, heightened the volcanic energy of her performance.[100] Graham Robertson described her ensuing entrance: "Not a whit of her shrewishness did she spare us; her storms of passion found vent in snarls, growls, and even inarticulate screams of fury; she paced hither and thither like a caged wild beast, but her rages were magnificent like an angry sea or a sky of tempest, she blazed a fiery comet through the play, baleful but beautiful."[101]

After demonstrating the magnitude of Katharine's ferocity, Daly collapsed Shakespeare's several taming scenes into a single episode set at Petruchio's residence in the country, where the husband insisted upon taking his wife immediately after the nuptial ceremony. Thus, in Daly's version most of the taming process coincided with the occasion of marital consummation in a place distinctly beyond city borders. As he readied himself for this conquest, Petruchio declared:

> I will be master of what is mine own:
> She is my goods, my chattels; she is my house,
> My house-stuff, my field, my barn,
> My horse, my ox, my ass, my anything.[102]

Arriving at the country outpost ahead of Katharine and Petruchio, Grumio recounted to Curtis the struggles of the newlyweds to make the trip across rugged terrain on horseback. For American audiences in the late nineteenth century, this narrative invoked the Wild West. As the actual frontier was about to close, this drama revivified the promise of untamed wilderness to regenerate national masculinity. The hero ventured away from civilization to prove his manhood on the frontier, whose savagery his ferocious new bride embodied.

In Daly's iconic scheme these rough circumstances mandated Petruchio's brutish behavior. With his sword holstered conspicuously over his groin, the debonair Drew managed to play the brute convincingly by cracking a whip and angrily hurling food, dishes, and verbal bluster to impress his might on Katharine (fig. 7). If, as a few commentators argued, Katharine's conversion came too rapidly and defied the logic of human character development, it ful-

7. *John Drew as Petruchio, in* Taming of the Shrew. *Courtesy of the Museum of the City of New York. Gift of Mrs. John S. Garrity.*

filled the logic of ennobling atavistic struggle on the frontier. Invoking the image of a spirited horse, Rehan described her character as "a grand creature, a very noble nature, of high breeding . . . high-strung and nervous, though, at the same time, strong and thoroughly healthy." In her estimation, the very qualities of extraordinary nobility and power by which the horse had heretofore defied domination enabled her to realize when "she had, at last, met her master. No one knew this better than she. She braced herself for her last grand fight, and fought it with vigor. As with a true soldier, after being defeated her submission was absolute, and she acknowledged her conqueror as frankly as she had defied him."[103] Through this encounter, Daly's Petruchio transformed himself, conquering his own bestial nature and acceding to a fuller, nobler manhood.

In celebration, the hero returned with his trophy to her father's house for the final banquet scene, literally and symbolically a lush spread of the fruits of conquest. For the spectacle Daly had his scene painters and carpenters copy the Paolo Veronese painting *Marriage Feast at Cana* and filled the palatial structure with an anachronistic mélange of authentic Italian, French, and English antiques and Oriental rugs.[104] When the curtain opened on this imperial splendor (fig. 8), audiences were so dazzled that they called Daly himself out for a triumphant bow, acknowledging him above Petruchio as the play's ultimate conqueror.[105]

Daly's personal quest further superseded that of his Shakespearian analogue in the ensuing wager scene, in which the three new husbands—Petruchio, Lucentio, and Hortensio—bet their manhood along with their money on the obedience of their wives. When they dispatched messengers to see whose wife would obey her husband's summons, only Katharine passed the test. Her sister Bianca, seemingly the more gentle and obedient before marriage, and the Widow conspired "by the parlor fire" to defy their husbands.[106] The capitalist who had ventured farthest and engaged with the greatest savagery won the truer wife and, in so doing, became the truer man. Following this theme, Daly's own victory was greatest of all; he had conquered the theatrical wilderness and made a true—and truly civilized—woman out of an actress, one truer, by implication, than the seemingly more respectable women in the audience. In the play's last moments, his Katharine bowed before the banquet table, submissively deferring to the lion king enshrined within the palatial architecture. Repeating, open-ended classical archways receded into the mist toward an indeterminate vanishing point, a scenographic realization of the fantasy of unlimited frontier and its close

8. *Banquet Scene, in* Taming of the Shrew, *arranged by Augustin Daly. Courtesy of the Folger Shakespeare Library, Washington, D.C.*

corollaries, infinitely expanding empire and untrammeled masculinity. This theatrical conquest promised continued triumph over both feminine savagery and overcivilization; Sly never woke up to close the frame, which kept Daly's American dream a reality.

In its initial run, *Taming of the Shrew* played 121 performances, a remarkable record for a Shakespeare play during the period. The show remained a regenerative force in Daly's career through frequent revivals for the next thirteen years.[107] According to Rehan, "Mr. Daly watched and directed most every performance."[108] With each one, he reasserted his prowess as a maker of iconic femininity and induced consumers to continue copying his leading lady while reminding them of his possession of her. This message became particularly apparent on the occasion of *Shrew's* one hundredth performance, when Daly distributed to all the ladies in the audience specially bound volumes containing both the verbal and iconic texts of his adaptation of the play. Each book was fronted with side-by-side photographs of himself and Rehan.[109] After this performance, he hosted a banquet on the set. The fifty-member guest list included many important literary, theatrical, media, and business figures, notably Horace Howard Furness, Mark Twain, Laurence Hutton, William Winter, Bronson Howard, Lester Wallack, and Wilson

9. "Mr. Daly Reading a New Play to His Company," with Ada Rehan and the Chinese boy Leong Loey seated at his feet, 1888. Courtesy of the Theodore Leavitt Collection, University of Illinois Library.

Barrett, whose admiration and respect Daly had earned over the years. With his longtime friend, General William Tecumseh Sherman, as toastmaster, the event confirmed Daly's place within an elite fraternity.[110]

Shrew's perennial triumph furthered the material growth of Daly's enterprise. This is reflected in a second photograph Daly had made of himself reading a play to his company (fig. 9).[111] The setting of this 1888 image is the same lush drawing room with Daly seated in the same thronelike chair as in the 1882 picture, but the company grouped attentively around the manager has grown more numerous. Signaling Drew's diminishment in the company as a result of Rehan's greater stardom, his position in the composition has shifted from the center opposite Daly to one of the seats behind the leading lady. An increasingly disenchanted Drew would leave Daly's to join Frohman's company in 1892. In the place formerly occupied by Drew sits the grandfatherly Charles Fisher, not a leading figure, but along with Mrs. Gilbert and James Lewis, part of a phalanx of elders separating Rehan from the younger actors behind them.

Rehan herself still has the distinction of sitting on the floor, and she reclines in much the same pose with her body facing her manager's on the diagonal. Still flanked by several young women, Daly sits with his legs spread toward his *grande maitresse* and his toe poking suggestively under the hem of her dress. The presence of young actors in the same grouping suggests he might be more secure in his power, although achieving a balanced pictorial composition with this many people may also have necessitated his putting them on that side. The well-worn Persian carpets are more visible in the foreground in this later image. Rehan reclines on a larger animal pelt that resembles royal ermine in its lushness and whiteness. She is joined on the floor not by any other actors or actresses but by another emblem of the impresario's imperial self-styling. The Chinese boy, Leong Loey, whom Daly employed to hand out programs to audience members in his theatre lobby, is clad in Oriental costume and seated cross-legged at his feet.[112]

Such image making helped earn Daly his most symbolically significant career tribute. In 1892, officials selected his Irish-born leading lady as the model for an allegorical statue of Justice (fig. 10) to be Montana's exhibit at the World's Columbian Exposition in Chicago, the era's most elaborate display of American imperial power. The *Chicago Herald* reported:

A statue of Justice in solid silver, eight feet high, costing $50,000 [almost $1.1 million in 2006] and standing upon $250,000 worth of gold compressed into a pedestal, this will be one of the exhibits at the World's Fair coming from Montana. The pedestal will represent the largest lump of gold ever seen. . . . Miss Ada Rehan was one of the first thought of [to be the model], as she is considered to be physically one of the most perfect types of American womanhood.[113]

The statue conflated Rehan with the emergent national feminine ideal whose neoclassical features were also inscribed in the fair's central icon, Daniel Chester French's towering Republic amid the Grand Basin, as well as other female allegorical statues.[114] While neoclassical styling had long been characteristic of American monumental sculpture, that styling in the 1890s correlated with the newly codified visual form real American women were supposed to embody.[115] On a more human scale, the American Girl (fig. 11), definitively rendered by illustrator Charles Dana Gibson, shared Republic's statuesque bearing, upswept hair, and "chiseled patrician" facial features.[116] Through new print technologies such as halftone engraving, her image was mass reproduced in a dizzying array of media, from magazines, newspapers,

*10. Montana Silver
Statue depicting Ada
Rehan as Justice, 1892.
Courtesy of the Museum
of the City of New York.*

and coffee-table books, to table and bed linens, matchbook covers, leather goods, and even wallpaper for bachelor apartments, all of which compelled men to possess and women to become her.[117] Another famous American Girl illustrator of the period, Howard Chandler Christy, deemed her a singularly WASP goddess, a "veritable queen of the kingliest of races." His rhetoric heralded her as "the culmination of mankind's long struggle upward from barbarism to civilization," feminine perfection "won from the tight fist of nature's grudging hand," the archetypal American trophy wife.[118] Montana's Justice emblazoned the same classical feminine features in unprecedented quantities

11. *The national feminine ideal, the American Girl, as the Debutante, by Charles Dana Gibson, 1899, in* Eleven Gibson Books in Two Volumes, *n. pag.*

of precious ore mined from the western wilderness. Even more thoroughly than the only superficially gilded Republic, she embodied the frontier conquest that Frederick Jackson Turner, in the famous speech he delivered during the fair, argued had defined America and Americans. As Justice poised walking atop the world on the back of a winged eagle, scale in one hand, sword in the other, Rehan literally became a trophy, one symbolizing both her impresario's victorious ascent to WASP respectability and the nation's self-righteous claims to world superiority. Daly's taming of Rehan inspired a cultural icon signifying continued conquest of savage nature and shrewish Others on an ever-receding frontier line.

Even as Daly reached the summit of his success, the balance of power between him and his leading lady continued to shift with an unsettling volatility. He had made Rehan so famous that she had become synonymous with his enterprise. She gained the ability to make or break him, as she demonstrated before *Shrew's* London opening. When she bit his hand, he was at her mercy, awaiting her agreement to perform. The enormous risk he took in provoking her may have sweetened his ultimate triumph, but it was Rehan who commanded the play to begin that night. Recognizing her power and indispensability, Rehan in 1894 demanded of Daly and received star billing. While she had arguably been the de facto star of his company for years, his conferring that status upon her officially was still a major concession. Rehan obtained this agreement by threatening to leave him, a prospect which by that point he could not countenance.

Although Daly was clearly vulnerable to Rehan's demand behind the scenes, this single instance of retracting his long-standing policy worked more to augment than detract from his public image. Making Rehan a star made her a more brilliant trophy, which he displayed not only on stage but also in his theatre lobby in the form of a full-length portrait by John Singer Sargent and a marble bust of her as Katharine. Like the Montana statue, these were not only tributes to her but emblems of his conquest and cultivation of her.

With Daly's death in 1899, Rehan claimed that she lost her spirit and much of her will to perform. In her letter to William Winter, she wrote: "I am very indifferent to the future. If I ever go on again with my work, I fear it will be more of the machine than the artiste."[119] Otis Skinner, who had acted with her under Daly, toured with her in 1904–1905 and noticed the change: "The exquisite comedienne with whom I had the happiest memories of five years' association was no more. . . . Augustin Daly was dead, and without him she was helpless."[120] Rehan was not exactly helpless, since she managed to act credibly for several years after Daly's death, but her attitude and feelings about her work had markedly changed. By her own admission, as well as by the characterizations of associates like Graham Robertson and Otis Skinner, she had, in significant ways, like Trilby, "lost her voice."

For Daly, Rehan's fate may have constituted a final victory—if he had to make her a star, he made her one who, unlike the more independent women with whom he had struggled in earlier decades, could not function well without him. Yet as his career had progressed, neither could Daly function without her. By the end of their time together, the practical and emotional needs of impresario and actress for each other had equalized. The conquest myth that structured the relationship, however, made Daly the lionized self-reliant individualist forged from the encounter and Rehan, in all her glory, still the emblem of his evolutionary attainments, the raw Irish matter that he had refined to attain American manhood. Nevertheless, the reality of mutual need and the inherent instability of the power achieved through conquest of feminine savagery would continue to drive the relations of successive impresarios and female stars.

3

Birds of a Feather

THE QUEER THEATRICAL EMPIRE

OF CHARLES FROHMAN AND

MAUDE ADAMS

. . . the world owes much of its beauty to [the] combination of
feminine sensitiveness and of virile accomplishment. Each
attribute supplements the other, and art has often become
the richer for this duality. The mind of a man with the
heart of a woman makes an ideal exotic that should not be
despised, and how frequently they go
hand in hand where artists are concerned.
—Theatrical agent Elisabeth Marbury
in her memoir, *My Crystal Ball* (1924)

The year after Augustin Daly triumphed with the 1888 London engagement of his *Taming of the Shrew*, starring Ada Rehan, a younger manager, Charles Frohman (1860–1915), scored his career-launching hit in New York with Bronson Howard's *Shenandoah*. From that 1889 opening until his untimely death on the *Lusitania* in 1915, Frohman would far surpass Daly in the scope of his impresarial achievements. By the time Daly, the venerable owner of an illustrious theatre in New York and one other in London, died in 1899, Frohman had acquired controlling interests in forty-two American theatres and had bought into the first of a string in London. He had also become a founding partner and the chief producer of the Theatrical Syndicate, a conglomerate of six lawyers and businessmen that controlled bookings in "first-class" theatres across the country and threatened to put smaller, independent theatre companies like Daly's out of business.[1] Completed in 1893, the New York base of his operations was appropriately named the Empire Theatre, a lavishly decorated 1,099-seat playhouse echoing the beaux arts style popularized by the Chicago World's Fair as the architecture of American imperialism.[2] Contemporary critics dubbed him "the Napoleon of Managers."[3] In America and overseas, admirers heralded him as "the pioneer and the builder."[4] Figure 12 shows him astride the deck of one of the many cruisers he boarded to cross the Atlantic. At the height of his career, by Barnard Hewitt's reckoning, he "owned theatres in New York and London worth more than $5 million [about $98.2 million today], paid $35 million [about $687 million today] in salaries to over ten thousand employees, and spent over half a million [about $9.8 million today] annually in advertising."[5] Samuel E. Moffett, who included Frohman in his Captains of Industry series of articles for *Cosmopolitan*, remarked: "The dramatic profession of the world has known no such universal ruler since that imperial connoisseur, Nero, dictated the programs of the theaters of Athens, Alexandria, Antioch, and Rome. Let us hasten to add that the parallel extends no further, for Mr. Frohman is as amiable as Nero was the reverse."[6] Nevertheless, under the aegis of Frohman and his Syndicate partners, especially Marc Klaw and Abraham Erlanger, who handled the centralized booking of his productions, theatre became a major capitalist monopoly.

While Frohman worked with many stars in the course of building his empire, including such luminaries as John Drew (a defector from Daly's), Ethel Barrymore, and Billie Burke, his longest-serving and most profitable performer was Maude Adams (1872–1953). She appeared in twenty-seven productions under his management from 1890 to 1915 and became the star

12. *Charles Frohman on the deck of the* Mauretania, *sister ship of the* Lusitania, *in* Charles Frohman: Manager and Man, *by Isaac F. Marcosson and Daniel Frohman, op. p. 384.*

with whom he was most closely associated. In 1913, William de Wagstaffe calculated that New Yorkers had paid $2.5 million [about $49 million today] and Chicagoans $1.525 million to see Adams in various plays over the years. The combined totals for other cities across the nation amounted to even more. "A week's receipts of $20,000 [about $393,000 today] for Maude Adams on tour is commonplace,"[7] observed Wagstaffe. By several even more conservative accounts, Adams's earnings far surpassed those of her contemporaries.[8] Gustav Kobbe pronounced her "the best piece of theatrical property in the world."[9] She was the primary vehicle by which the theatrical Napoleon conquered so many audiences.

Beyond their economic successes, Frohman and Adams extended the moralistic, civilizing work of impresario and actress relationships established by Daly and Rehan. Adams's stardom advanced a managerial agenda that Frohman's biographers summarize with the pithy declaration that "his entire theatrical career was a rebuke to the salacious."[10] In a 1911 article entitled "Maude Adams: A Public Influence," David Gray synthesizes wide-ranging opinions about why she so epitomized Frohman's enterprise: "this devoted woman has used the stage as a means to celebrate and glorify noble sentiment and the high, purifying emotions." Unlike Ada Rehan and other leading ladies of the era, "She has no grasp of the fierce, elemental passions of animal sex. To depict these things does not interest her. The fountainhead of her personality is nun-like and virginal."[11] Many accounts attributed her virtuous star power and resulting popularity chiefly to her impresario's strict control over her life and image on and off the stage.

Frohman's campaign for Adams served several aims, including his desire to counter the widespread prejudice in the United States against actors and the theatre profession. The suspect status of women in the theatre was a notable problem. But beyond these general conditions, which the profession as a whole was attempting to address (as Benjamin McArthur has charted in *Actors and American Culture, 1880–1920*), Frohman also confronted another prevalent prejudice of the times, one reinforced by the reigning Social Darwinist ideology about "race." People of northern European and Protestant background, especially of Anglo-Saxon heritage, were the preferred norm in the United States; people of all other regions and religious belief were widely perceived as inferior. African Americans, Native Americans, and Asians were, without question, deemed "lower." Rather than ethnic groups, Irish, Jews, and Italians were also categorized as "races" and were considered nonwhite to varying degrees relative to Anglo-Saxon ideals.[12] The rising tide of immigrants from southern and eastern Europe in the decades around the turn of the century prompted virulent xenophobia and anti-Semitism. Frohman came from Jewish roots in Germany, and Adams from lapsed Mormon roots in Utah. Along with "racial" and religious prejudice against Jews, lingering anti-Mormonism raised the stakes for Frohman to mould and Adams to embody a transcendently chaste Gentile stardom.

But even while seeking social and cultural advancement with conquering displays of male dominance and female virtue, Frohman and Adams also queered the established paradigm for impresario and actress relationships. In part because of the legacies of duos such as Daly and Rehan, journalists often speculated not only that Frohman controlled her every move, but that he and Adams were romantically involved and even secretly married. Rumors of romance began with Adams's rise to the first rank of stardom with *The Little Minister* in 1897 and were widespread enough that cartoonists picked up on them. One amusing drawing shows actress and impresario dancing hand in hand (fig. 13). Yet both, in fact, lived in long-term, same-sex domestic partnerships, and Adams exercised considerable authority in the Frohman organization. Shielded by presumptions of normality and their enormous wealth and privilege, they managed to manipulate their public images to hide their unconventional private lives. Behind the scenes, they worked with a wider network of theatre practitioners who formed professional associations based on shared tastes and understandings about secret desires and lifestyle choices. In the years around the turn of the last century, when modern sexual identities—the binary categories of hetero- and homosexuality—were just coming into formation, this network was part of an emerging queer subculture that not only enabled and inspired Frohman's and Adams's careers but was instrumental in the growth of Broadway. The term "queer," meaning "odd," and vernacular expressions such as "queer bird," meaning "odd one," came to connote sexual difference in contradistinction to "straight" or "normal" people.[13] How impresario and actress negotiated these sexual categories, along with those of "race," gender, and class, is crucial to understanding their relationship, their attraction to particular plays and playwrights, and the appeal of Adams's performances to differently desiring audiences.

The Woman Within and the Actress Without

Frohman, Adams, and their queer network understood their sexual difference in terms of sexual inversion, the era's prevailing theory for explaining same-sex

13. *Cartoon of Maude Adams as Lady Babbie in* The Little
Minister *(1897) dancing with her impresario, Charles Frohman.*
Part of an odd-looking artifact, the cartoon was cut out of another printed
source and pasted onto an advertisement page of a theatre program.
Adams's fans engaged in this type of scrapbooking practice.
Courtesy of the Museum of the City of New York.

sexual desire. According to leading sexologists of the 1870s and 1880s, Karl Heinrich Ulrichs and Richard von Krafft-Ebing, one's attraction to a person of the same sex derived from a "spirit" or being of the opposite sex trapped inside one's body.[14] The reigning image of the male invert in New York around the turn of the century was that of the fairy whose inner female spirit or being was akin to a prostitute. An effeminate working-class type prominent in the Bowery, the waterfront, and parts of Harlem, the fairy flagrantly wore the outward signs of femininity—including bleached hair, tweezed eyebrows, and painted face—to signal his proclivities and seduce other men.[15] Members of the middle and upper classes could but did not have to "slum" in the fairy's haunts to encounter him. Beginning in the 1880s and 1890s, the genre of periodical press led by Pulitzer's *World* and Hearst's *Journal* burgeoned by capitalizing on the sensational appeal of stories of crime, scandal, and the urban underworld, many of which offered vivid glimpses into "degenerate resorts" and "fairy backroom salons."[16] The fairy's high visibility made his type, in George Chauncey's words, "the primary pejorative category against which male normativity was measured."[17] Other vernacular expressions such as "she-man," "nance," and "sissy" were used synonymously with "fairy" to denote the flamboyant or "flaming" type of man.[18] All of these terms registered the widespread belief in such a manner being the outward expression of a sexually desirous inner femininity, the manifestation of a seductive woman within.

Regarding female inverts, the primary image was that of the "masculine" or "mannish" woman with an "unnatural passion" for members of her own sex. As Krafft-Ebing explained in 1886, this passion "may nearly always be suspected in females wearing their hair short, or who dress in the fashion of men, or pursue the sports or pastimes of their male acquaintances; also in opera singers and actresses who appear in male attire on the stage by preference."[19] Discussion of female sexual inversion remained largely confined to the medical profession until 1892, when the sensational case of two Tennessee belles, Alice Mitchell and Freda Ward, made national headlines. The two planned a secret elopement in which Alice, adopting the name "Alvin," would dress as a man. After Ward's family disrupted the plot and separated the two women, Mitchell fell into a deep depression. Several months later, she accosted Freda in the street and cut her throat. Close coverage of Mitchell's insanity inquisition in the *New York Times*, the *New York World*, and other papers around the country pushed female "sexual perversion" and its supposed manifestation in cross-dressing into wider public discourse.[20] Reports that Mitchell aspired to be an actress also further tied such proclivities to the theatrical profession.[21] The possible incidence of female sexual perversion widened as Havelock Ellis, the leading English sexologist of the turn of the century, argued that women's growing claims to higher education, professional careers, and political power could "develop the germs" or "cause a spurious imitation" of the invert.[22] Such reasoning, frequently invoked by American antifeminists, implied that women who acted socially mannish could turn sexually mannish, and vice versa.[23]

Thus, for Frohman, Adams, and their fellow inverts, dodging stigma meant containing the seductive impulses of their opposite-sexed inner selves and avoiding cross-gender signs in their outward appearance and conduct. Because of the sexism inscribed not only in long-standing social attitudes and institutions but also in newer currents of Darwinian thought, male and female inverts did not meet those challenges on equal ground. Sexologists and more popular commentators categorized sexual inversion as a form of degeneracy. Those at the top of the evolutionary scale (predominately WASPs) were marked not only by racial superiority but also by optimum differentiation of the sexes—that is, the greatest absence of femininity in men and masculinity in women—and therefore the straightest alignment of biological sex and inner and outer selves. These "straights"—male and female—also claimed the highest levels of sexual and bodily purity defined in terms of continence and self-control; however, men could surpass women in reaching the pinnacle of evolution because "lower" attributes of barbarism and susceptibility to carnal appetite were themselves feminized as well as racialized. Women by dint of being female were intrinsically less capable of overcoming these weaknesses and therefore needed male control and protection, a perception that provided a powerful justification for male dominance in the theatre and other social institutions. For both men and women, sexual inversion signaled sexual incontinence and devolution to a less gender-differentiated, less healthy, and by implication, less racially pure state. But because men were supposed to be more evolved than women, that descent was theoretically greater.[24]

Most significantly for impresario and actress relationships, sexual inversion crystallized in gender-specific images a central tenet of evolutionary theory: recapitulation, which held that ontogeny recapitulated phylogeny, meaning that the development of the individual recapitulated that of the species. According to the logic of recapitulation, even "straight" men had to pass through feminine and savage stages on their way to adult manhood. Moreover, in the course of evolution, the male "originated" the acquisition of desirable onto- and phylogenetic traits, whereas the female "perpetuated" or "conserved" them.[25] The instigating role privileged men as the heroes of the evolutionary struggle, while the concept of female "conservatism" contributed to women's deification as repositories of the attainments of their race. Through revivals of *Taming of the Shrew*, Augustin Daly publicly reenacted his mastery of the "lower" attributes he personally had to overcome to achieve upward mobility. His star, Ada Rehan, became an evolutionary trophy, a vessel containing his acquired refinements and symbolizing the feminized savagery he conquered within as well as outside himself. For a man like Frohman, who sexually desired other men and fit the category of sexual invert, those "lower" attributes constituted not a temporary developmental phase but an enduring part of his person fully figured as a woman within. Rather than sexual domination, her taming involved an ongoing dance of containment and release, which Frohman enacted through his relationship with Maude Adams. More than any of his female stars, she served as the outward embodiment of the queer impresario's inner woman.

Frohman and Adams's quarter-century *pas de deux* crisscrossed their private and public lives, as each engaged the other from a home base of same-sex partnership. The year Adams first starred under Frohman's employ, 1892, was also the year he met Charles Dillingham (1868–1934), the man who became his domestic partner. Although they came from different backgrounds, the two men's paths converged in the theatre. Frohman was born in Sandusky, Ohio, the youngest son of a German Jewish immigrant cigar maker who in the early 1860s moved his family to New York, where he hoped his boys would have better prospects. The Frohman cigar store was located in the heart of the theatre district and frequented by many of its leading practitioners. That proximity prompted the boys—Gustave, Daniel, and Charles—to enter the theatrical business as entrepreneurs with aspirations to management. Charles served as an advance agent for a traveling minstrel show, which undoubtedly heightened his awareness of racial and cultural hierarchies, before signing on as the producer of *Shenandoah*. The success of that play enabled him in 1890 to establish his own stock company, with which he "hoped to maintain the traditions established by Augustin Daly, A. M. Palmer, Lester Wallack, and the Madison Square Company."[26]

Dillingham hailed from Hartford, Connecticut, the son of an Episcopalian minister. According to a newspaper account,

He ran away from home when a boy of some 18 years, and tried cow punching for a while. Then he drifted to Chicago, where he "covered" the hotels for the Tribune. Next he went out to Seattle, or Tacoma, or one of those cow towns of the far Northwest, got newspaper work, and ultimately bobbed up in Washington as a secretary to Senator [Watson Carvosso] Squire. The next we heard of him he was writing the dramatic column of the New York Evening Sun. His work attracted the attention of Charles Frohman, and that is how he got into the managerial line. Dillingham has been uniformly successful in everything he undertook, with the possible exception of matrimony (he and his wife Jennie Yeamans, having agreed to get a divorce and did so), and in playwriting.[27]

Not surprisingly, his non-normative sexual proclivities go unmentioned in this account. But same-sex sexual desire might explain some of these turns in his early career, from the rupture with his doctrinaire family, to seeking refuge in the male homosocial world of cowpunching, to gaining advancement through the help of older, more powerful men who took an interest in him, to failing at matrimony.

Dillingham first crossed paths with Frohman at the Bijou Theatre in the spring of 1892 during a performance of Dillingham's short-lived *Twelve P.M.* The play was running across the street from Frohman's hit and Adams's first starring vehicle with John Drew, *The Masked Ball*, adapted from the French of Bisson and Carré by Clyde Fitch. Frohman admired enough of the play to invite Dillingham to his offices to discuss whether he would be willing to adapt another French farce for him. According to Frohman's biographers, Isaac F. Marcosson and Daniel Frohman, "'Twelve P.M.' was a dismal failure, but it brought two unusual men together who became bosom friends."[28] Dillingham's lackluster playwriting did not provide a sustainable basis for their relationship; rather, their connection quickly deepened for more personal reasons.

Frohman invited Dillingham to accompany him that summer on his annual trip to London, where he had just established his first offices in Henrietta Street. Apparently confident that he would be provided for, Dillingham abandoned his newspaper post to join his new friend. Without much business to transact, the two spent most of their time seeing plays. Frohman's biographers refer to Dillingham as his "sort of secretary," a frequent euphemism of the era for an intimate same-sex companion. Among the tastes the pair shared was a common sense of humor; both delighted in pranks, puns, and epigrams. When a haughty English businessman told Frohman his "secretary" had claimed to be too busy to help him because he first had to wash the windows,

Frohman reportedly "laughed so heartily he nearly rolled out of his chair. After the Englishman left, he went out and congratulated Dillingham on his jest. From that day dated a Damon and Pythias friendship between the two men. They were almost inseparable companions."[29] (See fig. 14.)

Direct evidence of the nature of their intimacy is scarce because the two men were highly circumspect. Frohman, in particular, was notoriously secret about his private life. *The Theatre* characterized him as "the greatest man ever unknown," *Metropolitan* declared him to be "Charles Frohman—An Enigma," and the *New York Times* proclaimed him "Probably the Least Photographed Man of His Prominence in America."[30] Yet some clues to the relationship between the two men remain. In his unpublished memoir Dillingham writes that he and Frohman "worked together like the pitcher and the catcher." They were able to signal each other with subtle winks and body language not only to make an unsuspecting interloper the butt of a joke but also to gain the advantage during a business negotiation.[31] Dillingham's appeal may have been physical as well; he was a handsome dandy, whom the press dubbed "the Beau Brummell of Broadway." His appearance prompted one journalist to proclaim: "He looked cute enough to kiss, in a staggering waistcoat and lemon colored gloves."[32] Frohman, by contrast, was described as short and stout. "Nature did not bother about the physical length of our manager, but put all of his stature in his head," quipped one wag. But the same writer granted that he still possessed attractions, "chief among them being an even disposition, good humor, philosophy, and kindliness."[33]

Certainly, Frohman was extraordinarily kind to Dillingham. He used his wealth and power to back him in numerous ventures with a generosity that went beyond common business sense and the usual bonds of male friendship. Along with assigning him various office duties, Frohman sent Dillingham on occasional short trips to do advance press work for his touring shows. He also dispatched him on occasion as a charming and safe escort for his unmarried female stars, for example, Ethel Barrymore, who reputedly needed special handling because of "nervousness."[34] (Adams did not need such assistance because she had her protective female companion.) In addition, Frohman gave him a small interest in plays, such as Augustus Thomas's *The Only Girl*.[35] He took greater risk than these assignments when he enlisted Dillingham to manage certain of his theatres, first briefly the Garden and then, for several years, the Criterion.[36] Concerned about how well he was doing by his dapper companion, Frohman remarked to a mutual friend: "The money I pay Dillingham as manager of the Criterion won't keep him in

14. *Charles Frohman strolling with his partner, Charles B. Dillingham, from the* Chicago American, *n.d. Courtesy of the Museum of the City of New York.*

waistcoats. I have got to do something for him." Whereupon, Frohman began giving him stars to manage, beginning with Julia Marlowe, which "marked the beginning of Mr. Dillingham as an independent manager."[37]

As long as Frohman was alive, however, he continued to provide both financial and personal support for Dillingham. For example, when he was in London, usually for several months per year to attend to theatre business, he often relied upon Dillingham to take care of some aspects of his New York theatres—in conjunction with his business manager, Alf Hayman.[38] And Frohman often authorized Hayman to advance Dillingham large sums of money. He also authorized Hayman to sign banknotes for Dillingham to acquire loans for his theatre ventures. Moreover, Dillingham obtained this support without having to provide specific records to Frohman's office of how he spent the money. Occasionally, Hayman expressed concern that Frohman was putting his own financial well-being and credit at risk. On 26 March 1907, Hayman wrote: "There are some ugly rumors running around town about Dillingham and his financial position. I don't know how true they are and presume it's none of my business. But as you are regarded by everybody both in and out of the business as his partner and financial backer thought it best to write you and tell you of the rumor." Dillingham reputedly was in gross arrears on bills for *The Red Mill*, and now he was coming to Hayman for more money for another production. Hayman continues in the same letter: "If Dillingham does *The Hoyden* with Elsie Janis it's only fair for me to think you will be interested and whether you can afford to go along with him at the present [gait?] he is going presuming all the rumors are true, you alone can decide. Personally, I'm sorry to see it for I've failed to see Dillingham's qualifications as a businessman." Two days later an alarmed Hayman wrote that Dillingham told him Frohman would be endorsing a note so he could borrow $30,000. Hayman felt duty bound to tell Frohman that such a loan is not advisable, given Frohman's other obligations. Such a transaction could exhaust his borrowing capacity for the coming season.[39]

At the same time that Frohman was funding Dillingham's ventures, Adams was also requesting large sums from Frohman's office for productions, but Hayman viewed these differently. In one letter to Frohman dated 1 April 1909 as Adams was preparing for the *Joan of Arc* pageant, a huge extravagance that he feared from the start would result in large deficits, Hayman wrote that he had given the star $13,000. He explained to his boss that he preferred to give it to her in cash because she had already received $22,000 drawn in bank notes. Those notes, together with $24,000 recently borrowed for Dillingham, amounted to more than he wanted to owe the bank.[40] Yet Hayman did not question the wisdom of Adams's requests as he did Dillingham's, even though both—especially both combined—were financially risky. Covering Adams's expenditures fit within cultural assumptions about how an impresario would take care of and indulge his leading actress. Those assumptions did not, however, carry over to his male companion.

In addition to their financial dealings, Frohman and Dillingham shared living quarters and attendant intimacies. For many years, the two jointly owned a country retreat, Hiddenbrook Farm, in White Plains, New York. Newspapers record that during the week, the workaholic Frohman spent most of his time at the theatre and kept rooms at a nearby hotel such as the Waldorf-Astoria or the Knickerbocker for sleeping. But he often spent weekends and holidays at the farm with Dillingham. In his memoirs, Dillingham recounts a special surprise he arranged for Frohman's birthday one year at Hiddenbrook. Frohman had returned from London raving about the perfect waiter, Max Boppler, who had dutifully served him breakfast precisely to his specifications in bed at the Hotel Savoy every morning. Obligingly, the waiter never made small talk or even uttered a word while he performed these services. Dillingham secretly brought Boppler over from London and the morning of Frohman's birthday had him silently enter and serve his astounded domestic partner breakfast in bed just as the waiter had done at the Savoy.[41]

With a similar sense of shared humor and intimacy, Dillingham also took care of Frohman's health. Because he loathed going to the doctor, Frohman would sometimes send Dillingham to impersonate him and gather the information as to diagnosis and treatment. On one of these surrogate outings, Dillingham recounted Frohman's symptoms as his own and reportedly received shock therapy, after which, the partners joked, Frohman's health markedly improved.[42] When Frohman was ill, friends, business associates, and the media depended on Dillingham as the primary source of information about his condition.[43]

Along with tending to each other on the home front, Frohman and Dillingham also regularly vacationed together abroad. Papers chronicled their comings and goings, as in this report from the *New York Telegraph*: "Charles Frohman and Charles Dillingham have been doing Paris, London, and Berlin together this spring, taking in all the sights."[44] On such travels, they shared sleeping quarters. In his unpublished memoirs, Dillingham recounts an episode that occurred in the middle of one of their nights together in London where Frohman was trying to sustain a struggling repertory company:

This repertoire theatre financially embarrassed Charles Frohman and one morning at 2 o'clock he was walking the floor.

I said, "What's the matter?"

He said, "I've got to get $40,000 within a week."

It was in the spring and I put a light overcoat over my pajamas and went down into the city where there is a cable office open all night and wired A. L. Erlanger to telegraph $50,000 to Charles Frohman. At noon we got a wire from Mr. Erlanger saying "You bet your life I'll do it!" That's the way the theatrical giants did business in those days![45]

Apparently recognizing Dillingham's closeness to Frohman, Erlanger responded as though the request came from Frohman himself.

Although some of the intensity of their earlier companionship may have waned, this known special connection between the two men continued even after Dillingham remarried in 1913. He was forty-five when he wed actress Eileen Kearney, whom the papers described as "many years his junior." No stranger to the operations of same-sex desire, she had been part of *The Marionettes* company with Alla Nazimova, a well-known actress notorious for bisexual liaisons.[46] It is possible the marriage served as a cover for one or both parties. A private ceremony was performed in the Little White Church in Purchase, New York, in Westchester County, near Dillingham and Frohman's country place. The *New York World* reported that the marriage was kept a secret until bride and groom were on board the *Kronprinz Wilhelm* at sea, when "an intimate friend"—in all likelihood, Frohman—wired an announcement to the press.[47] After the wedding, Frohman expanded his joint car insurance policy with Dillingham to cover Kearney.[48] Dillingham took Frohman to the dock for his fateful trip on the *Luisitania* in 1915. Bidding Frohman good-bye, he promised to be at the dock upon Frohman's return—a reunion that German torpedoes nullified.[49]

Following Frohman's untimely death, Dillingham received numerous condolence letters acknowledging the two men's longtime companionship. Among the most heartfelt was the one from Lee Shubert:

my deepest sympathy goes out to you in the loss of your dearest friend.

I have always had the greatest admiration and respect for Charles Frohman and your loyalty to him and his to you has been one of the finest expressions of friendship I have ever seen.

I know through my own sad experiences what your grief must be but the sympathy of one's friends is a help and among the number of yours, I want you to believe no one feels more deeply for you than

Yours very sincerely,

Lee Shubert[50]

Alf Hayman wrote that it was the "fervent wish" of C. F.'s family that Dillingham serve as one of the honorary pallbearers at the funeral.[51] Of course Dillingham accepted the invitation.

More direct evidence of the homosexual nature of Frohman and Dillingham's partnership comes from the unpublished memoirs of George James Hopkins (1896–1988), the award-winning Hollywood designer who began his career in New York theatre. According to Hopkins, turn-of-the-century New York theatre was saturated with gay culture, but "homosexuality wasn't the casual topic of conversation it is today." Talented and delicately handsome, he moved easily in gay circles in his teenage years as a number of powerful men took an interest in him. Among the first to do so were Frohman and Dillingham, whom he understood to be a couple. From about 1912 until Frohman's death in 1915, the pair often made him their dinner guest and introduced him to others of like persuasion and influence. Later mentors included the Shuberts' costume designer, Melville Ellis, whom Hopkins also refers to as Lee Shubert's lover, which may explain Lee's especially heartfelt understanding of what Frohman meant to Dillingham. These recorded memories position Frohman and Dillingham, even after Dillingham's marriage, as senior members of New York's emerging gay subculture.[52]

From the earliest months of their relationship, the couple also participated in an international gay subculture. As for others of their class and proclivities, annual travel abroad provided time away from the American press and greater freedom to pursue their pleasures. Whereas in New York, Frohman, the perpetual bachelor, was notoriously reclusive, in London write his biographers, "he seemed a different human being. The inaccessibility that hedged him about in America vanished. He emerged from an unsocial shell; he gave out interviews; he relaxed and renewed his youth and jaunt and jest. His annual trip abroad therefore, was like a joyous adventure. It mattered little if he made or lost a fortune each time."[53] For Frohman, pursuit of the freedom to be less closeted, perhaps even more than the expanded business opportunities, was a major part of the appeal of venturing abroad.

On Frohman and Dillingham's first trip together to London in 1892, the summer after they met, they established a lasting connection to Oscar Wilde.

Among the many plays they saw was *Lady Windermere's Fan*, Wilde's first major comedy hit. Their lesbian colleague, the theatrical agent Elisabeth Marbury, whose home offices were in Frohman's Empire Theatre, probably arranged for them to meet the British cultural sensation. Marbury counted Wilde among her international clients, along with G. B. Shaw, J. M. Barrie, and Victorien Sardou. As a result of the meeting, Frohman became Wilde's American producer. He arranged the American road tour of *Lady Windermere's Fan* that began in October 1893 and then, two years later, produced the American premier of *The Importance of Being Earnest*.[54] After Wilde's trials began on 2 April 1895, Frohman went ahead with the scheduled opening on 22 April and kept the play running until it no longer attracted patronage, which was longer than George Alexander kept it playing in London.[55] Both his American producer and agent remained loyal to Wilde during his imprisonment. Marbury prepared a refuge for him next to her Versailles estate, and Frohman offered him a play commission to get him back on his feet after his release.[56] Sadly, Wilde died before he could take full advantage of these accommodations.

Frohman's close connection to Wilde during these years shaped his understanding of same-sex sexual desire and its possible consequences. In 1892, when Frohman became involved with Dillingham, met Wilde, and began starring Adams, Wilde was not only penning brilliant social comedies; he was also combining themes of sexual inversion and racial decadence in a darker poetic work, *Salome*, which he originally wrote in French, *la langue sexuelle*. Salome, a first-century Judean princess, was depicted in several internationally famous canvases by Gustave Moreau in the 1870s. This Jewish Lolita, whose seductive wiles bring down a king and a prophet, became a lightning rod for fantasies of feminine evil in the *fin-de-siècle*.[57] Her name was also a favorite among the flamboyant monikers that fairies chose to construct their queer personas.[58] By the time Wilde created his Salome, he had also begun his affair with Lord Alfred "Bosie" Douglas, who first translated the play into English. An ominous embodiment of the male invert's woman within, *Salome* forecast Wilde's own downfall three years later, which he attributed to having been "prey to the absolute madness" of transgressive desire.[59] Those like Frohman and Dillingham who knew Wilde personally in the early 1890s and became aware of that madness were undoubtedly alarmed by it. The reckless behavior in which Wilde and Bosie engaged contrasted sharply with the discretion Frohman and his intimates practiced. When the trials that condemned Wilde for gross indecency began in 1895, their worst fears were realized. Indeed, the public spectacle of Wilde's demise greatly heightened the risk factor for those with same-sex affectional preferences and alternative lifestyles throughout Anglo-American society.[60] Wilde's cautionary example stands as a foil for how Frohman managed his leading lady onto whom he projected his own inner femininity. If the Jewish inner Salome brought down the Gentile Wilde, the Jewish Frohman would fashion a chaste, Gentile Adams to further his climb up the social and cultural hierarchy. Frohman's desire to contain female sexuality embodied in Adams became one of his primary career motivations.

Queer Star Making

Born in Salt Lake City, Utah, Adams came to New York in 1888 at the age of sixteen as part of E. H. Sothern's company in *The Paymaster*. She first appeared under Frohman's management in *All the Comforts of Home*, by William Gillette, which opened in New York on 8 September 1890. In 1890, Frohman hired her to join his newly formed Empire Theatre Stock Company. The young actress's background as well as her talents fit her well for Frohman's managerial agenda. Although she was not, as some believed, a descendant of the Quincy Adamses of Massachusetts, her lineage nonetheless traced back to *Mayflower* passenger John Howland. Her grandfather, Barnabas Lothrop Adams, "did a very incorrect thing," in the words of Walter Prichard Eaton. With her grandmother, Julia Ann Banker, he joined Brigham Young's Mormon expedition and subsequently married two other women. Maude's mother, Asenath Ann (Annie) Adams, shared a home with thirteen siblings born of three different mothers.[61] When Annie was eight years old, Brigham Young's "favorite wife" Emmeline chose her to play children's parts in the town theatre his followers erected. As an adult, she crossed Utah's Mormon-Gentile divide and left the church to marry James H. Kiskadden, whose lineage was Scottish and Irish Catholic. While James, a bank employee, moved their home first to Virginia City, Nevada, and then to San Francisco, she pursued an acting career. Maude was their only surviving child. Her father did not want his daughter to become involved in theatre, but her mother prevailed and took little Maude with her on stage from the age of nine months. The disapproving James would not let her perform as a Kiskadden; he insisted that she use her mother's maiden name instead, which is how her stage name became Maude Adams.[62]

Maude spent her early childhood years touring with her mother, periodically returning home to see her father and attend school and visiting her Mormon grandmother in Salt Lake. At her grandmother's house, she relished the freedom of tomboyish pursuits like climbing trees and barn rafters, riding horses, and swinging from cow's tails.[63] From ages ten to twelve, she stayed with her grandmother full time so she could obtain more formal education. Whether the choice was made primarily for financial or religious reasons is not clear, but she attended the Salt Lake Collegiate Institute, a preparatory school run by the First Presbyterian Church that offered free tuition to children to try to convert them out of Mormonism.[64] When she was eleven, word came to the Institute that her father had died. Her mother moved back to Salt Lake and took a job in business to help support Maude in school. Finding the income insufficient, she left within a year to return to an itinerant theatrical life and took Maude with her. Thus, although Maude was still a teenager when Frohman first hired her, she had had years of experience as a member of traveling stock companies with her mother. She had also learned of the need to overcome the social taint that accrued to both her profession and her polygamous Mormon heritage.

Twelve years Adams's senior and just breaking successfully into management with his own stock company, Frohman took charge of her career as her producer, agent, and publicist. From the outset, their needs to overcome cultural stigmas harmonized. Like Jews, Mormons saw themselves as a chosen people entering a promised land (complete with its own Dead Sea—Salt Lake) and enduring persecution by Protestants and Catholics. Moreover, they viewed all non-Mormons as Gentiles, including, ironically, Jews. As Simon Bamberger, the only Jew ever to run for the Utah governorship, quipped in 1916, "As a Jew, I have been called many a bad name, but this is the first time I have been called a damned Gentile." Nonetheless, recognizing common experience, Mormons rallied around him as an Israelite, and he won the election.[65] For Frohman and Adams, shared nonGentile heritages provided a basis for affinity, while Adams's Puritan blue bloodlines and turns away from Mormonism offered the prospect of upward mobility. To bring out her northeastern gentility, Frohman compelled her to drop the western "r" in her pronunciation and set about to ensure that she project an image of youthful innocence and virtue. While he generally demanded a high standard of decorum from his employees both on- and offstage, he was particularly exacting about female sexual conduct, to the extent that whenever one of his female stars married, he refused to acknowledge the relationship to the public, the press, and even the actress herself.[66] He took a paternalistic interest in other female luminaries in his "stable," notably Ethel Barrymore, Julia Marlowe, and Billie Burke. But with Adams, whose background was unique among his stars, he developed a special bond and became the most protective of all. As she matured and adopted a secret lifestyle akin to his own, that bond and the need for protection only deepened.

Two playwrights, Clyde Fitch (1865–1909) and James Matthew Barrie (1860–1937), aided Frohman in fashioning Adams's star image. Both wrote pivotal debut vehicles for her. Early clients of agent Elisabeth Marbury, these writers also became part of the same professional network and developed close personal relationships with the impresario and actress on the basis of common sensibilities. Fitch, who kept a painting of Salome over his hearth, had been Wilde's lover from 1889 to 1891, years that saw Fitch's commercial breakthrough with *Beau Brummell*, written in tribute to Wilde and dandyism, and Wilde's *Picture of Dorian Gray*. True to Wilde's principle, life was imitating art. Just as Lord Henry seduces Dorian and Beau entices Reginald, the older Wilde initiated Fitch into the world of forbidden desires. But then Wilde broke his heart by taking up with Bosie Douglas in 1891. As Wilde's former lover with whom he continued to share professional and social connections, Fitch remained attuned to his fate. He was acutely aware of the dangers that Wilde's reckless sexual behavior with Bosie could and, of course, eventually did pose to his brilliant career. The need to control his own potentially destructive feminine desires by staging idealized female characters, which he often impersonated in rehearsal, impelled Fitch's dramaturgy.[67]

Fitch's social comedy, *The Masked Ball* (1892), with which Maude Adams rose to fame as John Drew's co-star, bears the early signs of this impulse in the portrayal of Suzanne Blondet. Adapting the play from the French of Alexandre Bisson and Albert Carré, Fitch mitigated the raciness of the original by making the young heroine's reputation for dissolute behavior only a ruse her husband deploys to ward off the attentions of a former suitor. The starmaking moment for Adams came at the end of the second act when Suzanne, to punish her husband for misrepresenting her, decides to feign tipsiness during a masked ball. Adams recalled struggling with the scene in rehearsal until "someone"—she doesn't specify who—gave her a flower, "a lovely, long-stemmed rose."[68] Holding the rose in her teeth while teetering about the stage enabled her to avoid coarseness and strike an appealing note of delicacy, coyness, and apparent spontaneity.[69] Since authors were among the few people Frohman allowed into rehearsals, it may well have been Fitch who handed her the rose to help her find the right business to make the scene work.[70] While Fitch had not yet established himself professionally as the director of his own plays, he had staged numerous full-length comedies and fraternity skits at his then-all-male alma mater, Amherst College, in which he also cross-dressed into ingenue and soubrette roles. The business with the rose was just the sort of charming detail in feminine characterization for which he became famous in college and would later on Broadway as well.[71]

After the success of *The Masked Ball*, Adams remained Drew's co-star for four seasons, and Fitch became the most prolific and financially successful playwright for Frohman's Syndicate. In her memoir, *My Crystal Ball*, Marbury described the special bond that developed between Frohman and Fitch, or "C.F" and "c.f.," as they called each other. "They shared many personal tastes," including private dessert orgies at Sherry's. Fitch, the more flamboyant and dandified of the two, represented to Marbury a "commingling of the masculine and feminine." She defends him in terms suggestive of sexual inversion: "The mind of a man with the heart of a woman makes an ideal exotic that should not be despised, and how frequently they go hand in hand where artists are concerned."[72] Given her own proclivities as the long-term domestic partner of the sometime Frohman actress and stage designer, Elsie de Wolfe, and her position as Fitch's and Wilde's agent and Frohman's colleague, she would have understood Fitch's relationship with Wilde and Frohman's with Dillingham. The homes she shared with de Wolfe in New York and Versailles, France, were frequent social gathering places where members of this queer circle interacted and fostered their personal and professional relationships.[73] The bond she and de Wolfe helped nurture between Frohman and Fitch sustained "C.F." and "c.f." through dozens of productions over two decades.

Following Adams's seasons with Drew, Frohman raised her to top billing when he cast her as Lady Babbie in Barrie's *The Little Minister* (1897), the first of several vehicles that made her Barrie's primary stage interpreter. Next to Charles Dillingham and Clyde Fitch, Barrie became Frohman's most intimate friend, and the two were frequently together during Frohman's annual months in England. Elisabeth Marbury brought the two together in order to foster Barrie's transatlantic success. Numerous accounts testify to the extraordinary sympathy they had for one another. Like Frohman, Barrie was short, not much over five feet tall, only much slighter in build. He was married, but according to his wife, who eventually left him, the marriage was unconsummated. His closest personal relationships, apart from that with Frohman, were with young boys. In assessing Barrie's work, recent critics have taken into account his latent homosexuality, which would help explain the connection with Frohman.[74] Although the two friends came from different countries and had different personalities, they shared certain interests and passions, including a common need to closet their inverted sexualities. The reassuringly chaste Maude Adams became the ideal actress and Muse for the Scottish bard, as she was for her impresario.

With the character of Lady Babbie in *The Little Minister* (1897), a play derived from his novel of the same name, Barrie helped Frohman fashion a star persona for Adams that enduringly countered the threat of the Wildean inner Salome. Marbury encouraged her client to do the stage adaptation so that Frohman would produce it in America. When she brought the first draft to Frohman, he rejected it because it adhered too closely to the novel. "It is a man's play," he told her, "whereas I am looking for a play for Maude Adams."[75] As "a man's play," the script focused primarily on the Reverend Gavin Dishart who falls in love with the gypsy Babbie. Not only was this chiefly a vehicle for a male star, but Babbie, although a fanciful and folkloric creation, was still too dangerous and seductive a figure to suit Frohman's agenda. Realizing Adams's potential star drawing power, Marbury prevailed on Barrie to consider rewriting the script to suit her. Barrie went to see Adams's charming performance in *Rosemary* and was inspired both to make Babbie the leading role and to lighten the tone of the piece. The *New York Times* headlined the change: "Maude Adams as Babbie, But the New Make-Believe Gypsy Is Not the Eerie Babbie We Used to Know So Well." Barrie turned Babbie into Lady Barbara Rintoul, the unquestionably Gentile maiden daughter of a blueblood family, who only dresses up as a gypsy for amusement and captures the heart of Dishart when she is in disguise. Because "she is no gypsy," she "does not suffer from the recurrence in her nature of the wild and savage traits and instincts of wandering ancestors." Rather, "she is a sprightly girl." Her gypsy dance—certainly a far cry from Salome's Dance of the Seven Veils—is but a lighthearted, comedic masquerade. "The little romance of the New Babbie . . . and her Gavin is piquant and dainty, with just a touch of pathos," observed the *Times*.[76] To effect Babbie's transformation, Barrie drew upon the long British theatrical tradition of well-born female characters adopting disguises to move the plot but then safely returning to their prescribed social roles. The New Babbie's underlying good breeding is never in question, and her marriage to Dishart ultimately enhances the social standing of both minister and maid.

Adams's performance triumphed over an insubstantial and improbable plot. As E. A. Dithmar quipped, "She is obviously not enough like a gypsy to be mistaken for one even in the moonlight."[77] This was all to the good, as far as Frohman's virtuous agenda was concerned. Adams enchanted audiences with an appeal entirely unlike that of the deceptive femme fatale, or even the coquette. She kept the entertainment "clean, bright, and wholesome" by projecting an image "of an innocent and lovely girl, artless, buoyant, piquant, brisk."[78] Apparent artlessness and youthful playfulness and innocence were the keys to her special appeal. Dithmar found Adams's "most striking artistic trait" to be "her absolute simplicity and naturalness of utterance.... There is never a hint of the conventionally theatrical in her poses and gestures."[79] Walter Prichard Eaton held her up as a consummate example of the "personality" actress adored for the "personal charm" that shone through her performance, reassuring audiences that they were seeing the underlying truth and goodness of her nature.[80]

Other "personality" actresses were also praised for their uplifting "wholesomeness" and sincerity. But their charms were recognized as more "womanly" and, by implication, more adult and sexually mature. Adams was not, like Julia Marlowe, "an enthralling influence of sweet and lovely womanhood." Nor did she possess the "tantalizing, delicious, feminine caprice" of Ada Rehan.[81] Her frame was more petite and less curvaceous, as she stood just five feet tall and weighed barely one hundred pounds. The prevailing image Adams codified as Babbie was "girlish," "dainty," and "winsome," but also "impish" and "elfin."[82] More than other actresses in what Garff Wilson has termed "the Sisterhood of Sweetness and Light," Adams sidestepped the heterosexual economy of desire. Rather than a sensually alluring potential wife or lover, she remained, as Lewis Strang said of her Babbie, "some dear friend, a cherished companion." Because she did not appeal to men sexually like other actresses, Strang could write that she "inspired us to look up and seek beyond."[83] Many women, however, felt very passionately about cherished female companions. These women, as the next chapter will elaborate, made Adams, more than Rehan or Marlowe, an object of ardent desire.

At the core of public belief in the charming artlessness and innocence of Maude Adams was the widespread perception, fostered by earlier vehicles such as *The Masked Ball* and lastingly imprinted by her incarnation of Lady Babbie, that she was incapable of expressing and therefore supposedly of feeling the more savage, elemental emotions. As J. Ranken Towse put it, "the passion that shakes the centres exceeds her range."[84] Leading Victorian gynecological theory situated women's emotional production in the reproductive organs. Outbursts of fierce passion stemmed from sexual arousal and appetite and thus exceeded the bounds of respectable bourgeois conduct.[85] Historically déclassée, actresses could excel at torrid emotional roles because, like prostitutes, they were allegedly highly promiscuous. In the late nineteenth century, as powerful managers raised the social status of the theatrical profession, critics reconciled passionate female performance with respectability by theorizing that actresses increased their capacity for expressing strong emotions after undergoing marriage and childbirth. The young Ethel Barrymore reportedly shared Adams's "exquisitely girlish personality" but then underwent a transformation.[86] Seeking to explain "The New Ethel Barrymore," Walter Prichard Eaton claimed the actress had deepened as a result of conjugal relations.[87] The most famous emotional star of Adams's generation, Mrs. Leslie Carter, had experienced marriage, motherhood, sordid alleged love affairs, and divorce before the fierce training of David Belasco made her safe for bourgeois theatrical consumption. If some critics found the perpetually unmarried Adams's lack of raw emotional power to be a limitation, this deficiency proved an asset to Frohman's civilizing agenda because it purportedly indicated absence of sexual desire and sexual activity. Apparent lack of passion signified virginity, and the failure of Adams's emotional range to deepen over time, perpetual chastity.

Launching her virginal, sprightly, Gentile star persona, Adams played Lady Babbie for a record of three hundred successive performances and gross profits of $370,000 (about $8.65 million today). Among the notable personages to attend this initial run were the former president Benjamin Harrison and the sitting mayor William L. Strong.[88] Adams's triumph in this role prompted Frohman to elevate her to the rank of First Lady of his Empire.[89] He offered to give her a substantial raise, but instead she shrewdly requested a percentage of gross receipts, an arrangement that allowed her to build her own large fortune. He also used the wide reach of the Syndicate booking apparatus to make her stardom a national phenomenon by sending her on tour following the New York run. To preserve her pure and profitable star image, he resolved only to showcase her in "clean plays" and to keep her offstage life entirely shielded from public view. A 1930 retrospective reported:

> The "secrecy" that has surrounded every movement of her private life was set for her by Frohman, the result of his innate showmanship.
>
> With a star on his hands after the tremendous recognition accorded her Lady Babbie, said Frohman—
>
> "You will continue as you are. You will say nothing. You are not to be

interviewed. You are not to be quoted in the press. You will be to the public only Maude Adams of the stage. People will wonder at you; yearn for details of your private life; your off-stage pursuits and inclinations. Let them. It will only spur their interest and desire for you."[90]

In the words of his biographers, Frohman "exhausted every resource to keep her aloof and secluded . . . [so that] she be known through her work and not through her personal self."[91] The guiding presumption was that if audiences had no other information to contradict her assiduously maintained persona, they would continue to assume that who she was on stage was who she was, that she was virtuous through and through, and that so, by extension, was Frohman's enterprise.

The impresario's victory over corruptive femininity was solidified when his star was chosen as the model for a solid gold statue to be exhibited by the State of Colorado at the Paris Exposition of 1900. Herbert M. Wells, the former governor of Utah, drew an analogy between heroic frontier mining and female starmaking:

> You see, Maude Adams was like one of the great silver or lead or copper mines that abound in this region—we walk all around it every day for perhaps a generation, never realizing that a hidden treasure lies at our door, and then some bright day a David Belasco or some other Napoleon [i.e., Frohman] swoops down upon us, is attracted by the formation, discovers the mine, and develops it.[92]

Adams was chosen because her virtues qualified her to embody what the statue was supposed to represent: "The Type of American Woman," that is, the national WASP ideal of femininity. Her selection made her, literally, an evolutionary trophy for the Jewish Frohman, much as Ada Rehan became for the Irish Catholic Augustin Daly when she was cast in silver for the World's Columbian Exposition of 1893. Rendered by the noted Chicago sculptor, Bessie Potter Vonnoh, the statue of Adams comprised six hundred pounds of fourteen-karat gold valued at $150,000. According to newspaper accounts, she was depicted in a gown of "charming simplicity" whose design was "modest in the extreme," fittingly more modest than the sleeveless, off-the-shoulder tunic and barefooted, sword-wielding pose of Rehan's Justice. For Adams, "The arrangement of the hair in the statue is classic, and the pose is admirable, with the hands hanging naturally by the side and the drapery falling gracefully about the figure."[93] Following its display at the Paris Expo in the summer of 1900, the statue returned to the United States for a national tour that further publicized Frohman's achievements with Adams.

The victory was not only personal for Frohman. In an 1898 editorial, *Life* magazine linked the Syndicate's commercialism with the Jewishness of its leadership and accused the conglomerate of debasing the theatre. Along with Frohman, the Syndicate included Abe Erlanger, Al Hayman, Marc Klaw, Samuel Nixon, and Fred Zimmerman. An accompanying cartoon entitled "The Drama in New York" (fig. 15) shows a bearded, hook-nosed, cigar-smoking impresario eyeing a "whiter" actress who asks him about her prospects for success on the stage. He responds "Well, did you bring your tights?" As it degraded the theatre, the Syndicate also threatened to defile Gentile womanhood.[94] Garnering highly public credit for protecting and touting Maude Adams's virtuous, nunlike star persona, Frohman counteracted some of the anti-Semitic charges of lechery and vulgarity that tarred the Syndicate.

For her part, Adams appeared scrupulously dutiful in abiding by Frohman's strict paternalism to ensure that her private life never countered her pure public image. She rarely spoke to the press, never married, and as journalists repeatedly noted, took respites in convents.[95] An association first with the Augustinian Convent in Tours, France, and then with the Cenacle of St. Regis, a Catholic order at Seton Hall, where she often stayed when in New York, became a recurring motif of her Gentile performance. Standard accounts of her life offstage portrayed her as living alone on a farm in simple, rustic surroundings in spite of her wealth and fame. Here, alone with her thoughts, she devoted herself to reading, studying her art, and taking fresh air, either on foot or on horseback.[96] Her bedroom at the farm reportedly replicated the layout and décor of her humble accommodations at the Cenacle.[97] When she finally sat for an extended interview in 1937, long after her Broadway retirement, she entirely reinforced Frohman's agenda with her comments:

> I declined to give interviews and to read what was said about me because it seemed to me I had compensated my public by what I gave it over the footlights. It seemed to me, too, that I needed all my resources to prepare myself for each successive message. Obviously, others are not affected as I am, but with me lively contacts with the world would have been so disconcerting to my work that I could not have given it the concentration I felt imperative.[98]

In a commencement address she gave in 1939 at Stephens College, where she was teaching, she reiterated that Frohman "delighted in what he called

15. *"The Drama in New York," Life, 12 May 1898, p. 405.*

'clean plays.'" Echoing his philosophy, she asserted that "the theatre is a civilizing force."[99]

But espousing Frohman's agenda as her own and giving the impression of a reclusive, ascetic lifestyle was not simple obeisance to her impresario. The arrangement served the actress's queer interests as it facilitated a private life lived exclusively with other women, first with Lillie Florence who died prematurely in 1901, and then with Louise Boynton from 1905 until Boynton's death in 1951.[100] As with Frohman and Dillingham, the evidence of these relationships is sparse because the parties were highly circumspect. But the absence of evidence is itself indicative. On her farm, with the help of the property master for her company who poured the kerosene, the actress threw all her personal correspondence into a pit and set it ablaze. Since Adams did her best to ensure that public knowledge of her private life never contradicted her star persona, such deliberate destruction of her personal papers suggests that their content might have been threatening to her pristine image. The only letters she spared from incineration were those from J. M. Barrie, for whom she remained the salutary muse.[101]

Adams wrote an autobiography, but it sheds little light on her private life. The document was published in six installments in the *Ladies Home Journal* in 1926 under the evasive title, "The One I Knew Least of All."[102] She opens with the following declaration: "It is one of the many blessings of life in the theater that we are delightfully busy being someone else, and need have scarcely an inkling of ourselves. That doubtful pleasure can always be deferred. And what a mercy! If we really knew ourselves, how could we endure it?"[103] Hiding behind her profession, she relieves herself of the burden of self-revelation; she cannot disclose what she allegedly never had time or inclination to discover. She further distances herself from her own story by maintaining a third-person stance. The subject throughout is "she," "the one I knew least." Nowhere in the six installments does she refer to either Lillie Florence or Louise Boynton even as acquaintances, though they were the closest people to her. The only female friend whose name she mentions is that of Elizabeth Alexander, wife of the designer John Alexander with whom she collaborated on several productions. These self-deflecting narrative strategies continue her career-long practice of keeping her offstage life shrouded. They also call to mind some of the reasons why many queer people have been drawn to the theatre. Opportunities for masking, make-believe, and public approbation have strong appeal to those whose real life circumstances make them leery of fully inhabiting their own skins.

While Adams herself left few revelatory traces, and media accounts persisted in describing her as living alone, her close friend Phyllis Robbins's biography, titled *Maude Adams: An Intimate Portrait*, registers the importance of her domestic partners in her life. According to Robbins, Adams was utterly distraught over the loss of Florence in the fall of 1901, especially since she had to leave her, just days before her death, to begin a tour.[104] By the following spring, Adams was so run down by the strain on her "nervous system" and bouts of insomnia that she had to take an extended holiday abroad and withdrew from the stage for the entire 1902–1903 season. She spent the summer of 1902 in the Swiss Alps taking a rest cure in St. Moritz; wintered in seclusion on her New York country estate; and then, beginning in March 1903, traveled to Turkey, Egypt, and Palestine and returned through Germany, France, and England.[105]

The media attributed the malaise that necessitated these getaways to over-work from her rise to stardom, but those closer to her understood it also to be the result of the loss of the companionship and support that Florence had provided. By coincidence, Clyde Fitch was also taking the cure at St. Moritz that summer and staying at a nearby hotel with his travel companion, Ferdinand Gottschalk. Fitch contacted her and offered their company to help cheer her up. While generally keeping herself secluded, Adams felt comfortable enough with these two to go out for occasional meals and let her hair down. According to Gottschalk's account of their return from a dinner, she climbed on top of the carriage with the coachman, tossed off her hat, "shook her hair out to the breeze," seized the whip, and helped drive the horses home.[106] For companionship on the desert trip, Adams took along her maid and a Miss Ray Rockman, "who, it is said, Barrie 'got' for her."[107] She was also briefly joined by Nora Davis, the daughter of the author Rebecca Harding Davis and L. Clark Davis, the editor of the *Philadelphia Ledger*.[108] In 1905, still concerned about Adams's well-being, her physician, Dr. William B. Wood, sent Louise Boynton (1868–1951) to her to fill the void left by Florence. Four years older than Adams and a native of Maine, Boynton had moved with her family to New Jersey, where she and her sister briefly ran a local newspaper. Robbins says she had a gift for writing that she used in letters, essays, and occasional translations of plays from the French. But mostly she assisted Adams as "a friend, companion, secretary, and buffer against any unwarranted intrusion, a delightful dragon. . . . She dedicated herself to Miss Adams and won her lifelong love."[109]

Further insight about the nature of Adams and Boynton's partnership comes from the correspondence of another female friend, Nan Hodgkins, who met Adams in 1902 and was close to her until the mid-1930s.[110] These letters speak to the circulation of female desire around Adams. In addition to shared feelings of adoration for the star, correspondents discuss jealousies among Adams's friends for her attentions and various pleasures and strains in their respective domestic partnerships. In a letter to Hodgkins dated 3 January 1953, a correspondent mentions her own "close friend" with whom she lived from 1911 until her partner's death in 1935, commenting that they had a "companionship" such as Nan enjoyed with her longtime domestic partner. Three years later another friend of Hodgkins, Adams, and Boynton comments on the published material on Adams, which had resurged with the actress's recent death: "It is strange reading books and articles about people. If one doesn't know one accepts all the story, but if one does know so many mistakes are written, not intentionally, of course."[111] Her remarks allude to another reality behind the official story of Maude Adams. All of this correspondence locates Adams and Boynton within a circle of female same-sex couples.

Although Adams left no written documentation of her love for Boynton, the actress made a poignant declaration in the manner of her burial, which involved the partners' longtime association with convents. Having had such a meaningful rest at the Augustinian Convent in Tours, France, in the summer of 1901, Adams sought a similar respite from the stress after Frohman's sudden death in 1915. Boynton, who had herself stayed in the Tours Convent, started looking for a comparable haven in New York. With the help of Adams's costumer, Boynton located the Cenacle of St. Regis, whose Mother Superior agreed to accommodate their needs. From this first visit onward, the room at the Cenacle remained at Adams's disposal for lodging when she was in the city. In 1921 Adams gave her Lake Ronkonkoma, Long Island, farm to the Cenacle to use as a retreat and retained a small white house on the property for herself and Boynton, where they continued to reside together among the nuns.[112] Predeceasing Adams by two years, Boynton was buried in the cemetery the Cenacle established on the estate. Between her partner's death and her own, Adams suffered a bout of pleurisy and was temporarily unable to talk. During a visit, Robbins exclaimed, "Your dear voice has come back!" to which Adams responded, sharing a laugh with an old friend, "Did you say my 'queer' voice?"[113] When Adams passed away, the *New York Times* reported with characteristic euphemism that the actress's burial place adjoined that of "her friend and secretary."[114] The names of Maude Adams and Louise Boynton are engraved on the same modest tombstone, a simple square slab lying flat on the ground, under the inscription "In Grateful Memory."[115] There they rest, together for eternity, as they had lived for nearly half a century, on the land they loved.

With mutual understanding about each other's private devotions, Frohman and Adams actively helped facilitate each other's lifestyles. When Adams was still living in a boardinghouse with her mother in 1895 and gossip began to circulate about possible romantic liaisons with other actresses in "Maude Adams's Adamless Eden," Frohman's office issued a decoy announcement to the *New York Clipper* and the *Dramatic Mirror* that his budding young star was engaged to be married to the popular author Richard Harding Davis.[116] There is no evidence to suggest any romance between the two, though Frohman might have thought he could make the ruse credible because Adams was friendly with Davis's sister, Nora. In 1900, when Adams was still with Lillie Florence, Frohman took out a $35,000 mortgage to help her buy "a house of her own."[117] In subsequent years, Frohman made it company policy that when Adams traveled, arrangements had to accommodate Boynton as well.[118] But what afforded the most mutual protection was that Frohman and Adams both allowed the rumors of their romance and secret marriage to each other to circulate. Only once out of the myriad occasions on which Adams was publicly asked about her marriage to Frohman did she respond with a denial.[119] Otherwise, she and Frohman either refused to respond or reiterated the high regard in which each held the other.[120] They even let stand the speculation in 1902–1903, when Adams took a year off from the stage, that she had gone away to have Frohman's baby. The story helped cover for the real reasons: work-related strain and stress compounded by the recent loss of her female partner. Belief that she and Frohman were married also quelled questions about why neither was romantically linked with anyone else of the opposite sex and why, as one paper put it, "it was said through her life that she exhibited a calculated coolness toward men."[121]

Intriguingly, these stories of Adams's secret marriage to her manager and even birthing his child did not damage her nunlike, virginal reputation. If she had experienced loss of virginity and childbirth, the expectation, given prevailing beliefs about the production of female passion, would have been that she would deepen as an emotional actress. But that deepening, according to the critical reception of her work, never occurred. Even as rumors of a sexual liaison surfaced, seeming evidence of lack of consummation persisted. This contradiction simultaneously allowed for many people to continue believing in Adams's chastity and for others to entertain different possibilities. As the next chapter will elaborate, Frohman and Adams joined hands in bringing a subtext of sexual inversion and same-sex desire elaborately into play in Adams's breeches roles, which she began enacting in 1900. A circle of queer intimates and associates continued to provide crucial personal and professional support, while an emerging queer audience helped further Adams's stardom and her maker's empire.

4

Through Fairy and Fowl

A woman can play a boy's part, because she
can look as much, or more, like a boy than a man
can. But a woman cannot play a man's part as
well as a man. . . . She may succeed in creating
something strange and wonderful, but for the
normal audience she will never create the
character intended by the dramatist.
—Walter Prichard Eaton,
"Playing the Piper," 1911

"My stars! He's falling in love with a hen dressed
up as a cock!"
—Louis N. Parker, trans., *Chantecler*, 1911

On 19 May 1900, Charles Frohman and Maude Adams sat down to dinner with Sarah Bernhardt, perhaps then the most famous actress in the Western world. The American impresario and actress were visiting Paris to see the French diva in *L'Aiglon*, or *The Eaglet*, Edmond Rostand's play about the frail son of Napoleon I, in which Adams was to appear that fall. Bernhardt hosted the dinner in Adams's honor with twenty distinguished authors and members of the Comédie-Française. The American entourage included Frohman's domestic partner, Charles Dillingham, and Elsie de Wolfe, an actress in Frohman's company and the domestic partner of theatrical agent Elisabeth Marbury.[1] In addition to illustrating the queer network of theatre practitioners that supported and enabled Frohman's and Adams's careers, the occasion marked the beginning of Adams's career as a breeches performer. Through their breeches productions, star and impresario would most fully engage their own queer sensibilities as well as those of an emerging queer audience that patronized Frohman's theatres along with masses of straight spectators.

Adams donned breeches for five major Frohman productions. After *L'Aiglon* came *Peter Pan* (1905), by James M. Barrie; *The Jesters* (1908), by Miguel Zamacois; *Joan of Arc* (1909), adapted from Friedrich Schiller, and *Chantecler* (1911), by Rostand.[2] These five comprise a set of historical costume dramas and fantasies that trade heavily on bird and fairy motifs rife with queer connotations when understood within the era's emerging homosexual lexicon and social practices. Intriguingly, except for *Peter Pan*, Bernhardt preceded Adams in her aspiration to play all of these roles. She played the lead in *The Jesters* in 1907 and in *Jeanne d'Arc* in 1890 as well as in *L'Aiglon*. When Benoit-Constant Coquelin died before *Chantecler*'s 1910 premiere, she pleaded with Rostand to let her take over the title role.[3] Crossing paths with Adams on American soil, Bernhardt toured the United States nine times between 1880 and 1916. Furthering the queer cultural work of Adams's breeches productions, the French diva served as both inspiration and shadow for the American star.

The decades during which the careers of Adams and Bernhardt overlapped were ones that saw a marked decline in the popularity and acceptability of breeches roles on the American stage. According to Elizabeth Reitz Mullenix, reasons for the decline included the advance of realism, the rise of "leg shows" that linked women appearing in hose to a burlesque "low other"; and, most damningly by the 1890s, the specter of the sexual invert.[4] Leading sexologists explicitly named and connected sexual inversion in women to cross-dressing and the acting profession.[5] As Mullenix demonstrates, the broader currency of these ideas began to arouse suspicion about actresses who essayed breeches roles.[6] Adams's unique reputation for inviolate virtue, thrown into relief via comparison with "the divine Sarah," enabled her to remain beyond suspicion even in male attire for those repulsed by purported perversity. At the same time, the widening discourse of sexual inversion helped make her breeches performances more queerly legible and enticing for those aroused by the possibilities of same-sex desire.

An extraordinarily compelling performer, especially in emotional, tragic roles, Bernhardt came to represent much that Frohman and Adams purported to contravert with their civilizing agenda. Bernhardt excited American audiences with her virtuosic embodiments of forbidden French passions in roles such as Racine's incestuously lustful Phèdre, Legouve and Scribe's doomed actress, Adrienne Lecouvreur, and Dumas-*fils*'s prostitute with a heart of gold, Camille, as well as Jeanne d'Arc and L'Aiglon. Her disreputable family origins included a Jewish courtesan mother who bore her out of wedlock and left her to be raised in a convent. Moreover, she was known to "wear the breeches" offstage as well as on. She ran her own theatre, pursued sexual liaisons with both women and men, and supported an illegitimate son as a single parent. Both a visual and a stage artist, she also wore pants when she painted and sculpted.[7] Beginning with her first tour in 1880, American newspapers ran anti-Semitic caricatures accentuating her curly hair, prominent nose, and perverse and serpentlike thinness, along with her penchant for cross-dressing. The main theme of the satire was her allegedly rapacious and deceitful desire to profit from her performances, not only by her acting, but also by selling her own sculptures and paintings while touring her plays.[8] Compounding her domineering and potentially destructive Jewish persona, she played the *belle juive* (beautiful Jewess) heroine of *Leah, the Forsaken* during her 1891–1892 star tour. While on that tour, in February 1892, she also went to a Tennessee prison to visit Alice Mitchell, then the most notorious female invert in the country on account of her murdering her beloved Freda Ward. Bernhardt was considering playing Mitchell in a proposed new drama based on the murderess's life to be written by Sardou. The project never materialized, but Bernhardt's visit and plans to play Mitchell were well publicized.[9] The following June, she began rehearsing for a London premiere of *Salome* that the Lord Chamberlain curtailed. That Wilde reportedly wrote the play for her and that it was censored became part of her legend.[10]

Against Bernhardt's dangerous, perverse French Jewish image, Adams was fashioned to represent the Gentile, nunlike American antithesis. In diametrical opposition to Bernhardt's Camille, Adams's most famous female character was Lady Babbie. When Adams played Bernhardt's breeches roles, the American press drew direct comparisons which claimed that Adams's star qualities were morally superior and often artistically preferable to those of the French star in spite of her relative lack of emotional force. For the queer Jewish impresario Frohman, the contrast with Bernhardt helped make Adams the saving antidote to the sexual invert's Wildean inner Salome. Even though he and his leading lady became extremely wealthy from Adams's stardom, her anti-Bernhardt image and Frohman's well publicized propensity for lavishing exorbitant sums on her productions without thought of profit countered some of the charges of rapacious commercialism leveled against the Jewish-run Syndicate.[11] Yet as their continued socializing with Bernhardt and imitation of her repertoire suggest, Adams and Frohman displayed a need to reveal as well as conceal forbidden desires. Aspiring to civilize the dangerous passions Bernhardt embodied by reincarnating several of the same roles, Adams also invoked some of those very passions. Her ostensibly more respectable breeches productions conveyed ambivalent meanings, as the shadow of the bisexual French diva became part of a system of representational codes that different audiences could read in different ways.

She Would Be an Eagle

With their lush production values and thick tapestries of poetic allusions and allegory, historical costume dramas and fantasies offered Frohman and Adams particularly rich vehicles for pursuing their civilizing agenda while engaging queer interests. L'Aiglon opened at the Knickerbocker Theatre in New York City in October 1900 for a run of seventy-three performances. It moved to Boston where it played for several weeks before going on a national tour for the rest of the season.[12] While Rostand's play captured some of the moodiness and profligacy of the historical Aiglon, the English translation by Louis N. Parker glossed over these more complex aspects of the character. This revision helped foster the belief that Adams's inviolate virtue could triumph over the perverse potentialities of cross-dressing. L'Aiglon, or the Eaglet, is the pale, consumptive, twenty-year-old son of the deceased Eagle, Napoleon I, and Maria Louisa of Austria. Titled the Duke of Reichstadt, he is held a pampered captive at the Hapsburg Court. He yearns to defy his maternal grandfather, the Austrian emperor, and return to France to claim his imperial destiny. Napoleonic loyalists operating under cover in Austria help him plot his escape, but the scheme, like its leader, proves ineffectual. En route to France, he spends the night on the battlefield of Wagram, where exposure to the elements brings on greater illness and feverish delusions. Austrian soldiers recover him and return him to the palace. With his destiny unrealized, he dies a few days later. The potential threat of a woman in pants is defused via infantilization, a reiteration of the actress-as-boy trope that had worked to contain female sexuality and render breeches roles acceptable earlier in the century.[13] Although the Duke dreams of full-blooded manhood and conquest, he never gets beyond playing with toy soldiers; the Eaglet remains a virginal fledgling who ultimately cannot leave the nest.

The comparison with Bernhardt's version became strikingly acute when, a month after Adams had opened at the Knickerbocker, Bernhardt brought her production to play for sixteen performances at New York's Garden Theatre in repertory with *La Tosca, La Dame aux Camelias, Hamlet,* and *Cyrano de Bergerac.*[14] With her greater maturity (she was almost thirty years older than Adams), scandalous reputation, and proven virtuosity in tragic roles, Bernhardt was credited with bringing much more emotional force and complexity to the role.[15] But many American observers preferred Adams, whose lack of passional force and appeal to pathos better suited the frail hero, at least as he came across in Parker's translation.[16] The Chicago critic Amy Leslie commented that Adams "has not Bernhardt's combination of thinness and leonine force of grace, her lithe elegance, or animal suppleness." Five-feet tall, slender, flat chested, and straight through the waist and hips, the shorter, younger Adams looked more boyish. In that boyishness, she also appeared to be prepubescently feminine, which reassuringly signaled greater innocence than commentators perceived in the French star.[17]

Moreover, if Bernhardt wielded disconcerting power as a businesswoman and ran her own theatre in Paris, Adams seemed to operate as the subservient protégée of an autocratic male manager. Advance press noted that the production would be "under the personal direction of Mr. Frohman."[18] The play itself helped foster the image of her deference to Frohman because audiences could read in the Duke's paeans to his father during the play Adams's admiration of her manager, who was famously known as the "Napoleon of the Theatre."[19] They could also read in the Duke's failure to reach maturity and carry on his father's conquering legacy the impossibility of Adams ever overpowering her manager's control. She would remain the perpetual Eaglet to Frohman's Eagle.

While those who needed to could assuage themselves with these reassurances against possible threats posed by the play and performance, there was plenty to prompt alternative readings and stir subaltern desires. The Duke's fledgling, unactualized manhood was itself a sign of inversion, as immaturity was considered a feminine trait, a stage to be passed through en route to full masculinity in both ontogenetic and phylogenetic development. Aware of his abnormally prolonged immaturity, the Duke asserts that his brain is not "ripe" enough to rule.[20] He and others repeatedly question the nature of his inner self—is he an effete, blond Hapsburg through and through, or does a dark, virile Corsican lurk underneath? When he startles and offends his mother by intervening with uncharacteristic force in a flirtation she has with her fiancé, the Marquis de Bombelles, he explains:

> For this cry, this movement
> Were not my own. Within me still remains
> A reverence for my mother and her freedom!
> 'Twas he—'Twas he by whom my soul's possessed,
> Who sprang upon you with this tragic force!
> Thank God! I'm saved! The Corsican leapt out![21]

Such explicit references to the nature of the man within would have resonated strongly with public understandings of sexual and gender inversion when the role was played by an actress in breeches.

The possibilities of inversion are further elaborated through the Duke's connection to his cousin, the Countess Napoleone Camerata. She is his twin in stature, facial features, and political allegiances but is outwardly female, physically robust, and dark-haired. Parker's translation describes her as

> the strange, unarmored amazon, who bears
> Her father's likeness proudly in her face,
> Seeks dangers, rides unbroken horses, fences. . .[22]

In her, the dark, virile Corsican, not the pale, effete Hapsburg has ruled. She becomes the Duke's chief inspiration and agent for his escape and return to France to assume his father's legacy. The plot involves the Duke and Countess switching places during a costume ball so that he can escape while being mistaken for her. She dyes her "sable tresses fair" like his, and the two don twin Napoleonic costumes that are identical except for differently colored capes. His is violet, the color of the flower Napoleon adopted as the symbol of his party. Violet has also been a color associated with same-sex-desiring men and women since the classical Greek period. Her cape is brown, a mixture of green and red, two other colors used to code same-sex desire in the late nineteenth century.[23] When the Countess approaches the Duke to make the switch, he exclaims, "My very image! I'm coming toward myself as in a glass." She says "Well met, Napoleon!" to which he replies "And Napoleone."[24] This exchange by two actresses in imperial drag both highlights inverted gender play and hints at subversive female power.

The inversion motifs that entwine these two characters extend to same-sex sexual desire. From the opening act, the Duke, a role known to have been originated by Bernhardt and translated for Adams, is portrayed as an object of female affection. Numerous women at court swoon over him, but two capture his special attention. He embraces Fanny Elssler, who smuggles to him forbidden historical information about his father. A production photograph shows Adams handsomely clad in a black waistcoat, breeches, and riding boots, with both arms around Fanny and their cheeks turned in to each other (fig. 16). He wants to return even more affection to beautiful Theresa de Loget. Lamenting how his breeding has made him different from his father, the Duke rationalizes his aptitude for sexual over military conquest:

> O splendid blood another has corrupted,
> Who, striving to be Caesar, was not able;
> Thy energy is not all dead within me.
> A misbegotten Caesar is Don Juan!
> Yes, 'tis another way of conquering . . .
> The adventurer landed in the Gulf of Juan,
> He felt Don Juan's thrill; and when Don Juan
> Pricked a new conquest in his list of loves,
> Did he not feel the pride of Bonaparte?
> . . . 'Tis well the legend closes thus,
> And *this* conqueror is the other's son.
> I'm the fair shadow of the dusky hero,
> And, as he conquered nations, one by one,
> So will I conquer women, one by one.
> Moonbeams shall be my sun of Austerlitz![25]

Clad in Napoleonic regalia (fig. 17), which shows off her flat-chested, boyish figure to a most elegant tee, the Duke proposes a secret assignation with Theresa that night at his hunting lodge. She delightedly agrees, exclaiming "I am to come—!"[26] When he learns that the escape plot also must unfold that night, he has to get word to Theresa of the change in plans. As he and the Countess rendezvous to exchange identities at the costume ball, he tells her to

16. Maude Adams as the Duke of Reichstadt embracing Fanny Elssler (Margaret Gordon), in Maude Adams in *L'Aiglon:* A Pictorial Souvenir.

17. *Maude Adams as the Duke of Reichstadt in full Napoleonic regalia. Courtesy of the Philip H. Ward Collection of Theatrical Images, Rare Book and Manuscript Library, University of Pennsylvania.*

meet Theresa at the lodge in his stead. "Swear you will tell me later if she comes," he implores his cousin.[27] When they switch cloaks, the group of court women fawning over the Duke turn their ardor to the Countess and hover around her to provide additional cover. She leaves vested with the Duke's garment, mission, and ability to arouse female desire.

While the Duke's assignation with Theresa is thwarted, and thus the purity of the character Maude Adams played is left intact, the play tantalizingly raises the prospect of a lesbian consummation in which the Duke remains implicated. As he makes his way to France via the battlefield at Wagram, where his father famously outmaneuvered the Austrians, the Duke is told that Theresa's brother has learned of the secret tryst and gone to the hunting lodge to kill him. Fearing for the Countess's life, he wants to return to help her, but his aides prevent him. The Duke exclaims in anguish "To leave her were to cast my soul away!"[28] He identifies the Countess as his inner soul, the female inside the inverted male character; however, that soul is itself inverted, a woman with a man inside. So constituted, the Amazonian Countess, it turns out, did not need assistance. She appears before the Duke having killed the murderous brother with her sword and escaped on horseback. When the Duke asks her whether or not Theresa came, she tells him Theresa did not appear for the tryst. This is a lie, but she hopes the deceit will make him feel freer from romantic entanglements and hasten his escape. However, Austrian soldiers soon recover the Duke and take him back to the Hapsburg palace. His mother, Theresa, and the Countess gather at his bedside as he lies mortally ill from exposure. All three profess to have acted out of love for him. Although she would prefer to keep him to herself, his mother brought the other two women because she knew he would want to see them. Theresa reveals that her passion for the Duke did, in fact, drive her to the hunting lodge for the tryst that night. The Countess explains how her love for the Duke prompted her to deceive him. The Duke dies a virgin in his mother's grief-stricken embrace, an image to evoke outpourings of pathos, a respectable womanly emotion. But transgressive female eros occupies the picture as well, for next to this Pietà stands the Duke's Amazonian alter ego, who wielded a potent sword and to whom Theresa came after all.

The female passion circulating on stage among the Duke, his mother, the Countess, and Theresa also aroused and implicated the audience. Adams's most numerous and ardent fans were women. As Acton Davies notes, "Hers is the popularity of the woman even before the artist, and, curiously enough, it is for her own sex that her personality makes its greatest appeal."[29] According to the *New York Herald Tribune*, "Adolescent girls and single women were particularly susceptible to her charms."[30] Moreover, "A Maude Adams audience is of every class, from the shop girl, who saves her fifty cents to go and see her, to the more pretentious theatregoer," observed William de Wagstaffe.[31] Adams was a special favorite among the swelling demographic of Matinee Girls, young unescorted women who could attend the theatre in the afternoon. Inside the theatre, female enthusiasm erupted in deluges of flowers, dozens of curtain calls, and ovations that extended performance times beyond usual limits.[32]

Adams's starring premiere in a breeches role occasioned particularly intense ardor. During *L'Aiglon's* pre–New York opening in Baltimore, "The actress's first appearance, in dark trousers and a long coat [fig. 16], was the signal for a burst of applause that delayed the performance for several minutes."[33] While Adams, unlike Bernhardt, was not rumored to wear pants offstage, a review of the New York premiere noted that "she wears her garments as if used to them all her life."[34] Another photograph of an Act I scene shows the apparent ease with which Adams adopted the spread-legged seating posture of a young man (fig. 18). Several months later, a Boston reviewer commented: "Maude Adams still remains the idol of the matinee girl. . . . She has met the test of their affection and admiration in boy's costume, and from the exclamations heard on every side they evidently consider her lovelier than ever." The papers also noted how "thousands who had seen her before in the character of the Eaglet thronged to the theatre to repeat their enjoyment of the performance."[35]

After her shows, crowds of adoring female fans waited for her at the stage door. The *Burr McIntosh Monthly* recorded the phenomenon:

> All they want is to meet the glance of her eye, share in the warmth of her smile, hear her "good night," and they are rewarded—every mother's daughter of them, for however many hours' waiting and however many suburban trains home consequently missed. A small army of fair-faced girls and cultured looking women have been known to gather thus and wait for hours, simply to exchange smiles with Miss Adams. It does not look so much like a crowd as a gathering of disciples. Almost nothing is said, and in a moment after the object of it all disappears, everybody goes their different ways wreathed in smiles of happiness.[36]

This author explained the fans' attraction to the star as "simply an instance of goodness of life attracting goodness." Another writer asserted: "she is peculiarly liked by women because her manifestations are so sexless."[37]

*18. Maude Adams as the Duke of Reichstadt seated in a male pose,
in* Maude Adams in L'Aiglon: A Pictorial Souvenir.

Yet this sexlessness was more a function of cultural presumption than actuality. Many of the white middle- and upper-class women who were a large portion of Adams's fan base developed deep same-sex friendships involving intense exchanges of passion that merged gentility with eroticism.[38] These allegedly "passionless" attachments often began as school-age crushes that Havelock Ellis identified as being more prevalent among girls than boys.[39] The cases of two individual fans demonstrate how both adolescent crushes and the adult passion of romantic friendship fueled same-sex ardor for Adams. One such fan is her adoring biographer, Phyllis Robbins, author of *Maude Adams: An Intimate Portrait* (1956) and *The Young Maude Adams* (1959). *An Intimate Portrait* is as much a chronicle of Robbins's passionate friendship with Adams as it is of Adams's career. Robbins was an upper-middle-class single woman raised in Boston by her unmarried aunt, Frances Horton. When she was fifteen, her aunt took her to see *The Little Minister*. On that date, 19 November 1898, Robbins first became smitten with Adams.

The biography proceeds from this encounter rather than beginning with an account of Adams's childhood, which later became the subject of *The Young Maude Adams*. From that first sighting, Robbins began filling her multiple volumes of meticulously and lovingly arranged scrapbooks. In addition to reams of newspaper and magazine clippings, ranging from full-length articles and reviews to the briefest mentions of Maude Adams in the news, these scrapbooks contain photographs, theatre programs, and ticket stubs for the many times she saw each of Adams's productions in Boston and New York. Asserting her physical placement with respect to the performance, she wrote "My seat" beside each of these stubs. When applicable, she also noted the name of her companion—for example, "went with Aunt Fanno." Underneath the ticket stubs, she inscribed the extemporaneous curtain lines Adams delivered at the behest of the wildly cheering crowds of which she was a part.

Watching Adams come and go from the theatre, Robbins and Horton perceived that she had a "friend"—Lillie Florence at the time—through whom they might gain an entrée to the star. In March 1900, Horton prevailed on the "friend" to accompany her and her niece to lunch and the matinee so that afterward she might take them backstage for young Phyllis to meet her idol. The meeting occurred, and the women struck up a friendship. Having attended the New York opening of *L'Aiglon* and numerous Boston performances, Robbins recorded how touched she was in the season of 1903–1904 when Adams sent her violets, the queer encoded flowers of the production, because illness kept the star from making offstage visits.[40] The relationship progressed as Adams made Horton and Robbins's Boston residence a safe haven away from home. When the star augmented her Gentile status by becoming a lifetime member of the Massachusetts Society of Mayflower Descendants, she listed their address as her own.[41] Eventually, Adams invited the two women into the homes she shared with Louise Boynton in New York. This friendship, founded on fan worship and common lifestyle choices, endured for more than half a century. It lasted through the deaths of Aunt Fanno in 1927 and Boynton in 1951 and only ended with Adams's death in 1953. Robbins's devotion resulted in the fullest surviving documentation of the life of the nation's biggest star during the American theatre's most profitable and culturally influential era. In addition to the two published books, the scrapbooks and papers Robbins bequeathed comprise the bulk of the Maude Adams Collection at Harvard's Houghton Library, the major Adams archive.

Another individual female fan who left a written record is a woman from Chicago named Laura Kennedy. Like Robbins and legions of other

"Adamites," she was unmarried and made Maude Adams a hobby for decades before she met her. Along with collecting memorabilia and following Adams on tour, she wrote fan letters to the actress. Robbins reports that after Kennedy learned of her friendship with Adams, she wrote "long, gushing letters" to her as well and sent handmade Christmas presents to them both. In 1934, when Adams briefly returned to the stage in *Twelfth Night* and played in Ogunquit on summer tour, Robbins overheard the ticket teller say to a friend, "There's a woman who came from Chicago by bus, and she wants a seat for every performance!" "It could have been no one else," writes Robbins. "We hunted her up, and at last she met Maude." Meetings became more frequent after Kennedy moved to Oneida, New York, when a friend left her a house there. She also visited Adams in Columbia, Missouri, where the star taught and directed plays for several years at Stephens College after her retirement from acting. Kennedy saw a number of Adams's college productions.[42] Her extensive notes describe not only the performances in great detail but also fleeting exchanges of affection with Adams. She rapturously records those moments when the actress embraced or kissed her. Along with Robbins's materials, Kennedy's notes, letters, and memorabilia reside in the Adams archive at Harvard. They provide some of the most personal insight available into the star and the adoration she engendered.[43]

In spite of the intensity of the female ardor circulating around Adams, her appeal could remain "sexless" for those still clinging to older Victorian concepts of sexual activity that required a male initiator and focused chiefly on sexual intercourse.[44] The 1892 Mitchell-Ward case, while raising awareness of sexual inversion in women, could be dismissed as the result of aberrant insanity. Public suspicion of female same-sex passion among a wider range of respectable white women gained more momentum as women pursued higher education and political power. Many people perceived women's same-sex affiliations to be the basis for increased activism and lifestyles independent of men and marriage. Opponents of women's rights mustered charges of sexual perversion as a means of defusing threats to the male-dominated social order.[45] Spanning these transitional decades around the turn of the century, Adams's career remained respectable in part because she was not a college woman but rather a reclusive autodidact. Moreover, unlike some other actresses of her day, she adamantly eschewed taking a position on controversial women's issues such as suffrage and birth control.

Even among those who recognized dynamics of sexual inversion in her performances, Adams could occupy a relatively safe position according to prevailing sexologist theory. Ellis distinguished between a small group of congenital inverts who posed a real threat by seducing other women and a larger group who harbored a genetic weakness that made them susceptible to female seduction but who would remain "normal" when placed in a hetero-sexual environment.[46] In June 1901, after the close of Adams's season in *L'Aiglon*, Frohman attended another dinner *chez* Bernhardt at which the French actress suggested she and Adams co-star in a production of *Romeo and Juliet* in which she would play the male lead and Adams the female.[47] Bernhardt later retracted the proposition, claiming to have made it in jest, but Frohman took it seriously. He began making arrangements about which the press caught wind and ran several stories that piqued the interest of American audiences. Just prior to doing *L'Aiglon*, Adams had appeared as Juliet oppo-site a male Romeo, and her performance was considered inadequate because she could not muster all of the necessary passion.[48] The prospect of this other production both suggested she might respond more fully to Bernhardt and positioned the French actress in the more dangerously seductive male role. Again aided by contrast with Bernhardt, Adams could be delineated as the more passive, feminine type of invert. Since the production never took place, Adams remained unseduced, which further reduced the prospect of her becoming a corrupting influence on her throngs of female fans.

While women were by far the more prominent contingent in Adams's audiences, her breeches performances also played to the emerging gay male culture chronicled by George Chauncey in *Gay New York*. This group was less visible in turn-of-the-century Broadway houses, both because it was less numerous and because it was more actively trying to be discreet. Since the 1870s, gay male culture in New York City had been centered primarily in working-class districts, such as the Bowery and the waterfront, where its most visible type was the "fairy." According to Chauncey, this term "generally denoted any flamboyantly effeminate homosexual man (whose self presenta-tion resembled that of a female prostitute)."[49] Same-sex-desiring middle- and upper-class men who may or may not have solicited sex from fairies neverthe-less sought to distance themselves from the fairy's lower-class flamboyance in their own personal styles. They adopted a more refined, urbane demeanor and traded in subtler, more artistic and literary codes.[50]

As gay culture moved uptown to the Times Square area in the 1890s, Broadway theatres such as Frohman's drew gay patrons and employees with their highly fashionable front-of-house appeal and their reputation for greater tolerance of social deviance backstage than most other workplaces. From oral histories, Chauncey gleans that "the theatre and the district's other amuse-ment industries attracted large numbers of gay men who worked as chorus boys, actors, stagehands, costume designers, and publicity people; waiters and club performers; busboys and bellhops." One of his interviewees, a for-mer theatrical writer in the 1910s, described the theatre as "a sort of special world . . . with its own standards of fellowship and sexual morals."[51] Audi-ence members could fraternize with theatre workers after the show or with fairy prostitutes who, according to arrest records, were soliciting clientele on Forty-second Street in the 1890s. The trade grew in the theatre district so that by the 1920s, there was an established group of more well-dressed and "man-nered" hustlers who met their customers as they left the theatre and walked home on the west side of Fifth Avenue from Forty-second to Fifty-ninth Streets.[52]

An observer present at the first night of *L'Aiglon* commented that "it was an inspiring, cosmopolitan, and fashionable audience," descriptors that would have included same-sex-desiring men as well as women. In particular, the dandies of Continental taste and high fashion who were part of Frohman and Dillingham's social circle would have been in attendance.[53] The produc-tion offered them an array of queer delights. Literally a woman inside a male character, the exceptionally boyish, uncurvaceous Adams as the Eaglet signi-fied male as well as female inversion. The Duke's mother calls her son "my fop" and presents him with a collection of butterflies, insects long linked to dandies.[54] The Duke's aunt brings him violet perfume from Paris labeled "the Reichstadt scent." Visually, the production was a sumptuous recreation of the lavish, late baroque excesses of the Hapsburg court. Importing scenery, costumes, and drapes from Europe, Frohman reportedly spent more on it than on any of his previous shows.[55] Shortly after the Duke's first entrance, the Tailor enters with a display of the finest garments and fabrics to encour-age his client to "soar to fancy's wildest heights." He says that suiting unusual personal taste is his "special line." "Why we are Monsieur Théophile Gau-tier's tailors," he adds, dropping a reference to the dance, theatre, and art critic who penned a famous defense of aestheticism in the preface to his novel, *Mademoiselle de Maupin* (1835), about a bisexual protagonist.[56] Draw-ing on the queer palette of the *fin-de-siècle*, the Duke orders a green waistcoat with a scarlet lining, buttons engraved with eagles, and white cashmere breeches. As he takes his order, the Tailor reveals himself to be undercover for the Countess Camerata (a.k.a. Penthesilea, the Amazon Queen), who has entered disguised as the Tailor's assistant, along with the Young Man "dressed like a fashion plate." These agents of high fashion are Bonapartistes, members of the violet order, who lead double lives and conspire in secrets that mingle queer with seditious political codes. When the Young Man, speaking in flowery verse, tries to call the Duke to his imperial destiny, the Eaglet responds with a reference to another literary figure associated with bisexuality: "Your Byronism is too much like myself."[57]

Queer cultural tropes are also incorporated into the Duke's relationship with the older but still flaming Flambeau, "the torch," who once fought for Napoleon I and now poses as a servant in the Hapsburg palace. The Countess Camerata's former fencing master, Flambeau becomes a tutor to the Eaglet. By teaching him secret signals, such as pulling his ear with his thumb and forefinger like the Eagle used to do, he initiates him into the ways of the undercover culture. He offers the Duke snuff from his box on which his cherished Eaglet's head is pictured. In an intimate moment, he confesses that his one failing as a soldier "is overdoing things a little. I always add a trifle to my orders and wear a rose-bud when I go to battle: my little joke." When a dashing officer of the Noble Guard enters, Flambeau, "taking stock of him," comments aside to the Duke: "The beggars! Aren't they gorgeous swells!"[58] On the battlefield at Wagram, Flambeau stabs himself rather than surrender to the Austrian guards. He lies dying in his beloved Duke's arms, a queer *Liebestod* (love-death) legitimized as a tableau of loyalty to the Napoleonic cause.

Although critics continued to laud Adams as an icon of virtue, some anxiety about the intimations of sexual inversion in her performances informed the commentary in the periodical press. If Adams had exhibited chaste emotional limitations as Juliet, in breeches as the Eaglet she "was stirred to a depth of emotion that almost triumphed over sex," wrote the *Herald*. Another paper claimed that "her assumption of masculinity is, in the first place, as thorough as any actress could make it, and one never thinks of her as masquerading as a woman after the first few scenes of the play are over." However, reviewers also needed reassuringly to insist that "her sex asserted itself under her uniform. . . . She presented a heroic appearance. But she was heroine rather than hero."[59]

Adams and Frohman helped maintain the reassuring impression of the pure woman underneath the male attire throughout the rest of her career by interspersing breeches roles with female parts.[60] For example, after *L'Aiglon*, she reincarnated Lady Babbie as Phoebe Throssel in Barrie's *Quality Street* (1902). After *Peter Pan* (1905–1907) and *The Jesters* (1908), she played the similarly charming and wholesome Maggie Wylie in Barrie's *What Every*

Woman Knows (1908), which she also revived between *Joan of Arc* (1909) and *Chantecler* (1911). Given the presence of same-sex-desiring as well as "straight" audiences, this pattern of alternation did more than recuperate Adams into more traditional femininity. The spectacular and hugely publicized criss-crossing of gender roles that marked her repertoire was precisely what raised the possibilities of inversion and excited her most ardent fans. Performances of Viola and Rosalind, characters she played more convincingly than Juliet in summer productions at Harvard (1908) and Berkeley (1910), further highlighted her specialty of vacillation between male and female. Adams and Frohman periodically stepped back into the ingénue-centered productions only to push the boundaries of gender play further and appeal more strongly to variously desiring audiences with each successive breeches vehicle.

Fairy Plays

Adams's second foray into male impersonation, *Peter Pan*, became her most famous and lucrative role. She played Peter an estimated 1,500 times, including a 223-performance run at the Empire Theatre following the 6 November 1905 opening, a yearlong national tour, and two revivals. This play also initiated a move into fairy tales on which she and Frohman would continue to capitalize with *The Jesters* and *Chantecler*. Through the fairy-tale genre, their engagements with a queer lexicon proliferated.

By the end of the nineteenth century, the fairy tale was well established in Wildean circles as a rich vehicle for encoding queer tropes under the guise of innocent children's literature. As a well-known label for same-sex-desiring men, the term "fairy" resonated in double entendre.[61] Linking the world of the sprites with that of the queer subculture, Wilde autographed a copy of his book of fairy tales, *The Happy Prince*, for his lover and Frohman and Adams's close friend and collaborator, the playwright Clyde Fitch, with the inscription, "Faery stories for one who lives in faery land."[62] Fitch responded with a book of his own fairy tales, including "The King's Throne," a story he dedicated to Wilde that ends with the image of a long, hard shaft of a crucifix falling to rest over a softly blossoming floral circle.[63]

Beyond fairy terminology and homoerotically coded imagery, *Peter Pan* comprises other elements that made the fairy-tale genre appealing to theatrical producers and consumers across the spectrum of desire. The portrayal of Peter may be related to Barrie's own personal anxieties, shared to varying degrees by other contemporary queer men and women, about facing the adult demands of heterosexual marriage and the pressures of potentially destructive sexual desires.[64] While allowing for homoerotic fantasies under the cloak of childhood innocence and allegory, fairy tales also glorified youth and beauty as anodyne to the moral and physical degeneracy attributed to sexual inverts. In particular, fantastical flora and fauna created a pleasing aesthetic surface to counter the hideous ravages of syphilis, the then-ubiquitous and -incurable contagion that preachers touted as the wages of sin and "perversion." Syphilis permeated the world of *fin-de-siècle* literature and art, manifesting, for example, in the picture of Dorian Gray and various figures in the drawings that Aubrey Beardsley did for the 1894 English edition of Wilde's *Salome*.[65] Unlike Wilde, Barrie may have escaped the contagion, but his work circulated in a culture that both dreaded and prized syphilis as the sign of forbidden desire. On the grand scale of a hit Broadway production, *Peter Pan* offered queer as well as straight spectators the ultimate escape fantasy of never growing up. If Wildeans adored the decadence of syphilitic themes and the "divine Sarah," they also had reason to worship the more youthful, virginal Adams whose Peter defied the forces of time, gravity, and disease. Adams had queer male appeal in Barrie's fairy tale partly because it featured the one breeches part in her repertoire that Bernhardt could not credibly embody.

An elaborately rendered fantasy space outside the bourgeois family world, Peter's "Never, Never, Never Land" beckoned to same-sex desiring women as well as men. It was peopled by homosocial bands of Lost Boys played by girls "with full boyish zest," along with pirates, gender-ambivalent Indians, and the fey Captain Hook.[66] Adams deemed Peter Pan the "most delightful" of all her plays.[67] It allowed her to relive some of the tomboy pleasures of her own youth on her grandmother's farm in Utah as she performed Amazonian feats of climbing and swordplay in costumes that showed off her boyish figure. Swinging from cows' tails and barn rafters was her childhood preparation for swinging from fly wires.[68] The Eaglet even became the violet-coded Eagle when the star donned an iconic Napoleon costume to mark the hero's triumph over Hook and ascension to supreme power in this fairyland empire. Matinee girls idolized Adams's Peter and clamored alongside young children to see the production multiple times, while the mothers of those children swooned at the characters' search for maternal love.[69]

Thus, when Peter famously appealed to spectators to clap if they believed in fairies, differently desiring fans could join in the applause for a range of respectable and subversive reasons. Playing further on the double entendre, Frohman strategically posted "Do you believe in fairies?" placards in the theatre lobby. But because "Never, Never, Never" ostensibly meant never growing up and succumbing to sexual and other lusts, commentators asserted that Peter Pan's greatest Napoleonic feat was a moral conquest that Adams's virginal reputation secured. As Mark Twain told the star in a widely quoted statement: "It is my belief that *Peter Pan* is a great and refining and uplifting benefaction to this sordid and money-mad age; and that the next best play on the boards is a long way behind it as long as you play Peter."[70]

Peter Pan so magnified Adams's popularity and virtuous persona that following two seasons in that play, Frohman presented her immediately in her next breeches vehicle, *The Jesters*, by Miguel Zamacois, without an intervening ingénue role. Since Adams was playing another Bernhardt-initiated adult male character like the Duke of Reichstadt, the venture was more risky;[71] however, because the play was a fairy tale written in verse, Adams could still preserve her innocence and the civilizing agenda she shared with Frohman while engaging variously desiring audiences. In this fable, set in sixteenth-century France, Adams took the part of René de Chancenac, a wealthy young nobleman. Chancenac makes a bet with his friend, Robert de Belfonte (played by a male actor), that wit can prevail over good looks in seducing a woman. While hunting together in the forest, they spy the fair maid Solange through a hedge, and both fall in love with her. Solange's father, the Baron de Mautpré, fearing poverty, keeps his daughter from suitors but agrees she can employ a jester to relieve her sadness. René and Robert gain access to the Mautpré household by posing as jesters to audition for the post.

The personae these two jesters adopt resonate queerly in turn-of-the-century terms. Robert becomes Narcissus, the "love-bird," who compares his physique to that of classical Greek statues and effeminizes himself à la Wilde's Dorian Gray as the object of desiring gazes. The stage directions read: "He throws off his cloak, appearing in a well fitting suit of rose-colored silk. There is a murmur of admiration of his handsome figure." Solange's maternal male servant Oliver exclaims, "This young man will break hearts," while Solange herself finds his preening repellant.[72] Perceiving that Narcissus loves himself most of all, Solange proclaims him "too elegant by far," a dandy more for male than female adoration.[73]

René, by contrast, becomes Chicot, the "rare bird" who declares himself "not to be quite straight." He claims that his genius, overflowing his brain, has had to migrate to his back where it forms a hump that bends his posture. He confides to Robert that he knows when Solange approaches because of "a pricking in my thumbs," a phrase which alludes to phallic arousal and, when spoken by a woman in drag, suggests lesbian erotic practices.[74] But René's more openly declared virtuosity lies in wit and epigram, the Wildean stock-in-trade:

> To us our speech is like his sword
> To a brave belted knight. We jesters use a word
> As the wasps use their sting, as the hawks use their beak,
> And when we know its use to wound have but to speak.[75]

As Chicot, Adams got to utter verses that verbally took another woman's virginity. The jester seductively impresses upon Solange the power of his words:

> . . . in your shell-like ear
> I first have whispered them; trembling I first have drawn
> Upon that lovely cheek womanhood's early dawn
> Incarnate in a sweetly hot encarmined brush,
> Painted on velvet tissue with impassioned brush,
> Another's voice to you the selfsame words may say,
> But first from me, Solange, you have heard them to-day,
> And when that other comes he cannot take from me
> The treasure to-night stored in my memory.[76]

Such a declaration might have been particularly arousing, perhaps even familiar, to Adams's female fans involved in crushes or romantic friendships who faced the prospect of marriage and the intrusions of husbands on their same-sex intimacies. Letters, autobiographies, and popular fiction produced and consumed by women of the class and era of Adams's audiences echo these sentiments.[77] How pleasing, then, in Zamacois's fantasy, that no other suitor has to supplant Chicot. Like the Countess Camerata and Peter Pan, he proves himself an able swordsman in a duel. After casting off the hump and dispelling Solange's father's financial worries, he wins her hand in marriage. As the lovers kiss, Oliver declares, "The fairy prince is here."[78]

While Adams's most ardent fans embraced her as René-Chicot, others found this vehicle a letdown after *Peter Pan*, and the show closed after a modest fifty-three performances in New York and a short spring tour.[79] Troubled by the star's career trajectory, the reviewer of *The Jesters* in *The Theatre* commented: "What a queer idea this to persist in giving male roles to as womanly a little woman as ever trod our stage! The essence of Maude Adams's great success, the secret of her vast popularity with our public, is her innate sweetness, her lovable personality, her modesty and womanly charm."[80] These concerns were temporarily assuaged when Adams resumed her ingénue character in a revival of *What Every Woman Knows* in December of that year. Far more spectacularly, she played one of the greatest virgins of history in a massive staging of Schiller's *Joan of Arc* in Harvard Stadium in the summer of 1909, the year the historical Joan (1412–1431) was beatified. She played Joan for only a single performance, on 22 June, but the production became a prominent part of her legend. This role sanctified her image even as it proffered awesome delights to differently desiring audiences.

A Queer Ascent to Sainthood

Adapted from Anna Swanwick's and George Sylvester Viereck's translations of Friedrich Schiller's *Jungfrau von Orleans*, *Joan of Arc* was not technically a breeches vehicle since the character remained female. However, the Joan of the play, like her historical prototype, inverted gender norms in significant ways. Viereck linked her to Sappho in a chain of "unconscious precursor[s] of the emancipated woman . . . that stretched from antiquity to the middle ages."[81] She famously eschewed marriage and donned men's clothes to pursue her divinely inspired military mission to save France from the conquering English. In her ability to play such a role and challenge gender norms with impunity, Adams benefited yet again from comparison with her predecessor. The reviewer Edward Harold Crosby alluded to the allegedly profiteering, duplicitous Bernhardt when he asserted that in Adams's Joan, "Simplicity and humility seemed to be the dominating characteristics of the impersonation. Hers was not the Amazonian Joan that some have chosen to present in the past. It was always the gentle, guileless maiden, with never a thought of self-aggrandizement, always sincere and steadfast in following spiritual guidance."[82]

Yet in terms of sheer physical challenges, Adams's Joan was more Amazonian than those of her predecessors who confined their performances to the limitations of an indoor stage. Indeed, the feats the actress undertook far exceeded even her own previous onstage heroics, including those in *Peter Pan*. This production's definitive piece of iconography pictured Adams in full male armor astride a white charger in an era when women were still expected to ride sidesaddle.[83] (See fig. 19.) If the Eaglet dreamed of emulating his father and Peter Pan got to pose as the Little Corporal on the deck of the pirate ship, Joan commanded an army. Battery A of the Massachusetts

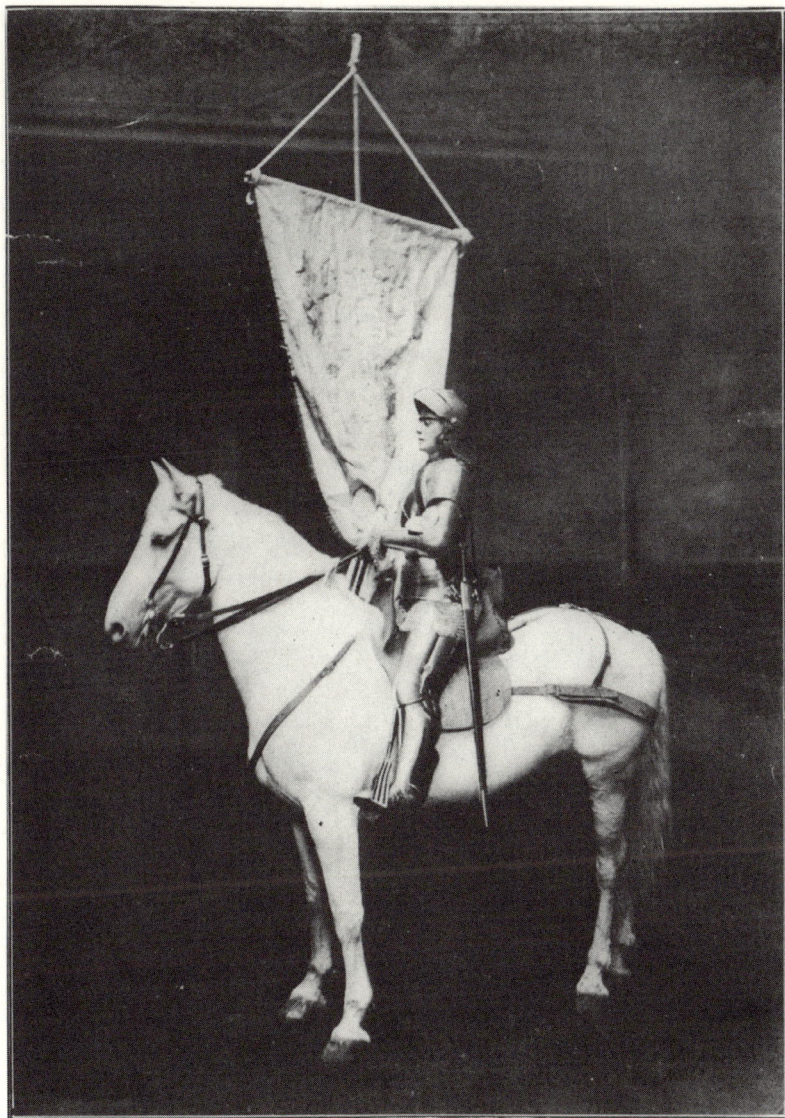

The first photograph taken of MISS MAUDE ADAMS, in the character of "JOAN OF ARC," in the play as given at Harvard University in the Stadium, Tuesday evening, June 22nd.

19. *Maude Adams astride her white charger in* Joan of Arc, *performed in Harvard Stadium, 22 June 1909. Courtesy of the Museum of the City of New York.*

State Militia provided many of the personnel and horses for the corps of 1,150 soldiers, mounted and on foot, who were all adorned with medieval costumes and armor for the production. Joan first appeared on her horse atop a "mountain," a twenty-foot high structure built for the show. She and the horse had to mount this structure in the dark so that glaring stage lights could suddenly reveal them when they reached the summit. Under lights, she rode down this hill to ascend another mound sixteen feet high. On that hilltop, two mounted armored knights posed with her for a tableau fashioned after Jean Louis Ernest Meissonier's *1807*, which depicts Napoleon reviewing a regiment, as Joan gazed on the army filling the stadium below. In the final battle scene, she charged across the stadium at full gallop, her thousand-strong army thundering behind her, while a two-hundred-piece orchestra played *Eroica*, the symphony Beethoven originally titled and dedicated to Bonaparte. When the show was in preparation, Frohman and his business manager, Alf Hayman, feared for Adams's safety and urged her either to eliminate the mountains or use a stunt double. Much to the thrill of the huge audience estimated at 15,500 she did neither.[84] Spectators were treated to an equestrian *coup de théâtre* that recalled Adah Isaacs Menken's *Mazeppa* in daring and far exceeded it in respectability.

Perhaps even more impressive than her Napoleonic efforts onstage were those she undertook offstage as the primary instigator and orchestrator of this massive spectacle. According to her mother, Adams had studied the Maid of France for years and aspired to surpass the attempts not only of Bernhardt but also of Fanny Davenport and Margaret Mather to play her.[85] When she performed in *Twelfth Night* in Cambridge the preceding summer (1908), the German Department approached her about mounting a German classic, and she seized the opportunity to do Schiller's masterpiece. She convinced Frohman of the necessity of mounting it outdoors on a grand scale. It is a measure both of Frohman's belief in the value of the endeavor and his faith in Adams that he approved the project, gave her fifteen stage managers, and put unlimited financial resources at her disposal. Moreover, he did not remain in the country to supervise but left for his usual trip to London.[86]

The extraordinary level of power granted Adams over *Joan of Arc* capped years of increasing responsibilities that she had assumed within the Empire organization because Frohman's managerial style allowed her to do so. Although Frohman personally directed some of Adams's shows, he did not exercise constant vigilance and micromanagerial authority after the fashion of Augustin Daly. He was no less a workaholic than Daly, but his approach was more mercurial and good-natured. Rather than focus obsessively on a single production and a single star's performance, he liked to mount multiple shows simultaneously and move from rehearsal to rehearsal, checking in on how the "soul" of each play was coming across. After watching a scene, his first impulse was not to scold but to praise so that employees would warm to his comments. His generally kind and jovial demeanor with employees also markedly contrasted with that of his rival producers, the Shuberts, who were notoriously abusive. Members of his companies were genuinely fond as well as admiring of him. They marveled not only at his astute theatrical instincts but also at the vitality of his line readings and spontaneous character impersonations, which seemed to exceed the physique of this "chubby little man."[87]

Moreover, unlike Daly, he was receptive to creative input from others, which enabled him to cede artistic control. Once Adams became a star, he let her run the initial rehearsals of her shows before he took over. He also left many of the external design elements and practical details to subordinates.[88] With Frohman's encouragement, Adams became keenly interested in these elements and made stage lighting a particular area of expertise. In addition to her private dressing rooms, she had her own office in the Empire Theatre. She did extensive historical research for her plays and was actively involved in costume and set as well as lighting design. Beginning with the tour of *The Little Minister*, Frohman put her at the head of her own company, over which she often personally served as stage director. She directed the final run-throughs of *Peter Pan* before its American premiere.[89] When the show embarked on its long tour, she had a special railroad car built, the Tinkerbell, in which a fully equipped theatre was installed for her to rehearse her company.[90]

All of this experience proved useful preparation for *Joan of Arc*. The production involved actors for some 60 speaking parts, 150 mounted knights in full armor, 1,000 foot soldiers, 200 Rheims citizens, 150 women and children, 120 musicians, 90 singers, and herds of sheep and goats, plus dozens of costumers, armor makers, scene painters, riding instructors, carpenters, electricians, and property men.[91] Adams had assistance from the designer John W. Alexander, the stage director Gustav von Seyffertitz, and a corps of stage managers led by W. H. Gilmore; however, correspondence and media reports clarify that she was the primary on-site authority.

Newspaper coverage of the production publicized both Adams's leadership over the huge operation and Frohman's absence. Some questioned her ability as a woman to handle the task, but she proved spectacularly successful. Any threat of her demonstration of power in "wearing the breeches" onstage

and off was assuaged by comparing her achievements to those of her character. As Chapin noted, "This is the biggest thing ever undertaken by any
woman, except perhaps the one she is representing. . . . She was not playing
Joan—she was living her. The two identities were merged. . . . [The produc-
tion] was a resurrection of Joan's personality, a reproduction of her environment."[92] The implication was that, like the Joan of Christian myth, Adams
would not ordinarily be able to perform such a task but could do so because
of divine inspiration. Papers stressed Frohman's high-minded ambition for
the production and direct bestowal of responsibility on Adams. His godlike
Napoleonic authority supposedly moved his star to fulfill this sanctified mission whether he was physically present or not.[93] As Joan responded to the
directives of an invisible higher power, so, too, did Adams.

The star's mission for her maker was one of multifaceted uplift. In an article
accompanying the iconic image of Adams as the armored Joan astride her
white charger, David Gray argued that America must recognize Adams as an
instrument to "further spiritual progress and civilization, . . . as an evolution-
working personality luminous with sweetness and light, even more than as an
artist; as a public influence, even more than as an actress."[94] Artistically, *Joan
of Arc* elevated the genre of paratheatrical spectacle. The reviewer Edward
Harold Crosby called it "an enormous production striving for the ideals and
standards of the fine arts, rather than those of the Kiralfy and Wild West
shows."[95] A not-for-profit, high-art pageant, *Joan* also elevated the Frohman
enterprise above the crass commercialism attributed to Jewish impresarios. To
keep this a high cultural venture, Frohman reportedly turned down $50,000
(about $1.1 million today) for the motion picture rights and dedicated the
$15,000 proceeds (about $321,500 today) of the production to the Germanic
Museum.[96] With this donation, *Joan of Arc* furthered Frohman's social ascent
by throwing into relief his German roots and eliding his Semitic ones. Heralding Frohman's cultural assimilation, Edward Congdon Cavanaugh proclaimed
him "a splendid type of the German-Americans who have done so much to
develop the Young Republic this side of the Atlantic."[97] The queer impresario
had spectacularly overcome his "lower" evolutionary attributes. Far from Bernhardt's Wildean Salome, his star, the outward embodiment of his woman
within, was now to the American public a Christian saint, beatified along with
Joan in Harvard Stadium. Adams herself could likewise not have overcome her
non-Gentile roots more spectacularly. As one critic asserted, she merited "secular honors comparable in a sense with the ecclesiastical dignity recently con-
ferred upon the original of the stage role."[98]

The media-generated mythology about how Adams met the production's enormous challenges under Frohman's aegis but without his physical participation kept hidden from view certain behind-the-scenes interactions that might have raised questions. Whatever inspiration she might have had from a higher power, she was a very capable, exacting, and determined director in her own right. For years, she had exercised considerable executive authority in the Frohman organization. Hayman's letters to Frohman document how she initiated projects and designs, requested tens of thousands of dollars at a time, and made contracts with employees. The seemingly "miraculous" stamina of this "little woman" through the arduous weeks of preparation and the strenuous four-hour performance does not seem so inexplicable when her genuine talents and the contributions of her invisible but devoted personal support network are recognized. Her partner, Louise Boynton, and close Boston friends Phyllis Robbins and Frances Horton saw to it that her household affairs were tended to and that she was well fed, rested, and escorted to her myriad engagements and planning meetings.[99]

Hayman's letters also offer some insight into the reasons for Frohman's absence. He writes that Adams fervently wished for Frohman to return from England to see *Joan of Arc*, but Frohman cabled back, "You must explain impossible."[100] The professed impossibility is curious given his usual desire to please Adams, his enormous resources, the frequency with which he made the Atlantic crossing, and the fact that he was not opening a show in London until late August. *Joan* was a massive one-of-a-kind event that garnered extraordinary attention from dignitaries and the media. The audience included Harvard president Lowell, former president Samuel Eliot, the entire university faculty, the German ambassador Count Johann von Bernstorff, Mrs. Grover Cleveland, and Bishop Greer of New York. Sir Charles Wyndam and members of the London press were among those who came from overseas especially for the show, but not its producer.[101] The letters suggest Frohman's reasons were personal. Hayman wrote him that Dillingham, who had been in New York without Frohman for much of the spring, would be sailing for London on Wednesday 9 June. The ship would have arrived around the date Frohman would have had to leave to make the crossing to New York in time for the performance of 22 June. Hayman's correspondence after mid-June indirectly implies that Dillingham is with Frohman. Hayman avoids being forthright or presumptuous about that possibility, which suggests that the nature of the overseas reunion of the two domestic partners was private. Evidently, it was also more important to the couple than attending the legendary Harvard spectacle.[102] If Frohman missed the show for love of Dillingham while his female star took charge, then his absence further queered the spectacle even as *Joan* brought him uplifting social acclaim.

Cock Fantasia

Whatever his reasons for staying abroad during *Joan of Arc*, Frohman was very present and engaged for Adams's last breeches vehicle, Rostand's *Chantecler*. Whereas Adams instigated *Joan of Arc*, this play was Frohman's inspiration. He went to Paris to see the original production. According to his biographers, "It thrilled and stirred him, and he bought it immediately," reportedly paying $20,000 (about $410,000 today) for the rights to produce it in America.[103] Upon return, he stunned the theatre world with the announcement that the saintly Maude Adams, who had won her greatest popularity as the boy Peter, was now to play a full-grown cock. In Rostand's fanciful animal fairy tale, Chantecler is a barnyard rooster, the cock of the walk amid a bevy of other fowl. It was general knowledge that Rostand had written this "Cyrano in feathers" for the virile French star Benoit-Constant Coquelin, who died before opening. Another virile French actor, Sacha Guitry, premiered the role. Thus, commentators expressed profound skepticism over Frohman's proposed effeminization of the character. But the impresario insisted: "'Chantecler' is a play with a soul, and the soul is its moral. This is the secret of 'Peter Pan'; this is why Miss Adams is to play the leading part." He vowed "to stand or fall" by this production and made *Chantecler* the ultimate test of his impresarial potency.[104]

The play's message was expressed allegorically through the rooster's valiant dedication to the hard and lofty work of crowing. In Louis N. Parker's adaptation used for the production, Chantecler proclaims:

> . . . I am
> As 'twere a speaking trumpet given by nature
> Through which the Earth sends up her cry to heaven!
> . . . I sing!—And sudden!— . . . I start,
> Dazzled to see that I am turned to gold,—
> That I, the Cock, have caused the sun to rise![105]

To persevere in his mission, Chantecler must overcome a number of challenges: derision and physical attacks by resentful night birds who conspire with fighting cocks to defeat him; the demoralizing realization that his voice is

not as beautiful as that of other birds like the nightingale; and, most dangerous of all, the seductions and demands of the alluring Pheasant Hen. When
he succumbs to seeking nighttime comfort under her wing, he misses the
dawn and must face the crushing fact that the sun actually rises without his
effort. Rather than give up, he crows on with revised purpose: "He may not
create light, but he can proclaim it to the world."[106]

For Frohman, Chantecler's triumph over the distractions of sex and his
glorification of work conveyed a profound moral. Adams had to play the part
because she embodied the civilizing enterprise of his Empire Theatre and,
most particularly, signified his conquest over female sexuality. Herself a devo-
tee of work and "clean plays," Adams dove enthusiastically into the project,
declaring "To play *Chantecler* is an honor international in its glory."[107] She
later confided to Phyllis Robbins, "Of all the plays that were trusted to my
care, I loved *Chantecler* best, and then came *Peter Pan*."[108] With Peter, she triumphed in a breeches role for which her French shadow Bernhardt was
never in contention; with Chantecler, she got to play the Cock to which the
divine Sarah fervently aspired but was denied the opportunity. Newspapers
reported that although Rostand chose the male actor Sacha Guitry over
Bernhardt, "who literally fell on her knees before him begging the privilege of
presenting herself as Chantecler," he approved of Adams for the American
production. Frohman's exorbitant payment for the rights likely warmed him
to the idea. As Louis V. Defoe explained, French authors were chiefly concerned with Parisian artistic opinion and, once that was garnered, could feel
"free to turn to America to gather a more substantial harvest."[109] Publicity
about Rostand's choice of the virginal Adams over the decadent Bernhardt
helped affirm the American impresario and actress's civilizing agenda.

Devoted to the project, Adams invested herself heavily in the staging.
Commentators spoke of Frohman as the orchestrator of the production, but
his star had more to do with the practicalities of its realization. She studied
the script assiduously, worked again with John W. Alexander on the designs,
and personally oversaw even the minutest details. According to her mother's
account, along with preparing to play the leading role, she conducted numerous rehearsals just to perfect the farmyard noises and hired a trainer to school
the actors in making proper fowl sounds. In addition, "she herself rearranged
and bettered nearly all of the fowls' costumes," for which Frohman spared no
expense and imported materials from France. With the sunrise being such a
key part of the show, she labored intensively over the lighting effects. She even
personally worked out the appropriate *entr'acte* music.[110]

While touting the purifying morality of the work ethic, the Frohman-Adams *Chantecler* also exceeded their earlier fairy plays in trading on coded allusions and appealing to queer as well as straight audiences. The queer cultural work of this piece was informed by the sense of humor for which Frohman was well-known among his family and associates. His brother Daniel Frohman and Isaac F. Marcosson, co-authors of his biography, devote an entire chapter to the subject titled "Humor and Anecdote." Frohman shared this famed sense of humor with Dillingham. The two were great lovers and practitioners of wit in the Wildean manner. Also notorious pranksters, they delighted in amusing each other and their friends by one-upping unsuspecting people they met in the course of their work and travels with improvised ruses and epigrammatic retorts. Decades after his death, Adams paid tribute to Frohman's humor by quoting, in her Stephens College commencement speech, some of the gentler puns he would quip during rehearsals.[111] He and Dillingham were also capable of more wicked wit. When Wilde was in his heyday in the early 1890s, Frohman and Dillingham indulged his love of mockery as flattery with an American production of a one-act satire of his work, *The Poet and the Puppets*. The piece featured a coterie of dandies cleverly talking of "tossing off" and a spritely fairy who flitted through a dizzying array of queer connotations.[112] Echoing such humor, the production of *Chantecler* was filled at many turns with a punning extravagance that no doubt delighted the impresario, his partner, and their knowing friends.

Not the least of *Chantecler*'s pun points were its manifold forms of cock play. According to the *Oxford English Dictionary*, the word "cock" had been in circulation as a term for penis since 1730.[113] In aiming to glorify Chantecler and his resolute pursuit of his mission, the production glorified the cock—and especially the queer or inverted cock, the eponymous cock who literally contained the nation's biggest female star as his inner woman. The more the establishment doubted the potency of Frohman's concept of casting Adams, the more determined and lavish Frohman became in planning her ambitious transformation into the "barnyard Romeo."[114] His biographers write:

> Never, perhaps, in the history of the American stage was the advent of a play so long heralded. The name of "Chantecler" was on every tongue. Long before the piece was launched hats had been named after it, controversies had arisen over its Anglicized spelling and pronunciation. All the genius of publicity which was the peculiar heritage of Charles Frohman

was turned loose to pave the way for this extraordinary production. It was a nation-wide sensation.[115]

The impresario used advance publicity to whip audiences into a frenzy of anticipation. Lines began forming outside the box office the day before tickets went on sale. By the second day of sales, some desperate would-be viewers were reportedly offering as much as two hundred dollars (four thousand dollars today) for a seat on opening night, an expenditure that surely gave new meaning to the term "cocksucker." The excitement only intensified when the opening had to be postponed a week at Adams's behest to tend to more production details. Deeming the Empire Theatre too small to accommodate *Chantecler*, Frohman announced he was moving the production to the larger Knickerbocker.[116]

When the Cock's revelation was finally at hand, first-time viewers were tantalized with some remarkable theatrical foreplay. To highlight her impending transformation, Adams appeared before the curtain in an evening gown to deliver the Prelude. In Paris, Jean Coquelin, son of the famous actor, had performed the Prelude in tux and tails, not Guitry, the star. Showcasing the femaleness of her body before it was encased in cock feathers, Adams reiterated her special métier of vacillation between genders. Moreover, her evening gown was rendered in the fashion of classical Greece, a culture long associated with same-sex erotics, which further signaled the queerness of the production. During her speech, as per Rostand's stage directions, the curtain twice playfully began to rise. Each time, the actress beckoned it back down, saying "No, not yet!" (Prelude, p. 1). The *New York Herald* described this intermittent flashing of the barnyard behind the resplendently Grecian Adams as "beautifully timed, artistic, and exciting to the curiosity." Mr. and Mrs. John D. Rockefeller were in the opening night audience, which Frohman's biographers characterize as "brilliant and highly wrought up." Several spectators were heard gasping "Lovely!" "Beautiful!" "How odd!"[117]

Upon completing the Prologue, the begowned Adams exited, and the curtain arose fully to reveal the barnyard scene. This was no simple, rustic country farm for the strenuous self-regeneration that Teddy Roosevelt had been advocating. The spirit of the setting reflected the fancy farm Frohman and Dillingham themselves shared. At their country getaway, they raised not ordinary livestock but a trick goat and lushly groomed, show quality Old English Sheepdogs, most notably the prize-winning pair they bought for $5,000 in 1904 (more than $109,000 today) and campily named Bouncing Lass and

20. The Peacock (A. Lionel Hogarth) displays himself at "The Guinea Hen's Five O'Clock Tea," in Chantecler, as Told in Words and Pictures.

Stylish Boy.[118] Running more wildly into make-believe, the barnyard of the play was a world of Brobdingnagian fantasy, whose exorbitant budget enabled extravagant glorification of the Cock. The set was not only peopled with fantastical fowl in Ziegfeldian costumes ordered from Paris, but, in a master stroke of wit and whimsy, was entirely scaled to the Cock's eye view. Figure 20 shows a five-foot-high wheelbarrow on the left and a fifteen-foot-high wall opening around a twelve-foot gate in the center. Illustrating how a human would appear to barnyard fowl, the fifteen-foot-high scarecrow costume hanging on the wall accentuates the scale.

Along with these enticing visuals, aural glorification of the Cock came in a veritable golden shower of allusions. While the star underwent her miraculous gender and species change, several plumed, polyamorous fowl of both sexes chattered the wonders of Chantecler to build excitement for his entrance. The White Hen exclaims, "He is the Cock!" to which the Blackbird responds, "Who doth all hearts unlock!" The Turkey tells of having seen him develop from a chick, while the Hens chirp a chorus of "Growing!" in tribute to his size. At the moment of his entry, the Blackbird cries "Ecstasy!" (Act I, pp. 7–17). Figure 21 shows Adams as the Cock in her most erect, fully plumed glory. As Chantecler proceeds to demonstrate his virile vocal emissions with an "Ode to the Sun," many barn fowl swoon over him; however, it is a Pheasant Hen flying in from the forest who catches Chantecler's queer eye. Because of her splendid coloring he mistakes her for another rooster. Production photos evince a striking similarity of silhouette between the two fowl (fig. 22). Patou, a sheepdog reminiscent of Frohman and Dillingham's pampered Stylish Boy, comments, "My stars! He's falling in love with a hen dressed up as a cock!" (Act I, p. 38), a wonderful irony given the casting.

But the most elaborate sequence of cock play comes in the third act, "The Guinea Hen's At-Home," set in her flower garden. Posing the Peacock near a sunflower, the hostess remarks, "Isn't that Burne-Jones?" referencing the pre-Raphaelite painter favored by Wildean aesthetes (Act III, p. 7). The Peacock, said to "ogle with his tail," as he is doing in Figure 20, is an outlandish dandy fowl. Aligned with the night birds against Chantecler, he has arranged for a group of Fancy Cocks to attend the At-Home and humiliate the barnyard Romeo. The Magpie announces the Procession of the Cocks of the World, each sporting a costume more exotic in plumage than the last: "They're wonderful!—Walk up and take your choice! Cocks of all shapes and sizes, small and great . . ." including:

> The Bantam Cock, the ancient Plymouth Rock Cock,
> The Wyandotte, the Orpington, the Tartar,
> Mesopotamian, Andalusian, Hamburg,
> Burmese, Cochinchinese, Bagdad,
> Malay, Albino, Negro, four-clawed, no-clawed,
> The Walikikili, called Choki-Kukullo,
> The Java Cock, the Bramah Cock, the Dutch Cock,
> Chili and Antwerp, and the Lord Knows Where. (Act III, p. 10)

When Chantecler enters, he tells the Magpie to announce him simply as "the Cock." Asked what he thinks of the exotic assemblage, he launches into a dizzyingly alliterative tirade that cleverly denounces their fanciness while glorying in the sound of "cock":

> I think they're nightmare cocks born on Cocytus—
> Crosses between cockleshells and cock-a-leekies;

21. *Maude Adams as the priapic, crowing Cock in* Chantecler,
as Told in Words and Pictures.

22. *Chantecler (Maude Adams) rebuffs the advances of the Pheasant Hen
(Josephine Victor, who replaced May Blayney) while the Sheepdog Patou
(George Henry Trader) looks on.*
In Chantecler, as Told in Words and Pictures.

Cocks of Cocagne, feeding on Coooloba.
They're sparrow-cocks—a sort of Coccothraustes
Cocks without coccyx, colored cochineal;
Cocks without cockades, like coachmen cock-a-whoop!
Cocks come in cockboats, snuggled without cockets
Conceived in cockle-oasts, under cock-hedges,
They're cockney cocks, cock sure and cockered cocks.
Cook-chafer cocks, not cocks according to Cocker;
Cocks dyed with Coccinite and cockleous-shaped.
Or are they plants? Cocciferous-cocklearia?
Or coccinellas born in cocalons?
Cock-horses, insects:—cockeyed coccuses—
They're anything and everything but—cocks! (Act III, p. 14)

23. *Chantecler (Maude Adams), the "plain" Cock, squares off against the fancy Game-Cock (Bertram Marburgh) in Act III of* Chantecler, *1911. Courtesy of the Museum of the City of New York.*

The verbal sparring escalates until Chantecler and the Game-Cock square off to fight in a sexually inverse matchup. The foofy fancy cock resembles a drag queen encased in a giant white feather boa; Chantecler, by contrast, sports a darker, more martial and butch cock suit topped with a coxcomb like a crest on a soldier's helmet (fig. 23). Armed with sharp spurs, the Game-Cock has the advantage until a hawk flies overhead. Chantecler scores a moral victory by bravely shielding the other fowl while his opponent wounds himself in cowardly confusion. Touting his manly triumph, he beckons the Pheasant Hen to accompany him to the woods, "Come, my wild Princess!" (Act III, p. 23)

Chantecler's—and, by extension, Frohman and Adams's—victory is one of queer style as well as morality. He declares, "I sing the rose," whereas the Peacock, speaking for his exotic entourage, retorts, "How obsolete! The green carnation—yes!" (Act III, pp. 15–16) Rostand based the character of the Peacock on Count Robert de Montesquiou (1855–1921), who also appeared as Jean des Esseintes in Joris-Karl Huysman's *À rebours* (1884), a key text for the Decadents, which in turn inspired *The Picture of Dorian Gray* (1891).[119] These inverted characters infamously indulge the lusts of inner women like the Salome who ruined Wilde. In Chantecler, Frohman could celebrate both the magnificence of his queer Cock and the saintly continence of the woman within, even as the spectacle offered a smorgasbord of more Decadent delights. Meanwhile, Adams's same-sex desiring female fans thronged to see her strut and vocalize in her putatively un-Fancy but still sumptuous cock suit. They were even treated to an ornithological lesbian kiss in Act IV when Chantecler and the Pheasant Hen emerge from their love nest inside a hollow tree trunk and "touch beaks" (p. 3). Many female fans attended multiple times. A woman named Ouida Meyer reported going to twelve performances.[120] But the fairy tale also allowed thousands of "straight" audience members to feast on the spectacle while denying, in the evening's greatest act of make-believe, that this edifying show about the Cock was really a queer cock show.

Chantecler ran at the Knickerbocker for ninety-six performances beginning 23 January 1911, opened the next season in New York in the fall, and then embarked on a North American tour that lasted until March 1912. Adams received twenty-two curtain calls after the last act on opening night and hundreds more from audiences around the country. Although the play did not garner the level of popularity of *Peter Pan*, it still had a successful life on the stage that enabled Adams to fulfill the dream denied to the divine Sarah. Yet numerous critics considered it not only a failure but a mistake. They argued that whereas the intrusion of Adams's "charming femininity" had been acceptable and even fitting in her earlier characters, such as Peter Pan or the Duke of Reichstadt, it was "somewhat appalling" to see her try to impersonate "the real Chantecler," "the lusty, aggressive, self-sufficient, vainglorious Cock."[121] Refusing to allow that Frohman and Adams could lay their own, different claims to Chantecler, these critics sounded a note of warning about future such attempts. The era in which Adams could push gender and sexual boundaries while trumpeting a civilizing moral with impunity was coming to a close. Changing sensibilities that interfered with her pursuit of the projects she most loved and Frohman's untimely death in 1915 helped precipitate her retirement in 1918. But emerging queer as well as straight cultural tastes, before the two were undeniably delineated, had helped make Adams the biggest star and Frohman the most powerful impresario of Broadway's Golden Era.

5

A Priestly Acting Pedagogy

DAVID BELASCO'S QUEST FOR SEXUAL KNOWLEDGE

Ah! I understand women. I have come in contact
with thousands of them! There is a strong strain of
woman in my nature. I know that it is there, and
I can understand woman in all her variations.
There is nothing hidden from me.
—David Belasco, quoted in the
New York Journal, 1901

In 1879 in his hometown of San Francisco, three years before he would move to New York, young David Belasco, a Jew of Portugese descent, stage managed Salmi Morse's *The Passion: A Miracle Play* portraying the life of Christ in ten acts. This was an extraordinary event on many counts. The huge stage of the Grand Opera House—80 feet deep by 106 feet wide—accommodated such vivid tableaux as "The Massacre of the Innocents," which involved one hundred screaming mothers and babies fleeing the charge of Roman soldiers.[1] James O'Neill's impersonation of the adult Christ marked the first time Jesus had appeared as a character in a biblical play performed by an American company.[2] Catholic authorities approved the script, although the circumstances of production were less than devout. The flamboyant Tom Maguire, whom Belasco called "the first Napoleon of the theatre," produced the show with backing from the famed gambler and entrepreneur, Elias Jackson "Lucky" Baldwin. *The Passion* played amid San Francisco's boisterous entertainment culture, whose fare included popular melodramas and Shakespearean classics, minstrel shows and other musical and variety entertainments like the magic trick "Mystery" at Egyptian Hall, and grand opera. A group of Protestant clergy and outraged laymen decried the commercialism and Catholicism of the venture and moved to halt the production on moral grounds. Initially, Maguire was pleased with the free publicity the controversy engendered; however, when the company defied a court order to cease performing, O'Neill and several other company members were arrested. Belasco escaped going to jail only because he had befriended the local sheriff, who forcibly kept him away from the theatre when the raid occurred.[3] Released on bail, the actors continued performing for a few more nights until Maguire bowed to social and legal pressure and closed the show. "Lucky" Baldwin reportedly lost all of his $25,000 investment.[4]

The experience of working on *The Passion* profoundly affected Belasco. He was at a crossroad, unsure of whether to pursue acting, writing, stage managing, or painting. The production catalyzed a number of impulses that determined his ultimate career path. Certainly the show fueled his love of theatrical spectacle, wizardry, and Barnumesque humbug. But more profoundly, it aroused priestly inclinations and an integrally related desire to move women to experience extreme emotion. He claims in his autobiography that O'Neill, who was "obsessed" with the project, persuaded him to join the team as a stage manager. He excitedly recalls scouring San Francisco churches, schools, and theatres for two hundred singers and four hundred performers, including children, to fill the massive ensembles. "In the process,

24. *A rakish Belasco, about twenty years old, ca. 1874, in William Winter,* Life of David Belasco, *vol. 1, op. p. 40.*

everyone seemed to be inspired," notably O'Neill, who forsook smoking, swearing, and "all the little pleasures of life" to assume the role of Christ. As "the boards of the stage became a Holy Land," Belasco writes, he himself "became a veritable monomaniac on the subject." He says, "I was never without a bible under my arm. I went to the Mercantile Library and there studied the color effects in the two memorable canvases there hung, depicting the dance of Salome and the Lord's Supper. My life seemed changed as never before." Recalling events of his childhood, he adds "once more my thoughts began to play with monastery life, and I thought of the days spent in Vancouver with my priest friend."[5] His manner of dress changed as well. Pictures (figs. 24 and 25) showing Belasco at about twenty and thirty indicate that it was sometime in his twenties—likely around the time of *The Passion*, when he was twenty-five—that he went from the more rakish loose bow tie of his youth

25. Belasco, about thirty years old, wearing his trademark priestly collar, ca. 1884, in William Winter, Life of David Belasco, *vol. 2, op. p. 16.*

to the starched, stand-up faux clerical collar that became his daily accessory for the next fifty years.

These priestly inclinations are especially remarkable given Belasco's religious origins. The playwright, Morse, was Jewish as well; but whereas Morse garnered the epithet "apostate Hebrew," Belasco never renounced his faith.[6] Yet his life-changing enthusiasm for the production suggests he shared some of Morse's religious ambivalence.[7] Believing that the Oberammergau passion play had been fashioned to inflame anti-Semitism, Morse contended his version would be different; however, in fulfilling his avowed purpose "simply to present an epitome of the life of Jesus, as described in the gospels," he and his collaborators who staged the play nonetheless perpetuated inflammatory biblical stereotypes of Jews.[8] After Simeon declares of Mary's baby, "This is Christ! The Messiah!," a Jewish messenger "rushes upon Jesus with his dagger drawn, as if to kill," then recoils upon realizing "God's luminous guard."[9] During the arraignment of Jesus before Pontius Pilate, murderous Jews press repeatedly for Jesus's crucifixion over Pilate's appeals to reason and mercy. Although subsequent historians have been unable to corroborate the account, William Winter, who interviewed Morse and Belasco about the events for his Belasco biography, reports that the play incited some people—he specifies "ignorant Irish"—to attack Jews in the streets.[10] Anti-Semitic attacks also appeared in print. A review in *The Argonaut* noted that Morse was Jewish and that "seven-eighths of the first audience were of his own faith," an exaggeration reflecting anxiety over post–Gold Rush San Francisco's high concentration of Jewish inhabitants. The review condemned the play as exploitation of "the holiest traditions of Christianity" for Jewish amusement and profit.[11] Anti-Semitic results thus clouded Morse's professed philo-Semitic intentions. If Morse was attempting to improve the representation of Jews, that effort consisted chiefly in his portrayal of Jesus. The script repeatedly asserts the Jewish identity of Christ and uses the bloodthirsty Jews to highlight the leading character's exemplary virtues by contrast.

Belasco also greatly admired Jesus, as he told interviewer Magda West many years later:

The greatest, and the most successful, and the most lastingly famous individual that the world has ever known was a carpenter who lived in Nazareth. His name was Christ Jesus. And whether men acknowledge or dispute His divinity, they agree at least that he was human, and that He achieved the success of fulfillment of His prescribed destiny. And men of almost all creeds agree, too, that He did this by discipline and denial, and that He so admitted when He bade His followers, "Take up the cross and follow me."[12]

Most of all, Belasco admired Jesus's impact on women. Christ famously demonstrated the virtues of discipline and denial in relation to the seductress Mary Magdalene, whom he then inspired to seek redemption. The play amply displayed the prophet's ability to stir a range of female emotion, from the Chorus of Women who open the first act and sing the praises of the Christ child, to Mary and the Daughters of Jerusalem wailing as Jesus is led to his crucifixion.

Through the production, Belasco's admiration of Christ became intermixed with his admiration of James O'Neill. Jesus the exemplary Jew was largely defined for Belasco by this Irish Catholic actor, the future Count of Monte Cristo, who "with his delicacy, refinement, and grandeur, typified the real Prophet."[13] Belasco recalled the awesome moment: "When O'Neill came up from his dressing-room and appeared on the stage with a halo about him, women sank on their knees and prayed, and when he was stripped and dragged before Pontius Pilate, crowned with a crown of thorns, many fainted. I have produced many plays in many parts of the world but never have I seen an audience awed as by the Passion-Play."[14] These comments about O'Neill's stage presence are tinged with envy. As another of his biographers, Craig Timberlake, notes, Belasco was "desperately afraid that he would not be tall enough to become a great romantic actor."[15] O'Neill was the kind of actor young Belasco aspired to be, but his hopes were frustrated because of his short stature (he stood five feet three inches) and features—in particular, his dark, curly hair, dark eyes, heavy brows, and prominent nose—that commentators often termed "Oriental." Through his collaboration with O'Neill on this production, however, he learned that although he did not have the actor's commanding presence and charisma on stage, he could contribute to the overall effect of the performance on actresses and audiences through backstage managerial and directing work. Posing as a priest and provoking female emotion became key strategies for Belasco to achieve success as an "Oriental" Jewish impresario in a predominantly Christian society.

The Call of the Cloth

When Belasco was frequently asked about his trademark clerical collar, which was actually a regular wingless collar made to stand up so it would look like a clerical collar, he cited the boyhood experience he recalled in his narrative of *The Passion*. He claimed to wear the collar in tribute to an old priest, Father McGuire, who had been his beloved teacher. Supposedly, as Belasco relates in his autobiography, he met Father McGuire in 1861 when he was seven years old and living in Victoria, British Columbia. His parents had moved north to follow the Gold Rush after first immigrating to San Francisco. Always self-conscious about his small size, Belasco refers to himself in these early years in the third person as "little David." With his father gone prospecting, little David was raised primarily by his mother, who resisted her husband's rabbinical hopes for their only child. Believing he was, like herself, too much of a "gypsy," she encouraged him to attend the theatre and engage in theatrical games with his friends. He stood out from his peers because of his size, dark eyes, and masses of blue-black hair whose curls his mother, much to his chagrin, would accentuate by twirling them tightly around a comb. Father McGuire watched little David on the playground for several weeks. One day, he approached him, asked him about his religion, and invited him to come visit him at the monastery.

During the visit, the priest bid little David to sit on his lap. As Belasco describes it, the encounter was eerily pederastic because the attempted conversion proceeded like a seduction in which the priest sought an intense intimacy via confession. "The old man," he writes, "inspired me with a holy love." Father McGuire reportedly told little David, "You've passed into my heart." Prompted to wonder "if the holy Father could see into my very soul," the boy divulged his deepest secrets. Father McGuire then invited little David to come live with him. Belasco claims his parents let him stay at the monastery for five years under the "special guidance" of the old priest. Belasco helped him do research in his library and perform his daily offices with the other brethren. Father McGuire used to tell little David, "There's much of the Catholic in you. You are tense and dramatic, sentimental and emotional, like all Catholic believers." However, the conversion did not take. Belasco left the monastery rather precipitously when, he reports with some delicacy, "the falseness of one of the monks to his vows rudely awakened me from my spiritual dreaming." He says he fled the monastery to join the Rio de Janeiro Circus on a tour of the Pacific Northwest. After a brief stint as a bareback rider sporting pink tights, he rejoined his family in time to accompany them on a move back to San Francisco where he commenced Hebrew lessons at age thirteen.[16] Unable to verify the existence of a Father McGuire in Victoria in the early 1860s, Timberlake dismisses this story.[17] However fabricated, this tale of Belasco's years of puberty in a monastery nonetheless evinces the childhood fascination with the priesthood that his later experience with *The Passion* rekindled.

Moreover, in telling the story, Belasco highlights his emotional temperament and casts himself in the feminine role as the object of religious and sexual seduction. Being cast in emotional and female roles had been a pattern of his early acting career. His grammar school teacher, a former actress named Nelly Holbrook, saw in him a special talent for enacting extreme emotion. She schooled him in highly charged recitations of dramatic poems, most notably "Curfew Must Not Ring Tonight," by Rose Hartwick Thorpe, and Monk Lewis's "The Maniac," which he was called upon to repeat on various occasions.[18] The poem gave him a singular opportunity for the pyrotechnic display of incontinent passion:

> Clad in a pair of disreputable trousers belonging to his father, crowned with a shock of hair for which he had levied upon his mother's mattress, and further adorned by spears of straw stuck through it, armed with a sponge full of red fluid, with which he used to deluge his face at the

moment when his ravings were supposed to have burst a blood-vessel, and bound with clanking iron chains, the boy David Belasco must have been a fear-inspiring object.[19]

With high hopes for stardom, Belasco turned professional in 1871, at the age of seventeen. But he found himself continually exoticized, infantilized, and feminized as he came up against the limitations of his physique. His small stature and high-pitched voice often relegated him to women's roles or to bit parts, such as Sambo in *Uncle Tom's Cabin*, a Nubian slave in *Pygmalion and Galatea*, and the dwarf in *Rip Van Winkle*. Occasionally, he got to play "first old men" such as Uncle Tom and Fagin in *Oliver Twist*.[20] However, leading roles with first-string companies, the mainstay of a starring career, eluded him. Dissatisfied with his acting career, Belasco began to take on more behind-the-scenes jobs.

While touring with the company of Piper's Opera House in Virginia City, Nevada, he witnessed an impressive event. He had taken pity on a young prostitute who had stopped by the theatre looking for more honorable work. Unable to secure a position there or elsewhere, she killed herself in despair. Belasco describes the funeral he attended in the brothel with her madam and fellow sex workers:

> Some stray man of the streets played a hymn upon the piano, and presently the little preacher arrived. Little of body the preacher was, but a great soul slumbered within him, to be awakened by just such a moment as this. And how he gripped the moment now; with what fire of genius he told the living the pitiful tale of all the dead girl had gone through; with what delicate sympathy he exhorted them to pure lives! There was not a woman in the room, hardened and callous as they were, that was not brought to tears by his pleadings. If they had been rehearsed, they could not have shown such perfect accord in repentance. If I had directed the scene, I could not have hoped to succeed as that little minister of the Gospel, asking the Magdalenes of Virginia City to be good women. I am sure that not one of these unfortunates but had a crucifix concealed somewhere about her person, and never shall I forget the unmistakable sincerity with which the repentant creatures sang hymns played by the stray man of the street.[21]

The demonstrable talent and power of this diminutive preacher served as a potential model for Belasco. Whether or not this event actually occurred,

Belasco uses it to signal a growing realization about how he might become more effective in his profession. It foreshadowed the kind of influence over actresses he would later achieve.

Returning to San Francisco, he pursued his managerial aspirations in earnest, primarily under the employ of the legendary Tom Maguire, an Irish Catholic immigrant, who had come to California from New York in the Gold Rush of 1849 and built eleven theatres, eight of them in San Francisco. The striking euphony between the names Father McGuire and Tom Maguire may be more than coincidental, since the latter's paternalistic mentorship had a profound effect on Belasco's career. Maguire, too, was short, but he was also a burly, proven pugilist, known at the time as the "Napoleon of the Theatre." Moreover, he did not look exotic.[22] When Belasco started as assistant stage manager at Maguire's theatres in 1874, he had problems asserting his authority, especially with leading ladies. He admired and wanted to impress these actresses, but they persisted in seeing him as a boy, though he was by then twenty and married.[23] Adelaide Neilson, a famous Juliet, looked maternally upon Belasco, offered him a bauble from her jewel box as a token of appreciation and wrote him a letter addressing him as "you weird, strange little fellow."[24] When Maguire introduced Belasco to the traveling star of the famed Wallack's Theatre in New York, she haughtily exclaimed, "What, that little brat direct me, Rose Coghlan?"[25]

Belasco was still embroiled in such struggles with actresses when he took on his most challenging assignment to date, that of stage managing *The Passion*. While others involved in the production were changing their behavior in deference to the material, Belasco may have adopted the mandarinlike priestly collar as more than a reverential gesture. The vestment was also a way of parlaying his "weird, youthful appearance" into a stance of greater authority, especially over the women of the stage. In emulation of Christ, priests such as the little preacher in Virginia City demonstrated particular influence over fallen women with whom actresses in the late nineteenth century were still often associated. Morse's *Passion* emphasized this aspect of Christ's influence. Two of the ten acts are devoted to showing the lascivious decadence of the court of Herod Antipas and Salome's dance for the head of John the Baptist. In the penultimate act of the play, "Taking Down from the Cross," Salome appears repentant, along with Mary Magdalene, Mary the mother of Jesus, and Mary the mother of James, weeping at Jesus's feet. The emotional climax of *The Passion* comes when Mary Magdalene, according to the stage directions, "rushes into the sepulcher, screams piteously, and falls to violent weeping."[26] While Morse's practical theatre experience was limited, Belasco, who had played female and highly emotional roles since childhood, could have provided the actress with effective coaching in this scene.[27] Whether he did or not, he was beginning to realize how the priest's pose could enable him to use to special advantage in working with female performers the very qualities that excluded him from playing romantic leading men.

Knowing Wayward Womankind

The Passion galvanized a preoccupation with fallen women that Belasco also pursued through nontheatrical activities. What he lacked in manly bearing to move the Magdalenes and Salomes of the stage, he more than made up for in acquisition of knowledge. The little preacher story was but one of the many Belasco chronicles of his forays into houses of prostitution and gambling during his days in San Francisco and Virginia City, as the anatomy of female waywardness became the central focus of a broader array of morbid interests. In his autobiography, he also writes of visiting asylums, where he studied "the conditions of the insane," and prisons, where he interviewed the condemned to gain insight into their emotions as they faced their fates and then witnessed their hangings. He also visited morgues to examine more closely the corporeal ravages of painful death.[28] While on tour for Maguire in Virginia City, he says he persuaded a hospital physician to let him know when someone was likely to die. "I would sit for hours watching the phenomenon of the passing of life."[29] Upon returning to San Francisco, he prevailed on his family physician to take him to hospitals to watch operations: "I was brought in to witness the death agonies of a girl under the influence of arsenic; I saw a man die from the effects of a knife wound." Realizing the earnestness with which he approached the subject, the doctor aided him in the study of poisons. "It was not long before I knew the exact length of time it took to fall under the influence of different drugs, and the physical effects which naturally followed them. Soon I became an authority on the subject, and many actors came to me to ask my advice about their death scenes."[30]

The most formative of these on-site researches, to which Belasco would repeatedly refer in his autobiography, interviews, and articles, involved another young girl he knew who led a stormy life. After a quarrel with her lover, she killed herself, but not before bequeathing her body to the San Francisco Medical College, where he obtained permission to watch her dissection:

I suppose, in my youthful imagination, I felt that when I could say "look upon the history of this heart," I could solve the whole riddle of humanity for myself. . . . There it lay, somewhat smaller than a closed fist. I sat for more than three hours facing the empty seats of the arena, thinking of the girl's history until the heart seemed to palpitate and throb with the memory of the grief of that unfortunate creature. Every emotion seemed to cry out from the heart, every vein told me a story. It taught me the ending of things; it taught me kindness; it taught me pity; it taught me to remember the dust under the flesh; in fact, it taught me to look for the *excuse*. Since that experience, whenever I rehearse a situation of passion, of crime, wrongdoing, I remember the heart. I make an excuse—seek out the motive to put the actor in touch with the culprit's point of view. The excuse is *always there*. . . . [31]

Belasco's morbid curiosity about female emotional anatomy went beyond the spectatorial; elaborating on his morgue experiences in a subsequent interview with Montrose J. Moses, he claimed he was only able to fathom a woman's heart after he had held one in his hand "that had just stopped beating, but was still flushed with warmth." Thus, when he later wrote that as a teacher he "found it possible to thrust my fingers into the open bosom and pluck at the very strings of the emotions, compelling them to do my bidding," he was pushing a metaphor to its literal condition. His quest to know and thereby control the workings of incontinent feminine passion extended to tactile and corporeal as well as emotional and psychological realms.[32]

Belasco's fieldwork at morgues, hospitals, prisons, and asylums provides a revealing context for the book collection he amassed that gave him his primary access to power through knowledge. Beginning in boyhood, he was an avid reader and book collector, haunting libraries and bookstores and befriending older men who gave him access to private collections.[33] William Winter says Belasco gave him the impression that "from an early age his mind has been interested in the study of those famous women of history whose conduct of life is shown to have been governed by their appetites and passions."[34] Catalogues of Belasco's books sold after his death include more than a hundred biographical works on extraordinarily powerful, lusty women associated with European monarchies and the theatre dating from the Roman Empire through the eighteenth century.[35]

But the category of Belasco's books that most vividly explores female waywardness is pornography. Not surprisingly, the notoriously prudish Winter does not mention this interest of Belasco's at all, and it is not until the final chapter of his biography that Timberlake offers the following unexamined observation: "He was a grossly sensual man, morbidly preoccupied with the bizarre aspects of sexual behavior as he observed them in life and in his extensive collection of pornography. Essentially a creature of the emotions and not the mind, he lacked intellectual distinction."[36] Timberlake takes pains to point out in a footnote that while he has seen a list of pornographic books, shown to him by Belasco's former secretary, Thomas A. Curry Sr., he has not seen the books themselves.[37] The book collection itself no longer exists, but copies of all the titles on the list—most in the same editions Belasco could have owned—can still be accessed. The editions consulted for this study are itemized at the end of the Bibliography.

Belasco's pornophilia illuminates aspects of his relations with actresses. As Tracy C. Davis has demonstrated, pervasive male consumption of pornography fueled the continuing association of actresses with prostitutes through the nineteenth century and into the twentieth.[38] Not only were actresses frequently depicted in pornographic serials, pictures, and novels, but as public women performing in the theatres, they served as readily available objects for male sexual fantasies, often aroused by the illicit consumption of pornography. During the era, producers and performers regularly provided theatrical stagings that manipulated sexual images of women's bodies for the delectation of pornographically literate spectators. Belasco came of age amid a burgeoning Anglo-American pornography industry, especially in the locales where he launched his theatrical career: Gold Rush San Francisco, which bourgeois moralists dubbed the Sodom and Gomorrah of the West, and New York City under the antivice agent Anthony Comstock, whose rabid attempts to curtail the spread of pornography abetted its subterranean efflorescence.[39]

Along with its obvious appeal to prurient interests, pornography has flourished historically because it has provided a rich source of supposed knowledge, especially for men, about female sexuality.[40] Belasco believed that the poet Aldrich "was never so entirely right and so delightfully felicitous as when he sang":

> The loveliest book that ever man
> Looked into since the world began
> Is Woman! As I turn those pages,
> As fresh as in the primal ages . . .
> I think that I am slowly growing
> To think no other work worth knowing![41]

A woman, like a book, could be opened to reveal her inner secrets. Translated literally from its Greek root words *porneia* and *graphos*, "pornography" means "whore writing," literature that reveals the desires and experiences of whores and those who pursue them.[42] Given the manifold ways Victorian culture elided the actress and the whore, pornography became, in a highly instrumental sense for Belasco the director, "actress writing." Pornography elaborated in graphic detail what fallen women supposedly desired, how they inwardly responded to sexual stimulation, and how they outwardly enacted high excitation and climax. With leading medical and popular discourses of the period linking women's mental states to their reproductive organs, and so many women being diagnosed as pathological "hysterics" for supposed uterine and ovarian malfunction, there was a widespread belief that female emotions emanated from the lower body.[43] In this context, pornographic knowledge of women's sexual functioning could also serve as knowledge of actresses' emotional production.

Young Belasco had ready access to pornographic material as well as to prostitutes in San Francisco and other mining centers such as Sacramento, California, and Virginia City, Nevada. Relatively inexpensive, ephemeral magazines and postcards would have been easy to come by. Among the odd jobs young Belasco sought while struggling as an actor was work in bookstores, including one affiliated with a cigar store that catered to a male clientele and probably introduced him to the higher-class, canonical pornographic books he collected as he made more money. His job entailed cataloguing and writing detailed synopses for the customers' guidance. Booksellers used such synopses especially for the marketing of rare antiquarian books, such as "curiosa" and "gallantiana," euphemisms for expensively bound, privately printed pornographic novels.[44] The list of books in the pornography collection Belasco subsequently amassed contains only the titles and prices of seventy-six items, some in multivolume sets. Publication dates range from as early as the sixteenth century to as late as 1930, which means that the list was probably made around the time of Belasco's death (1931) in preparation for sale.[45] However, he would have had access to many of the items in the period of his maturation as a director and maker of actresses, that is, from when he worked as a stage manager for Maguire in the late 1870s to when he made his first major female star, Mrs. Leslie Carter, in the early 1890s.[46] While the list cannot be taken as exhaustive or comprehensive (he probably consumed many more pornographic books than are listed), it does provide significant indication of his tastes. Dr. Clifford J. Scheiner of New York City, a specialist in the history of pornography and the author of the two-volume *Essential Guide to Erotic Literature*, comments that the books listed are fairly typical of those owned by knowledgeable, monied collectors of the period, but also highlight a particular interest in the psychology of women's sexuality. He characterizes most of the books as "very, very intelligent books, well written. You can learn something from them. They're not potboilers."[47] What Belasco learned from these books he would incorporate into the theories and practices of actor training he pursued after he left the West Coast and moved permanently to New York in 1882.

Exciting Emotional Expression

Arriving in Manhattan, Belasco confronted a different social dynamic than he had known in San Francisco. The California gateway city's multiethnic society forged during the Gold Rush lacked a Protestant hegemony because of the strong presence of Catholic immigrants. Although comprising a smaller percentage of the population than Catholics or Protestants, Jews were well integrated into the larger community. From the state's inception, Jews had the franchise, helped found the state's many Anglo-based institutions, and were elected to public office in San Francisco beginning in the 1850s. While anti-Semitism could flare up on occasion, as it did during Morse's *Passion*, it did not generally affect individual Jews' daily interactions with their neighbors.[48] In New York, on the other hand, there was a long-standing white, Anglo-Saxon Protestant hegemony, and Belasco arrived as widespread anti-Semitism surged with the massive influx of Jews from southern and eastern Europe in the late nineteenth century.

A cartoon entitled "Hints for the Jews—Several Ways of Getting to Manhattan Beach" (30 July 1879), which was published in the popular humor magazine *Puck* and also circulated widely as a single sheet, captures some of the anti-Semitism that Belasco confronted (fig. 26). Drawn by the magazine's founder, the Viennese-born and -trained artist, Joseph Keppler, the cartoon appeared after the resort owner Austin Corbin enacted a policy admitting only certain kinds of Jews. Its imagery draws on European racial stereotypes that gained currency with rising immigration to northeastern, urban American society. The immigrant Jews lining up for admission to the beach are grotesquely caricatured with short, squat, potbellied physiques; unruly masses of dark, curly hair; large, hooked noses; and thick lips. In the lower left foreground is a couple whose demeanor smacks of gender inversion. The

HINTS FOR THE JEWS.—SEVERAL WAYS OF GETTING TO MANHATTAN BEACH.

26. "Hints for the Jews—Several Ways of Getting to Manhattan Beach," by Joseph Keppler, in Puck, *30 July 1879.*

man displays feminine traits, and the woman masculine ones. Racial theorists attributed gender inversion to Jews as a sign of emotional and physical—especially sexual—incontinence and lower evolutionary status than WASPs. One way for Jews to improve their social status and achieve greater, although still not complete, gender differentiation is, of course, money. This is reflected in the inset cartoon in the upper left corner depicting the ostentatiously dressed duo labeled "Corbin's 'White Jew' and Whiter Jewess." Other ways, shown in the upper background of the main cartoon, involve fulfilling Corbin's posted mandates: "Kinky hair must positively be straightened out" and "Parabolic noses must be trimmed down in Christian style." The most prominent Jew to have fulfilled these mandates and gained admittance is cornetist Julius Levi, the main entertainment attraction at the resort. Levi is shown greeting and scrutinizing the new arrivals through his monocle in the lower right of the drawing. His hair, nose, and belly are all trim in the more genteel as well as Gentile fashion.[49] The preponderance of figures carrying horns in the foreground reflects both the special musical talent and gift for mimicry

David Belasco's Quest for Sexual Knowledge | 157

attributed to Jews and implies that they can gain admission to Manhattan Beach by acting, like Levi, more white and Christian.[50]

These anti-Semitic stereotypes raised the stakes for Belasco to manage his own Jewish identity as he pursued the highest ambition for success in his chosen field. In his autobiography he recalls that when he set his sights on New York after the uplifting experience of *The Passion*, "Wallack's or nothing, was my cry within myself, not a very modest cry inasmuch as Wallack's was the acme of the profession, both as regards playwriting and acting. It was the magic name for artistry, and difficult to enter. . . . I began to say to myself: 'There is the prestige I need. How shall I accomplish it?'"[51] Founded by the London-born actor-manager James William Wallack and passed on to his son, Lester, Wallack's in the 1870s and early 1880s was the favored legitimate house of the Protestant bourgeoisie and the benchmark of theatrical respectability, which Augustin Daly and Charles Frohman also sought to achieve. But because of his cultural background and appearance, Belasco faced greater challenges in pursuing this high professional and social goal than did the tall, handsome, Gentile Daly or even the queer, Jewish Frohman. For both Belasco and Frohman, short stature correlated with effeminizing stereotypes of Jewish men; however, Belasco looked more exotic than his bald, smaller-nosed, more conventionally dressed Levi-like colleague. Whereas Frohman could physically assimilate and keep his sexual difference hidden, Belasco's outward appearance made his supposed racial difference—and, hence, his supposed effeminacy—more visible. Moreover, his priestly pose compounded the ways his theatrical profession played into dominant cultural perceptions of Jews as expert in mimicry and therefore inherently deceitful and unoriginal.

In this climate, managing actresses' performances became more than a way of overpowering the women who reigned on the stage. It was also a means of demonstrating mastery over the effeminacy, emotional and physical incontinence, and duplicity that an anti-Semitic society believed Jewish men like Belasco embodied. Rather than containing his actresses' passions within a chaste persona, as Frohman did with Adams, Belasco learned to demonstrate that mastery by pushing actresses to putatively genuine emotional and physical climaxes and professing to control every phase and facet of the progression. Experience in formalized actor training during his early years in New York proved crucial to developing this strategy for success.

Soon after his arrival in 1882, Belasco found employment at New York's Madison Square Theatre owned by two brothers, the Reverend George S.

and Marshall H. Mallory, whom the *Morning Journal* dubbed "those cunning little Christians" because of their eye for turning religion into profit.[52] Professing to specialize in producing morally righteous drama, they hired the priestly Belasco as stage manager. In that capacity, he succeeded Steele MacKaye, who had moved to the Lyceum Theatre under the management of the Frohman brothers. Belasco had first become acquainted with the Frohmans when Gus Frohman came to San Francisco with a touring company.[53] Through these connections, Belasco left the Madison Square in the fall of 1884 and went to work at the Lyceum with MacKaye, who was developing the first formal curriculum for training actors in the United States. Although MacKaye soon departed the Lyceum because of a rivalry with his colleague, Franklin Sargent, he indelibly shaped the philosophy and training methods of the institute. Sargeant assumed leadership and renamed the institute the New York School for Acting (NYSA) in 1885. Belasco served as a founding faculty member at the school until the end of the decade.[54]

More than just gaining an entrée into the new actor training school, Belasco found the program quite conducive to his developing method of evoking highly emotional acting out of actresses. MacKaye's and Sargent's approach was steeped in the theologically based theories of the French Catholic guru, François Delsarte. Claude Shaver has observed that "the whole Delsarte system is primarily a method which enables the actor to achieve complete freedom of the imagination and the spontaneous expression of the emotional inner state in the truest possible manner."[55] Delsarte originally defined the composition of that inner state, its "truth," and modes of expression in religious terms. He conceived of each half of humanity's dual natures—spiritual and physical, or immanent and organic—as being divided and subdivided into sets of three elements, according to the Christian Trinity. These tripartite divisions were parallel and correlative so that each immanent aspect had an organic manifestation. Spirit and flesh became metonyms of each other. As MacKaye wrote in his notes on Delsarte:

> The immanent essence of life, mind, and soul [tied, respectively, to Father, Son, and Holy Ghost] are expressed through the organic acts of feeling, thought, and love, by the physical mechanisms. . . . Life, with its immanent acts of sensation, instinct, and sympathy, is expressed by the vocal mechanism [lungs, back of mouth, larynx]; mind, with its accompanying immanences, judgment, induction, and conscience, is expressed by the buccal mechanism [velum, tongue, lips]; soul, with its immanences of sentiment,

intuition, and contemplation, is expressed by the dynamic mechanism [torso, head, face].[56]

After studying with the master in France, MacKaye, "like a John the Baptist, came back to America to prepare the New World for the coming of Delsarte."[57]

Although detractors disparaged the Delsarte System as a superficial and mechanical mode of acting by set poses and gestures, MacKaye understood and practiced it as a way of accessing and exteriorizing what were held to be profoundly internal and invisible aspects of the human organism. And the system gave these immanences the authority of spiritual truth, which made their provocation and exteriorization not only an acceptable endeavor but a sacralized one. Sargent's discourse was more secular than MacKaye's, but the theological underpinnings remained. Charged with the mission of eliciting spiritual truth from the body of the student, Belasco could readily adopt the method as well as manner of a priest seeking to "save" a penitent.

At the school, the bodies from which Belasco and other instructors elicited these truths were primarily white, middle-class, and female. From its inception at the Madison Square Theatre through its lasting institution at the Lyceum, the acting school's legitimizing framework was one of moral and social uplift with particular concern for the reputations of young women who sought a livelihood in the theatre. According to an article by Philip G. Hubert in *Lippincott's* magazine written shortly after the opening of the school, the Lyceum managers sought to address a still-pressing social need, "the regeneration of the stage," by organizing "companies composed wholly of respectable people, among whom a young girl will be safe from moral injury." He reports that in the entering class of more than one hundred students who could afford the two-hundred-dollar tuition (more than four thousand dollars today), a large majority—two-thirds—were female.[58] The pitch to female pupils worked, but the school became so desperate for male scene partners that it had to lure men with free scholarships.[59]

If the preponderance of students was female, the gender distribution of the instructors was the reverse. For the opening term in the fall of 1884, only two of the twelve faculty members were women. In 1887, after the school was reconstituted under Sargent, a *Dramatic Mirror* article named eleven instructors, six men and five women, but their actual influence on curriculum and instruction was not as gender equitable as these numbers suggest. Sargent was firmly in charge and retained only those faculty who would strictly serve his MacKaye-Delsarte system. Of the 1,074 total hours of instruction tabulated for the school year, 745 hours were taught by men, and chiefly by Belasco (312 hours) and Sargeant himself (230 hours).[60] Sargeant dictated that the relationship between teacher and student should function like that between a stage director and an actor. In an era when stage directing was almost exclusively a male occupation, this credo strongly privileged male instructors at the school.[61] Thus, the larger moral and social agenda of regenerating the stage was to be achieved chiefly through the work of male acting teachers on female pupils.

The focus and methods of the training not only shored up Belasco's directorial power but, in spite of the school's high-minded ideals, also tapped into his pornographic imagination. Rather than preparation for comedy or farce, the training was geared to preparation for emotional drama, and women's emotions were understood to be both embodied and sexual. While MacKaye's rhetoric transmuted female sexuality and sexual arousal into a language of spiritual elevation, his focus on the body kept the sexual underside an active if unacknowledged force in the pedagogical dynamic. MacKaye contended that the emotional aspects of character were most fully revealing of the "soul." This was an intangible element that a performer could tangibly express through an "organic" or bodily "act" of "love" by using the "dynamic mechanism" of the torso, head, and face. In his elaborate schema, these soul-revealing emotional aspects could also radiate through other sections of the body and corresponding spiritual essences via "circumincession," a principle of dynamic exchange of energies among various parts of the anatomy.[62] The Delsartean metonymy of spirit and flesh compelled Belasco and his colleagues to provoke a woman's emotional expression through her body in the name of the Father, Son, and Holy Ghost. High spiritual and social purpose at once masked the sexual nature of the activity and justified great rigor in classroom instruction.

The priest's pose, which Belasco wore more explicitly than other teachers, itself fostered a slippage between spirituality and sexuality in exercising the school's philosophy and methods. If priests figured prominently as saviors in official society, they became infamous corrupters in pornography's world of inverted social values. With privileged access to sexual as well as theological knowledge, priests who abuse their holy offices to lure and defile the innocent are stock characters in the type of pornographic novels Belasco collected.[63] Pornographic depictions trade on the parallelisms between the spiritual and sexual transformations that male priests seek to effect in women. Both processes involve priests seductively eliciting confessions that save sinners or turn virgins into lusty whores. The most profoundly transformational confessions are not just verbal but involve the whole body in expressing inner passion. The fallen woman's joyful ecstasy when Christ enters her heart finds its pornographic correlative in the reluctant virgin's first experience of sexual penetration and orgasm that shakes every fiber of her being.[64]

To effect the woman's transformation and prove the priest's or seducer's potency, the confession must be genuine. This principle animated both the acting training at the New York School for Acting and the pornographic novels Belasco consumed. According to Delsarte and MacKaye, only a "true" or sincere emotion can reveal the "soul." Pornography, as Linda Williams has argued, caters to a pervasive male desire to know whether or not a woman has truly climaxed during a sexual encounter: "The woman's ability to fake the orgasm that the man can never fake (at least according to certain standards of evidence) seems to be at the root of all the genre's attempts to solicit what it can never be sure of: the out-of-control confession of pleasure, a hard-core 'frenzy of the visible.'"[65] As proof of his manhood, the sexual conqueror needs to turn the virgin not only into a whore but into a genuinely feeling performer of sexual experience. Because of the special powers of his office, the priest has advantages over the layman, even the most manly military hero or charismatic Romeo, in eliciting such confessional performances. For the priestly Belasco, with his storehouse of pornographic as well as theological knowledge, Delsarte-based acting training offered an elaborate system for making otherwise inscrutable female emotions visible on—and therefore knowable and controllable through—the body. As Belasco later exclaimed about this pursuit of knowledge, "The science of the body—how the body lends itself to the expression of the emotions—is a wonderful study! The shoulders, back, forehead, the eyes which shout out truth, the lips which mirror the heart's gaiety or break into the hysterical laughter of despair, the very toes—all enter vividly into the portraiture of the actual and must be taught to become willing, supple servants of the will."[66]

Because body revealed spirit, according to Delsarte, the mode of instruction that Belasco learned and practiced at the school was intensely physical. Breaking the body down into individual parts and then releasing and disciplining each part became means of solving the enigma of immaterial emotion and controlling every gradation of its expression—hence, the Delsarte System's focus on gesture and pantomime. Whereas, according to MacKaye, mental or intellectual energies are seated in the head and vital or physical energies in the limbs, moral or volitional energies are located in the torso, which contains the soul-revealing organs of deepest feeling. MacKaye devised two primary exercises for releasing and controlling these feelings, the Harmonic Gymnastics and Gamuts of Expression. Both were central to the curriculum taught by Sargeant and Belasco. One of MacKaye's early pupils, Genevieve Stebbins, vividly articulated the glorious potential of mastering the exercises: "The kingdom of heaven is within, and we must try to make such indwelling beauty visible in outward form, life, and action."[67] The effort could be exhilarating, especially when the exercises focused on the torso. The Harmonic Gymnastics, Stebbins writes, are movements that "free the channels of expression, and the current of nervous force can thus rush through them as a stream of water rushes through a channel unclogged by obstacles."[68]

Drawing on his military training as an officer in the Civil War, MacKaye made "drill" the operative verb of classroom instruction at the school.[69] Students were put through Harmonic Gymnastics drills in two phases, the first of which involved "decomposing" exercises to break down the stiffnesses and habits that clogged emotional expression. In the second phase, MacKaye taught students to manipulate the individual "expressive organs" to convey specific emotions. After they mastered the nine basic positions he charted for each organ, he drilled them in exercises involving bends and extensions of torso and limbs, including, according to Stebbins, Back Full, Front Full, Kneeling, Pivoting, Bowing, Rising from Sitting, Rising from Kneeling.[70] Throughout, MacKaye stressed the necessity of connecting each movement to an inner emotional source, harkening to Delsarte's caveat that "nothing is more deplorable than a gesture without a *motive*." In the Gamuts of Expression in Pantomime, students were given a "situation" calling forth an emotion that they were to express by using the intricate visual code they had mastered. Success was measured in terms of how well a student was able, on command, to make emotion legible on the body and thereby enable viewers, in MacKaye's words, "to see through [the gesture] to the soul."[71]

In order to allow for greater individuality in performers, Sargeant was less prescriptive than MacKaye in matching shades of emotion to specific gestures, but he was no less intent on connecting real feelings—especially powerful ones not considered expressible in bourgeois daily life—with outward physicality. The head of the Department of Action, Sargeant drilled students in Bodily Movements and Pantomime courses with the admonition that all gestures be accompanied by thought and feeling.[72] During Hubert's visit to the school, Sargeant shared his belief that while the average person is endowed with "all the requisite means or machinery for the expression of exceptional emotion, the machinery is rusty"; thus, the Delsartean exercises were necessary "to keep this machinery of emotion well oiled and in order for use."[73]

Belasco showed a keen aptitude for the school's methods and soon became a leading instructor. Where Sargeant taught gymnastics exercises "to facilitate acting," the task of teaching the students how to employ their well-oiled emotional machinery in the production of plays fell principally to Belasco, whose classes in "stage business and rehearsal" filled the greatest number of hours in the curriculum.[74] Hubert recorded his observations of Belasco at work at the NYSA in 1885:

> Mr. Belasco's class were rehearsing a scene from an emotional drama of his own. A husband, who has been deeply wronged, visits his home for the last time to demand his child. The scene between husband and wife is short, but Mr. Belasco, who sat in front of the stage, watching his pupils as a cat watches mice, was so particular about every detail that the young woman who personated the wife, and who is required to enter to slow music, clutching the furniture for support, had to make her entrance eleven times and to make seventeen attempts to sit down in a chair before Mr. Belasco was satisfied.[75]

In this exercise, which fittingly reveals his interest in wayward womankind, Belasco places particular emphasis on the actress's torso, seat of the passions that presumably caused the wife to wrong her husband. Having released the lower body's energies through the Harmonic Gymnastics, the instructor now must discipline the region through the bending motion of repeated sitting and rising. After just a year at the institution, Belasco is applying the pedagogy with all the authority and intensity of his drill sergeant mentor.

Belasco and the rest of the faculty at the NYSA could not have developed these methods without at least some level of collusion on the part of the female pupils. No one was forcing this well-heeled clientele to pay the costly tuition and endure the rigors of the training, and very few actually went on to professional acting careers. Hope for stardom is insufficient explanation of why so many eagerly enrolled. The writings of Genevieve Stebbins offer further insight into the training's appeal. Having studied with MacKaye and gone to France to work with a religious disciple of Delsarte's, the Abbé Delaumosné, Stebbins became the master's leading female proponent. She published several books, most popularly *The Delsarte System of Expression*, which was issued in multiple editions beginning in 1885, and she also founded and taught at the New York School of Expression from 1893 to 1907.[76]

Preaching self-regeneration through the embodiment and expression of "noble emotions," Stebbins encouraged her students to imitate classical statues.[77] Although, like MacKaye, she employed a rhetoric of high artistic and moral purpose, transgressive liberation lurked in her lessons. She taught the pupil not only to strike the pose, but also to practice the movement and release the energies necessary to emulate the figure. To cite just one revealing example from *The Delsarte System of Expression*, she invites her young female pupil to study a statue of a male nude in an action pose that shows off his very well developed musculature and prominent genitalia: "Ah! Fighting Gladiator! You indicate to me explosion, with your excited air and forward-bent knee. I am told that you are striving to seize the bridle of rearing horses with that outstretched arm, and you are running, not fighting. You have been much maligned."[78] Imitating such a figure demands special attention to normally shrouded, discreetly managed body parts. After isolating and working the thigh, Stebbins enjoins the student to use the muscles more vigorously by racing her in Central Park:

> Here is a by-path, no one observing but those two black swans with crimson beaks, sailing majestically on that tree-encircled lake. Catch me, if you can. Ah! I outdistance you, for, like all women, you roll instead of run. Recall the attitude of the fighting gladiator, . . . forward leg strong, knee bent, torso thrown well forward. The run is a continuous succession of these attitudes. Try for me. Very well; you are an apt scholar. Shall we race again? We cannot; a gray-coated policeman appears. He eyes us with suspicion. He thinks us "children of too large a growth" for such games. We will go home; the sun is setting.[79]

Away from the confines of the corset and the drawing room, well-heeled young women could enroll in Delsarte training and do what their repressive upbringings prohibited: exercise in unladylike ways and experience the exhilaration of venting excitement through explosive movement. Stebbins was known as a stern taskmaster who demanded rigorous effort and commitment to the training to maintain its integrity and respectability. In her popular manual, she warns her pupil: "if at the end of these lessons, you have not freed the channels of expression, you will simply be ridiculous, and will merit all the fun which is leveled at the mechanical mugging of so-called Delsarteans. Work! Work! Work!."[80]

As the wary gaze of the policeman indicates, however, women could not always train under Stebbins with impunity. When women conspired to engage in unladylike activity outside male supervision, their actions aroused suspicion. The greater authority vested in the male administrators and instructors at the New York School for Acting provided an added layer of control that reassured the guardians of respectable society. Women could practice many of the same exercises as Stebbins prescribed but posed less danger to the social order when they did so with a teacher such as Belasco, who wielded the combined powers of priest and military drill sergeant. More-over, the NYSA kept its pedagogy in the institutional confines of the gym and rehearsal hall rather than the open air of Central Park.

While the male authority of the NYSA may have been reassuring, the school's methods of having men "drill" respectable women into expressing sexually linked emotions—even in the name of the Holy Trinity—still might have been morally troubling to society and alienating to potential female pupils. Yet this does not appear to have been the case, at least not to any extent that prevented the school from thriving. Additional discourses were at work enabling the training methods Belasco was mastering and would use to great acclaim throughout his career. Such "drilling" of women by male experts had a much longer history at another institution that would have shared clientele with the NYSA, the gynecologic clinic. In a racial and class culture that placed a high premium on women's emotional and sexual conti-nence, hysteria was pandemic, and the demand for treatment widespread and lucrative. It was common practice for respectable white, middle- and upper-class women to make weekly visits to their male doctors for gynecologic mas-sage to relieve hysterical symptoms that could arise, paradoxically, from both too little and too much sexual arousal. The arduous task of massaging so many women to what was politely referred to as the "hysterical paroxysm" spurred technological innovations that material culture specialist Rachel Maines has recently chronicled in her history of the vibrator.[81] Some rather imposing apparati, powered first by water, then by coal, steam, and electricity, were applied weekly to the same class of women and thus likely to many of the same individuals who patronized the acting school. Figures 27 and 28 depict, respectively, the "Hanging type of Carpenter vibrator" and a similar model, the Chattanooga, set up in a clinic. Imagining these devices in use can help one understand how the rigorous physical methods deployed by male acting teachers, which may seem inappropriate or extreme by today's standards, seemed necessary and desirable for women in Belasco's day.

27. *"Hanging type of Carpenter vibrator" used for gynecologic massage treatments, in Mary Lydia Hastings Arnold Snow,* Mechanical Vibration and Its Therapeutic Application.

Maines argues that the professional, male-dominated clinical framework within which the treatments occurred allowed for a camouflage of potential scandal.[82] A satire of the NYSA's Delsarte-based exercises for generating and lubricating the expression of "exceptional emotion," entitled *Forty Minutes with a Crank, or the Seldarte Craze*, penetrates that camouflage to reveal more of how Belasco's contemporaries understood and enabled his methods. This one-act play appeared in 1889 while Belasco was still on the faculty. The playwright, George M. Baker, was a leading author of plays for amateur theatricals, a favorite social pastime of white and middle- and upper-class patrons, especially women, and an outlet for those who lacked the talent or wished to avoid the taint of professional theatre. The script plays upon the correlations between gynecologic therapy and actress training and the underlying sexual nature of both activities.[83] Baker offers a biting contemporary critique of the core training methods and their potential for abuse.

The main character is Archimedes Abbott, Principal of the Realistic School of Expression, who combines attributes of at least three notable figures at the NYSA. His position and pontifications evoke MacKaye and

28. *"Operating theater" where women went regularly for gynecologic massage treatments, in Mary Lydia Hastings Arnold Snow,* Mechanical Vibration and Its Therapeutic Application.

Sargeant, the school's founding and current directors, while the monastic reference in the surname Abbott also points the satire in the direction of Belasco, the clerically collared faculty member who taught the most hours in the curriculum. The character's first name refers to the classical philosopher and inventor who gave civilization the screw. Archimedes—a.k.a. "Old Screw"—extracts money from well-heeled and misguided female aspirants to the stage by wooing them with false flattery about their performance potential and eliciting real feeling from them. Because they are made to really feel something, they are supposed to believe they have gotten their money's worth from the acting lesson. This scam proceeds from an explicit pun on Victorian economic metaphors for sex replete in pornography but also in widespread colloquial use: Archimedes screws women into "spending"— that is, "putting out," both in terms of sexually linked emotions and money— with a curriculum that clearly favors big spenders.[84] The pun rang true, as complaints from actual female pupils at the school printed in letters to the editor of the *Dramatic Mirror* in the years immediately preceding Baker's publication of the play charged Sargeant with retaining students in proportion to their capacity to spend.[85]

The play opens with the sounds of voices from behind a curtained doorway upstage center over which is a sign marked "Curfew Department," which Abbott later declares is "the best paying department in the school."[86] One of Abbott's subordinates, Musty Knott, is administering a lesson to Minnie, otherwise known as Miss Moneybags, a thirty-five-year-old pupil pointedly costumed "too young" for her face. She is reciting Rose Hartwick Thorpe's poem, "Curfew Must Not Ring Tonight," while enacting the heroine's rescue of her condemned lover by seizing the clapper of the huge bell high in its tower that would alert enemy soldiers to his escape. The poem was a popular recitation piece among young women, and given that it had been a particular favorite of Belasco's since childhood, he may well have been the one who introduced it as an exercise at the school. Certainly the piece offered excellent opportunity for practicing the school's core method of physicalizing emotion, which made it ripe for Baker's satire and enduringly inspirational for Belasco, who would use the heroine's impassioned leap for the clapper as the centerpiece of his breakthrough commercial success, *The Heart of Maryland*, in 1895.

Baker's script provides elaborate stage directions for rigging a stage facsimile of the bell behind the door with a knotted rope from which Musty can vigorously swing the women. Standing in front of the curtain, Mary, who assists along with Musty at the school, comments: "There they go! The same old story from morning till night. 'Curfew Department!' Torture-chamber would be a better name for that museum of horrors. I know, for, like every pupil who enters here, I came with curfew on the brain." Musty commands his pupil from behind the curtain, "Now swing," and Minnie cries, "Oh, oh, professor! oh, oh!" Mary explains: "She's practicing the grand acrobatic feat, hanging by the tongue of the bell." More cries from Minnie: "Oh, oh!"[87] Musty draws back the curtains, signaling the end of the lesson, and Minnie comes forward rubbing her sore muscles. "I've nearly dislocated my shoulder-blades, and my wrists," she complains. Musty affirms the lesson:

> Yes; you now feel permeating your entire system the noble inspiration which caused the heroic Bessie to perform her feat of grand and lofty tumbling, that has convulsed the world. You now realize the situation, and can speak your little piece feelingly. Ah! shoulder-blades may crack, wrists give way; but the grand idea, the soul of poetry is with you evermore. (*Holds out hand.*) Five dollars, please.[88]

The satirical use of swinging as a form of acting pedagogy played on long-standing gynecologic practice. Physicians for centuries had prescribed swinging as a therapy for the relief of women's hysteria by realigning the pelvis to allow for proper expulsion of dangerously pent-up passions.[89] Minnie's rhythmic cries of "Oh! Oh, Professor! Oh! Oh!" from behind the curtain indicate that the treatment is working. Musty's assistant Mary reports that she, too, first came for the Curfew treatment and never left, which suggests it is not pure torture.

After this opening lesson showcasing the method, Archimedes enters with his would-be son-in-law, Arthur, to whom he explains more of his revolutionary theory:

> Behold the evolution of dramatic art. True expression slumbered in the little bell till Seldarte roused it to action. All other systems attack the outworks: we of the new school throw our bombs into the magazine of pent-up eloquence, and open at once the avenues of speech, glorious! ecstatic! superb! No artificial concentric, eccentric, and normal action of the legs, arms and torso; no passion save what the heart inspires. Feeling is the walking-beam of our engine: feel and act. Old systems play about the altar of eloquence, touching here and there with their little matches outhanging faggots; but we of the new school thrust our torches into the centre of the pile and send a blaze of glory through the fabric. Illuminating! transfiguring! enrapturing!

When Arthur expresses concern about the anarchistic implications of this pedagogy, Old Screw is quick to reassure him:

> No; everything is law and orderly. Like the old school, the human frame has been classified. The legs, being the vassals of the body, we call *vaseline*; the arms, from the cunning of the hand, we style *cuticura*; the body, which until Seldarte discovered its proper place, lacked art, we style *lactart*; the face, from its power of mimicry, *moxie*; and the head, whence flow ideas (tapping his head), *sapolio*. All original terms hypothecated by the great master. . . . The old school start the arms, legs, and face working, to draw fire from the heart and mind; we start with the fire, which we build in lactart, the centre of the system, generating the steam which, permeating and electrifying, sets vaseline, cuticura, moxie, and sapolio working; and the result is genuine expression. . . . [90]

Baker's farcical lens magnifies ways the system worked to draw extreme feeling outward through the body in a version of Linda Williams's "frenzy of the visible." The incendiary imagery of this satire contained at least a spark of truth;

Sargeant proclaimed in the school's catalogue that students "must surrender themselves to the feeling aroused. The great task of the instructor is to start the spark of feeling and to see that its expression is kept sincere. It does not suffice to indicate or describe emotion; the actor himself must learn to feel."[91]

The inducement of physical pain in the course of rigorous training, as the play indicates, could be an expedient means of starting that spark. This pedagogical technique invoked both priestly and pornographic discourses familiar to Belasco and many of his contemporaries. Because the activities in the Curfew Department, which Mary calls a "torture chamber," transpire behind a curtain, the audience does not see exactly how Musty is making Minnie swing, but the situation invites fantasies of the whip. Flagellation motifs replete in canonical pornography are strongly ecclesiastical in derivation.[92] As in confession, where the priest is privy to the naked soul of the penitent, in mortification rituals he is privy to her naked body and authorized to administer the rod. Flagellation is confessional because its ostensible purpose is to expiate sins arising from forbidden passions. Physical torture helps to guarantee a genuine confession; whereas a woman can speak false words or fake an orgasm, even with her priest, she cannot feign the marks of injury that rise on her body with each turn of the rope or stroke of the lash. Whether the instructor achieved it by subjecting the pupil to some degree of physical pain or to another kind of stressful "situation," visible proof that she actually felt the emotions he incited became the primary determinant of the success of NYSA pedagogy. Pursuit of that proof would remain a crucial goal of Belasco's training of actresses.

Bourgeois society could laugh knowingly at the sexual and sadomasochistic references in Baker's farce and yet tacitly condone the activities he satirized. Both gynecologic therapy and actress training served the dominant order by managing female emotions and the reproductive organs from which they supposedly sprang. Maines argues that most if not all of the women who made weekly visits to the clinic for massages to relieve hysterical symptoms knew "what was really going on." They sought the therapy (and many of their husbands and fathers paid for it) because it indeed provided relief and helped sustain the bedrock institution of bourgeois marriage in which female sexual satisfaction was neither properly understood nor actively pursued by either party.[93] Similarly, actress training provided an institutionalized outlet for full-bodied expression of forbidden passion. Moreover, because the training was theatrical, it made a spectacle of disciplining female emotional expression that was at once titillating and supportive of social values. These attitudes and institutional practices comprised a framework of social acceptability for Belasco's work that endured throughout his career.

After he left the NYSA in 1889, Belasco published numerous articles about his approach to training and directing that reflect the foundational influence of his experience at the school. Several of these appeared in women's magazines, which attests to the ongoing special appeal of the pedagogy to women.[94] His most comprehensive statement of his methods, "About Acting," published in the *Saturday Evening Post* (24 September 1921), begins by explicitly crediting the school with providing the basis of his ideas. As one who relied heavily on books for knowledge, Belasco also drew on an acting text he likely had known since his early years in the profession, *On Actors and the Art of Acting*, by the Victorian scientist and drama critic, George Henry Lewes. First published in 1875, the book was read and used by a number of leading actors whom Belasco admired and with whom he worked from the late 1870s through the 1890s, including Edwin Booth, Minnie Maddern Fiske, Joseph Jefferson, and E. H. Sothern.[95] To complement MacKaye's more theological system, Belasco found in Lewes a more scientific understanding of how to manipulate the passions called forth through the body. Indeed, he found Lewes so compatible with the approach he developed at the NYSA that he was caught plagiarizing him in a 1905 article.[96] In language and ideas, "About Acting" still smacks strongly of Lewes's influence, as well as that of the Delsarteans.[97]

According to Belasco, following Lewes, Diderot's famous paradox that "an actor must feel in order to act; but in order to act he must not feel" is only apparent.[98] While it is absurd, he acknowledges, to expect a performer who impersonates a violent criminal actually to have committed the crime to know what the criminal feels, she must be capable of feeling it. The actor, he insists, must possess "extreme sensibility combined with quick and powerful intelligence." What bridges the criminal's reality with the actor's performance of it (as also in Lewes and MacKaye) are imagination and memory. The interworking of these aspects in the actor he defines as follows:

> The imagination conceives and evokes all the emotional sensations and reactions of a special character which is to be represented, in the circumstances and situations prescribed; the sensibility—by which I mean the capability of being vividly impressed and the capacity for being profoundly moved—experiences those sensations and reactions to the fullest extreme; the quick and powerful intelligence minutely observes their

every effect and manifestation—registering in memory every inflection of voice, every play of feature, every movement of the body, every gesture—applies itself to creation of a perfect mental picture or record of them, and then to the reproduction and delicate exaggeration of them by means of all the artistic mechanism it has mastered and formulated.

This threefold process is repeated over and over again: at first in the lonely hours of study; then at rehearsals; finally during performance after performance in public, till at last the result is a reflection, a portrayal, a picture so vivid and exact in its apparent spontaneity and fidelity to truth that the fortunate spectators are enthralled and pronounce it perfect Nature. It is in fact perfect art.[99]

Belasco goes beyond Lewes in insisting that it was not enough for the actor to feel some or a semblance of what the character feels. Inspired by the intensely physical Delsarte-based work of MacKaye to "free the channels of expression" and fired by the pornographic desire to make women genuinely and transformatively feel, Belasco asserts that the actor must experience the character's sensations and reactions "to the fullest extreme." Nor is this phase of creation confined to the rehearsal period. The threefold process—of imaginatively conjuring, inwardly experiencing, and outwardly reproducing—emotion, he says, is also repeated "during performance after performance in public." Belasco aspired to push the line between preparation and performance, between "perfect Nature," involuntary experience of emotion, and "perfect Art," imitation of that experience, to the finest possible extent. Moreover, whereas Lewes describes a process the actor autonomously undertakes, Belasco describes a process that he, following MacKaye and Sargeant, orchestrates as priestlike pedagogue. Directing the actress through all the phases he enumerates, Belasco, not the actress herself, presumed to be the ultimate arbiter of when and how she was feeling and enacting the character's emotions. In his theoretical model, the audience could be fooled into mistaking the authenticity of her performance, but her teacher and director never should be.

To intervene in the actress's process and gain control over her expressive mechanisms, Belasco claimed to wield more than the male authority and knowledge of a Lewes or MacKaye. He came to believe that the effeminacy attributed to him as an "Oriental" Jewish man in a predominately WASP society gave him an advantage over other male teachers and directors in manipulating women's sexually based emotions. As he boldly declared in the epigraph to this chapter: "Ah! I understand women. I have come in contact with thousands of them! There is a strong strain of woman in my nature. I know that it is there, and I can understand woman in all her variations. There is nothing hidden from me."[100] The pornographic books in Belasco's collection helped foster his claims to hidden female knowledge. Signal works such as *The Memoirs of Fanny Hill* and *The Lustful Turk* are framed as epistolary exchanges that allow one woman to confess to another her deepest desires and record in the most intimate detail her sexual experiences.[101] Even while making men the provocateurs of women's most extreme sensations, canonical pornography tries to usurp women's special knowledge of the female body by concocting lesbian scenes in which a more experienced woman initiates a neophyte into the arts of lovemaking. Often the two women engage in a graphic show-and-tell for each other and the reader, detailing parts of their anatomy and what happens to them during arousal.[102]

Scenes of female intimacy in brothels include elaborate lessons for neophytes in how to stage sexual responses to please male clients. For example, the arts of feigning loss of virginity in *Fanny Hill* include not only false cries of pain-into-pleasure and flailing limbs but the insertion of prosthetic hymens of wax and, most ingeniously, the concealing of stage blood and a sponge in a spring-loaded chamber in the bedpost for timely application on the inner thighs.[103] These scenes serve as instructive cautionary tales for the would-be Casanova and the male acting teacher, who both need to prove their efficacy by eliciting genuine feeling from women. For Belasco, who bore the anti-Semitic stereotype of effeminacy and its corollaries of deceptiveness and emotional and sexual incontinence, the stakes for being able to tell—and thus to manipulate—whether the actress was feeling it or faking it were especially high.

Stebbins's textbook, *The Delsarte System of Expression*, whose many editions were well known to Belasco and his students, played right into the budding impresario's pornographic frame of reference and claims to female knowledge. The book is written in the first person as a series of lessons Stebbins is imparting to a younger woman whom she addresses as "dear pupil." At one point, she expresses sadness that her "dearest" has been called away, and the relationship becomes an epistolary one in which instruction continues amid an exchange of confidences. The obsessive attention to specific body parts and how to manipulate them obversely mirrors the anatomical elaborations in the lesbian instruction scenes of pornographic novels. Likewise, the mutual frissons of excitement when teacher and pupil emulate a statue in a risqué pose or indulge in the explosive burst of a surreptitious gladiatorial run in the park echo the sharing of new sexual sensations between the likes of Fanny Hill and her cohorts. Stebbins's repeated demands that her pupil connect outward gesture to inner feeling provide a counterpoint to the cunning fakeries of whores in the pornography Belasco was already reading.

Appropriating these knowledges, Belasco drew on both the allegedly feminine and masculine aspects of himself to master women. His exotic, racially marked appearance together with his growing expertise as a trainer of actresses prompted his contemporaries to circulate a myth that he actually was part female.[104] A writer for *Theatre Magazine* noted, "Mr. Belasco has the eyes of a woman of genius."[105] With his priestly pose and access to secret information, he colluded with his female clients in a system that allowed bourgeois women legitimately to express forbidden passions. Although Belasco's female pupils may not have been as pornographically well-read as their teacher, they—especially those who also sought weekly massages at the gynecologic clinic—were at least tacitly aware of the underlying sexual nature of the pedagogy and found the sensations it produced appealing. Respectable society accepted the acting training at the NYSA because, like the gynecologic clinic, the school provided a male-dominated institutional framework for managing potentially disruptive female emotions. There the priestly Belasco acquired an extraordinary expertise in orchestrating women's emotional expression in performance as a means of gaining power over others— both actresses and audiences—and negotiating the stigmas a racist society projected onto him as a Jewish man. In so doing, he sought to effect both his own and the theatre's social betterment. Belasco's methods became a highly profitable, if volatile, means of starmaking when he was able to work one-on-one with a series of handpicked female pupils. Private tutelage would prove to be his most challenging and productive pedagogical mode.

6

Drilling Her in the Emotional Parts

I, Svengali, . . . am going to make millions . . .
With Trilby! . . . Trained by me, she shall sing for
the world's delight. Hers will be the voice, mine the
knowledge—mine the genius. I have not studied
Mesmer's art in vain. . . . Trilby shall be the greatest
contralto—the greatest soprano—the world has ever
known, and I—Svengali will see that the world
prostrate itself in admiration at my feet.
—Paul Potter, *Trilby*

With the publication of Du Maurier's novel, *Trilby* (1894), its rapidly produced dramatization (1895), and the "Trilby craze" it spawned, the story of the bohemian artist's model and the darkly Semitic Svengali who made her sing gripped public imaginings of relations between impresarios and actresses at the turn of the last century. This fictional duo codified a view of the actress as an instrument that a subaltern male maestro—one whom Du Maurier terms an "Oriental, Israelite, Hebrew Jew"—could most expertly play. Driven by a will to compensate for his own cultural degradation, Svengali vows to make millions with his protégée and, through her, to conquer high-class western European society.[1] His malleable Trilby first appears androgynously clad in a man's military jacket and woman's slip. Her accent sounds "Scottish with a hint of French." She is unusually tall with wavy light brown hair, darker brows, prominent cheekbones and chin, and wide-set eyes. Perhaps hinting at some eastern European or Oriental blood, she bears a neck "of a delicate, privet-like whiteness that is never to be found on any French neck, and very few English ones."[2] These ambiguities signify her potential for movement along the cultural hierarchy, potentially upward toward greater purity but also downward into further decadence. Du Maurier notes "poor Trilby's one shortcoming—*quia multum amitavit*—what Christ said of Mary Magdalene, 'she loved too much.'"[3] Emotional and sexual incontinence haunt her performances, even as Svengali makes her into a neoclassical goddess, the physical form appropriated by Gentile culture for the racially pure feminine ideal. To her audiences, who are irresistibly and ecstatically stirred by her singing, she becomes the fallen and sanctified Teutonic Marguerite in Gounod's opera *Faust*.[4]

Perhaps no American impresario was more closely identified with the Svengali character than David Belasco, who scored his first major Broadway hit with his first female star, Mrs. Leslie Carter, in *The Heart of Maryland* (1895), the same year *Trilby* took the stage. Although Belasco's Jewish origins were Sephardic, and unlike the novel's tall, "spidery," bearded, antagonist, he was short and clean shaven, the nefarious eastern European Jewish stereotype still ghosted him. Commentators referred repeatedly to his "Svengali-like influence" over his performers, especially his female stars.[5]

Operating within an anti-Semitic cultural framework widely reproduced in Du Maurier's novel and its dramatizations, Belasco worked to appropriate the power Svengali gained through Trilby while countering some of the Jew's more negative attributes. His Catholic priest's pose proved instrumental in these maneuvers. Although Catholics, largely because of their greater numbers, had at times been more reviled than Jews, the Catholic position remained attractive to Belasco. Given the Darwinian logic of the era, Catholicism appealed by dint of its historical liminality. Having evolved from Judaism and, in turn, given rise to Protestantism, Catholicism offered the Jewish impresario a richly symbolic, aesthetically lush, and highly theatrical space of transformation, of moving from a putatively "lower" toward a "higher" position. Catholicism made the body of the wayward woman a primary site for the enactment of sin and redemption, a pivotal cycle of conversion potently construable as evolutionary force. Wearing the priest's collar, Belasco identified more closely than Svengali with the Catholic position into which he cast his actress Magdalenes. This pose at once distanced his personal image from Svengali's and made more explicit that what the subaltern impresario was working out through his female protégées were his own racial and moral stigmas; he pursued his own higher status and salvation by subjecting actresses to the cathartic cycles of sin and redemption that drive Catholic religious practices and aesthetics.

Following his apprenticeship at the New York School for Acting, Belasco further developed this Catholic paradigm in training Mrs. Leslie Carter, his first—and prototypical—star. Their seventeen-year relationship (from 1889 to 1906) was book ended by a legendary scene of "discovery" and an infamous breakup when she remarried without his foreknowledge and approval. Subsequent actresses came to him wanting him to do for them what he had done for her. The press and the public read his ensuing star-making relationships in terms of this primary liaison. Seeking to know—and thereby control—Mrs. Carter in the fullest sense, Belasco the priest poseur made auricular and corporeal confession the center of his enterprise. For redemption to occur, the sinful passion first had to be fully and truthfully divulged. Pornography continued to provide both a tool and a frame of reference as he pursued the arousal of real feeling in Mrs. Carter's body to the level of extreme climax. He sought a purportedly purifying mastery over his actress's passions by drilling her in techniques for reproducing her displays of emotional and sexual incontinence on demand in repeated performances. While many observers assumed that Mrs. Carter simply yielded to her maker's fierce, hypnotic control, she actively aided and manipulated that impression to serve her own ends. Her perception, need, and use of Belasco become crucial to understanding the cultural operations of their legendary relationship and their breakthrough success in *The Heart of Maryland*.

Mrs. Carter came to Belasco with both a notorious reputation and a fierce agenda for personal redemption in the eyes of society. The foundation of her celebrity was a sensational divorce trial that had publicly branded her a scandalous woman. This and other elements of her social background made her an especially apt pupil for Belasco's methods. Mrs. Carter is also a ripe case for historical analysis because she left behind more of her own reflections on her experience with Belasco than those who succeeded her. Not only did the press shadow and repeatedly interview her, but she wrote an autobiography, "Portrait of a Lady with Red Hair," published serially in *Liberty Magazine* in 1927, which rivals Belasco's in length and provides more of a sense of the actress's perspective and agency in the star-making process than that left by other Belasco actresses. These autobiographical accounts reveal how the respective points of view of impresario and actress reproduce dominant discourses of "race," gender, sexuality, and class. But each also displays a significant level of self-consciousness in playing to those discourses and using them to mutual and individual advantage in spinning compelling yarns and shaping their own legacies.

The daughter of a wealthy plantation owner, Mrs. Leslie Carter was born Caroline Louise Dudley in Lexington, Kentucky, in 1862. After the Civil War, her father moved the family to Dayton, Ohio. When her father died in 1870, her mother decided to send her to the Convent of St. Mary's in New York City for schooling. Her four years there prompted her to contemplate two career paths: "Religious observances are full of pageantry—and there comes a time in many a young girl's life when she wishes to become either a nun or an actress."[6] She did not pursue either of these options immediately, however, because she returned to Dayton, enrolled at the Cooper Academy for Young Ladies, and in the winter of 1876–1877 made her social debut. In 1880, when she was eighteen, she married Leslie Carter, scion of a wealthy and socially prominent Chicago family in the railway business.[7] They had a son, Dudley, but the marriage was troubled almost from the beginning, as Caroline chafed under what she described as the repressive, "mausoleum-like atmosphere" of the Carters' "tightly governed narrow Scotch home" run by Leslie's two spinster sisters. Tall, athletic, crowned with long, flaming red hair, and exhibiting a penchant for casting off her corset and engaging in daring feats of horsemanship, Caroline proved an affront to her in-laws, who branded her a harlot.[8] She rebelled by taking long trips to Europe and spending her husband's money with a vengeance—to the extent of purchasing a toilet seat set in sterling silver that cost four thousand francs, a sum worth more than sixteen thousand dollars today.[9] In September 1886, after a full year abroad, she returned to the United States without telling her husband. Complaining of a nervous condition, she sought sanctuary at her alma mater, the Convent of St. Mary's in New York. Leslie learned of her whereabouts, declared her mentally insane, and sent her to a sanitarium in Lake Geneva, Wisconsin, where she was diagnosed with paranoia and confined for ten months.[10]

A few weeks after her release, Caroline filed for divorce. The case went to trial in May 1889 and garnered sensational national headlines for six weeks. The *New York Times* called it "the most indecent and revolting divorce trial ever heard in the Chicago courts" and chastised other papers who saw fit to print the salacious details.[11] For the first seven days, Caroline took the stand, accusing her husband of mental cruelty and physical abuse, including forced acts of sodomy, which she could not document. Leslie's well-compensated team of attorneys denied all the allegations against him and charged her with several counts of adultery. They produced a series of witnesses who testified to seeing or hearing her inappropriate intimacies with other men, including a state senator, an actor, and a doctor. Caroline's attorney tried to claim it was too dark for the hotel maid to have seen from an overhead window whom New York state senator James J. Pierce was embracing, but the maid remained certain because she had dumped a pitcher of cold water on the couple and then seen Caroline enter the hotel in wet clothes. To little avail, Caroline tried to explain that she kept company with the English actor Kyrle Bellew in New York because he was giving her acting lessons. Most salacious were the details concerning the visits of the physician Dr. James Gilbert to Caroline's New York hotel room. A witness in the room next door testified to hearing first the sounds of rustling dresses and kisses, then the doctor's request for some water, then "a noise that might ordinarily accompany the working of a bulb syringe," and, finally, Caroline's parting query as to whether he had enjoyed himself as well with her as with the other ladies. Dr. Gilbert took the stand to say he was treating Caroline for a vaginal infection.[12] This account caused a sensation because the overt sexual implications of the doctor's visit violated the medical camouflage under which women of Caroline's social status regularly sought treatment, often in the form of hydrotherapy, for purported vaginal maladies and a host of hysterical symptoms.

If these countercharges were not damning enough, Leslie's attorneys undercut Caroline's allegations of spousal abuse by producing letters she had written to her husband during their marriage expressing continuing love and begging his forgiveness for her transgressions. The press reported that in one letter she asserted, "Satan gets into me and makes me so abominable."[13] The jury of twelve men acquitted her husband of all the charges against him, branded Caroline an adulteress, and awarded sole custody of their son to Leslie.[14]

By the end of the trial, she was a certifiably fallen woman—emotionally, sexually, and economically. Her status mobilized cultural assumptions that a shamed woman in her position, deprived of financial resources and without many marketable skills, would resort to prostitution.[15] Kyrle Bellew had told her she had acting talent, and the press had highlighted her highly emotional, apparently volatile, histrionic nature displayed at the trial. Acting was still a suspect profession but one gaining respectability with the theatre's taming by heroic impresarios such as Augustin Daly and the establishment of the first formal institution for actor training in the United States, the New York School for Acting. When Caroline received a letter from a friend, Marie Nevins, who spoke of having taken lessons from the school's most effective teacher of actresses, David Belasco, she determined to seek him out and implore him to train her for the stage.[16] Securing backing from an old friend of her father's, the pork-packing tycoon N. K. Fairbank, she moved to New York with her mother, fully aware that whatever the truth of her husband's charges against her in court, she had to climb back up a steep and slippery slope to regain her reputation and her son. She would prove more than willing to play the repentant spendthrift whore on and off the stage in order to do that.

In addition to providing financial support, Fairbank went to New York, met with E. D. Gillmore, the owner and manager of the old Academy of Music, and arranged to have him introduce Caroline to Belasco. Her recorded impressions of that initial meeting elaborately link his appearance of "racial" Otherness to his pedagogical effectiveness in the art of acting:

> One has often been in a crowd and the eye has been trapped by a face with a subtle kind of distinction that made it uncommon—some indefinable air, hard to explain. Mr. Belasco's was like that. I immediately became interested in him.
>
> Here was not one man but a hundred men. Judea was here in the sensuous curving lips. Rome was here in the tightly curled hair of a proconsul. Greece was here in the beautifully cut, clearly silhouetted profile, with the soft ivory pallor one finds in the faces of Orientals. The Florentine of Italy, too, was in the inset of the whole mouth, restrained and a little cruel. He

was dramatic in himself as his plays were dramatic, surprising and vivid. He was like a coin—not the coinage for an ordinary populace, but some delicately carved medal struck off for a special occasion.

His very way of dressing—as if in the absorption of some achievement of his own, he was completely unaware of fashion—engrossed me. An iron resolve formed in my mind. It was this: If this man would not teach me, no one else should.

When he asked her if she had a play she wanted him to write, she famously responded: "Nothing in particular; only I am a superb horsewoman and I should like to make my entrance on horseback, jumping a high fence."[17] Much bemused, Belasco put her off by saying he would call her for a lesson as soon as his busy schedule permitted. Along with teaching acting at the school, he was stage managing for Daniel Frohman and collaborating on a play with Henry de Mille.

After several weeks elapsed without word from Belasco, Caroline tracked him down at a remote cottage on Echo Lake in New Jersey, where he was hiding out with de Mille trying to finish the play. Finally gaining an entrance, she writes of how she was compelled to offer up a full confession:

I dropped into a chair . . . and began to cry softly and steadily, and he took his seat in the chair opposite me.

Then to this strange man, whom I had met only once before in my life, I told everything.

I kept nothing back—the eager young years, the bitter intense years, the big elemental things that touched you just to read you, the little uneventful things, all woven into a web at once tremendous and tragic that by the old, foolish social tests always failed you. He should know it all. He should hear once and forever everything—the lies, the truth.

"O Lord, give to this man an understanding heart," I prayed, never knowing then that this was his chief portion in the dower of genius God had already given him. . . .

I raised my face and thus I ended: "If being hurt by people can *make* me act, I can act."

He leaned forward and very simply took his handkerchief and wiped from my wet cheeks the black that had come off my eyes. Physically I moved to my feet; spiritually I was stiller than I had ever been in all my life.

"I am just beginning to think you can," he answered, rising and looking at me with great intentness.[18]

Belasco recorded the encounter from his perspective:

> She fairly overwhelmed me with tears and entreaties. I did the best I could to make plausible excuses, explaining that the play Mr. de Mille and I were writing for the Lyceum Theatre Company required all my time. There she sat, with eyes fixed upon me which expressed more than her torrents of words. As she begged my assistance her voice and face grew eloquent, and when she began to tell of her domestic troubles her manner became almost tragic. Nothing about her was beautiful or even pretty, but the radiance of her features, the eloquence of her soul, and the magnetism of her highly keyed, temperamental nature convinced me she would go far, if only her natural abilities could be developed and controlled.[19]

Hearing her confession, Belasco beheld a woman who could be to him what Mary Magdalene was to Christ and what the repentant whores of Virginia City were to the little preacher. Here was a woman who had sinned but now fiercely sought redemption by means of his artful manipulation of the very incontinent passions that had ruined her. In his "racial" Otherness, Caroline found a capacity for understanding and stirring her extreme emotions, which could help her attain her professional and deeply personal goals. She wrote: "With all Mr. Belasco's fineness and ideals, he was racially and fundamentally a Jew, with all the Jew's harboring of hatred. He was as unforgiving as any of the patriarchs of the Old Testament but had the same utmost capacity to swing as quickly to a great nobleness."[20] She believed he would fight for her and that the Jew's stereotypical penchant for vengefulness would serve her agenda. If Leslie had vowed never "to speak or listen to the mention of her name again," she resolved:

> I am going to be known to the world. Electric lights over the theatre lobbies will carry the name of Leslie Carter in five foot letters. I hate the name; consequently, I will bear it to the end. Newspapers shall spread it forth, the streets shall hum with it! Mrs. Leslie Carter! It shall be borne upon him by the printed word and the spoken word. He cannot escape. It shall hound him until his last day![21]

With Belasco's assistance, she aimed to have her revenge against her ex-husband, the all-male jury that convicted her, and the high society that ostracized her. Even more passionately, she sought to reclaim her son. Before leaving Echo Lake, she secured Belasco's promise in writing to contact her for her first lesson immediately upon his return to New York and took his gold watch to keep "as evidence of his good faith."[22]

Redemptive Instruction

To make Mrs. Leslie Carter into a star, the exotic Jewish tutor and the spectacularly lapsed convent girl assumed roles in a stock religiocultural metadrama through which they could prove both her redemptability and his priestly impresarial potency in effecting it. The whore's body became the primary redemptive site, and actress training the primary means of salvation. In his treatise, "About Acting," Belasco declared that he used "precisely the same methods of instruction" employed at the New York School for Acting to teach Mrs. Carter, only he took her on as a private pupil and presided over her training in the whole curriculum.[23] Because of Mrs. Carter's background, the task mandated greater stringency. Belasco's middle-class female pupils at the school, many of them mature and married, had not fallen from respectability. Their relationship to their emotions was constructed as passive. Supposedly, such women lacked the individual will to express rather than contain the passions that built up once their womb—still, at base, construed as Plato's "animal inside an animal"—was loosed from its moorings through conjugal relations. The presumption was that they needed a male acting teacher to make them "feel"—that is, embody extraordinary emotion—in the same way they needed a male gynecologist to help them attain relief by mechanical inducement of the "hysterical paroxysm."[24] Rather than lie there and be choked by the buildup of hysterical symptoms or seek proper relief in a supposedly chaste clinical setting, Mrs. Carter had exhibited shocking willfulness in endeavoring to express them herself through overspending, adultery, and disturbingly skilled and venturesome feats of horsemanship.[25]

Accordingly, to effect her salvation, Belasco needed not only to show that he could provoke expression of her passions but that he could overpower her will, and possibly that of Satan, who she claimed possessed her, in the process. The religiocultural narrative within which they were operating mandated a program of extreme rigor, including purgation to the level of exorcism and fierce training to gain control over her physical and emotional capacities. That rigor gained further sanction in a dawning Progressive Era increasingly preoccupied with policing sexuality through a variety of medical discourses, social reforms, and antivice campaigns, especially against prostitution.[26] Thus, intimate engagement with the whore's transgressive body and passions could justifiably be undertaken within a purifying ethos of harsh discipline and hard labor. As Mrs. Carter noted in describing "What My Career Means to Me," "It meant work, work, always work, and then more work, until by sheer force of circumstance, I came to learn that in any career, whether onstage or not, the greatest joy in life is to be found in work. That is the crown of life."[27] The Jewish priest and his lapsed Gentile protégée pursued upward mobility by touting slavish devotion to the Protestant work ethic.

Belasco began the process of gaining control over Mrs. Carter's expressive mechanisms in July 1889 by placing her on an intense program of physical culture involving a prescribed diet and exercise initially administered under a doctor's supervision. In her trainer's estimation she had lost too much weight and suffered nervous exhaustion from the stress of the divorce trial and needed to regain her stamina in order to endure the rigors of star making. During this early phase of physical restoration, Belasco, foreshadowing Shaw's *Pygmalion*, set about ridding Mrs. Carter of her stigmatized regional accent—in this case, southern—and other distracting mannerisms:

> I arranged a carefully laid-out plan of vocal instruction and gradually her breathing, enunciation, and the placing of her voice were corrected and improved. I had observed that she was a very nervous woman, given to too much facial expression, so I kept her at physical exercises until this dangerous fault was overcome. . . . When, finally, she began to get her voice under control I set her to work memorizing short poems and simple one-act plays, such as "The Happy Pair" and "The Conjugal Lesson."[28]

Along with exercises in vocal control, Belasco devised exercises for increasing her vocal capacity: "To begin with I had her inflate her lungs and hold her breath until she was not only red but blue in the face; then with filled lungs to pronounce the vowels softly, holding the tone as long as possible; then increasing from a low tone to a roar like a bull." He had her do this "in at least a thousand different ways—lying prone on the floor, running, jumping, in laughter and in tears." Then came what Belasco called the "wear and tear" exercise "to get the vocal chords strengthened so that they can stand the harsh tone and deep whispers without rasping the voice." He reported that "during the first week's practice she never finished a lesson without coughing blood."[29]

Belasco administered these lessons with Mrs. Carter intermittently throughout the day and after hours, as he had a regular job as stage manager of the Lyceum Theatre and was teaching classes at the New York School for

Acting. They worked mainly in the apartment she shared with her mother and in rented studio space. In his absence, she completed assignments and practiced on her own. By winter, she reportedly was fit enough to sustain twelve-hour work days. She described her schedule to an interviewer:

> I study all day and nearly all evening, from 9 in the morning until 9 at night, in various ways. First, there are the exercises which Mr. Belasco gives me, which are a sort of calisthenics, but not exactly the Delsarte System. They are to make the body pliable and willowy and to strengthen the muscles. It is wonderful what you can learn to do—almost make a contortionist of yourself and tie your body up in knots. It makes you lame at first, like horseback riding but you get over that after a little and learn to do something more every day toward being graceful. There are the kneeling and rising and falling and all that look so easy, but are anything but easy to do. I tried it the other day, the kneeling, I mean, and went down with a bang. Mr. Belasco told me to do that just once on stage and die. I practice the exercise two hours and a half every day. Then there are the fencing and dancing as well every day.[30]

The daytime regime of exercises was followed by a nighttime regime of studying parts from the established repertoire. Belasco chose these, he asserted, in order to suit Mrs. Carter's temperament. While this, like voice, speech, and movement work, has become a common technique of acting training, what is notable here are the micromanagerial extremes to which Belasco took these practices and the personal stakes he had invested in arousing in order to demonstrate mastery over the particular wayward feminine aspects Mrs. Carter embodied. He writes: "I commenced to lead her into the art of impersonation by drilling her in selected scenes from standard plays. I knew she was an enthusiastic horsewoman, so I gave her the speech in which Lady Gay Spanker describes the race in 'London Assurance,' which proved useful because it required rapid enunciation under stress of enthusiasm."[31] Within Belasco's pornophilic frame of reference, the figure of the equestrienne connoted a sexual dominatrix in need of taming. So did the name "Lady Gay Spanker," with "gay" then being a term for loose woman. Mrs. Carter expressed great enthusiasm for the role: "It was full of England, of color and action, of hunting fields, of hounds in full cry, and was good for two minutes of sustained applause from any audience from Dan to Beershaba. Lady Gay's speech was the perfection of craft in playwriting. It began on an even tone, then mounted, and ended in one fine, rounded, prolonged note of smashing climax."[32] The pupil thrilled to rise to the challenge, while the instructor got to orchestrate the build.

"To develop her in the formal mood of classical comedy," Belasco continues, "I had her learn and act whole scenes from 'She Stoops to Conquer,'" the randy, Restoration-inspired eighteenth-century classic by Oliver Goldsmith.[33] The plot turns on male suitors' confusion of a private home with an inn, which causes them to approach the heroine, Miss Hardcastle, not as a proper young lady but as a common bawd. Enacting scenes ensuing from this situation gave Belasco ample opportunity to provoke and direct the kind of playful, coquettish nature that Mrs. Carter had been accused of using to lure her paramours.

But even more indicative of her ultimate métier were the early emotional roles he assigned her: "to teach her to control her emotional ability, which she possessed from the first, I drilled her over and over again in the tearful parting scene between Father Duval and Marguerite in 'Camille.'"[34] Mrs. Carter's experience coughing blood no doubt helped her identify physically with the tubercular courtesan. The role resonated thematically for her as well, since *Camille* is arguably the signal drama of redemptive whoredom in the Western canon. In this gut-wrenching scene of self-sacrifice prompted by true love, the courtesan Marguerite promises her lover's father that she will cut off her romance with his son so that he might be restored to respectable society. The role, which presented the double threat of woman's physical and moral degeneracy, had a history of performance by unruly female stars. A review in the *New York Herald* had likened the greatest American Camille, that of Matilda Heron, to "a high-pressure first-class Western steamboat with all her fires up, extra weighs on the safety valve, and not less than forty pounds of steam to the square inch. The effect is fine but the danger of explosion is imminent."[35] Her almost as famous successor, Clara Morris, who played the part with similarly volatile emotional pyrotechnics and even more graphic mimicry of tubercular symptoms, did so after breaking her contract in rebellion against the authoritarian management of Augustin Daly. For Belasco, drilling Mrs. Carter in this role was a significant step in reaching historically higher degrees of female provocation and containment.

Tutor and pupil advanced to yet more torrid roles that resonated still more pointedly with stigmas each carried into their relationship and sought to overcome. Belasco writes: "To stimulate her vivacity Mrs. Carter learned from end to end the rôle of Cyprienne in Sardou's 'Divorçons,' and to cultivate the tremendous outbursts of passion which, as her development progressed, I became more and more convinced were eventually to become her forte as an actress, I drilled her in the violent curse scene from 'Leah, the Forsaken,'" the Jewess whose Gentile lover rejects her to marry a Gentile woman.[36] In these sessions, Belasco would often play opposite Mrs. Carter in the scene. *Leah* gave him the opportunity to take the part of the Gentile hero and curse the feminized Jewishness embodied in the heroine who threatened to ruin him.

This course of tutelage went on for six months before Belasco decided his pupil was ready for a more public venue. According to Mrs. Carter's recollection, Belasco introduced her to the new task as one might a green horse: "One late afternoon, he brought me over to the old Star Theatre, and ran me up and down the stage—just for the feeling of it. It was the first time in my life I had ever been on a real stage—it neither awed me nor interested me. In fact, my only sensation was that it was time for me to act."[37] Belasco arranged with proprietor Daniel Frohman that he would do some extra work in exchange for time on the Lyceum stage to rehearse Mrs. Carter when the Lyceum Stock Company was not using it. Within a few weeks, however, Frohman notified Belasco on behalf of the stockholders that Mrs. Carter was no longer welcome there; evidently, her scandalous reputation had offended the company's leading lady. Indicative of his identification with his protégée, Belasco took personal offence, replying curtly to Frohman: "rest assured I shall not forget their petty treatment of me."[38] He found alternate space at Palmer's Theatre to rehearse Mrs. Carter and in March of 1890 resigned his position as stage manager of the Lyceum, ending his association with both its theatre and acting school.

Because Belasco was struggling to cobble together a living and was obligated to fulfill other playwriting commissions, he relied on other authors to supply the first two vehicles in which Mrs. Carter played before a paying audience. As a result, neither proved an entirely advantageous fit for her. Both were in the vein of comedy, which, it became increasingly clear, was not Mrs. Carter's forte. However, each played upon aspects for which Mrs. Carter had been socially denigrated and thus appealed to her for the opportunity to turn these to professional advantage. For her debut, Belasco had Paul M. Potter (who would later adapt *Trilby* for the stage) script *The Ugly Duckling* based upon a Hans Christian Andersen fairy tale. Well aware of her deficiencies relative to dominant standards of female beauty, Mrs. Carter willingly took on the role whose very title underscored the arduous journey on which she had embarked to become an actress: "I was too tall, my hair was the wrong color, my gestures were wrong, my voice was not adequate. Instead of discouraging me, these facts of my limitations only nerved me with greater courage to overcome the obstacles."[39]

Before showtime on opening night in November in New York City, Belasco delightedly beckoned Mrs. Carter to peer through a hole in the curtain to behold the "brilliant audience" assembled to see her. She writes in her autobiography that "society turned out *en masse*. William C. Whitney, Flora Payne Whitney, and their friends occupied a lower box; De Lancey Nicoll, his wife, and Frederick Townsend Martin, with other friends, were in the opposite box."[40] However, *The Ugly Duckling* lasted only sixteen performances and then toured across the country, drawing crowds who were mainly curious to see what Belasco had made of his notorious protégée. The papers exaggerated Mrs. Carter's wicked past for sensational effect. The *San Francisco Examiner*, for example, wrote: "It will be remembered that Mrs. Carter is the heroine of a Chicago divorce suit in which it was proved that she had intimate relations with nearly everybody in that great and growing city, which is said to raise more hay than any other great aggregation of houses in this United States.... Her Chicago experience will no doubt prove a great help to her."[41] In spite of such coverage, the production lost money everywhere but Chicago, where curiosity was greatest among Mrs. Carter's former social set. *The Ugly Duckling* closed in March 1891 in Kansas City because her backer, N. K. Fairbank, on whose credit Belasco had arranged the tour, grew increasingly uneasy about the financial picture and the scandalous press and withdrew his support after investing more than $40,000 (about $860,000 today).[42]

Nevertheless, Belasco found the resources to set sail with Mrs. Carter, her mother, and maid Suzanne for Paris in April to see whether a French musical farce, *Miss Helyett*, might be adapted for their next vehicle. Belasco had heard about the play from Daniel Frohman's brother, Charles, with whom he was then still friendly and who offered to purchase the American rights. They liked the play and remained in Paris for a month for additional theatregoing and sight-seeing. The American press reported that Belasco and Mrs. Carter had secretly eloped, although the alleged bride was conspicuously chaperoned by her mother and maid and the groom was still married and the father of two daughters.[43] This reportage reflected the easy suspicion that Belasco's interest in Mrs. Carter was sexual as well as professional and artistic. The play humorously echoed her reputed appeal to her tutor while compelling further development of her voice. An artist hero seeks to make the eponymous Miss Helyett a model after he rescues her from a fall off a precipice that left her hanging bottom up over a fortuitously protruding tree branch. Opening in New York in November 1891, *Miss Helyett* held the boards for one hundred performances and then toured until the end of the 1891–1892 season. The show provided Mrs. Carter with a steady income of $40 per week (about $860 today).[44]

A report in the *New York Dramatic Mirror* entitled "Mrs. Carter Runs the Show" commented on the backstage dynamics between impresario and star and implied Belasco's task in training Mrs. Carter was far from complete. The report was based on an interview with Laura Bellini, a disgruntled supporting actress. She resigned from the company because she refused to accept cuts Belasco made in her part allegedly at the behest of Mrs. Carter, who feared she would steal the limelight. "There are wheels within wheels in the production of Miss Helyett," the article asserts. "Inside the ring Messrs. Belasco and [business manager] E. D. Price rush wildly around with an eye on Mrs. Leslie Carter and the others in a daze. In the centre stands Mrs. Carter, with a whip-hand over all. It is a gay spectacle. Turned inside out it is also comic." Servitude to the dominatrix was taking its toll, according to the embittered Bellini: "It is really pitiable . . . to see Mr. Belasco bandied about between Mrs. Carter and Mrs. Carter's mother. He seems to be growing thinner every day, and actually seems to have lost all his individuality. He serves all the purposes of a lackey for the Carters, and it is sad to see a man who certainly has ability as a playwright in such a position. Funny, isn't it?"[45] Whatever the truth of Bellini's claims and whatever pains and delights the parties may have taken in Mrs. Carter's figurative backstage whip-cracking and onstage obtrusions of her wayward posterior, it was clear to all that she still had far to go before becoming a star of the first magnitude.

After delivering on a promise to write a play for the opening of Charles Frohman's newly erected Empire Theatre,[46] Belasco decided to devote his efforts exclusively to the development of Mrs. Carter. He determined to write her a vehicle that would bring out her greater talents and over which he would own the rights. There followed a three-year period of economic sacrifice in order to go back into training mode and start over with renewed urgency until, as Belasco put it, "the foundation of her splendid equipment as an emotional star had been laid."[47] His recollections of this period reveal the extent to which his aspirations for success and independence were bound up in making this actress:

> Mrs. Carter was the pivot about which my new plans revolved. I was almost without funds; Mrs. Carter was raw material in the making, and my task was gigantic. She was fiercely determined; I was desperate.

Not for her the long novitiate, therefore. She must begin at the top or not at all. To this end I drove her tremendously, treating her as though she were the leading woman in a stock company, the one person who must play certain parts. She was difficult to handle, tears and occasional revolts marking her progress. But in fourteen months she memorized and rehearsed more than thirty heavy roles, each new experience bringing her some added power of expression both of tone and feature.[48]

To survive the months without regular income, Belasco, Mrs. Carter writes, "sold everything he could lay his hands on: the books he had accumulated—they were rare and they were many—his few antiques, all went. We were now dining off the very last of his historical volumes." Among the books sold may have been some of his rare pornographic volumes; books that had given him forbidden knowledge of women's purported nature and functioning now impacted his career in another practical, if more mundane, way.[49] Also willing to sacrifice, Mrs. Carter and her mother moved into cheaper accommodations and sold many of their possessions. The actress expressed aspirations that complemented those of her maker when the two splurged on a meal at Delmonico's, where they saw Augustin Daly and Ada Rehan dining at another table: "I looked at Mr. Daly and Miss Rehan, and whispered to 'Mr. Dave,' 'Shall we ever get there and be, like them, successful and accepted?' To which [he] confidently answered, 'Of course we shall.'"[50]

Mrs. Carter described the training process to which she dedicated herself:

> Belasco began by saying to me: "You have chosen a vocation to which you must give your body, your blood, and your bones. You must strip yourself to the foundations and become emotionally bare; then you will have to begin to build according to the best traditions. But be very careful you do not walk in a groove. A groove is a path made by the wheels of others."
>
> We engaged a small stage in a little hall on Sixth Avenue, and there for four, five, sometimes six hours at a stretch, he demanded of me one thing which I gave him with a single heart—work, work, and then more work. Every play was gone over with him—parts that allowed for expression, such as *Marco* in the Marble Heart; parts that allowed for diction, such as Shakespeare's plays; for the voice, such as *Julia* in the Hunchback; and parts of dramatic abandon, such as *Frou-Frou, Odette,* and *Adrienne Lecouvreur.*[51]

While Belasco used some comedies to inculcate versatility and technique, the major strength he sought to develop in his actress was in parts calling for extensive emotional expression. When he introduced Mrs. Carter to a new role, he would have her first work on it herself to see what she would give him on her own. "He read the other parts and I rehearsed my role. Nine times out of ten I was all wrong at my first trial. 'Not a bit like it,' Mr. Belasco would say, and then, in his corrections made upon my practical study, I learned my valuable lesson."[52] He would "drill" her to remake her interpretation and take control of her emotional expression: "Any criticism from him was like a blow that whipped the will into making a greater effort. Sometimes, thinking a loudly pitched voice would better express all my bottled emotions, I would shout. Then he would say: 'You are like a new, unplastered house where there are no draperies to deceive. Don't give so much of yourself—keep a little in reserve.'"[53]

To intensify the level of feeling she could bring to a particular role, Belasco would surprise Mrs. Carter with sudden injunctions to improvise. He told her: "You have just discovered you are in love. . . . The business in your part has been omitted intentionally at this point. Supply it yourself—now!"[54] In another interview, she describes how he used intimate knowledge gleaned from their personal relationship to provoke her:

> I lived with my dear mother, the bond between us was very close, and no one knew this better than my tutor, yet a certain day that Mr. Belasco came to our little apartment is indelibly impressed upon my memory as an example of his stringent yet wonderful manner of teaching a lesson.
>
> He sat down for a moment or two, looked at me gravely and silently. I was beginning to feel nervous when suddenly he said, "Suppose I told you your mother was dead, how would you act?"[55]

Belasco described the intensity of his efforts: "I feel as if I were using a surgeon's knife. I probe and probe and probe, and finally I find what I was looking for, what the person herself may have had no knowledge of."[56] Mrs. Carter viewed both Belasco's methods and her endurance of them as "heroic measures" necessary for the attainment of their mutual goals. Looking back on these sessions, she wrote:

> It takes not only heroic health, but a soul nerved to heroic tests. The master can but heat the metal in the crucible. Time alone will prove whether it be pure or base. A teacher of the drama, Mr. Belasco, for instance, has given his marvelous methods to many; how few of the many have had the courage to serve the necessary apprenticeship to realize his ideals, to present the idea as he has seen it in the marble ere he commenced to chisel![57]

Along with these one-on-one tutorial sessions, Belasco assembled a group of supporting actors solely for the purpose of rehearsing Mrs. Carter in a designated repertoire of plays. "The practice was what she needed—practice—practice—practice—to work the stiffness out of her, to teach her to shift from one emotion to another—high comedy, low comedy, melodrama."[58] Mrs. Carter reports: "He would say, 'In a week we are to put on Camille, I shall expect you to be letter perfect on Monday night and to rehearse every day until then.' The rehearsals took place, the minor parts being filled by actors only too glad of the opportunity to be coached by a master's hand. In this way I became a qualified stock leading lady, ready to play on a day's notice any of the standard leads."[59] In his reminiscences, Belasco's secretary, Thomas Curry, aptly analogized Mrs. Carter's process to that of an opera singer learning to sing the masterpieces.[60] The aim was to achieve the same finely calibrated level of control over the physical mechanisms of expression in spoken drama as is required of a singer to perform the most demanding aria. Indeed, an image endures in the biographical film, *The Lady with Red Hair* (1940), of Belasco actually using a piano and striking keys to define the emotional pitch he wanted her to reach in a particular scene.[61] Mrs. Carter reports with pride how she won praise from her teacher in meeting the arduous demands of mastering the repertoire by these means: "Mr. Dave was a wonderful man to work with. And my tirelessness and ability to work appealed to him. He often said that I was the only person he had ever seen who could outwork him. (You know he too is tireless.) I loved it all. I had wanted to work, forget and live again."[62] Her desired redemption and rebirth would come with the breakthrough success she shared with Belasco in *The Heart of Maryland*.

Saved by the Bell

It was amid the intensity of remaking Mrs. Carter as an emotional actress that Belasco created his first original vehicle for her. The process he developed to create *The Heart of Maryland* became paradigmatic for creating original star vehicles throughout his career. It involved exteriorizing his own feminine emotions, beginning with the climactic scene, transferring them to the actress, and mastering them by directing her in the lead role. The overall aim, charged with evolutionary implications, as one Belasco interviewer aptly summarized it, was the "lifting of the primitive emotions toward joy and happiness."[63]

The personal emotions Belasco invested in the project are evident from the story he often repeated about his inspiration to write the play. He drew upon childhood memories of his Jewish mother, whom he credited with encouraging his theatrical "gypsy" spirit, reading to him the poem by Rose Hartwick Thorpe, "Curfew Must Not Ring Tonight."[64] Set during the English Civil War of the seventeenth century, the poem begins with the heroine Bessie expressing fear of her imprisoned lover's impending doom. He is a nobleman sentenced to die at the stroke of the curfew bell that night for spying against the Puritan regime. Thorpe's verses dwell on the impact on Bessie's body of the terror of her lover's execution and the daunting task before her of trying to stop it. Emotion is written on her flesh, as trembling with fear, she rushes past the old sexton and scales the slimy ladder up the high bell tower to muffle the sound of the clapper:

> She has reached the topmost ladder; o'er her hangs the great dark bell;
> Awful is the gloom beneath her, like the pathway down to hell.
> See, the ponderous tongue is swinging! 'tis the hour of curfew now!
> And the sight has chilled her bosom, stopped her breath and paled her
>   brow.
> Shall she let it ring? No, never! Her eyes flash with sudden light,
> As she springs and grasps it firmly: "Curfew *shall not* ring to-night!"[65]

Bessie gains a reprieve from Cromwell himself when she turns her hands, bruised and bleeding from being smashed between the clapper and the insides of the bell to stop the sound, toward him to plead for mercy. This sign of expiation of her transgressive—and, by implication, more Catholic-leaning—passion "Touched his heart with sudden pity, lit his eyes with misty light. / 'Go! Your lover lives,' cried Cromwell. 'Curfew shall not ring to-night!'"[66] Belasco recalled listening to the poem: "'Can't you see her, Davey?' my mother would say, and I, closing my eyes as I have always done in order that I might the better concentrate, would answer, 'Yes, Mother, I see her. She is young and slim and tall, and she wears a white dress. And I can see her arms straining.'"[67] Widely reprinted in elocution manuals, the poem was chiefly popular among girls for recitation, but Belasco, identifying with the passionate female, made it part of his own repertoire in grammar school.[68] Thus, he writes, "The picture of that swaying young figure hanging hero-ically to the clapper of an old church bell lived in my memory for a quarter of a century. When the time came that I needed a play to exploit the love and heroism of a woman I wrote a play around that picture. It furnished me the idea for 'The Heart of Maryland.'"[69]

The heroine's emotions that Belasco himself had embodied as a young actor he projected onto Mrs. Carter in writing the play. Hers was the heart of the title, which Belasco conceived of both viscerally, as in the heart of the dissected prostitute he had held in his hand at the San Francisco medical college, and metaphorically, as a stringed instrument best played by a master. Recalling how that disembodied heart contained the secrets of the fallen woman's tragic life story, he wrote: "As the violin is an instrument for the musician, so the human heart is an instrument for the artist."[70] Mrs. Carter's heart became both surrogate and sounding board for his own, as he tuned the instrument while writing the play in a studio in her apartment and on a retreat they took in Maryland, where the action is set.[71] The actress described the process in her memoir:

> In a little town called Oakland I became drenched with the spirit of the South. The provincial, slowmoving, lovely old hotel was its very essence. I slept with Maryland Calvert, ate with her, lived with her, breathed with her.
>
> Mr. Dave joined us there. Day by day he grappled with his closely woven structure of language. Hour by hour I listened eagerly to it, first in one form, then in another. It was exactly as if a piano tuner, with a tuning fork, were striking chords, and when they came back in the form of a wrong note, he would begin all over again.
>
> I shared in the plays he wrote for me to this extent: I reacted to his material like the echo of an Aeolian harp. If a thing struck me wrong, he would never touch it. He had faith in my instincts, just as I had faith, wholehearted, unending, in what he told me.[72]

Belasco conceived the range and texture of emotions to be played on and through the "Aeolian harp" of Mrs. Carter as Catholic. Setting the play in Maryland, he not only transposed the action of Thorpe's poem from the English to the American Civil War, but he also extended the religious history and dynamics of the story. The heroine's name, Maryland Calvert, refers to the state's founder, Cecil Calvert, Lord Baltimore, who named the land in honor of Queen Mary, wife of Charles I, as a gesture of gratitude for the charter the king granted him in 1632 to establish a haven to which Roman Catholics could escape English religious restrictions.[73] To Belasco, the name also connoted that of an earlier British queen, Mary, Queen of Scots, who was herself Roman Catholic. From his youthful forays into library and bookshop stacks, this Mary had been a favorite "wayward woman" of history, relished for the demise, ultimately at the hands of Elizabeth I, Protestant ruler par excellence, that historians attributed to her too passionate, sexually appetitive nature.[74]

Like Mary, Queen of Scots, and, of course, Mary Magdalene, Maryland Calvert "loves too much"—that is, transgressively relative to cultural mores. Echoing Mrs. Carter's personal history, Maryland hails from a prominent, plantation-owning Confederate family. In spite of her allegiances, she falls desperately in love with Yankee colonel Alan Kendrick. But this same runaway passion that causes her to betray her family is also what carries her up the belltower to save Kendrick by making her heroic leap for the clapper in the climactic scene. Where Thorpe's Bessie only has to get past a benign old sexton to enter the tower, Belasco's Maryland has to overcome an attempted rape by the villainous soldier standing guard. "With a cry of disgust, horror, and rage," she wrenches a bayonet from where it had been driven into a wooden tabletop to serve as a candlestick and stabs him repeatedly in the chest shouting "You Devil!" before commencing her feverish ascent.[75] "The lifting of the primitive passions toward joy and happiness" is achieved at the end when, as the sun rises to the soft strains of "Maryland, My Maryland," the rescued hero takes her tenderly in his arms. Playing the heart of Maryland, Belasco exceeded even Thorpe's melodrama to turn Catholicized feminine emotion into a force of redemption fueling Northern victory and, by extension, the growth of American nationhood.

In spite of the play's winning message, Belasco had considerable difficulty securing a production. A number of producers eschewed the project because of Mrs. Carter's still questionable acting credentials and scandalous reputation, which the naughty *Miss Helyett* had done little to change. His longtime friend and associate, Charles Frohman, who had helped him acquire *Miss Helyett*, said he would produce *The Heart of Maryland*, but not with Mrs. Carter in the lead role, a stipulation Belasco found unacceptable and offensive. Belasco also believed the Frohmans—Charles and Daniel—would not back him and his leading lady because they feared that a hit in which he had the controlling interest might make him their rival instead of their employee.[76] To Mrs. Carter, his willingness to sacrifice an opportunity and stick by her was a manifestation of the "great nobleness" that she attributed to his more primal "Oriental" Jewishness, as opposed to the more assimilated German Jewishness of the Frohmans.[77] Desperate, Belasco finally managed to convince the three lessees of the Herald Square Theatre, "Charlie" Evans, F. C. Whitney, and Max Blieman, to back the venture.[78]

While all three lessees signed on initially, Whitney and Evans dropped out, leaving Blieman to shoulder the risk alone and cast about for a space. Unable to secure a booking in New York for this seemingly dubious, untried venture, Belasco decided to go to Washington and Baltimore for out-of-town tryouts where, at last, he did find accommodating stages. Blieman reportedly emptied his accounts to finance the premiere at D.C.'s Grand Opera House on 9 October 1895. Audiences enthusiastically affirmed the production's potential, but they were small in number because of financial panic in the capital city. Thus, proceeds barely covered salaries and expenses. Neither did the company turn a profit when they moved to Baltimore, where they found themselves stranded without funds to bring the production back to New York. Blieman, a dealer in "antiquaries" and "pictures" with a shady reputation, borrowed $1,500 on a $30,000 painting (or about $35,000 on a $695,000 painting today) to finance their return and the opening at the Herald Square.[79] Blieman obtained the $1,500 from Al Hayman, Charles Frohman's business partner, who, as Belasco's and Mrs. Carter's accounts imply, would not back the show himself but would make this lopsided loan. Mrs. Carter offered the following meditation on Blieman's extraordinary willingness to take risks to back the show:

> I should like to speak of Max Blieman, the most curious medley of human complexes wrapped up in a man potentially big, but just never able to measure up to it. Some hidden flare in his temperament made him react to everything in art, especially the drama. Some twisted quirk in his nature made him traffic in the marketing of unauthentic masterpieces of painting. Still, you felt that here behind this uncultured Russian Jew was a man who instinctively loved beauty.[80]

Whereas others had eschewed the venture, this Russian Jew, lower on the cultural hierarchy and supposedly more susceptible to art and corruptive desires, stuck by them. Belasco called Blieman "a boy after my own heart!"[81]

Belasco, Blieman, and Mrs. Carter's faith in the play to move audiences was vindicated with the famed New York opening on 22 October 1895. Mrs. Carter recalled the exhilaration of the audience's response: "After the second act there were twenty curtain calls, after the third act, thirty. When it finished with the ringing of the curfew with a woman's body used as a human tongue in the bell, it was the first time I was ever to see an audience flare like tinder to its emotions and pandemonium break loose. High on its tiptoes, it shouted, it clapped, it bravoed."[82] In his curtain speech, Belasco charted his long climb toward success in the profession for the cheering audience:

> This production tonight is the culmination of twenty-five years of work—of hard, hard work, and often bitter disappointment. I have been a supernumerary, a call boy, an actor, a stage manager for others, an adapter of plays—now I am encouraged to hope I have proved myself a dramatist. . . . It is many long years since I first dreamed of an independent success in New York—a success I might keep in my own hands. If this is the turning of the tide that leads on to fortune, I shall never forget my debt to you.[83]

Afterward, with the applause still ringing, he went to Mrs. Carter's dressing room exclaiming, "You hear that? Do you know what it means? It means that never—never—never again will we have to eat in a Third Avenue restaurant."[84] Indeed, it was the turning of the tide. The play ran for 229 consecutive performances in New York in 1895–1896, toured nationally for the next two seasons, and closed with a sensational engagement in London in June 1898, grossing close to a million dollars (about $23.4 million today).[85]

According to many testimonials, the primary reason for the play's success was Mrs. Carter's performance in the climactic bell tower scene, which one reviewer accurately described as "the excuse for the play's existence and its constructive starting point."[86] The sensational thrill derived chiefly from the audience's belief in the reality of her enactment and accompanying assumptions about the prowess of the man who made her do it. The visual impact of the staging and the discourse surrounding the production fueled these beliefs. Belasco's Act III stage directions call for a rapid change from scene ii to scene iii to mark the escalating emotion. Scene ii takes place in the villainous Colonel Thorpe's office in the old church vestibule from which the staircase leading up the tower is visible. After stabbing her would-be rapist with the bayonet (fig. 29), Maryland grabs a lantern and runs up the staircase. There is a blackout, and then, tracking her climb, the quick change to the belfry, a multistory, see-through structure. A ladder comes up from below the stage floor and extends upward inside the structure to the bell platform three stories high. Maryland enters climbing up the ladder from below the stage floor. The stage directions read:

> BLOUNT [officer serving the wounded Thorpe]: Ring—the bell! *[Maryland is seen as she climbs the ladder. She has a lighted lantern in her hand which she throws away when she reaches the second story of the belfry (from*

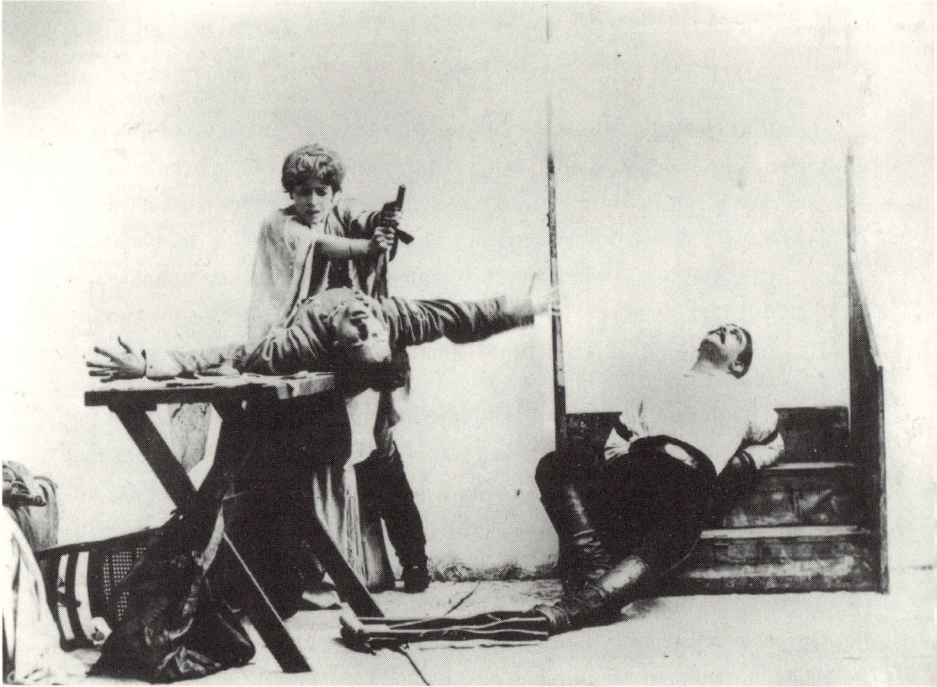

29. *Mrs. Leslie Carter as Maryland Calvert stabbing Colonel Thorpe (John E. Kellerd) in* The Heart of Maryland, *1896. Courtesy of the Byron Collection, Museum of the City of New York.*

stage). With exalted exclamation she rushes to the top story. As she is appearing through the top opening, Blount is heard shouting from below, angrily but faintly] Ring the bell! *[The ponderous tongue begins to move and strikes faintly the lip of the bell just as Maryland stands facing it]*
MARYLAND The bell shall not ring! *[Maryland leaps and clings with both hands to the tongue of the bell. The bell moves higher and higher; she is dragged backwards and forwards by the swing. Shouting, etc. keeps up until the curtain falls]*[87]

Commentators marveled at the sheer physical exigencies of what Craig Timberlake terms Mrs. Carter's "marathonian performance."[88] They wrote over and over of the extraordinary gymnastic ability required to fight off her attacker, stab him repeatedly, scale some seventy-five rungs of the ladder to a height of thirty-five feet above the stage, leap for the clapper, and swing high overhead, trailing her long, red tresses in the breeze (fig. 30).[89] Program copy for the show, most likely prepared by Belasco and his staff, called her "a veritable well

30. *Mrs. Leslie Carter swinging from the bell clapper at the climax of David Belasco's* The Heart of Maryland. *Published by Strowbridge Litho. Company, 1895. Courtesy of the Museum of the City of New York.*

of emotion" and highlighted her genetic affinity for the role: "A Kentuckian by birth, she has the soft, almost transparent skin and full-blooded blue veins to be found only among our women of the South." Mrs. Carter herself is quoted in the program declaring, "I do not play Maryland, I am Maryland!"[90] Audiences were inclined to believe her because they bore witness to her live performance of arduous and daring feats that caused real excitement and terror in the moment. The extreme physical demands of the part worked as a guarantor of the actress's emotional authenticity in playing it.

Other contemporary associations with the swinging action may have heightened many audience members' appreciation of the performance. Covering the Victorian period in his *History of Pornography*, H. Montgomery Hyde notes the "subtle insertion by artists of indecencies into their works" and cites Fragonard's famous painting, *The Swing* (c. 1766), as an example. A gentleman lolling on the grass is treated to a view up the skirts of his mistress arcing high on a swing overhead. Fragonard's canvas imported into a more aristocratic scene the dynamics of the circus and variety theatre, where the flying trapeze was a thrilling way to proffer athletic bodies to admiring spectators.[91] In a respectable milieu where the exposure of feet, ankles, and undergarments was considered scandalous, Mrs. Carter's in-the-flesh danglement thirty-five feet over the stage floor would have induced viewing pleasures similar to those Fragonard depicted. Hyde writes, "It is astonishing how much thinly veiled pornography the Victorians were able to 'get away with' by the exercise of a little ingenuity."[92] Well-versed in pornographic codes, Belasco was nothing if not ingenious. The belfry scene was a signal example of the "petticoat humor" that became a staple of his productions.[93]

Swinging enticed viewers by dangling not only Mrs. Carter's athletic body but also her long, glorious red hair, once aptly described as "one shade hotter than Titian."[94] When respectable women were expected to wear their hair pinned up as part of proper dress, the loosening of the locks suggested preparation for the boudoir. Public display of the fallen tresses telegraphed a loosening of conventional morality. Victorian melodramatic theatre used exigent circumstances to justify frequent appearances by leading ladies with their hair down. Mrs. Carter's appearance in the belfry scene followed almost to the letter key attributes of the long popular image of the damsel in distress. Moralists had expressed grave concern about the damsel's visual impact, especially on the young male spectator: "when the [leading lady] appears in some thrilling scene clad in a white robe, her hair flowing loosely in extravagant luxuriance down her back, her white arms bared to the shoulder, her neck and bosom by no means jealously guarded from the vulgar gaze, he loses his head in the enchantment of her presence, and carries away a mental impression of her which can do him no good and may do him much harm."[95] When the hair was red, the pornographic effect could be even more potent, like a red flag to a bull. Long-standing popular beliefs about redheaded women, as noted in an item preserved in the Mrs. Leslie Carter Clipping File in the New York Public Library, included their lack of moral character compared with that of blondes and brunettes, and even their lack of souls.[96] Another article in the same file reports that Mrs. Carter enhanced her natural endowment throughout her career with hair pieces and wigs:

> The Carter hair became a Broadway trademark and drove critics ga-ga as six feet of it flaunted while the actress swung from a belfry tower in the "Heart of Maryland." But it was made from locks of hair shorn off peasant girls in Austria-Hungary.
>
> For services rendered, Mrs. Carter paid to Hair Merchant Albert Simonsen $50,000 [about $1.16 million today].
>
> In sixteen years on Broadway with David Belasco she bought ten new sets of hair at $3,000 [almost $70,000 today] a time. She paid $20,000 [almost $463,000 today] for repairs.
>
> Only a very few knew it was false. Yet Mrs. Carter had to bring it in frequently for cleaning and re-weaving. "Broken hairs had to be replaced," Simonsen said.
>
> Altogether La Carter's hair weighed an even pound and contained four times the quantity of hair on an average woman's head. It was garnered from 300 peasant girls, who, in impoverished pre-war Europe, raised hair crops to trade for dowry funds.
>
> In Simonsen's workshop were remaining carrot-red strands, left from the last Carter order in 1925.[97]

Clearly Mrs. Carter, as well as Belasco, was heavily invested in making and keeping her spectacular hair a signature attraction of her performances.

Most significantly for starmaker and star's mutual aggrandizement, these erotic thrills were presented within a legitimating frame of institutional control over female emotion and sexuality. Many New York spectators may have made the link between the rigors of the belfry scene and the gymnastic methods that by 1895 had been employed at the New York School for Acting for over a decade to break down inhibiting stiffnesses and provoke "real feeling" in the bodies of white, middle-class female pupils. Knowledge of the school's curriculum had been disseminated in the press, and given the demographics of the clientele, some women in the audience may themselves have been pupils at the school. George M. Baker's *Seldarte* (1889), the one-act parody of the Delsarte System underpinning NYSA methods, featured the "Curfew Department," where the guru's lackey, Musty Knott, swung female pupils from a rope hanging from a makeshift bell. Since sharp parody cuts close to its source, it is possible that bell swinging inspired by the popular Thorpe poem was an actual exercise employed at the school. Whether or not swinging was part of the NYSA curriculum, the association between the activity and medical therapy to realign the hysteric's pelvis so she could express dangerously pent-up passions would have been familiar to Belasco and his audiences as it was to George M. Baker.[98] Accordingly, the production's titillations derived not only from petticoat views but also from a voyeuristic spectacle tied to techniques of acting training that echoed those of the gynecologic clinic. As administered in clinical and instructional or directorial contexts, swinging could involve more direct male control over the hysteric than alternate therapies such as rapid horseback riding. Directing Mrs. Carter in the belfry scene, Belasco showed that he could take control over—literally realign and thereby "correct"—the wayward pelvis of his infamously unruly equestrienne. Thus, his pornographic display could work to improve rather than worsen his leading lady's scandalous reputation and ultimately raise his own moral standing.

The redemptive possibilities of Belasco's staging were magnified in his audiences' imaginations by testimony he gave at a trial the summer following *The Heart of Maryland*'s opening season. The testimony came in a lawsuit Belasco had filed against Mrs. Carter's former backer, N. K. Fairbank, in November 1893 that took two and a half years to bring to trial. At the time of the original filing, Belasco and his protégée were still struggling for their breakthrough success and found Fairbank reneging on previously promised support. Mrs. Carter described Belasco's heroic efforts on her behalf: "He told Fairbank's attorney, Morrison: 'He is a welsher who refuses to pay his losses because the horse he picked didn't win. I am so sure of Mrs. Carter's ultimate success that I am willing, by any process you will arrange, to bind myself to a promise to pay everything back.'" Only when this magnanimous offer was refused, she claims, did Belasco press the suit.[99] In the case presented at trial, Belasco sought $65,000 (almost $1.5 million today) in compensation for his salary for the initial months of Mrs. Carter's training (July 1889–March 1891) and production costs of her debut vehicle, *The Ugly Duckling*.[100] To justify his request for such a large sum, Belasco had to show just how arduous had been the task of taking a stiffly mannered, "nervous" former socialite with no professional skills and turning her into a stage actress. He offered graphic testimony about how he gained control of her body through hours spent on teaching her to relearn simple physical tasks, such as entering and exiting a room, sitting down and standing up, turning pages of a book, opening a letter and carrying on dialogue at the same time. In addition, under his tutelage she learned boxing, wrestling, fencing, and dancing. While he conceded Fairbank paid for her supplementary instruction in music and jig dancing, he asserted: "I taught her to use her muscles and limbs—to be limber. I taught her to become the embodiment of the poetry of motion—a great nerve trial."[101]

Even more arduous was the effort required to inculcate proper expression of emotion. In a striking illustration of the mechanics of how he worked out his own emotions through his actress, Belasco described teaching her ways to weep: "I would weep myself for hours until I looked like a wet rag. I would tear and scratch myself. I taught her to weep for the different emotions in a different way. So many, nearly all of the actresses on the stage weep in one way—they only know one way to weep. I instructed her in thirty to forty roles." But it was Belasco's description of the exercise he devised for "drilling her in sudden transitions of emotion" that generated the most riveting and memorable testimony of the trial. He elaborated how they would rehearse together the horribly climactic scene from *Oliver Twist* where Bill Sykes beats his Nancy to death. Rising from his seat and pantomiming the action for the jury by grabbing an imaginary head, Belasco testified, "I dragged her around by the hair, just as Bill Sykes dragged Nancy. I would hit her head on the floor and haul her about until she had reached the proper pitch and could express just what she felt."[102] The major New York papers broadcast this testimony with headlines such as "Dragged Her by the Hair."[103] A quip made by a former champion pugilist in response to Belasco's widely publicized testimony quickly circulated as a joke: "I ain't good for anything now, I reckon, but training actresses."[104] The jury and audiences fixated on this moment in part because Dickens himself had primed the public imagination with his own famous enactments of the scene during readings of his novel. Along with Dickens's own readings, numerous play adaptations were available to inspire Belasco. With the spectacular image of Mrs. Carter's flowing locks in the belfry scene of *The Heart of Maryland* fresh in their minds, trial watchers could well imagine the ready handle those tresses provided for her fiercely driving Dickensian tutor. The court proceeding and accompanying media coverage also turned the red-hair flag of arousal into a tool of impresarial discipline.

The one signification symbiotically entwined with the other, indelibly emblematizing the Belasco method.

By today's standards, such training methods would no doubt raise questions of abuse. But far from drawing censure or criminal charges, Belasco prevailed in the lawsuit and managed to recoup $15,000 (almost $350,000 today) of his original claim. He might have won more had not Fairbank's attorney, Deming, forced Mrs. Carter to admit on the stand that Belasco had not raised her weekly salary in proportion to the increased earnings of her star vehicles. This enabled Deming to deliver a closing zinger containing the "racial" slur that Belasco was "jewing" his leading lady and now was trying to "jew" Mr. Fairbank: "There's the whole story. Belasco owns this woman at $50 a week [about $1,200 a week today] and farms her out at $200 or $300 a week [about $4,700 or $7,000 a week today] and puts the rest in his pocket. That's the interest he has in this woman, and that's what he trained her for."[105] However, other cultural discourses were at work in the 1890s to justify Belasco's training methods and the still-substantial settlement he received for his expenditures of time, effort, and money. Along with the Progressive Era's policing of female sexuality, those discourses included the prevailing understanding of hysteria and related feminine emotions as embodied; hence the need for physical treatment whose rigor had to match the perceived degree of pathology. Since the highest levels of pathology were generally thought to exist in "fallen" women, reversal of a lapsed female's downwardly spiraling moral gravity mandated extreme physical remedy.[106] Mrs. Carter's fall had been so spectacular that she deserved a treatment of such ferocity as could be administered by a man deemed racially more "savage." The beating, pounding, and dragging were understood as what was required to drive her back up the moral spiral and up what spectators could read as its theatrical metonymn, that thirty-five-foot ladder to the belfry and starring success.

Following the trial, media coverage of the production highlighting the dangers of the role and strain on the actress augmented public belief in the authenticity of the climax and, by extension, the prowess of the trainer who elicited it. In February 1897, *Munsey's Magazine* reported:

> Mrs. Carter studies faithfully every day, knowing well that the highest niche in the temple of fame can be worn only by persistent, toilsome climbing. And, yet, after the physical exertion required by the role of Maryland every night, an actress might well be excused for thinking of nothing but relaxation during the day. To swing from the bell in the lofty church tower

requires real pluck. A relaxation of the grasp would result in a drop to almost certain death on the stage below. Then the performer's nerves have been wracked pretty thoroughly by the exciting scene immediately preceding. When Mrs. Carter is called before the curtain at the end of this act, the audience sees a woman who has for the moment masked with a smile the tremendous nervous strain she has undergone. Once in the wings again, she falls to sobbing hysterically.

"It is the feeling that I must be there in time to keep that bell from giving out a second peal," she says. "If I failed in that, the whole scene would fall to pieces. One does not quickly recover from such high wrought tension."[107]

Later in the season, when the production was on tour and reached the West Coast, the *San Francisco Daily Report* marveled at her daring: "Not one woman in five hundred, unless they had trapeze experience, would risk herself as does Mrs. Carter."[108] Indeed, according to publicity accompanying the production, Mrs. Carter had initially been so terrified that she had become dizzy in rehearsal and could not actually perform the feat until the excitement of the first performance carried her away. A prominent blurb in the tour program boasted that this was "The Original Production in Every Way," itemizing "40 men employed behind the scenes alone to handle the stupendous production. One thousand two hundred electric lights used. Eighteen calciums [lime lights]. Ten carloads of scenery."[109] The full apparatus was there to recreate the dangerous material conditions in which Mrs. Carter could relive the terror of the first time for audiences across the country and fall into hysterical sobs behind the scenes of theatre after theatre. The *San Francisco Daily Report* proclaimed her "without equal on the American stage in the expression of grief. Her cry is from the heart and her agony wells up from despair. She is a child of nature in the absolute realness with which she depicts a woman's soul. Through months to come, the puny sobs that will reach our ears will only accent the storm-sodden wall that is borne back from Maryland Calvert's heart."[110] Such press worked to verify the caption under a publicity photograph of the actress being embraced by co-star Maurice Barrymore in a love scene from the play: "The Star 'Whose Face Expressed Every Emotion of Her Heart.'"[111] And the name above hers on the masthead, the one who administered her training program, wrote the play, conceived the huge apparatus on which she executed her death-defying feat, and drew the extreme emotion outward through her body to read on her face was, of course, Belasco's.

Mrs. Carter's dangerous climb and bell swinging, together with the violent methods that drove her to this sensational climax night after night, became the defining tropes of her virtuosity as a star and Belasco's as a star maker. Reviews and other popular media commentary indicate that many theatregoers relished the seeming reality of what they witnessed on stage and the possible reality of what they heard went on behind the scenes. At some level, both Belasco and Mrs. Carter realized it was to their advantage to cater to this audience fascination regardless of what they knew to be the truth, or what else they thought the public may have needed or wanted. It does appear from testimony of company members, even years after the fact when it might have been safe or even gainful to suggest otherwise, that Mrs. Carter did all her own stunts throughout the run of the production and not a double in a long red wig.[112] However, it is highly unlikely that the belfry scene was not fully rehearsed before opening night. The stage directions specifying the instant in the clapper's backswing from the first faint sounding against the outer rim when Mrs. Carter had to execute her leap make clear the precise timing and high level of technical coordination that were required. Neither Mrs. Carter nor Belasco could have afforded the ruinous anticlimax or possible injury that could have resulted if she failed to leap at the right time or otherwise missed her mark. But both impresario and actress wanted to foster the perception that that was the risk they were taking.

The levels of physical violence Belasco used to "make" his star are also questionable in that they likely went beyond what would be allowable today but were not as punishing as many reports asserted. Again, neither Belasco nor Mrs. Carter could have afforded to have her incapacitated, but both played to the public perception of behind-the-scenes abuse. Little in the archival record indicates that Belasco mobilized the publicity machine he deployed in other instances to stem the tide of stories that flowed from his trial testimony about the *Oliver Twist* scene, which suggests some willingness on his part to let those stories go unanswered. His few printed denials, appearing decades after the events allegedly transpired, do not really debunk the myth. In 1914, he told an interviewer for the *New York World*, "The fact is that I did nothing more than play Bill as the part was played in the good old violent days. It was the custom then to drag Nancy across the stage by a band hidden beneath her hair. But people generally believed the story that I had trained Mrs. Carter by brute force."[113] Using such a band might make the exercise easier on the actress's hair and save her the pain of having her hair pulled, but her head and body would still be subject to "the good old violent" pounding and dragging. Even when he purported to "explode the myth" once and for all in the *Ladies' Home Journal* article of 1917 that became a chapter in his official theatrical memoir and advice book, *The Theatre through Its Stage Door* (1919), he left room for the myth to persist because he did not offer a direct denial. Rather, he claimed that what he described in court was what the character Bill did to Nancy in the play, and that the reporters could not resist taking this as what he did to Mrs. Carter. But his testimony had clearly stated that he pounded her head and dragged her around the floor "just as Bill Sykes dragged Nancy," so the exculpatory distinction he tried to draw between the character and himself as actor was largely semantic.[114] After this supposed official denial, he would recall the training technique with even further embellishment in interviews for publication: "Hour after hour we rehearsed this scene until she was letter perfect in all the presentments of emotion."[115] "I acted the part of Bill Sykes to her Nancy, seized her hair, pulled her around the room and beat her face upon the floor until she yelled with natural excitement, and I told her that was the natural, right tone, and to remember it."[116] Thomas Curry, looking back over Belasco's career, wrote of the story's persistence: "The papers loved this and for years told how he dragged young ladies around by the hair (of the head) to train them for the stage."[117] Curry's compulsion to insert the parenthetical clarification as to which hair on her body the actress was dragged by may be read as another indication of popular suppositions about the sexual as well as violent nature of the training.

Mrs. Carter's public handling of questions about the backstage violence to which she had been subjected likewise left room for suppositions to continue. In her 1927 autobiography, "Portrait of a Lady with Red Hair," she wrote:

> I have denied the story many times, for I would never believe the public wanted some highly spiced, unnatural, acrobatic, mesmeric training by him. It was said he twisted my long braids around his wrists and, using them as ropes, dragged me about the room as if punching or hurting a woman's body could make her act. . . . The whole truth is that Mr. Belasco did with me only what a musician would do with a musical instrument."[118]

Although she claims at this late point in her career to have denied the story many times, the printed record during her years with Belasco yields little in the way of direct denials. Her primary strategy with interviewers was to lavish praise on her trainer and put the rigors of his methods in the context of her extraordinary capacity for and professed love of hard work. Her assertion that Belasco did with her "only what a musician would do with an instrument" hardly puts the rumors to rest when such wildly virtuosic, bow-plunging, and string-plucking violinists as Pagannini and churning and roiling pianists as Franz Liszt shaped popular late-nineteenth-century images of musicians. Although she scoffs here at the story of Belasco twisting her long braids about his wrists, the 1940 film, *The Lady with Red Hair*, based on her autobiography, coyly refers to that alleged technique. In a rehearsal scene, Belasco (Claude Rains) stands on a crate, takes the ends of Mrs. Carter's (Miriam Hopkins) braids in his fist, and pulls them up to straighten her posture and make her walk properly, as a trainer might do with a show poodle on a leash. Given that Mrs. Carter's second husband, Lou Payne, whom she met and married while still with Belasco and to whom she willed control of her interests, served as consultant on the film, this moment suggests a deliberate continuation of the actress's own tendency to let the legend persist.

Complicit in these sensational stories of backstage violence and onstage danger and exigency, both star and starmaker acted out with at least some degree of self-consciousness aspects attributed to them according to prevailing racial and sexual stereotypes of their time. While it would have been unseemly for a bourgeois Gentile man to mete out the extreme punishment warranted by Mrs. Carter's extreme sinfulness, it was fitting—indeed expected—that the Svengali-esque Belasco would do so. By taking on this task in so visible a fashion, Belasco performed a public service that made him in some ways heroic and respectable. Forcibly realigning Mrs. Carter's hysterical body, he demonstrated mastery over the socially threatening corporeal incontinence attributed to Jewish men as well as fallen women. The critic Wendell Phillips Dodge acknowledged both Belasco's triumph and identification with his star: "When Mrs. Carter swung from the belfry, it was Belasco swinging; he worked the strings."[119] With the highly publicized rehearsal process and production of *The Heart of Maryland*, star and star maker together effected a spectacular expiation that earned them upward mobility through the liminal Catholic space of the old church bell tower.

The Payoffs of Pelvic Control

Once he had demonstrated such apparent mastery over Mrs. Carter's wayward pelvis and its unruly passions in this breakthrough production, Belasco proceeded to cast his star as fallen women through whom he could enact more morally and culturally charged feats of salvation. After *The Heart of Maryland*, Mrs. Carter essayed the *Camille*-like *Zaza*, featuring a far more risquée and declassée heroine.[120] Zaza is a Parisian music hall singer who does not solicit sex for money but is nevertheless construed as a prostitute because of her profession. Passionately involved with a bourgeois gentleman, Bernard Dufrene, she descends to a level of vengefulness worthy of Salome or Leah when she learns he has been deceiving her about his family and harboring an underlying contempt for women of her class. Subsequent scenes depict her transformation to more Christian, madonnalike self-sacrifice as she realizes the need to protect his innocent child and ultimately renounces sexual engagement with men altogether.[121] Zaza's cultural background and behavior made her transformation all the more resonant in Belasco's American adaptation, given contemporary statistics showing high percentages of French and Jewish women among prostitutes in New York City.[122]

For the priestly Jewish Belasco, the production brought added recognition of his power to convert and control the actress as an extension of himself. Dodge praised Belasco's directorial prowess:

> In "Zaza," more than in "The Heart of Maryland," was Belasco's magic influence felt in Mrs. Carter's acting. Every step, every movement, every look, every wink of the eye, every toss of the head, every gesture, every rise and fall in the voice—all was Belasco. It was as if it were Belasco on the stage acting in Mrs. Carter's costume! And during nearly all the long run of "Zaza" Belasco was to be found on the stage, watching Mrs. Carter from the wings, standing very close to the side of the proscenium. At the tense moments of Mrs. Carter's acting her master stood there as if glued to the spot, which soon came to be regarded as almost sacred. No one ever stood there but Belasco. It was as though he put the words into Mrs. Carter's mouth, and had strings attached to every muscle of the actress, which he manipulated.[123]

As the puppet master, Belasco could simultaneously exploit the scandalous material for its entertainment value and controvert fears that this potentially dangerous woman would seduce him and the husbands in his audiences away from their families as Zaza had threatened to do to Bernard. If he controlled her "every muscle," he could presumably prevent her from ensnaring other men, a valued attribute in an era of crackdowns on prostitution.

For Mrs. Carter, following Belasco's dictates and playing the fallen woman saved through the demands of the performance and its conversion plot brought the social redemption she ardently desired. As with *The Heart of Maryland*, media reports about the rigors of the role fueled audience belief in the genuineness of the extreme emotional expression. The headline "Mrs. Carter's Physical Endurance" appeared over an article attesting to the enormous strain of playing Zaza and how "after the fourth act, she is completely exhausted" and must do two hours of calisthenics daily in her apartment to stay fit for the part.[124] Nightly strenuosity effected nightly expiation. Belasco's adaptation played upon a key tenet of Victorian sexual ideology, the "pro-natal hypothesis," whereby, in the interests of middle-class propriety, women's desire for sex was construed as a desire for motherhood.[125] Driving Mrs. Carter to a series of putatively real climaxes, Belasco made a redemptive reverence for the maternal bond appear visibly to overcome sinful lust in the actress's body. Like the star herself, who sought this mode of upward mobility to shed the stigma of adulteress, Zaza, in relinquishing her affair with Bernard in the interests of his child, resolves to move up the cultural hierarchy as a performer. In the last act, she appears as the featured singer in the "Concert des Ambassadors." Her theatrical legitimacy marks the moral uplift she has attained through her realization of the pro-natal hypothesis.

More connections between the play and its star's own story and ambitions were forged when Belasco took the production to Chicago so that Mrs. Carter might enact her redemption in the very city of her fall from social grace. She writes of how she very nearly lost her nerve and would not have been able to go on had it not been for "Mr. Dave": "he watched me closely, never taking his eyes from mine. . . . The lines of my cue were nearing. . . . His eyes never left my own. . . . Finally my cue came. Mr. Dave gave me a gentle push, and my feet bore me on the stage. In the recesses of that confident pressure lay belief unending. With that touch, that bond behind me, I faced them."[126] Her performance moved even the hostile Chicago audience. When her ex-husband refused to let her see her son while she was in town, Belasco accompanied her to the Carter house and threatened Leslie with publicizing his heartless thwarting of maternal desire, whereupon the reunion of mother and son was quickly allowed and duly noted by the press.[127] Writing Mrs. Carter's story into Zaza's, Belasco showed how this fallen socialite, as a legitimate actress, could earn the right to see her son. Thus, for Mrs. Carter, the production of *Zaza* publicized and made more credible the agenda she had claimed from the beginning of her pursuit of a stage career.

Most lucrative for the star and her maker was *Zaza*'s further realization of the power initiated in *The Heart of Maryland*—the power to conquer respectable audiences by moving them and gaining their patronage and approval. An illustrated souvenir history of Mrs. Carter's career and the production of *Zaza* shows Belasco reveling in that victory:

> And when at last the outraged, heartbroken woman drove her lover from her presence in an outburst of indignation and then tottered across the room and bowed her head in a paroxysm of grief and bitterness, the pent-up feelings of the audience, relieved suddenly of the intense strain, found vent in such a storm of enthusiasm and applause as has not been heard within the walls of a New York playhouse in many a year.
>
> The whole audience, almost hostile in its attitude an hour before, had melted under the sway of her genius into one great pulsating human heart.
>
> Men of learning and men mighty in affairs; women of society and of the stage; critics, artists, stood up in their places and shouted and waved handkerchiefs and threw flowers at the feet of this sobbing, overwrought woman who had conquered them by her art; who had awakened their hearts to pity, and had compelled them to echo, with eyes streaming like her own, her own words, "Poor Zaza"! The house had risen at her.[128]

Playing Mrs. Carter as the instrumental extension of himself, Belasco drilled not only his actress in the emotional parts but, through her, their audiences. He may have tasted some of Svengali's revenge as he made society's finest subject to the same excessive emotions that had marked him as an emotionally and sexually incontinent male Jew and his leading lady as a whore.

However, if Belasco and others believed that he pulled the strings, Mrs. Carter was also awakening to her own power as a performer in these early starring successes. Reflecting on what she learned from the experience, she told an interviewer:

> Its effect on myself was to disclose to me my limitations and my powers. Without undue egotism, I may say that it showed me that it had been given to me to move the hearts of men and women; to stir their deepest emotions, and play upon them as an organist upon his keys. And with this knowledge came to me an understanding of the responsibilities that my gifts entailed.[129]

In her 1927 autobiography, she reflected again on how she became "exquisitely aware" of "the audience seizing the emotion through me and vibrating to it."[130] She first had the effect in *The Heart of Maryland*, but *Zaza* perhaps allowed her to feel it more acutely because her climax occurred on the terra firma of the stage floor closer to the audience rather than thirty-five feet over-head swinging from a bell. While Belasco played her like an instrument through which he could demonstrate command over the emotions she embodied and thereby move the audience, Mrs. Carter felt the more direct audience impact she had as the instrument of arousal itself. As long as Belasco could believe that Mrs. Carter's power as audience "vibrator" was an extension of his own potency and not a tool she wielded independently, relations between star maker and star remained harmonious, and audience assurance of his control of her waywardness intact.

Notwithstanding this potential for instability, Belasco by 1900 had secured the basis of a theatrical regime and a place for his leading lady in the pantheon of stars. Whereas he had needed the backing of Max Blieman for *The Heart of Maryland* and Charles Frohman, who owned the American rights, for *Zaza*, the profits of his success now brought financial independence.[131] More importantly for Belasco's social and cultural as well as economic ascent, Mrs. Carter, heralded as "the Bernhardt of America," had become a potent embodiment of her maker's feminized Jewish nature.[132] Impresario and actress had achieved seeming public triumph over the Judaized whore's body, first through the extreme form of gynecologic therapy employed in *The Heart of Maryland* belfry scene, and then through Zaza's conversion from lust and vengeance to maternal sainthood. With the wealth and fame attained in these productions, Belasco would extend his putative mastery of feminized and racialized passion embodied in the actress into more lavish spectacles and exotically Othered worlds.

7

Imperial Expiations

*If one idea has prevailed above another in
fashioning this new theatre, it has been the hope
that all interested in its undertakings should look
upon it as an annex of their own. Not only has
Mr. Belasco now his own theatrical domicile, so to
speak—dedicated by him as the dramatic home of
Mrs. Leslie Carter and her productions—but it is
his wish that the public, who have so liberally
favored him in the past, may find here a sort of
domestic atmosphere which will lend an added
comfort to the occupation of playgoing.*
—"Home," program note for *Du Barry*
to mark the inauguration of the
Belasco Theatre, 1902

In George Du Maurier's *Trilby*, Svengali and his protégée tour the richest concert halls of Europe, culminating their cultural climb at Paris's once dazzlingly exotic arena, the Cirque des Bashibazoucks. Rapturous audience members, including powerful dignitaries, reel in thrall to Trilby's uncanny voice. Through her, Svengali possesses and rouses them to ecstatic emotional states that shatter the normal bounds of bourgeois sentimentality. As potent and lasting an impression as this duo makes on its audiences, Svengali and Trilby are forever gypsies, always guests in strangers' houses, welcome to offer momentary pleasure but not to stay. They do not own the buildings in which they perform, nor are the stages specially outfitted for them. Trilby sings in a simple classical gown with only a small footstool for a prop (fig. 31). The stool helps her keep one leg bent as she stands, hands behind her back, transfixed à la the Venus of Milo. Treated to more auditory than visual splendor, the audience sees only Trilby's immobile form in front of the curtain, with Svengali's head and wand bobbing mesmerizingly over the orchestra seated in the pit.

While contemporary commentators remarked that Svengali found a real-life analogue in David Belasco, the performances the Bishop of Broadway orchestrated with his star actresses developed to an operatic scale that far exceeded the fictional maestro's concerts with Trilby. Continuing his appropriation of Catholic tropes of expiating sin, the clerically collared Belasco pushed the expression of unruly passion further outward from the female body into the wider materiality of theatrical space in an overwhelmingly visual effect. Unlike Svengali, Belasco made his star the centerpiece of an immense *mise-en-scène*. Ever more lavish realistic sets depicted morally and often racially Othered spaces that worked to verify and magnify his actress's climactic performance.

Thickly woven into these massive stagings was Belasco's own identity formation as an exotically marked Jew, one whom many, including his primary leading lady, Mrs. Leslie Carter, termed "Oriental." Belasco played to the white Orientalist imagination that pegged Jews as expert mimics and often linked them to "darker" peoples "lower" in the evolutionary hierarchy. On at least two occasions in print, Belasco talked about how he could identify with various Others to write plays, how he would "saturate" himself with research until he would "become as a native of that country" at issue in a particular script.[1] He declared: "Though my address be in the Sixties or Seventies in New York, I am a Japanese or a Mexican or a Frenchman for the time. I feel and

31. Svengali conducts Trilby's song, "Au Clair de la Lune," in Trilby, *novel and illustrations by George Du Maurier, 1894, repr. 1998, 211.*

think as a Jap or a Greaser or a Frenchman."[2] Belasco interiorized these constructions in order to exteriorize them in production, chiefly through his star's performance and surrounding scenery. By eliciting female confessions and giving audiences titillating touristic glimpses into putatively real worlds of the Other, the impresario, as in Edward Said's concept of exteriority, "ma[de] the Orient speak."[3] While Said specifies that "the Orientalist is outside the Orient," Belasco worked from inside the construct. His plays exteriorized multifarious aspects the dominant culture projected onto him and gave theatrical form to the wide range of cultural exoticisms his upwardly aspiring but downwardly stereotyped Jewishness mobilized. These included explicitly Oriental but also Orientalized Western representations, such as decadent historical empires, barbarous frontier spaces, and dangerous dives of the modern urban underworld. For Belasco, exteriorizing Otherness onstage provided a means of working upon, gaining control over, and purifying racialized and feminized passion. He could thereby signal self- as well as theatrical mastery on a grand public scale.

The personal gains to the impresario from this enterprise hinged on audience impact. Amid the nation's imperialist zeal that escalated following the Spanish American War and the ascendancy of Teddy Roosevelt to the presidency, Belasco's stagings of exotic worlds both titillated and reassured spectators of transgression and Otherness being mastered before their eyes; the more lavish the physical and material exteriorization of sin and climactic the correction, the more thrilling for audiences and more socioeconomically and morally aggrandizing for the star maker and his star. However, Belasco's position relative to the nation's power structure remained ambivalent. An ardent admirer of Roosevelt and a collector of his writings, Belasco was still a target of the WASP nativism the president's policies propounded. It was thus a heightened victory for the impresario when his productions, in colonizing foreign aspects he himself allegedly shared, also turned the conquering impulse back on spectators to arouse their sensual natures and drill them as well as his actresses in the emotional parts they would deny in themselves and project onto Others.

In this theatrical conquest, Mrs. Carter remained the central figure, at least until 1906, when her marriage to a fellow actor precipitated her infamous break from Belasco. Her most massive star vehicle was *Du Barry* (1901), set in the decadent regime of Louis XV that fanned the flames of revolution in late-eighteenth-century France. Although it was not the first explicitly imperialistic work Belasco staged, it was the first that he mounted for his prototypical leading lady following her rise to stardom in *The Heart of Maryland* (1895) and *Zaza* (1899), and it epitomized the directorial vision he developed with her. The production of *Du Barry* not only extended the expression of extreme feminine passion into the materiality of the stage but also into the entire theatre building. The lavishness of *Du Barry's* Bourbon court, as conquered and purportedly purified by Napoleon, became the stylistic keynote of Belasco's first theatre, the Republic, which institutionalized his operations. The impresario's disciplining of the exotically climactic female, the centerpiece of his theatre, grew into his command of a vast production apparatus manned by innovative designers and technicians and a small army of stagehands and office personnel. The imperialistic architecture and decor of the theatre building itself, along with the collections of objects, most notably Napoleana, as well as books that it housed, became further instruments of female star making and additional venues for demonstrating mastery over

Otherness via artfully managed exteriorization. The dynamics of Napoleonic collecting and conquest established around *Du Barry* indelibly informed Belasco's work on subsequent productions.

Enshrining the Courtesan Queen

By the time *Du Barry* premiered, fittingly for the impresario's imperial ambitions, in the nation's capital on 12 December 1901, Belasco's growing agenda of Orientalist exteriorization and conquest was already evident. With Mrs. Carter occupied in the long runs and a tour of *Zaza*, he had taken advantage of the opportunity to profit from other material. He acquired two additional stars, Blanche Bates and David Warfield, whose respective early vehicles exoticized the worlds of the Japanese geisha (*Madame Butterfly*, March 1900), the French Algerian camp follower (*Under Two Flags*, February 1901), and the peddling New York Jew (*The Auctioneer*, September 1901).[4] However, he never developed the same kind of relationship with Bates and Warfield as he did with his first protégée. They came to him already seasoned, Bates with Augustin Daly's company and Warfield in vaudeville, which made them less susceptible to his formative manipulations. As a male vaudevillian, Warfield lacked the emotional and sexual vulnerability and appeal possible with actresses. The strikingly beautiful and athletic Bates, "with lovely dark eyes and hair," had some of those qualities, but her prowess was more physical than emotional; she excelled in "picturesque" rather than torrid parts.[5] Thus, for various reasons, while Bates's and Warfield's early Belasco vehicles depicted Othered worlds, they did not enact the extreme dynamics of exteriorization as expiation of sin. That required the sexual and emotional force of a "boudoir tigress" like Mrs. Carter.[6] It was owing to the merger of torrentially climactic female performance with orgasmically profuse imperialistic scenery that Belasco's methods reached an apogee in *Du Barry*.

The play is based on the historical case of the French milliner, Marie Jeanne Bécu, who agreed to an arranged marriage with the titled Guillaume du Barry in order to succeed Madame Pompadour as the mistress of Louis XV. Belasco and Mrs. Carter came upon the topic while in France the summer following the London run of *Zaza*. Belasco had been ransacking his history books in search of a suitable subject for his leading lady's next vehicle, but had not yet been adequately inspired. "None of them seemed to clutch at his imagination or to *drive* him," Mrs. Carter notes in her autobiography. "They had to possess him entirely and ride him, or he could not *see* them."[7]

She tells of a dinner the two had in Paris where Belasco described what he was looking for:

> At Paillard's Restaurant, where the wheel is seen in full circle, one night dining near us was the Maharajah of Kapurthala with his brown-faced suite. Weary, satiated, sybaritic. What a study! At his table was a frail young French girl not more than eighteen, like an ornament of white jade, with sultry eyes, around her neck enormous strands of heavy pearls.
>
> "There!" Mr. Dave nodded his head toward the picture. "If I could once seek out the motive for that, I would find the excuse. For the excuse is always there."
>
> "Turn your head from her as one may," he would say of a woman of the half-world, "she cannot be eliminated in that way. She is behind the thrones; she sits under the chair of the political leader; she is powerful in the lives of men. As long as she is the force she is, plays like mine can never be useless."[8]

If such women ruled world leaders, Belasco's theatrical expiation and mastery of their sinfulness could both do great public service and further his own interests. Gaining dominance over seductresses who initially possessed him and who could dominate royalty would augment his own power. Moreover, if his heroines continued to function as embodiments of his own culturally effeminized nature, vindicating women who had fallen into even greater cultural decadence than Zaza could bring him further personal vindication.

Shortly after the dinner at Paillard's, during a visit to Elisabeth Marbury and Elsie de Wolfe's home in Versailles, Marbury suggested the Comtesse du Barry, whose pavilion still stood at nearby Louveciennes, because she seemed to spring ready-made from history to fill Belasco's needs. Although Louis XV was not, of course, an Indian pasha, his reign represented a level of corruption and excess that could be elaborated to fit the impresario's racialized and sexualized scheme. Picking up readily on Marbury's suggestion, Belasco determined that Louis XV, "His Most Christian Majesty," presided over "the most gorgeous, extravagant, and dissolute court that Europe has ever known," and at the core of that decadence was the love-lorn monarch's weak-willed indulgence of his mistress's insatiable appetite for luxury.[9] The noted French author, Jean Richepin, whom Belasco initially enlisted to write the script, commented while driving with him and Mrs. Carter through Paris, "See, madame, they call her the 'Holy Courtesan.' Is she not rightly named? She is a great phallic temple set down like a huge trull in the midst of her

Notre Dames, her Madeleines, and her St. Roches. She can burn like some white candle in a holy place, or blaze like Venus before the fires of Vulcan."[10] She purportedly burned so hot for Louis that he opened state coffers to her extravagant desires and thereby enraged the starving masses.

Such an infamous seductress exceeded Zaza as a subject who could engage the pornophile Belasco's imagination. An historical icon, Du Barry was a fallen woman on a far larger scale, and she inspired pornography of the ilk Belasco collected. According to Mrs. Carter's hyperbolic prose, Belasco "bought every book ever written that gave the faintest reference to [Du Barry] or the times in which she lived."[11] Belasco himself claimed "to read at least a hundred books before writing a line of my play."[12] Although it is impossible to account for every book Belasco read or owned during his life, at the time of his death in 1931, he still had a number of relevant works in his collection. The catalogue of books sold at public auction included:

> # 52 *Du Barry (Comtesse). Anecdotes sur Madame La Comtesse du Barri* (Mairobert), n.p. 1775; *Pièces Historique de la Vie de Madame La Comtesse Du Barry*, Paris 1775; and others. Together 10 vols.

> # 76 French Biography. *Vie Privée de Louis XV*, 4 vols., Londres, 1785.[13]

Given his interests and extensive traffic in higher class pornography, it is likely that he also encountered well-known works in underground circles available in multiple editions, such as *The Authentic Memoirs of the Countess de Barre, the French King's Mistress,* and *Louis XV. Intime et les Petites Maitresses.*[14] (These may even have been among the "others" listed in #52.) Many if not most of the Du Barry–related books available to Belasco were written in French, a language he did not speak. Mrs. Carter, however, was fluent in what Anglo-American culture regarded as *la langue sexuelle.* Serving as Belasco's research assistant and interpreter in their sessions with the francophone Richepin, she literally spoke the arousing stories of Du Barry's amorous career to her maker through her body.

Richepin's script, however, proved a large disappointment. In spite of the author's expressed phallic ardor for the "Holy Courtesan," his version of the play, while historically accurate, did not adequately convey the excitement and passions star and star maker found in the material. Rejecting Richepin's efforts, Belasco commenced to rewrite the script and claim authorship. As a result, he forfeited $3,500 (about $81,000 today) in advance royalties and weathered a lawsuit over copyright.[15]

While Belasco used many of the same techniques he had used to create *The Heart of Maryland* and *Zaza*, this project demanded even greater rigor because of the greater degree of the heroine's sinfulness. He wrote in his autobiography:

> History paints Du Barry as the most despised woman of her time. She is said to have been the most evil creature antedating the French Revolution. I had a vast number of books relating to Du Barry, and ransacked them all for one redeeming trait in her character: not one kind word. Alas! Not *one*! For the first time in my life I found myself in the hands of a really bad woman. I had never met one before (bad men I have met, but women, — never!) I felt a desire to rush to her defense."[16]

In a defense of the character printed in the play program, Belasco indicated that her sinful nature went beyond that of the historical Du Barry to a more primordial source: "Redoubtable, faulty, and charming, her personality comes down to us so utterly feminine that we see in her Eve with all her faults, standing in naked frankness, quite as unclothed morally. She is the gamut of the woman who always has been, who always will be."[17] Running from the biblical archetype Eve to the imperial French courtesan Du Barry, that gamut also extended from Jewish to Catholic, and from East to West. Du Barry became a prodigious vehicle through which Belasco, the Jewish priest poseur, could expiate the feminized and Orientalized aspects of himself.

With his leading lady as his intimate collaborator, Belasco embarked upon a fourteen-month process to redeem Du Barry. He declared his intentions to Mrs. Carter: "I am going to take the lady down to the colonial atmosphere of Fredericksberg and there let her show me whatever of good she has."[18] Working out the good in the whore entailed excoriating the bad by eliciting confessions and molding their expression. If Mrs. Carter had first aroused him with her translations of the raw history from the French, Belasco began mastering those passions by writing *Du Barry* in bits and trying each one out on his leading lady to test her emotional response. She recorded the process in her autobiography:

> With her growth, I would sit and listen to his interminable, "Mrs. C., Mrs. C.," while with clear, cold logic he would watch me as he read me her unfoldment day by day. If my face was sterile of emotion, he eliminated it. He would rewrite it again and again until, focusing it to the right perspective, just as a photographer does to a subject, I would react to it.[19]

Following the writing of the script, the next developmental phase became still more physical for Mrs. Carter. According to her account, "There were two months' hard mechanics of the play before even attempting to study the lines." She explains "mechanics" as follows:

> No play of Mr. Belasco's was ever rehearsed until prefaced by what we call mechanics. These are the physical movements that subordinate themselves to the requirements of the action. These mechanics are equivalent to rhythm in verse—the meaning sometimes lies latent and can be brought into life by a gesture, a walk across the stage, a look. Every move, every action, must be placed to its right tempo; every action, every move to a certain pace.[20]

"Hard mechanics" helped Belasco gain control over the physical instrument of the actress's body in order to play the passions through her and regulate their outward expression.

Du Barry extends the outward expression of passions from the female body into the wider materiality of the stage and scenery chiefly through the trope of overspending. Along with being excessively emotional and sexual, the character Du Barry, like her historical prototype, is also infamously economically incontinent. On the grandest imaginable scale, she is both a courtesan and a spendthrift, which enables the play to trade continuously on financial metaphors of "spending," which were rife in pornography and common parlance alike from the eighteenth century through the Victorian period, for attainment of sexual pleasure. As Du Barry's sexual career grows more profligate, the stage becomes increasingly filled with the decadent trappings of luxury.

The character's indulgences and ultimate suffering and punishment for her sins served as an expiatory vehicle for the actress who embodied her because Belasco exploited Mrs. Carter's own admitted propensities. As the actress confesses in her autobiography,

> Certain lines were incorporated in the play exactly as they were brought forth on the occasion of being scolded for the magnitude of my bills. The only thing I really lower my head with regret to in my life has been my extravagance, and I said: "I'm so sorry. I am always sorry for things, but I always become sorry too late. I love pretty things. They are my curse. I get a touch of madness when I go to buy."[21]

Belasco's scoldings echoed those of her ex-husband, who had publicly excoriated her for her willful extravagance at their scandalous divorce trial. (Recall the four thousand francs she spent in Europe on a toilet seat cast in sterling silver.) On a larger scale, the role of Du Barry positioned the actress as a martyr for an expanding capitalist society morally anxious over rising patterns of female consumerism.[22] But Belasco was also working out through his leading lady his own propensities for overspending in the material as well as the sexual sense. He no less than Mrs. Carter was given to indulgence in exorbitant luxuries as the two became wealthier through their theatrical successes and he amassed his collections of exotic objects.

While allowing for expiation of mutual passions, the play's central trope of overspending also had implications for the power dynamic between impresario and actress. Greater wealth and fame meant greater stakes for the public perception of who was manipulating whom. In the play, Du Barry's inordinate economic and sexual overspending evokes the age-old specter of the whore as actress, a professional woman who "fakes it" for a living. An ongoing secret romance with the antiroyalist soldier Cossé Brissac throws into relief the falseness of the love she repeatedly shows other richer, more powerful men who can better afford to buy her pretty things. While Mrs. Carter as Du Barry forestalled conjugal bliss with Cossé and seduced the king on false pretenses, her impresario claimed a position beyond her ability to refuse or deceive him. As the author and director of the actress's performance, he remained the putative master of both her fakery and her truth telling and the orchestrator of her physical and emotional climaxes.

Out of Du Barry's conflicting propensities for true love on the one hand and false love on the other, Belasco created increasingly stressful situations to provoke the actress and drive the plot. Cossé wants to vitiate her weakness for luxury, while those for whom she fakes sexual attraction demand a fuller, more genuine response. In each act, the scenery both reflects and stirs her inner desires. When it comes to pretty things, her appetite for overspending is insatiable; the more she acquires, the more she wants. If, in the story of the play, Du Barry's material acquisitions and decorative excesses signal her success as a seductress and her royal keeper's loss of control, in the dynamics of theatrical production, these goods became instruments of impresarial authority. Belasco aspired to an unprecedented level of realism in staging this script in order to make the strongest impact on his actress and, through her, his audience. He used masses of fully built, historically accurate scenery and props to play on Mrs. Carter's own appetite for luxury, make her feel the conflicts Du Barry felt, and force true confessions from her to catalyze redemption.

The play opens in the Parisian workplace of the milliner, whom Belasco has renamed Jeanette Vaubernier. A fetishist's paradise replete with ladies' corsets, silks, ribbons, hats, and high-heeled slippers, the shop caters especially to *femmes declassées*, notably opera singers and dancers. As in the prototypical porn novel, *Fanny Hill*, milliner's shops were often fronts for brothels. Jeanette ended up here because of her "vagabond nature," the result of heredity as well as environment; she is the daughter of a "weak-faced" lapsed monk and a prostitute. "Pretty things are necessities to me," she explains to the other shop girls. "I cannot live without them. . . . It must be heaven to live for the mere luxury of living, like a great, fine flower in the hot sun; to deny yourself nothing—nothing at all; to laugh in the face of the whole world; to squander money—make it fly—buy everything you see—throw it away, eh? Ah, heavenly!" Rich admirers have bought her the fancy undergarments she dons with seductively visible lace that visually links her body to the lingerie filling the shop. Seeing her as synonymous with her surroundings, Jean du Barry, a pimp and a gambler, hires her as a "petticoat" to lure clientele to the Marquise de Quesnay's gambling rooms. She quits the milliner's shop, declaring "It is against my nature to work."[23] The scene changes "to a luxurious salon with silken walls and draperies. . . . The rich rugs, the gilded carvings—in fact, the entire surroundings—show that the little milliner of the rue St. Honoré has taken a step up (or down) in the world."[24] Effecting another merger of body and set, Mrs. Carter's famous flaming locks keyed the color scheme: "Under a high light the actress's hair blends in exquisite harmony with the red walls and curtains."[25] Moreover, Jeanette's salon was equipped with a peephole for surveying the clientele to be seduced, a scenographic play on the voyeuristic pleasures of the whole spectacle.

While Jeanette successfully lures the gamblers to the table, she does not, at this point in her career, grant them ultimate sexual satisfaction. Instead, much to the consternation of her employer the marquise, she bids them good night and slips away to drive out to the country in a carriage with Cossé to see the sunrise. But, signaling her propensity for further lapse, her *demi-monde* surroundings win out over the salubrious countryside. Although she now says she genuinely loves Cossé, her appetite for luxury keeps her from going away with him permanently and soon makes her far less accessible to him. The king, having seen her at the opera, made his attraction known to courtiers, who want to procure her for him to curry his greater favor. The socially ambitious Jean du Barry, once again acting as her pimp, tells these emissaries: "The King . . . My God, I hold a trump card and never guessed how to play it!

Thank you for reminding me that a petticoat has always ruled France and Jeanette wears a damned enticing one."²⁶ He knows that to become the king's mistress she must have a title and so concocts the scheme for her to marry Guillaume, his sot of a brother, whom he can then pay to disappear. Meanwhile, a gypsy mendicant appears and reads Jeanette's fortune: "Lady, I see Paris at your feet . . . I see power . . . I see triumph. More: wherever the name of France is read, yours is read, too."²⁷

Torn between the temptation of this triumph and true love, Jeanette offers her first major confession of the play to Cossé when he arrives to see why she has missed their usual driving date and is horrified to learn of what she is contemplating. She explains that she was distracted by the promise of trinkets— "I love pretty things: they're my curse." Repentant and afraid of losing him, she admits "There's something in me—whatever it is, it's bad—that I cannot tear out. . . . It's in my blood . . . it's my destiny to have everything in the world and to be utterly wretched because I have it."²⁸ She wavers, almost letting Cossé take her away, until the king arrives to woo her in person. The lifestyle he promises her proves too great a temptation. Barely able to contain his rage, Cossé leaves, his antiroyalist sentiments now inflamed for deeply personal as well as political reasons. If she managed to avoid it with lesser men in order to save herself for Cossé, Jeanette will now have to "put out" for the king and play the spender in both senses.

The heroine's incontinence culminates in the high-voltage emotional and scenographic climaxes of the third act. When the curtain rises, she is Madame La Comtesse du Barry holding a midday *petite levée* in the Palace of Versailles. Belasco's stage directions describe the scene depicted in Figure 32:

> SCENE: At a glance, one recognizes the room as a beautiful bedchamber occupied by a great lady of a frivolous turn of mind. The richness of the peignoir thrown carelessly over a chair, the splendid buckles on the high-heeled slippers lying on the floor, the drawn curtains at this late hour of the morning—all proclaim the fact that a lady of fashion has not roused herself to the dull cares of the day.
>
> An entrance at the back lets in or keeps out those that would pay court to the acknowledged favorite of His Most Christian Majesty, Louis XV. And here, in bed, we find Jeanette, the milliner,—now Madame la Comtesse du Barry, wife of the drunken and exiled brother of Jean, the gambler, sitting up in the midst of furs, lace flounces, silken sheets, pillows boasting embroidered crowns—in fact, all the kickshaws of the period.

32. Mrs. Leslie Carter as Du Barry, "The Doll of the World," conducting her petite levée *from her sumptuous bed in Act III, of Belasco's* Du Barry, *1901. Courtesy of the Museum of the City of New York.*

Madame la Comtesse du Barry wears jewels and a wonderful night-robe, and resembles nothing so much as a doll sitting up in state at a child's party. Above her head, Cupids smile down, and above the Cupids is a high gilded cornice holding soft draperies cunningly caught back at the sides to allow an unobstructed view of the lady in bed.[29]

The scene is rendered so that the "something bad" in the royally bedded courtesan spills out visually from her body in an orgy of material objects that signify the ruinous spendings she elicits from the king. Mounds of richly embroidered pillows, yards of flounces and draperies, piles of exotic carpets, ornately carved tables, candelabra, chairs, and columns fill a room whose walls and ceiling fairly drip with baroque splendor.

These objects were not only massively plentiful but, like the actress's unquenched passions they exteriorized, were also putatively authentic. Belasco commissioned James L. Ford, author of such popular works as *Hypnotic Tales and Other Tales* (1891) and *Cupid and the Footlights* (1899), to write two volumes to accompany the production: *The Story of Du Barry* (1902), a 288-page purported biography of the character's historical prototype laden with photographs of Belasco's production, which authenticates the impresario's work by attesting to his vast research; and a shorter book (60 pages), *Mrs. Leslie Carter in David Belasco's* Du Barry (1902), which is both a chronicle of Mrs. Carter's performance and a paean to the historical reality of the *mise-en-scène*. According to Ford, Belasco and Mrs. Carter "studied with the utmost care the social and political conditions which existed in France during the period...; and they made a close study of the furniture, dresses, ornaments, fans, and wigs which were used in court at that time."[30] Belasco aimed to put the profligate Bourbon court "upon the stage in such a manner that it would be possible for his auditors to imagine that they saw before them the real Jeanette Du Barry and the real King of France, setting the pace of reckless living, extravagance, and corruption that eventually brought upon their unhappy country the terrors of the Revolution."[31] Ford claims that Belasco and Mrs. Carter "procured detailed descriptions of everything pertaining to [Du Barry's] private life and that of the King, so that the various things that were made to order were, generally speaking, exact copies of those which had been in actual use."[32] The List of Illustrations for *Mrs. Leslie Carter in David Belasco's* Du Barry reads as a catalogue of prize possessions singled out for special viewing pleasure, including "Objects Seen in the Milliner's Shop," "Corset of the Period," "Spinnet of the Period," "Sedan Chair," and "A Corner of Du Barry's Bedchamber in the Palace at Versailles," which shows the highly ornate decorative details reproduced on the set. Offered as *pièces de résistance* were a number of objects that were not reproductions but were purportedly the things themselves, special sinecures of the production's authenticity: "Screen and Dressing Table Actually Used by Du Barry" and "Veritable Night Table Actually Used by Du Barry at Versailles" on which rested "The Du Barry Coffee Cup." The well-advertised actual use of the objects by the historical prototype brought traces of her bodily reality into the material space for the actress to inhabit. Mrs. Leslie Carter's lips touched the same cup rim as Jeanne Bécu's had more than a century earlier.

The key scenic emblem of the character's, the actress's, and the impresario's sexual and economic overspending was the bed in which Du Barry was discovered and from which she made her *petite-levée*. Ford calls the bed depicted in figure 32 "the crowning achievement of this act . . . in every detail an exact copy of the one in which the real Du Barry sat."[33] Mixed into its extravagant baroque styling are a number of exotic details that reflect Du Barry's degeneracy. The bed rests on a pedestal piled with carpets, some made of fur, with the topmost one of Orientalist design. A pair of life-sized cupids caressing the legs of a naked Venus stands atop the headboard. Over the whole bed looms an ornately carved canopy and heavy drapery in the "peculiar green" that was Du Barry's favorite color. Unable to obtain the actual coverlet Du Barry used to keep herself and her lovers warm, Belasco went to exorbitant expense to have a copy made. Mrs. Carter reports: "The coverlet for her bed from which she held her court was a copy taken from the Bibliophile [sic] Nationale, drawn by Cesare of the Comédie-Française, and made under his artistic supervision. The velvet, to get the width to cover the huge bed and have it seamless, was woven especially for us at Lyons. The entire cost of the spread alone was $12,000 [about $275,000 today]."[34] The intricate beadwork on the coverlet, the bedcushions, and Mrs. Carter's bed-clothes also suggests sybaritic Eastern influence. That and the actress's red tresses wrapped around her head rather than a powdered white wig distinguish Du Barry from the more conventionally baroque-clad visiting ladies, including the hostile young fashion maven, the princess Marie Antoinette.

But the most Orientalizing feature of this sumptuously appointed bed scene is the turban-headed black dwarf named Zamore, played by the juvenile actor "Master Sams." Ford offers the following historical background:

> Madame Du Barry has received Zamore at the hands of the penurious Duc de Richelieu, who turned him over to her, clad in his native garb of pleated grass and adorned with bracelets, earrings and necklace of solid gold, fashioned in barbaric style. He was a hideously ugly little savage with no more respect for persons than one would have looked for in a monkey. He was funny, however, in a rude simian way and could make grimaces and distort his puny body in such a way as to set his mistress off into roars of laughter.[35]

As he hovers around his lavishly bedded mistress tickling her fancy, Zamore, whose character also recalled Nabo, the black dwarf beloved by Louis XIV's Queen Maria, explicitly racializes the spectacle. His lower evolutionary status signals the degeneracy of so much indolence and expenditure emanating from Du Barry's body. Another image, figure 33, shows Du Barry propping herself up with her elbow atop Zamore's head. Her strings of beads echo those festooned over his turban, and the patterning on the wide hem of her dressing gown echoes that of the Oriental carpet beneath their feet.

From the luxuriant folds of Du Barry's bedclothes, her small denuded feet make naughty periodic appearances. Foot fetishism, a particularly intense sexual preoccupation in an age of corseting and full-body sartorial coverage,

33. *While propping her elbow on the accommodating head of her diminutive servant,*
Zamore (Master Sams), Du Barry (Mrs. Leslie Carter) holds out her foot so the
admiring papal nuncio (H. R. Roberts) can slip on her shoe in Act III of Belasco's
Du Barry, *1901. In James L. Ford,* The Story of Du Barry, *153.*

liberally spices the stage business, bringing the pornographic subtext of the scene closely to the surface and scandalizing some observers. Another historically accurate prop, offered as the final image and most fetishized object in the Ford chronicle of the production, is prominently featured in this scene: the Du Barry slippers. One of these slippers sported a buckle "which was property of Madame Du Barry and was worn by her on just the sort of occasions being represented."[36] Early in this act of the play, when her secret lover's father, the captain of the King's Guard, arrives to see her, she makes him wait outside her door. Thrusting her bare feet into her slippers, she tells her porter, Denys, "When a woman loves someone—she is cunning." She summons Zamore to help her effect an alluring presentation to extract information about Cossé from her visitor. Belasco's stage direction details her actions: "Zamore enters. Du Barry points to her feet. He throws himself down. She slips her foot from under the spread, using his back for a footstool." "Now show him in," she commands. Figure 34 depicts her pose, in which she also holds up an open fan beside her upgathered, flower-bedecked tresses for an additional Orientalizing effect. More stage directions describe the captain's response: "She offers her hand. He appears not to see it, standing with his eyes downcast, his hand on the hilt of his sword."[37] In spite of himself, he is aroused. Compelled to look down, he gazes upon her exotically presented feet and grips his weapon. Beyond Brissac-*père*, Belasco and Mrs. Carter were titillating viewers in the audience with the racy display of Du Barry's exposed feet bizarrely cushioned on the prostrate Zamore's posterior.

An even more suggestive sequence of fetishistic foot business occurs later in the scene when Du Barry receives the papal nuncio, the court priest who has now become her father confessor. Du Barry is emotionally primed for his entrance, because Brissac-*père*'s news that Cossé has called her a courtesan has distressed her and awakened her repentant impulses. She is recovering on her bed when the announcement of the nuncio's arrival prompts her to powder her face. Her attendants scramble to neaten the room and lay out the papal red cloth on which he will approach her bedside. Like the red décor in the previous scene, the holy cloth also extends her red hair in a visual double entendre to ensnare the nuncio in her allure. As the priest enters bearing a large bunch of grapes to share with her, a sexual play on the host wine, she is wiggling her toes over the edge of her bed in search of her slippers, which have been stashed under the night table. Richelieu tries to help her by picking them up and then quickly hides them behind his back as the nuncio approaches. While priest and would-be penitent eat grapes, Richelieu quietly puts the slippers down and withdraws. Seeing her toes still moving in search of her slippers, the nuncio offers to assist. Belasco's photographer captured the moment in figure 33, entitled "Ecclesiastical Homage," a wry poke at Christian piety. Once a footstool, now an armrest for his mistress, Zamore draws her skirts aside to expose her raised naked foot for the nuncio. Down on one knee, the nuncio holds the ball of the slipper in one hand, cups the heel of her foot in the other, and slides her toes into the shoe while staring fixedly at the slope of her arch. This mutually seductive encounter elicits a confession and a blessing. The nuncio motions others away so he and Du Barry can whisper a private exchange:

NUNCIO: I shall ever hope for my daughter, Jeanette—
DU BARRY:—the sinner—
NUNCIO:—until I receive into our fold, Jeanette the saint.

34. Du Barry (Mrs. Leslie Carter) uses the posterior of her black dwarf servant Zamore (Master Sams) as a footstool, in Act III of Belasco's Du Barry, 1901. In James L. Ford, The Story of Du Barry, *op. p. 144.*

DU BARRY: Ah, Monseigneur, the man I told you of—the one man—
could have made me one of the Saints of Heaven! But now—(*She
kneels—he raises his hand over her.*)
NUNCIO: God bless you, my girl. [38]

Overwhelmed with regret for abdicating the true love she had with Cossé,
a conscience-stricken Du Barry tells the king's scheming ministers that she
has changed. They have been bribing her to use her sexual wiles to get Louis
to do their bidding, which makes clear that she has never really loved the king
but has shown him affection for money. However, only her ulterior motives
have changed, not the falseness of her royal love. Sitting on the bed "cross-
legged like a Turk, throwing bon-bons to Zamore, who catches them in his
mouth," she resolves to seduce Louis into suspending the *pacte de famine*
("famine treaty") enacted to subsidize the very material lavishness that sur-
rounds her. When the king enters through his private door in a flirtatious
mood, she playfully hits him with her slipper. In a striking repeat of the
tableau just staged with the nuncio, the king kneels and puts the slipper on
her foot. But whereas the priest's fetishistic attention to her lower extremity
elicited a truer confession, here the stage direction reads: "It is plain to be
seen that she forces herself to submit to his caresses."[39] She is just getting him
to agree to suspend the *pacte* by threatening to leave and pretending to dress
herself to do so when word comes that the leader of the revolutionaries that
the king's army has been trying to capture is none other than Cossé. Du Barry
drops the hatbox she is holding, which betrays her inner alarm. Knowing she
had loved a young man and having bribed Jean du Barry to disclose his name,
the king is inflamed with jealousy and fear that her infidelity is tied to state
treachery. He exits in a rage.

Cossé enters wounded but determined to kill the monarch who lured
Jeanette away from him. His arrival gives Du Barry the opportunity to express
the true love she has withheld from the king to the real object of her affection.
While Belasco could push the envelope of public decency with a little foot
fetishism, he could not stage an explicit sex scene, so he maneuvered the lovers
into bed by other means. He devised an especially macabre situation to draw
passion outward from the whore's body into a climax that matched the orgas-
mic scenic investiture. As Du Barry starts to pour out her pent up passion, the
physical tension escalates with the roll of drums below and the approach of
soldiers and the king himself, who start pounding for entry. Fearing that he will
expose himself to certain death at the hands of the royal guards, Du Barry

35. Jeanne Du Barry (Mrs. Leslie Carter) pommels Cossé Brissac (Hamilton Revelle) on his chest wounds to "save" him in Act III of Belasco's Du Barry, 1901. Courtesy of the Byron Collection, Museum of the City of New York.

wrestles with Cossé to contain his mounting desire to stab the king. Their physical contact causes Cossé to "forget himself" and take the palpitating woman in his arms. But the sound of the king's voice moves him to rise and, fully erect, draw his sword. Whereupon, Du Barry, desperate to keep him from being discovered, throws herself on him, pounds him on his open chest wounds with her bare fists, and sends him falling backward, unconscious, on the bed (fig. 35). She rushes to loosen the door bolt and then tumbles into bed beside him, hiding his unconscious body under the twelve-thousand-dollar cover, as the king and his attendants burst into the room. The characters have discharged enormous passion, but Cossé's condition when he hits the sheets spectacularly guarantees that activities in the bed remain chaste and acceptable to respectable audiences.

With one lover improbably concealed in the bed and the other at her bedside demanding to know his whereabouts, Du Barry finds herself at the moment of most excruciating conflict between true and false love that Belasco devised to play his actress's emotions. The impresario developed the stage business with special ferocity. Working alone in his rented room when inspiration struck, he took the part of Du Barry himself and grabbed an unsuspecting workman passing by in the hallway to play Cossé. A fire had broken out in the building next door to which the workman was rushing to attend, but Belasco kept him in such a grip, repeatedly pushing him down on the bed and pounding his chest, that he could not escape for more than twenty minutes.[40] When Belasco brought the business to Mrs. Carter, he had to make her rise to his desired level of intensity, not only to beat her lover on his wounds with her bare hands but to contain the anxiety of hiding him once the king and his guards arrive. Mrs. Carter writes of how, in a session conducted in her private residence, she first attained the appropriate pitch:

> I am cursed by a prenatal mark of fear of electrical storms. This fear has been my torment—so much so that, in any house I have ever lived in, my bed rested on those cups of glass used as nonconductors on telegraph poles. . . . There was [a storm] while we were in Fredericksburg that was the most dreadful of my experience.
>
> Mr. Dave began the reading of the tremendous third scene, which begins with Du Barry in bed, her heart stricken with panic for her lover. She must hold her petite levee from her golden bed; but she must show no sign of distress. . . . Each peal sent me into convulsive crying.

Belasco scolded her to stop until he realized he could make use of her surges of emotion: " 'Good! Keep it up! Splendid!' he cried exultingly. 'I'll put it in. The whole thing is an avowal in itself of coming events.' "[41] Thereafter, each time she played the scene in rehearsal and performance, she was compelled to relive that "prenatal" terror.

When the king and his soldiers burst in on this bed scene, Louis tries to use his royal will to extract a truthful response from his mistress: "I know that man came into this room. I know where he is. I could hand him over to the police . . . but I want you to confess to me." But, having already given her emotional and bodily confession to Cossé, she bluffs the king and his attendants into leaving the room with a show of indignation over his suspicions. When she thinks they are alone, she uncovers Cossé to check on his health. However, the treacherous Jean du Barry has been spying on her and demands monetary payment in exchange for silence, forcing her to spend again—in material terms—before the act curtain.

In Act IV, she manages to distract Louis for a while with another huge expenditure, a grand bacchanalian fete featuring "Scalo, a big Nubian," high-kicking dancers, a troupe of clowns, two cupids, and a harp player who strums an ode to Du Barry's crowning sensual glory, her hair. But the evil Jean, seeking royal favor, divulges her secret to the king. "His Most Christian Majesty" forces her to remain his concubine in exchange for letting Cossé live.

Trapped but defiant, Du Barry operatically excoriates her royal keeper: "You can laugh at him, mock him, madden him, take my body, degrade it . . . torment it; make me your slave . . . your dog to kick . . . your Court fool; make me a traitor . . . a Judas—that is the price I pay for his life; but you cannot tear Cossé out of my heart, you cannot, you cannot; for he is there!" She hurls in the king's face that for all his vaunted authority and the cruelty of his blackmail, he cannot displace her true love. The stage direction has him exiting in a rage—"The King has gone off to pray that he might forget the milliner, and the Court has gone off to laugh at the King"—while Du Barry is left alone on stage.[42] Ford writes of the memorable picture "of the actress . . . at the moment when the curtain, falling on the fourth act, hid her from view as she stood, her hands before her face, her whole form shaken with sobs, completely unnerved by the storm and passion and suffering of the mimic scene through which she had just passed."[43] As the king is ridiculed for his impotence, the impresario proved spectacularly successful in emotionally unhinging his actress, or so Ford and Belasco would have audiences believe.

The play ends more than fifteen years later, after the death of Louis XV, when a repentant Du Barry has been living in exile, ironically—but, in Belasco's scheme, fittingly—in a convent in Louveciennes, and the Revolution is in full swing. The march of the Reign of Terror has reached Du Barry's door; she is slated to follow Louis XVI and Marie Antoinette to the guillotine. Clad in a white penitential robe, her famous flaming hair cropped short, Du Barry is rolled along the street past her old milliner's shop in a horse-drawn cart to the plaza for public executions. The old nuncio sits beside her in black to hear her last confession. A derisive crowd of "cart swallows" and sansculottes taunt and jeer at her to the strains of "La Carmagnole." In addition to the working cart pulled by a live horse, Belasco used a prize prop, another antique treasure procured for the production, to put Mrs. Carter more fully into the reality of the scene and ratchet up her emotions. She writes of the moment when he first presented it to her:

> Lady Meuse, Cora Potter, and I were in my hotel on an afternoon when Mr. Belasco entered with an enormous package, which he set before us with much satisfaction. He had been to the Morgue in the old part of Paris. In his graphic and dramatic way he began to describe those melancholy

forms that lay behind glass in the city of death, the little jet of water playing over each forlorn body, the only sign of life in that house of decay. We put our hands over our ears to silence him when he unwrapped his parcel. . . . It turned out to be what is now one of the valuables of his rare collection, which we used at every performance of Du Barry—a viol; in other words, a sort of medieval hurdy-gurdy.

It is strapped around the neck of the player, and rested, when not in use on four pegs. It is the instrument from which developed the violin, and was formerly employed at fairs, weddings, and festivals; but later, and more horribly, it was invariably in the back of the tumbrel, as an escort to the guillotine.

This particular viol was covered with bloodspots that had turned into rust and had eaten into the wood. By much patient research in after years, with the assistance of Sanford White, it was definitely established to have been used as an accompaniment to the furies in their carmagnoles as they danced around the melancholy freight in the tumbrels.[44]

If Belasco aspired to play his actress's body and evoke her passions like music from a violin, with this morbid instrument he orchestrated Du Barry's final expiation. To render the representation respectable, character and actress had to appear to be punished as hugely and violently as they have spent. For the play's concluding tableau, Cossé fights his way through the crowd for a last good-bye, and the nuncio calls for her final confession. With "her whole attitude one of abject and awful terror,"[45] Jeanette cries "Cossé—I loved you— through it all!"[46] She holds his gaze, her eyes pouring out tears of fear and sorrow for the purer life her indolence and material appetites prevented them from having together, as the horse draws the cart offstage to her beheading.

In meeting the goal of emotional impact on actress and audience, Belasco's lavish realism succeeded resoundingly, according to published accounts. After chronicling the story of *Du Barry* in terms of its massive scenography, choice antiques, and precisely reproduced props and costumes, Ford concludes his volume with the lines "at the core of it all—underneath the modest garb of the milliner's girl, the gorgeous robes of the pampered favorite of the Bourbon king, and the coarse gown of the condemned prisoner—is the soul of the woman who has created the part."[47] That soul announced to the press: "I am Mme. Du Barry. I am Mme. Du Barry reincarnated. I believe—I have always believed that in a previous existence I was that unfortunate woman."[48] Consequently, she viewed the play as more hers than Belasco's: "Do you wonder that I claimed Du Barry as my very own? I was the instrument from which he struck his resonances. The play represented a period in civilization in which the senses ruled; the whole of it swung on a great drive of passion, sex, intrigue, and color—every scene roared with an undying torrential beating of human emotions."[49]

Ford writes of how Du Barry's sumptuously displayed reincarnation moved the audience on opening night at New York's Criterion Theatre on 25 December 1901:

> It is safe to say that no one who was present on that memorable night will ever forget the moment when the audience that had doubted and questioned at eight o'clock, only to lose itself in the absorbing interest of the drama that was unfolded to them, rose at last with shouts of enthusiasm and waving of handkerchiefs, while tears streamed from women's eyes, and bouquets, torn from breasts that throbbed with emotion, fell at the feet of the great artist who had again conquered cold, critical, sneering New York.[50]

That this opening occurred on Christmas Day made Belasco's conquest with his actress all the more meaningful. If any of the audience harbored residual puritanical concerns over their lifestyles of conspicuous consumption that peaked during the holiday season, they could displace those onto a putatively more decadent imperial regime and feel righteous over the due punishment suffered by the heroine. Belasco might also have taken satisfaction from the ironies of his accomplishment. The Jewish impresario had compelled the high-class Protestant society that had disdained and doubted him, on a night when Christians might have been thinking about their savior's birth by immaculate conception, to feast on visual pleasures, indulge prurient interests, and cry over the fate of a whore.

Audiences allowed themselves the indulgence not only because of the play's ultimate moral message but also because the mode of production made them feel safe; the excesses to which they were exposed were controlled by established structures of impresarial management. Advance press and reviews sustained the impression that Belasco, like Augustin Daly before him, shaped the whole with a commanding artistic vision. He reportedly supervised the design and building of the sets and the acquisition of so many material goods, as well as directed the performances of all fifty-five cast members, chiefly, of course, that of his star. Reviewers understood how he used such extravagant scenic materiality to justify and provoke her performance. Drawing from Alan Dale's comment that only Mrs. Carter, with her supreme emotional powers, could triumph over such trappings, Craig Timberlake suggests: "The stifling atmosphere of such a heavy production may have prompted Mrs. Carter to lower the safety valve on her extraordinary reserves of 'hot hysteria.'"[51] The famously prudish William Winter was initially appalled by Mrs. Carter's performance because of how she appeared to lose self-control and violated the bounds of decency. He complained about the unseemly exposure of bare feet, noting "they were not even pretty feet," and decried her method—"to work herself into a state of violent excitement, to weep, vociferate, shriek, rant, become hoarse with passion, and finally to flop and beat the floor"—as "the ready resource of a febrile, unstable nature." But even he conceded that "there were, nevertheless, executive force and skill in Mrs. Carter's performance after it had been often repeated under the guiding government of her sagacious and able manager."[52] It was precisely the thrill of the appearance of her being out of control coupled with the reassurance that she was indeed strongly governed that made the performance so enjoyable.

Perhaps the most dangerous aspects of Mrs. Carter's performance that audiences needed to believe were under strict managerial control were the deceptive powers of the seductress that threatened catastrophe for imperial regimes. Both she and her manager actively contributed to the public perception that Belasco had these particular powers well in hand, that her character might have deceived the king but that the actress was not deceiving her maker; Mrs. Carter was acting for Belasco out of true love, not chiefly for material gain. Moreover, hers was not merely base physical love, although the belief that Belasco sexually controlled her also served this agenda, but a higher affectional and reverential form. The star made a huge show of this love when, on the set of *Du Barry* after the New Year's Day performance, she presided over a public presentation of a silver loving cup to Belasco. The engraving read "Mrs. Leslie Carter in David Belasco's Play 'Du Barry'/ Presented to Mr. David Belasco by the Members of His Company" and concluded with an adaptation of Du Barry's dying confession to Cossé, "Remember that we loved you; we loved you through it all."[53] The playing of "Maryland, My Maryland," the theme song from the leading lady's breakthrough star vehicle, *The Heart of Maryland*, during the ceremony underscored that the love, while extended by all the company, was the most personally and enduringly felt by Mrs. Carter.

Other visual emblems signaling Belasco's supposed control over his actress's body and sexuality included publicity photographs distributed around the production. One striking example shows Du Barry standing in

36. Mrs. Leslie Carter in her Du Barry *traveling costume
monogrammed with the initials "DB" over her hip, 1901–1902.
In William Winter,* Life of David Belasco, *vol. 2, op. p. 42.*

sumptuous "street clothes" dressed to leave the palace (fig. 36). She never fully dons this attire during the play, which suggests that the photograph was posed for purposes beyond documentation of the production. Her body stands sideways to the picture frame but her head is turned over her shoulder to cast a come-hither look at the viewer. Elaborately embroidered over her hip, which is angled slightly into the foreground almost dead center in the frame, are the letters DB entwined in a heart shape and topped with a crown. The initials ostensibly stand for Du Barry but could just as easily mean David Belasco and thus signify sovereignty like a brand on prize livestock.

Such publicity, together with Belasco and Mrs. Carter's onstage manipulations, helped respectable audiences indulge with impunity in the decadent spectacle of the Great Whore of History. Indeed, the play's popularity made it the duo's most sensational hit. After its Washington premiere, *Du Barry* played for thirty-six weeks over two seasons in New York and then toured for an eight-week engagement in Boston, six weeks in Philadelphia, and eight weeks in Chicago. Belasco boasted in his autobiography that "the expenses of the production were such [$98,000, about $2.4 million today] that there was no profit to be made" because "the mere 'suggestion' of luxury would not do."[54] However, by Charles Harper's accounting, *Du Barry* garnered more than $404,000 (about $9.16 million today) in box office receipts.[55] If Belasco and Mrs. Carter spent in various ways to mount the production, so, too, did the fashionable spectators who flocked to partake of *Du Barry's* charms in these major American metropolises.

Imperial Architecture and Napoleonic Collecting

Belasco's vaunted mastery of the feminine passion embodied in his actress and exteriorized in her emotionally excessive performance and the lavish materiality of the *mise-en-scène* extended into the momentous construction of his first theatre. As Belasco's biographers have pointed out, it was not until he acquired his own theatre that he attained full independence as an impresario and entered the ranks of the most powerful producers. With the death in 1899 of Augustin Daly, writes William Winter, invoking *Richard III*, "the chair of artistic managerial sovereignity was empty, 'the sword unswayed, the empire unpossessed.'" Belasco's opportunity to take possession came on 7 January 1902, during *Du Barry's* run at the Criterion, when Oscar Hammerstein, who owned the 1,100-seat Republic Theatre and was struggling against the Theatrical Syndicate's increasing monopoly on play production in New York

City, offered to lease him the building.[56] With this structure, the impresario styled his regime in an imperial manner that echoed the themes and material details of *Du Barry* in order to magnify his leading lady's star power and, by extension, his impresarial prowess as her maker.

Hammerstein had originally built the theatre to rival the Comédie-Française and the Imperial Opera House in Berlin, and it featured a dome that the *New York Times* described as "a replica on a slightly smaller scale of the dome at the Capitol in Washington."[57] Belasco kept these outer trappings of empire and commissioned extensive remodeling to enlarge the theatre's capacity for showcasing his leading lady to their mutual advantage. Belasco spent more than $150,000 on renovations (about $3.4 million today). Work-men gutted the interior and blasted a twenty-five-foot crater into underlying rock to enlarge the basement for scene change machinery, including traps, ele-vator lifts, and turntables.[58] The blasting, which the excited Belasco claims to have ignited himself, tapped an underground spring that flooded the building and cost $125,000 in repairs, which comprised most of the total bill for the ren-ovation but also garnered Belasco another biblical appellation for his persona. He told William Winter, "My boys in the theatre used to call me 'Moses' after that, for I did smite the rock and there came water out of it."[59] In addition to the building's elaborate scenic apparatus, Mrs. Carter was favored with a two-room dressing area on the stage level and a suite of rooms over the stage adjoin-ing Belasco's own suite. While his included a private studio, a library, and the theatre's offices, hers included an oak-paneled den "with divans and an open hearth" and a "serving room" supplied with "appropriate luxuries and con-veniences" for "dining after matinees."[60] Newspaper reports detailing these features made rival producers and the public aware that the new theatrical emperor was installing his consort in the palace.

If this arrangement evoked the disreputable paradigm of the conspicu-ously kept woman, Belasco and Mrs. Carter strove to ennoble it through the discourses of "home" and "work." The program for the inaugural production of *Du Barry* in the newly remodeled theatre was fronted with an essay enti-tled "Home," which declared: "Not only has Mr. Belasco now his own the-atrical domicile, so to speak—dedicated by him as the dramatic home of Mrs. Leslie Carter—but it is his wish that the public, who have so liberally favored him in the past, may find here a sort of domestic atmosphere which will lend an added comfort to the occupation of playgoing."[61] Providing the morally suspect "gypsy" actress with a permanent home and making the atmosphere more homelike for patrons was to civilize and uplift the theatre with the ideology of bourgeois domesticity. Moreover, the new theatre's luxuries, rather than merely enhancing pleasure, were to accommodate the impresario and actress's already well-publicized work ethic. Mrs. Carter's labors had been in the papers again the preceding spring when Belasco was compelled to send her to Europe for complete rest after the rigors of *Du Barry*'s first season.[62] Such reporting assured audiences that while grandiose indolence corrupted Du Barry, arduous effort was purifying the actress who played her. Belasco insisted that because it was his leading lady's "custom" to "devote her spare time to work and study," her apartment adjoining his studio was to give her a "home for these pursuits."[63] In his curtain speech after *Du Barry*'s third act on the new theatre's opening night, Belasco paid tribute to the actress as "my friend and companion in work."[64]

According to Mrs. Carter's autobiography, Belasco put the hardworking mistress of this theatrical domicile in charge of interior décor. The star carried the aesthetics of *Du Barry*, the crowning vehicle of her repertoire, into the design and invested the décor with the heroine's passion for material splendor. The stage curtain and draperies for the boxes were fashioned with rose Du Barry velvet, while the seats were upholstered "in delicate reseda green, toned with silver shading" that echoed the famous greens of Jeannette's bedroom.[65] Female patrons could freshen up in the Marie Antoinette cloakroom on the lower level appointed to give "the visiting lady" the impression of "entering her private boudoir."[66] When opening night approached, and the decorators had not finished on schedule, Mrs. Carter "with [her] own hands. . . helped to hang and tack and hammer the draperies in the boxes." She wrote of how she "began to have a peculiar feeling about the place, as one does about a home one loves." But, more than a home, it was a "church, wherein I could find my statues and my saints," and she infused the space with a religious ardor: "I could stand on its stage alone, among the shaded lights, in the austere stillness, and weave a mysterious secret tapestry of prayer as sacred as that called forth by altars and choirs. I named it myself."[67] She claimed that it was she, not Belasco, who first pronounced the name change from the Republic to the Belasco Theatre, at once signaling her worship of her clerically collared maker and her own agency in her making. However, press and program copy, as well as William Winter's biographical account, asserted that Belasco was the "executive force" that "drove through to completion" all facets of the renovation.[68] The public was to feel assured that Mrs. Carter's decorative spendings, like her passions in performance, were well under his control.

While Belasco's priestly image continued to lend an air of authority and sanctity, if not moral propriety, to his enterprise, a Napoleonic pose, magnified by the production of *Du Barry*, provided a more explicitly imperialistic sinecure of control. The five-foot-three Belasco had admired the "Little Corporal" who became emperor at least since the 1870s, when he apprenticed in San Francisco with Tom Maguire, who styled himself as the "Napoleon of the Theatre."[69] Over the years Belasco gathered Napoleonic books and objects, eventually amassing hundreds of items, including dozens of miniature statues and busts, army flags and drums carried by the emperor's legions, jewel-studded gold coffee cups used by Napoleon and Josephine, and even a lock of Bonaparte's hair. These would be given their own room in his second theatre, the Stuyvesant, in 1909.[70] But the collection was well underway by 1902 and was a prominent feature of Belasco's studio in his first theatre. A photograph (fig. 37) of that studio shows a statue of the emperor on top of a curio cabinet containing Napoleonic figurines and cups next to a lion-footed imperial brocade chair. One figurine visible on the top shelf inside the cabinet shows Napoleon wearing his trademark hat and long coat with arms crossed defiantly over his chest, the very costume and pose in which Belasco would later have himself photographed (fig. 38).

The inspirational qualities of Napoleon for Belasco entailed more than being short of stature and gaining great power. As Western history's preeminent "self-made" emperor, Bonaparte was a hero not only for Tom Maguire but for other theatre potentates (notably Charles Frohman, who was dubbed "Napoleon of the Drama" and wore a Napoleon ring) and captains of industry (Ida Tarbell famously compared John D. Rockefeller to Napoleon) in the high class of men to which Belasco sought acceptance. But for Belasco the appeal may have been even more specific. Writing in "Behind the Scenes with Belasco" about her visit, Jane Dransfield mused: "One wonders why this admiration of the imperialistic Corsican? Is it because of the exotic strain in the ancestry of both, making them spiritually kin? Or is it because Napoleon, too, believed in his 'star,' as has always David Belasco?"[71] Both men aspired to move from degraded, culturally Othered positions to the top of their societies. Napoleon may also have set an inspiring example for Belasco by not allowing feminine influence and the susceptibilities of the heart to deter him from his conquering mission. Magda West cites as indicative of "Belasco's Views on Love" his 1912 production of *The Governor's Lady* in which Bonaparte was repeatedly praised because he "rode over poor old Josephine's heart" and "let nothing stand in his path."[72] A workaholic bent on achieving

37. *"Belasco's 'Studio' in the First Belasco Theatre,"* in William Winter,
Life of David Belasco, *vol. 2, op. p. 54.*

theatrical success, Belasco could not afford to be overly deterred by the personal demands of a wife, two daughters, and numerous actresses who vied for his attentions.[73]

The opening of the new theatre with *Du Barry* worked in various ways to enshrine Belasco as Napoleon. In his account of the play and its historical sources, John L. Ford included the portentous note that "within three months after the formal presentation of Madame du Barry at the court of her king and lover, Napoleon Bonaparte was born on the island of Corsica."[74] While the Little Corporal never appeared in the play, the production lionized him by making as vivid as possible the extreme decadence and chaos from which he would save his nation on his way to becoming "the world's conqueror."[75] Extensions of the stage décor into other parts of the building linked Belasco's enterprise with Napoleon's. Positioned over the stage with a window for monitoring activities below, and featuring the Napoleon collection plus myriad artifacts from the Bourbon and revolutionary eras, Belasco's studio served as an imperial throne room.[76] Ada Patterson commented on one object whose outer edge is discernible in the studio photograph (fig. 37): "If [Belasco's] eyes turn upward, in search of inspiration, they encounter . . . a lion rampant and encircled by a curiously wrought wreath of iron, which hung before the door of a Paris tavern, in the path taken by the tumbrils that bore the royalty and nobility of France to the guillotine."[77] In the more public space of the auditorium, the "Napoleonic bee" embroidered on all 950 seats and embossed in the plaster facades of the boxes made a more visible link between the Little Corporal and the impresario.[78] Playing on the letter "B" for Belasco and Bonaparte, the bee was also a "sign of indefatigable industry," which highlighted Belasco's desired image as "a tireless toiler . . . attempting to wrest order out of chaos."[79]

A pointed attack by the rival Syndicate highlighted Belasco's Napoleonic investments in his new theatre. During the first performance of a revival of *Zaza* in the Belasco Theatre's second season, a young man leapt from one of the boxes onto the stage and accosted Mrs. Carter upon her entrance.[80] Unbeknownst to Belasco, Charles Frohman had sold the rights to *Zaza* to the actress Eugenie Blair, and her manager, Henri Gressitt, was trying to enjoin Mrs. Carter from appearing in the role. The young man who leapt onto the stage was the process server hired by Gressitt's attorneys to deliver the summons. Belasco attributed the plot to the Syndicate and blamed Frohman in particular.[81] The disruption of the performance was bad enough, but the affront to his leading lady on the stage of his palatial imperial "home" could not have been more insulting to Belasco. Believing that the established Napoleon was trying to "crush" the new Bonaparte, he attributed Frohman's motives to jealousy.[82] As a result, these former close friends and business associates would not speak to each other for twelve years.

While defending his empire against the Syndicate, Belasco adopted a more expansive Napoleonic vision of conquest in pursuit of his ambitions, a development that can be seen in his activities as a collector as well as an impresario. More than an eccentric display of increased wealth, his collecting worked in conjunction with his theatrical producing as a mode of imperial self-fashioning. Here again, Napoleon served as a model. A voracious plunderer with a taste for the exotic, Bonaparte commissioned Dominique Vivant Denon, infamous pocketer of the mummy's foot in Egypt, to organize the

Louvre, a palatial warehouse and showplace for art and imperial trophies.[83] He also established one of the world's premier pornography collections. As part of a containment program that also involved imprisoning the Marquis de Sade and cleaning up the smut trade around the Palais Royale, Napoleon had two copies of all books seized as immoral stored in an underground library, the Enfer, to which only the privileged few were allowed access.[84] He undertook such seizures on the hubristic presumption that possession of those objects meant control over the forces they represented.

Where Napoleon amassed national collections housed in state institutions, Belasco built a private collection. The accumulation of objects that had to proceed more slowly when he had less money and space could grow apace after he acquired his own theatre. As figure 37 reveals, he packed the studio in his first theatre from floor to ceiling with books and objects and continued to acquire more things, so that by 1909 he would fill multiple rooms in his second theatre. When the collection was sold after his death in 1931, the catalogue of objects spanned 188 printed pages and listed 1,239 lots, many of which comprised multiple items. These numbers do not include Belasco's vast book collection, which was dispersed separately.[85] In a brief foreword to the catalogue, Leslie Hyam notes:

> We are concerned here for a moment with the collector Belasco—the indefatigable collector of porcelains, glass, jewelry, watches, arms, and armor, fabrics, prints, bronzes, and a score of other categories of bibelots, the student and admirer of Napoleon, the whimsical worshipper of elephants— all one and indivisible. We have thus a picture of a man of astonishing breadth of interest, tireless curiosity and childlike wonder at the world's pretty things, which may be also, perhaps, to those who knew him well, a fair quarter-length portrait of the man himself.

Hyam's final comment about Belasco's collection serving as a kind of self-portrait points to a question a number of theorists have examined: how collections reveal their collectors. Writing about modern Western traditions of collecting, Susan Stewart observes: "The function of belongings within the economy of the bourgeois subject is one of supplementarity, a supplementarity that in consumer culture replaces its generating subject as the interior milieu substitutes for, and takes the place of, an interior self." In this context, the private collection becomes a device for the objectification and management of desire as the collector acquires, classifies, and fits objects into his own narrative to "invent a realizable world, a world which 'works.'"[86] For Jean

Baudrillard, in a section titled "The Object as Passion," the primary desire being objectified and managed through the collection, especially in male collectors over forty, is sexual and compensatory: "Man never comes so close to being the master of a secret seraglio as when he is surrounded by his objects."[87] But Stewart also addresses other identity issues bound up in desire. In collecting exotic objects, the collector manages his own capacity for Otherness, both by signaling survival of encounters with foreign cultures and by making himself appear more worldly and powerful.[88]

Many of the categories in the impresario's collection indicate objectification of the feminized, racialized, and sexualized passions the dominant culture projected onto him as an exotically marked Jew. An interest in rare—and, specifically, pornographic—books not only as knowledge sources but also as collectible objects registers a need for management as well as stimulation of sexual desires.[89] A feminine love of "pretty things" and exotica is overwhelmingly manifest in the scores of Chinese porcelains; Oriental and Alpujarra rugs; Bohemian, Rhenish, and English glass; bibelots and carved ivories; semiprecious mineral snuff boxes and carvings; necklaces of semiprecious minerals (including thirty-eight rosaries); other jewelry, cameos, watches, and miniatures; damasks, brocades, velvets, and embroideries; and French, Italian, English, and American furniture and decorations.[90] That Belasco also owned many books about these artifacts—in particular, in the category of Oriental arts—reflects the impulse to manipulate various aspects of the Otherness subsumed in his "racial" stereotype through accumulation of both knowledge and things.

The nature and volume of the objects in Belasco's collections reveal the extent to which the desires excoriated and expiated through *Du Barry* were the impresario's own. Montrose J. Moses, who witnessed the impresario's operations, wrote of how, in preparation for the play, "Mr. Belasco was in his element. The collector's instinct in him was given full rein; and he soon found added to his collection of curios an invaluable assortment of furniture, glass, and silks."[91] But whereas the character had to be punished for her overspending and the actress rigorously directed to control her emotional and physical outbursts, the impresario claimed the freedom to pursue and the power to control his appetites. He did so with the Napoleonic hubris that continued accumulation of objects would enable him to tame even as he indulged the passions they exteriorized and to build up rather than bring down his empire.

After *Du Barry*, both the accumulation of objects and the taming of passions in material form so evident in Belasco's collections also became increasingly evident in his productions, as the two activities overlapped and fueled each other. A brief look at his last two plays for Mrs. Carter, *Adrea* (1904) and "Repka Stroon" (1905), shows how Belasco extended his vaunted mastery of desire by venturing into more exotic subject matter that bore still closer relation to aspects of his stereotyped Jewish identity.

Set on a mythical island in the eastern part of the deteriorating Roman Empire in the fifth century CE, *Adrea's* massive scenery and operatically tragic performance by Mrs. Carter grandly exteriorized aspects of pre-Christian, Oriental "barbarousness" and licentiousness that were also part of early-twentieth-century negative Jewish stereotypes. The study of ancient Rome provided a font of material for Victorian pornophiles like Belasco, who likely drew from accounts of the late empire's more bizarre blood spectacles in formulating the heroine's provocation to climax.[92] Adrea is a blind princess tricked by her evil sister Iulia and faithless fiancé, the Northern Praetorian Tribune Kaeso, into having conjugal relations with the dwarf court jester Mimus, "a painted, hideous, gibbering thing in red and white; a dog from Pluto; an effigy of devils; not half a man"[93] (fig. 39). The plan is to conceal Mimus in Kaeso's Nordic armor and have him take Kaeso's place on the wedding night. Along with Roman sources depicting dwarves jesting at court and copulating with full-sized women for spectator sport in the arena, Belasco, a fan of Wagnerian opera, may have been inspired by the Mime of the Ring Cycle, who was recognized by contemporaries as a Jewish figure.[94] A lecher and an expert impersonator, Belasco's Mimus exhibits the mimicry, duplicity, and sexual incontinence attributed to Jewish males. Playing on the assumed links between Jews and "lower" races, Belasco dressed the actor in a dark corn-rowed wig, which further blackened the racial identity behind the jester's mask of white clown makeup. Because antique armor was another feature of Belasco's collections, the impresario had considerable hands-on knowledge and access to objects with which to work out the mechanics of this sexual ruse that exploited the heroine's lack of sight and consequent reliance on touch.[95]

After Adrea's cruel loss of virginity, Mimus's Jewish seed spawns a terrible vengeance in her. This is expressed in the lavish materiality of her next costume: a sensual gown whose highly ornate beading around the chest and over the hips, converging at the groin, invoked Gustave Moreau's well-known Orientalist canvases of Salome (fig. 40). As Salome demanded the head of John the Baptist, so Adrea rises from her throne and demands Kaeso's body.[96] She orders her minions first to flog him and then have him drawn and quartered by wild horses. However, before they can haul him away, he expresses

39. *Belasco's perverse love triangle in* Adrea *(1905): the blind princess (Mrs. Leslie Carter), flanked on the right by her warrior fiancé Kaeso (Charles A. Stevenson) and on the left by his trickster surrogate Mimus (J. Harry Benrimo). Courtesy of the Byron Collection, Museum of the City of New York.*

remorse that rekindles her love. Unable to let him suffer such a horrible death, she seizes a sword from a table and stabs him herself in a highly physical climax that rivals Du Barry's pummeling of Cossé in his open wounds. Her expiatory—and, by implication, Christianizing—conversion to mercy and forgiveness is completed when she passes the throne to the innocent son of her sister and Kaeso's incestuous union, the scion of the Nordic blood that will now govern the realm.

With the premiere of *Adrea* in Washington, D.C., Belasco scored one of the greatest triumphs of his career in a battle waged over the prerogative of showcasing his emotional star with all the material trappings of a full production. Signaling his imperial ambitions and desire to conquer the most powerful as well as fashionable of American audiences, he had insisted since *The Heart of Maryland* on premiering his plays in the nation's capital before opening them in New York. By 1905 the Theatrical Syndicate, seeking to thwart Belasco's string of successes, had shut him out of Washington's theatres, virtually all of which the conglomerate controlled. Not to be denied, Belasco went to tremendous expense and effort to outfit the available but

40. *Mrs. Leslie Carter as Adrea, after ascending the throne, in her Salome costume à la Gustave Moreau, 1905. In William Winter,* Life of David Belasco, *vol. 2, op. p. 186.*

ramshackle Convention Hall to accommodate *Adrea's* massive scenic demands. To give the interior a high-class aura, his crew festooned the auditorium with the green velvet drapes from the set of *Du Barry's* opulent boudoir.[97] The opening night audience included President Theodore Roosevelt and his fellow Spanish American War veterans, Admirals George Dewey and Winfield Scott Schley, who applauded the play even while being covered with green rain when the overhead drapes grew sodden under the leaky roof during a cloud burst.[98] The play was transferred to the Belasco Theatre in New York, where audiences stayed drier and whiter for a run of 123 performances. Belasco revived it the following season for 23 more. Although these numbers fell short of *Du Barry's* 165 initial performances and three subsequent revivals, *Adrea* still had a significant life on the stage.[99]

"Repka Stroon" was the final vehicle Belasco wrote for his prototypical star. The script was never produced, but it is still extant and warrants analysis for what it reveals about the impresario's developing vision. Furthering his Napoleonic project set forth in *Du Barry* of mastering the putative sins of his own Otherness, the play daringly engages the imagined world of Svengali. The action is set in New York City's far East Side "in a quarter where the Hungarians, Hebrews, Germans, and Bohemians are found," which Belasco would have realized with the collector's preoccupation with material objects and exotic pictorial detail that had come to characterize his *mise-en-scènes*. Whereas the Svengali figure lumps various perceived alien characteristics into a single image of a nefarious Jew, Belasco parses them more specifically to deflect the worst qualities onto more exotic "races." The Svengali-esque Stroon is a "dark man, half Bohemian, half gypsy," the latter a term with Hindu as well as Semitic associations. A heavily indebted drunkard and gambler, Stroon is driven to pimp his wife Repka to the villainous Micaela Eskier, an Andalusian fakir of the Basque province. In contrast, Belasco creates Judah of Portugal, "a little pale, large-eyed Jew," who bears both the author's short stature and land of family origin. Abjectly and chastely devoted to Repka, "Little Judah" seeks to protect her from Stroon's and Micaela's machinations. Belasco specifies that "no article of his dress should be copied after the wearing apparel usually worn by the stage Jew."[100] Along with behavior, Belasco wanted to use costume to separate the play's purest Jew, an echo of "little David," from prevailing stereotypes.

The heroine Repka is a "strange bird in the nest" with a "mixed ancestry" that includes both Portugese and "gypsy" elements. As in the case of Du Maurier's Trilby, her ambiguous "racial" identity and the stipulation that "she is uncorseted and should show it" suggest transformative potential for movement both upward and downward along the social, racial, and moral hierarchy. Like Belasco's priest's collar, her observance of All Saint's Day and a religious motto over the door to her room gesture toward "higher" spiritual aspirations. Only desperate circumstances pushed her into a "low" marriage to Stroon that she has tried stoically to endure. But when Stroon is not so mysteriously murdered, and the evil Micaela tries to blackmail her into sexual bondage, she lets loose with an expiatory tirade. Refusing to stand any longer for the abuse and degradation forced upon her, she will hearken to a higher law than that which Micaela threatens, no matter the consequences. Little Judah pledges loyalty to her to the end. In directing his actress to reach this emotional climax amid a fully realized, naturalistic rendering of the ghetto, Belasco could have boldly vented anger and desire for dignified triumph over the negative associations projected onto Jews as a group regardless of individual differences.

However, the summer before "Repka Stroon" was to go into rehearsal, Belasco called Mrs. Carter, who was vacationing in upstate New York after her tour, to ask whether rumors of her secret marriage to actor Lou Payne were true. When she confirmed that they were, Belasco, after seventeen years of partnership, cut off all dealings with her. Apart from some communication exchanged through Belasco's secretary toward the end of the impresario's life, the formerly intensely intertwined duo never directly spoke to one another again after that phone call. What crushed Belasco was not simply the fact that she had gotten married without his approval but that the marriage took him by surprise. Before he contacted Mrs. Carter, the press had gotten wind of the marriage and approached him for comment. He publicly dismissed the story as preposterous and declared: "I would as soon think of the devil asking for holy water as of Mrs. Carter taking a husband."[101] He had built his ascent to imperial theatrical power on his reputation as this actress's father confessor and maestro of her body and emotions. Her surprise wedding stingingly revealed a lapse in his power over her and, by extension, over aspects of himself exteriorized through her and the *mise-en-scènes* of her star vehicles. Making "Repka Stroon" respectable as a spectacle that so closely mirrored his own identity formation would have mandated a level of control over his actress that he could no longer boast. With the breakup of impresario and star, the project was permanently shelved, never to be mounted, even with another actress.

After Mrs. Carter, Belasco trained his Napoleonic sights primarily on "races" more distant from his own over which he could more firmly claim conquest.[102] With his two subsequent long-term leading ladies, Belasco dipped "lower" in the racial and moral hierarchy to vaunt impresarial power. He launched Frances Starr to stardom as the Mexican Juanita in *The Rose of the Rancho* (1906) before casting her as the Lower East Side prostitute in *The Easiest Way* (1909). Venturing into yet more exotic territory, he made racially Othered roles Lenore Ulric's stock-in-trade. She played a Comanche maiden in *The Heart of Wetona* (1916), a "French Canadian primitive" in *Tiger Rose* (1917), a bartered Chinese bride in *The Son-Daughter* (1919), a Turkish princess in *The Harem* (1924), and a Harlem nightclub singer in *Lulu Belle* (1926). Although different in "color," all these plays were *Du Barry*-esque in at least two key ways: they showcased female stars in cathartically melodramatic plots that reiterated a fundamentally Catholic cycle of the sin and redemption of wayward womankind; and they featured lavish settings that gave material—and therefore more visible and controllable form—to their variously raced and classed expressions of extreme feminine passion. As Napoleon conquered Bourbon France and expanded its colonial empire, so Belasco claimed to master these cultural terrains as the orchestrator of the theatrical apparatus that gave them representational form.

But more than demonstrating mastery over his actresses and the Otherness they and their *mise-en-scènes* exteriorized, Belasco gained a certain power over dominant cultural audiences that denigrated him. His conquest of "cold, sneering New York" was complete when his exotically displayed female stars succeeded, in Mrs. Carter's lively terms, as audience "vibrators"; that is, when the performance aroused in spectators the excessively emotional and sexual aspects they would deny in themselves and project onto Others. Belasco thrilled to record the multiple curtain calls his leading ladies' climaxes elicited, especially as spectators appeared to lose themselves in their enthusiasm, rising to their feet in a sea of unrestrained clapping, shouting, and bosom heaving. He achieved the desired effect most extravagantly in the torrential emotional outpourings catalyzed by *Du Barry*, but he spelled out its meaning perhaps most literally in *Adrea*. When the dwarf Jewish jester was revealed inside the Nordic warrior's armor, the joke was not only on Adrea but also on the dominant culture. The Bishop of Broadway's greatest feats of impresarial wizardry lay in drawing the most powerful and fashionable audiences into his theatre and stirring in them an inner Jew while seeming to affirm their racial and cultural superiority.

Epilogue

Phantom:
"Sing once
again with me
our strange
duet . . .
My power
over you
grows stronger
yet . . ."

Christine:
"Those who
have seen your face
draw back
in fear . . .
I am
the mask you wear . . ."

Phantom:
"It's me
they hear . . ."

—from "The Phantom of the Opera," 1986

The original novel, *The Phantom of the Opera*, by the French journalist and suspense fiction writer Gaston Leroux, first appeared in the United States in 1910.[1] It has since spawned numerous film, stage, and television versions, most famously the 1925 silent film produced by Carl Laemmle starring Lon Chaney and the 1986 Andrew Lloyd Webber musical, with lyrics by Charles Hart and Richard Stilgoe, still running on Broadway in 2006. While Leroux, as others have pointed out, owes a considerable debt to DuMaurier's *Trilby*, his knowledge of internationally famous real-life Svengalis—Daly, Frohman, and Belasco among them—likely sparked his imagination as well.[2] In fact, the year before *Phantom*'s publication, Belasco adapted a play by Leroux and Pierre Wolf called *The Lily*, whose production coincided with an extensive remodeling of Belasco's studio in his second theatre.[3] It is unclear whether Leroux traveled to New York to see the show and the Bishop of Broadway's inner sanctum, but the unveiling was widely covered in the media. This studio comprised a Gothic maze of ten rooms, several outfitted with secret compartments and trick doors used for the display of erotic art. These features, together with the famous underground lake workers encountered while dynamiting the basement to enlarge Belasco's first theatre, are highly suggestive of the Phantom's lair. Other key bits of impresarial lore that circulated widely and would not have escaped Leroux's notice included both Daly's and Belasco's penchants for seducing actresses and Belasco's crossing into opera through his collaborations with Giacomo Puccini on *Madama Butterfly* and *La Fanciulla del West* (*The Girl of the Golden West*).[4]

Drawing on historical impresarios for inspiration, *The Phantom of the Opera* provides a rich encapsulation of key themes that emerge from their careers. In the novel, the high-class audience at the Paris Opera seeks intense pleasure but refuses to acknowledge the depths of its own desires. It demonizes those baser appetites and projects them onto a reviled Other, the monstrously disfigured Phantom. His name, Erik, suggests vaguely Germanic and Scandinavian roots, but his eyes and skin color mark him as "Oriental." A freakishly wide singing range enables him to ventriloquize a soprano's repertoire.[5] Spectators thrill to the exquisite voice and beauty of his pupil Christine while driving her maestro underground, where he rules the palatial Opera from below. Christine gives in to and uses his power because of her own need to overcome deep personal loss and social marginalization by achieving fame and fortune.

Although Daly, Frohman, and Belasco were not hideously disfigured and thus could assimilate and work above ground to greater degrees than the

Phantom, their "low" origins were no less reviled. Seeking to rise up, they colluded with audiences in repressing aberrant traits in themselves and projecting them onto Others. But, like the Phantom, these impresarios also reveled in moving audiences in ways that often subverted dominant values. Their contributions to American theatre history and the meaning of what they put on stage derive from all the dynamics of repression and projection paradigmatically suggested in the *Phantom* story and played out through their onstage and offstage relationships with their leading ladies and their appeal to different groups of spectators. In that complex mix of interactions, boundaries between private and public break down; personal biography merges with wider social history; play texts become inseparable from modes of production and consumption; and forces of "race," class, gender, and sexuality are inextricably intertwined.

Redolent with ghosts of impresarios past, *Phantom* has resurged in various adaptations throughout the twentieth and into the twenty-first century.[6] In its most recent major incarnation, Andrew Lloyd Webber and his collaborators turn Leroux's disturbing tale into a spectacular musical that has become the longest-running show in Broadway history.[7] Lloyd Webber purports to restore elements of the original story, but his highly romanticized Phantom, a role he wrote for the handsome, English tenor Michael Crawford, glosses over the character's demonic racial and sexually predatious aspects. The original duet that Leroux's Phantom played with Christine Däae is far stranger than the one enacted on the Majestic Theatre stage for the last two decades. Nonetheless, two sentences from Lloyd Webber and lyricists Charles Hart and Richard Stilgoe's title song are particularly haunting: "I am the mask you wear," Christine sings to her tutor, to which he responds, "It's me they hear." The luminous actress is a mask for her impresario to conceal his reviled traits, assert his power in high society, and gain public approbation. She is a mask also for the audience to remain in denial about the repressed sources of its pleasure.

That denial has intensified with the restoration of New York's historic theatre district that has coincided with *Phantom*'s run. Construction and gentrification have driven historical Phantoms further underground even as their fictional analogue surfaces nightly at the Majestic. While Daly's Theatre and Frohman's Empire Theatre lay long buried beneath the Great White Way,[8] Belasco's first theatre has been restored as a crown jewel of the 42nd Street Development Project (42DP), a large-scale civic enterprise founded in the early 1980s to clean up Times Square, "the sleaziest block in America." After

housing Belasco's productions and collections, the Republic became a burlesque venue under Billy Minsky in the 1930s. Its reputation improved during
the Second World War when it was transformed into a second-run movie
house and patriotically renamed the Victory. But in the 1970s, the Victory
became the district's first XXX-rated cinema. The Durst Organization purchased the building in 1989 and partnered with 42DP on a full-scale renovation in 1994–1995, which not only restored its architecture and décor to the
glory of its Belasco days, but transformed it into a children's theatre renamed
the New Victory. The success of that restoration inspired the Disney Corpo-
ration to renovate the New Amsterdam and erect a skyscraper of vacation
condos and a huge Disney theme store on the square to further the district's
conquest by corporate capitalism and middle-class family values.[9]

Two blocks away at 111 West Forty-fourth Street, the second of Belasco's
theatres still stands after many renovations. The building continues to bear
his name, though it has remained mostly dark since the 1970s. Legend has it
that the ghost of the impresario haunts the halls.[10] He must relish the irony of
recent reports that while Disney and 42DP have so publicly cleaned up one of
the world's centers of sleaze and smut, pornography, with the aid of new
media technologies, has ballooned to a ten-billion-dollar annual industry,
bigger than professional football, basketball, and baseball combined. As the
New York Times columnist Frank Rich writes, "porn is no longer a sideshow
to the mainstream, like, say the $600 million Broadway theater industry—it is
the mainstream." Yet, he notes, very few of the masses of Americans who con-
sume "adult entertainment" admit to doing so.[11] Echoing down to the present, the strange duets of leading impresarios and actresses of Broadway's
Golden Age hauntingly suggest how such denial can fuel yet more projections of forbidden appetites onto racial, ethnic, and sexual Others.

NOTES

INTRODUCTION

1. Joseph Francis Daly, *The Life of Augustin Daly*, 461.

2. This episode is recounted by Otis Skinner, who worked with Daly and Rehan, in *Footlights and Spotlights*, 164, and by his daughter, Cornelia Otis Skinner, in *Family Circle*, 88–92.

3. The *Era*, 2 June 1888, Daly's Theatre Scrapbooks, vol. 20.

4. While the term "actress" is now eschewed on grounds of sexism, and "actor" is applied generically to both male and female performers, "actress" is used in this study because it was the prevailing term in the period, and it calls attention precisely to its gendered connotations, especially alongside the male-gendered term "impresario." According to the *Oxford English Dictionary*, "impresario," derived from the Italian *impresa*, or "undertaking," as in a business enterprise, means "one who organizes public entertainments; especially the manager of an operatic or concert company." The term was commonly applied to theatre as well as opera managers by the late nineteenth century. In contrast, the term "diva" for the leading female singer in an opera company was rarely used at that time to apply to theatrical performers, in part because operatic singing and acting were understood to be two distinctive talents. *Divus*, or "divine," the Latin root of diva, referred chiefly to the sublime sound of the singing voice, especially that of the soprano. See also John Warrack and Ewan West, *The Oxford Dictionary of Opera*, 194, 346, 571. Theatrical impresarios and others in the business used "leading actress" or "leading lady" to refer to the women at the heads of their companies. To keep performers' egos in check, Daly for most of his career fought the star system and long refused to use the term "star," even though Rehan had achieved that status well before he allowed her the title. A generation younger than Daly and more comfortable with and savvy about exploiting the celebrity culture, Frohman and Belasco often used "star" or "star actress" to refer to their leading ladies and boasted about those they "made."

5. Lawrence W. Levine, *Highbrow/Lowbrow: The Emergence of Cultural Hierarchy in America*.

6. See, for example, Felicia Hardison Londre and Daniel Watermeier, *The History of North American Theatre*, 178.

7. See, for example, Don B. Wilmeth and Rosemary Cullen, Introduction to *Plays by Augustin Daly*, 13–14.

8. Daly, *Life of Augustin Daly*, 456, 463.

9. See Faye E. Dudden, *Women in the American Theatre: Actresses and Audiences, 1790–1870*, 123–148.

10. Qtd. in Thomas Beer, *The Mauve Decade: American Life at the End of the Nineteenth Century*, 57.

11. Pendennis, "Clyde Fitch Conducting a Rehearsal—His Knowledge of Women," *New York Times*, 1 October 1906, Part 3, p. 6.

12. Belasco liked to shave years off of his age and so claimed to have been born in 1859. In his *Life of David Belasco* (1918), William Winter, seeking to set the record straight, asserted that Belasco was born on 25 July 1853, a few months after his parents first arrived in California by boat from England. The year 1853 has become the standard one given in scholarly sources for Belasco's birth. Recently, Mary Ellen Kelly located the passenger list for the ship *Margaret Evans* bearing the names of Belasco's parents, Humphrey and Rayna (sometimes spelled Reina) Belasco, for that transatlantic voyage. The list, available at http://www.immigrantships.net, is dated 19 April 1854, which means they immigrated a year later than Winter claimed. While other infants with their ages noted in months and children of various ages noted in years are listed on the manifest, David Belasco is not listed with his parents, presumably because he was not yet born. If he was born on 25 July following his parents' arrival in America, then the correct year of his birth is 1854, not 1853. Kelly speculates that Belasco, known to be vain about his appearance, likely knew the true year of his birth to be 1854, but by 1917, when Winter's biography appeared, preferred the earlier date because it made him look younger for his age. Mary Ellen Kelly, e-mail message to the author, 22 March 2006.

13. See Matthew Frye Jacobson, *Whiteness of a Different Color: European Immigrants and the Alchemy of Race*, 39–90.

14. "Legitimate theatre" is a term loaded with high cultural connotations dating back to the royal monopoly granted to the Patent playhouses in Britain during the Restoration. Applied to drama, the term "legitimate" has historically referred to plays accorded high literary and theatrical merit. By the late nineteenth century, however, the term referred less to the quality of the plays produced than to the greater cultural prestige the legitimate theatre claimed in relation to other competing forms of commercial entertainment. See Mark Hodin, "The Disavowal of Ethnicity: Legitimate Theatre and the Social Construction of Literary Value in Turn-of-the-Century America" *Theatre Journal* 52 (2000): 212.

15. Charlotte Porter, "Boston Discovers Miss Nance O'Neil," *The Critic*, June 1904, pp. 525–530. O'Neil left Rankin to star in *The Lily* under David Belasco's direction in 1909.

16. Margaret Knapp, "'Presented with Appreciation': Minnie Maddern Fiske as Producer and Director," *Journal of American Drama and Theatre* 1 (Fall 1989): 55–72. See also Tracy C. Davis, "Fiske, Minnie Maddern," *American National Biography*, vol. 8, pp. 35–36.

17. For more on the radical restructuring of the American theatre industry in the late nineteenth and early twentieth centuries, see John Frick, "A Changing Theatre:

New York and Beyond," in *The Cambridge History of American Theatre*, edited by Don B. Wilmeth and Christopher Bigsby, vol. 2, *1870–1945*, esp. 196–218.

18. See Warren Susman, "'Personality' and the Making of Twentieth-Century Culture," in *Culture as History: The Transformation of American Society in the Twentieth Century*, pp. 271–285.

19. In addition to Susman, standard sources on this broad transformation include Alan Trachtenberg, *The Incorporation of America: Culture and Society in the Gilded Age*; Robert Wiebe, *The Search for Order, 1877–1920*; and John Higham, "The Reorientation of American Culture in the 1890s." On challenges to WASP manhood in the period, see Gail Bederman, *Manliness and Civilization: A Cultural History of Gender and Race in the United States, 1880–1917*, 10–15. Regarding threats posed specifically by the New Woman, see Carroll Smith-Rosenberg, "The New Woman as Androgyne: Social Disorder and Gender Crisis, 1870–1936," in *Disorderly Conduct: Visions of Gender in Victorian America*, 245–296. On the emergence of homosexuality as a modern category of identity, see John D'Emilio, "Capitalism and Gay Identity," and John D'Emilio and Estelle B. Freedman, *Intimate Matters: A History of Sexuality in America*, 225–227.

20. Richard Butsch, *The Making of American Audiences: From Stage to Television, 1750–1990*, 66–80.

21. Albert Auster, *Actresses and Suffragists: Women in the American Theater, 1890–1920*.

22. Simone de Beauvoir, *The Second Sex*, 661–662.

23. See Martha Banta, *Imaging American Women: Idea and Ideals in Cultural History, 1876–1918*, 85–91, and Martha H. Patterson, *Beyond the Gibson Girl: Reimagining the American New Woman, 1895–1915*, 31.

1. PIONEERING ON THE THEATRICAL FRONTIER

1. Stanley Kauffmann, "Two Vulgar Geniuses: Augustin Daly and David Belasco," *Yale Review* 76 (Summer 1987): 500.

2. Joseph Francis Daly, *The Life of Augustin Daly*, 88.

3. Bruce A. McConachie has aptly termed this impresario an arriviste in *Melodramatic Formations: American Theatre and Society, 1820–1870*, 209. On the formation of this masculine gender ideal, see Dana D. Nelson, *National Manhood: Capitalist Citizenship and the Imagined Fraternity of White Men*. On its development in the late nineteenth and early twentieth centuries, see Gail Bederman, *Manliness and Civilization: A Cultural History of Gender and Race in the United States, 1880–1917*.

4. Richard Slotkin, *The Fatal Environment: The Myth of the Frontier in the Age of Industrialization, 1800–1890*, 282–296.

5. Letter to Joseph, 15 January 1865, Augustin and Joseph Daly Correspondence, 10 vols. In assessing Augustin Daly's career development, Joseph Francis Daly's account of his experiences and perceptions as presented in his *Life of Augustin Daly*

and the brothers' voluminous correspondence are especially significant because of their extraordinarily symbiotic relationship. As is well documented, Joseph was Augustin's closest adviser and frequent ghostwriter of his plays, reviews, speeches, and managerial policies. See, for example, Don B. Wilmeth and Rosemary Cullen, Introduction to *Plays by Augustin Daly*, 24–27.

6. Daly, *Life of Augustin Daly*, 15.

7. Ibid., 8–16.

8. Ibid., 14.

9. Ibid., 16–18.

10. Anna Cora Mowatt qtd. in Claudia D. Johnson, *American Actress: Perspective on the Nineteenth Century*, 11.

11. Joseph Francis Daly, *Life of Augustin Daly*, 19.

12. Dawes's performances are documented in classified ads in the *New York Daily Times*, 11 March 1853, p. 8, and 10 June 1853, p. 5.

13. A *New York Times* ad dated 5 August 1858, p. 6, documents the fifth week of her performance at Wallack's as the Yankee Gal, Aulda Cornduffer, with her husband as Irish Boy in *Advertisement for a Wife*. Mrs. W. J. Florence (Malvina Pray) is listed as doing the songs and dances.

14. Even though the most sensational part of her life, her career as the titled mistress of Ludwig I of Bavaria from 1846 to 1848, had passed, her reputation for scandal followed her. See, for example, "Outbreak of Virtuous Indignation—Letter from Lola Montez," *New York Daily Times*, 16 July 1852, in which she lashes out at the paper for invoking her as a benchmark of shameless fallen womanhood. Over the next few years until her death in 1861, she would find God and be redeemed. See Bruce Seymour, *Lola Montez: A Life*.

15. Qtd. in Joseph Francis Daly, *Life of Augustin Daly*, 37.

16. Ibid., 13.

17. On the impact of the star system on the old resident stock companies, see David George Schaal, "Rehearsal-Direction Practices and Actor-Director Relationships in the American Theatre from the Hallams to Actors' Equity," 184–190; Douglas McDermott reports that stars took a greater share of box office and forced managers to pay supporting players less, which prompted many actors to leave their resident managers and try to make it on the road as stars. See McDermott's "Structure and Management in the American Theatre from the Beginning to 1870," in the *Cambridge History of American Theatre*, vol. 1, *Beginnings to 1870*, 211. On antebellum audience sovereignty, see Richard Butsch, *The Making of American Audiences: From Stage to Television, 1750–1990*, 44–66.

18. McConachie, *Melodramatic Formations*, 200–203. See also McDermott, "Structure and Management," 202–204.

19. According to Joseph Francis Daly, *Life of Augustin Daly*, 23, Brooklyn, known

as the City of Churches, did not build a freestanding playhouse until the following year. Eschewing the label "theatre" on moral grounds, civil officials determined that it should be called the Academy of Music.

20. The male leads of both *Pillicoddy* and *Toodles* were popular features of Burton's repertoire.

21. Joseph Francis Daly, *Life of Augustin Daly*, 23–29.

22. Receipts and expenses are tallied in Marvin Felheim, "The Career of Augustin Daly," 541.

23. Joseph Francis Daly, *Life of Augustin Daly*, 13.

24. Felheim, "Career of Augustin Daly," 494.

25. See Rosemarie K. Bank, "Actor Training at the Mid-Point in Nineteenth-Century American Repertory," *Theatre History Studies* 8 (1988): 158–159.

26. Letter dated 22 December 1855, qtd. in Faye E. Dudden, *Women in the American Theatre: Actresses and Audiences, 1790–1870*, 128. See also McDermott, "Structure and Management," 206–209.

27. Qtd. in Dudden, *Women*, 130.

28. Albert A. Asermely, "Daly's Initial Decade in the American Theatre, 1860–1869," 14–15.

29. Joseph Francis Daly, *Life of Augustin Daly*, 30.

30. Asermely, "Daly's Initial Decade," 7.

31. Ibid., 29.

32. Ibid., 30.

33. Daly qtd. in ibid., 148, 156.

34. Daly's review of Vandenhoff's *Leaves from an Actor's Notebook*, *Courier*, 12 February 1860, p. 5.

35. Garff Wilson, *A History of American Acting*, 124.

36. Daly, Review of *Love's Sacrifice*, *New York Times*, 7 May 1868, p. 4.

37. See David Pugh, *Sons of Liberty: The Masculine Mind in Nineteenth-Century America*, 70–74.

38. Qtd. in ibid., 72.

39. Anne Norton, *Alternative Americas: A Reading of Antebellum Political Culture*, 53.

40. John F. Kasson, *Rudeness and Civility: Manners in Nineteenth-Century Urban America*, 150.

41. Carroll Smith-Rosenberg and Charles Rosenberg, "The Female Animal: Medical and Biological Views of Woman and Her Role in Nineteenth-Century America," *Journal of American History* 60 (September 1973): 334–335.

42. Norton, *Alternative Americas*, 56; Karen Halttunen, *Confidence Men and Painted Women: A Study of Middle-Class Culture in America, 1830–1870*, 92; Kasson, *Rudeness and Civility*, 156–170.

43. Halttunen, *Confidence Men*, 190.

44. William Winter, *Vagrant Memories, Being Further Recollections of Other Days*, 71–72.

45. Wilson, *History of American Acting*, 110–111.

46. *Citizen*, 24 August 1867, p. 8.

47. Asermely, "Daley's Initial Decade," 15–17, 62.

48. *Courier*, 17 March 1861, p. 5.

49. Asermely, "Daley's Initial Decade," 9.

50. Marvin Felheim, *The Theater of Augustin Daly: An Account of the Late Nineteenth Century American Stage*, 5–6.

51. *Taming a Butterfly* was adapted from *Le Papillon*, by Victorien Sardou; *Lorlie's Wedding* from *Dorf und Stadt*, by Charlotte Birchpfeiffer; *Judith* from Friedrich Hebbel's *Judith*, as adapted by Paolo Giacometti for Ristori as *Giuditta*; *The Sorceress* from *La Sorcière* by Bourgeois and Jules Barbier.

52. McConachie, *Melodramatic Formations*, 206.

53. Augustin Daly, *Leah the Forsaken* [1862], act II, scene ii, lines 49–52.

54. For an excellent analysis of the Jewish representations in *Leah*, see Harley Erdman, *Staging the Jew: The Performance of an American Ethnicity, 1860–1920*, 43–50.

55. Felheim, *The Theater of Augustin Daly*, 51.

56. Ibid., 158–159; Erdman, *Staging the Jew*, 51.

57. On "naturalized" femininity in sensation melodramas, especially as represented in Laura Courtland, see McConachie, *Melodramatic Formations*, 198–230.

58. *Under the Gaslight* (III, i), 157–161.

59. *Flash of Lightning* (I, i–II, i), 61–69.

60. Augustin Daly, *A Flash of Lightning*, in *Plays by Augustin Daly*, edited by Wilmeth and Cullen, 49.

61. *Flash of Lightning* (II, iii), 71.

62. Felheim, *The Theater of Augustin Daly*, 51, 63.

63. "Minor Theatrical Matters," *New York Times*, 18 July 1867.

64. The logic of the frontier myth is explicitly spelled out in Frederick Jackson Turner's famous 1893 essay, "The Significance of the Frontier in American History." But the operations of the myth are evident much earlier, as in the Leatherstocking Tales of James Fenimore Cooper and Natty Bumpo's need to escape the oncoming settlers he guides into the wilderness, to cite just one famous example.

65. *New York Clipper*, 20 March 1860, qtd. in Renée M. Sentilles, *Performing Menken: Adah Isaacs Menken and the Birth of American Celebrity*, 74.

66. Sentilles, *Performing Menken*, 22–23.

67. Joseph Francis Daly, *Life of Augustin Daly*, 20.

68. "The End" first appeared in the *Sunday Mercury*, 2 September 1860. It was renamed "Judith" and reprinted in Menken's *Infelicia*. Lines 47–51 from the *Infelicia*

version are quoted here. See Sentilles, *Performing Menken*, 79–83, for a fuller discussion of this poem.

69. "Passion" appeared in the *Sunday Mercury*, 18 November 1860. See Sentilles, *Performing Menken*, 85–86.

70. See Allen Lesser, *Enchanting Rebel: The Secret Life of Adah Isaacs Menken*, 48. Sentilles, *Performing Menken*, 55, lists Gus Daly of the *Sunday Courier* and Frank Queen of the *Clipper* as two journalists who favored Menken throughout her career.

71. Elizabeth Reitz Mullenix, *Wearing the Breeches: Gender on the Antebellum Stage*, 62; Sentilles, *Performing Menken*, 91–93.

72. Lesser, *Enchanting Rebel*, 88.

73. Letter to Augustin Daly, 6 Dec. 1865, Adah Isaacs Menken Correspondence.

74. Felheim, "Career of Augustin Daly," 528–529.

75. Letter from Menken to Daly, written from London in 1865, qtd. in Lesser, *Enchanting Rebel*, 215.

76. As the title indicates, Sentilles's *Performing Menken* analyzes the various facets of her celebrity image as self-consciously fashioned performances. See also Lesser, *Enchanting Rebel*, 215.

77. Sentilles, *Performing Menken*, 216.

78. Joseph Francis Daly, *Life of Augustin Daly*, 70, reports that Menken pressed Augustin Daly to write a play for her in the fall of 1864 after he returned from his tour with Avonia Jones. He furnished scripts to other actors and actresses, but not to her. See also Lesser, *Enchanting Rebel*, 104, 179.

79. "Adah Isaacs Menken: Some Notes of Her Life in Her Own Hand," *New York Times*, 6 September 1868, p. 3.

80. Sentilles, *Performing Menken*, 124–125.

81. Joseph Francis Daly, *Life of Augustin Daly*, 20.

82. Ibid., 43.

83. See Yvonne Shafer, "Count Johannes and the Nineteenth-Century American Audience," *Journal of American Drama and Theatre* 3 (Fall 1991): 59.

84. Report dated 30 January 1860. Qtd. in Dennis Strangman, *Lamplough Name Index*.

85. "Drury Lane Theatre," *London Times*, 6 November, 1861, p. 10, col. A.

86. Letter from Avonia Jones to Augustin Daly, 26 November 1863, qtd. in Asermely, "Daly's Initial Decade," 54.

87. Letter from Avonia Jones to Augustin Daly, 11 January 1864, qtd. in ibid., 55, and Joseph Francis Daly, *Life of Augustin Daly*, 58.

88. Ibid., 58.

89. Winter's review appeared in the *Albion*, 30 April 1864, p. 211. The *Sunday Times* review appeared on 1 May 1864. Both are quoted in Asermely, "Daly's Initial Decade," 59–60.

90. Augustin Daly, "Obituary of Avonia Jones," *New York Times*, 8 October 1867, p. 5.

91. Felheim, *The Theater of Augustin Daly*, 9.

92. Asermely, "Daly's Initial Decade," 72–73.

93. Letter to Joseph, dated only "September 1864," qtd. in Joseph Francis Daly, *Life of Augustin Daly*, 60.

94. Letter to Joseph, 15 September 1864, qtd. in ibid., 60.

95. Letter to Joseph, 6 November 1864, Daly Correspondence.

96. Letter to Joseph, 2 October 1864, qtd. in Joseph Francis Daly, *Life of Augustin Daly*, 61–62.

97. Letter to Joseph, 9 October 1864, qtd. in ibid., 61–62.

98. Letter from Joseph to Augustin, 4 November 1864, qtd. in Asermely, "Daly's Initial Decade," 83–84.

99. Letter to Joseph, 6 November 1864, Daly Correspondence.

100. Letter to Joseph, 12 November 1864, qtd. in Joseph Francis Daly, *Life of Augustin Daly*, 68.

101. Asermely, "Daly's Initial Decade," 89.

102. A letter Jones wrote Daly after the tour was over is addressed "My dear Brother" and signed "Your affectionate Sister." Qtd. in ibid., 85.

103. Letter from Joseph to Augustin Daly, 15 October 1864, Daly Correspondence.

104. Asermely, "Daly's Initial Decade," 85.

105. Letter to Augustin Daly, August 1866, qtd. in Felheim, "Career of Augustin Daly," 195–196.

106. An item in the *New York Times*, 17 August 1863, p. 5, reported that "Laura Keene's Theatre has passed into the hands of Mr. Duff, who has leased it to Mrs. John Wood for a period of years."

107. See, for example, Marion Victor Michalak, "The Management of Augustin Daly's Stock Company, 1869–1899," 130. In a 2 September 1880 letter to Joseph in the Daly Correspondence, Augustin complains of having to bow to his father-in-law's ideas about what to produce because of his financial dependency. Felheim reports that two days later, Duff withdrew his support, and Daly turned to Joseph for dozens of loans over the next few years until his company began to make lasting profits. See Felheim, "Career of Augustin Daly," 556.

108. Menken, Jones, and Bateman all played Jewesses. Bateman was also Jewish by birth, and Menken by her own acclamation.

109. Anne Hartley (Mrs. G. H.) Gilbert, *Stage Reminiscences of Mrs. Gilbert*, 222–223.

110. Cornelia Otis Skinner, *Family Circle*, 82.

2. A TROUBLED REPUBLIC

1. The morality-laden "homelike" advantages of the resident stock company over the star system were articulated in retired manager William Wood's *Personal Recollections of the Stage, Embracing Notices of Actors, Authors, and Auditors, during a Period of Forty Years*, 457–458. For most managers, the Panic of 1873 would deal a lethal blow to the stock company system. But Daly maintained a resident company throughout his career. He did, however, vary the repertory pattern with long runs when he produced a hit show, and as will be discussed later, he eventually allowed Ada Rehan star status. On the general transition from the stock to the combination (of a star plus supporting players hired for each production) system of production, see Jack Poggi, *Theater in America: The Impact of Economic Forces, 1870–1967*, 4–11; Peter A. Davis, "From Stock to Combination: The Panic of 1873 and Its Effects on the American Theatre Industry," *Theatre History Studies* 8 (1988): 1–9; and Rosemarie K. Bank, "A Reconsideration of the Death of the Nineteenth-Century American Repertory Companies and the Rise of the Combination," *Essays in Theatre* 5 (November 1986): 61–75.

2. Lea S. VanderVelde, "The Gendered Origins of the *Lumley* Doctrine: Binding Men's Consciences and Women's Fidelity," *Yale Law Journal* 101 (January 1992): 828–832.

3. See Richard Slotkin, *The Fatal Environment: The Myth of the Frontier in the Age of Industrialization, 1800–1890*, 282–295.

4. Grant Inaugural Address, printed in "The New Administration," *New York Times*, 5 March 1869, p. 6.

5. Qtd. in Joseph Francis Daly, *Life of Augustin Daly*, 548.

6. Ibid., 14; Augustin Daly editorial, "Minor Theatrical Matters," *New York Times*, 18 July 1867.

7. George Parson Lathrop, "An American School of Dramatic Art: The Inside Working of the Theatre," *Century Magazine* 56, new series 34 (June 1898): 273–274.

8. Quoted from contract issued to Miss Fanny Davenport, 13 February 1873, in Augustin Daly Personality File, Theatre Collection, Museum of the City of New York.

9. See David George Schaal, "Rehearsal-Direction Practices and Actor-Director Relationships in the American Theatre from the Hallams to Actors Equity," 349–360: Appendix II, "Articles of Agreement signed by the actors of the Chestnut Street Theatre under the management of William Warren and William B. Wood, 1815"; Appendix III, "Rules and Regulations of the Boston Theatre under the Management of Thomas Barry, 1854"; Appendix IV, "Rules and Regulations of the Salt Lake Theatre, ca. 1860"; and Appendix V, "Rules and Regulations of the Boston Museum under the Management of R. M. Field, 1880."

10. See, for example, Margaret Hall, "Personal Recollections of Augustin Daly," *The Theatre* 5 (June 1905): 150–153; (July 1905): 174–178; (August 1905): 188–191;

(September 1905): 213–215; Deshler Welch, "Augustin Daly, Dramatic Dictator," *Booklover's Magazine* 3 (April 1904): 491–504; W. W. Austin and Matthew White Jr., "A Famous American Manager," *Munsey's Magazine* 21 (August 1899): 736–744; Clara Morris, *Stage Confidences: Talks about Players and Play Acting*, 270–271; Dora Knowlton Ranous, *Diary of a Daly Debutante, Being Passages from the Journal of a Member of Augustin Daly's Famous Company of Players*; and Otis Skinner, *Footlights and Spotlights: Recollections of My Life on the Stage*, 135–136.

11. Lathrop, "An American School," 273–274; Otis Skinner, *Footlights*, 135–136.

12. Ranous, *Diary*, 53–54.

13. Ibid., 156–157.

14. Ibid., 66.

15. Marion Victor Michalak, "The Management of Augustin Daly's Stock Company, 1869–1899," 236–237.

16. Otis Skinner, *Footlights*, 135–136.

17. Ibid., 145–147.

18. Cynthia Eagle Russett, *Sexual Science: The Victorian Construction of Womanhood*, 56, 74.

19. For examples of physical manipulations of performers, see Ranous, *Diary*, 6; Clara Morris, *Life on the Stage*, 24. On forbidding any outsiders to witness rehearsals, see Hall, "Personal Recollections," Part III *The Theatre* (August 1905): 190.

20. Joseph Francis Daly, *Life of Augustin Daly*, 92.

21. See, for example, May Irwin's account of her experience with Daly in Lewis C. Strang, *Famous Actresses of the Day in America*, 180–183.

22. Isadora Duncan, *My Life*, 41.

23. For more on players' working conditions, see Benjamin McArthur, *Actors and American Culture, 1880–1920*, 62–73.

24. Ranous, *Diary*, 122.

25. Rose Eytinge, *Memories of Rose Eytinge*, 116–117. In another incident, James Lewis and Digby Bell, mistakenly believing Daly was not in attendance, introduced some impromptu funny business at a matinee performance. Daly did not reprimand them and let them remain in ignorance of his presence even though the infraction constituted a breach of one of his most stringent rules. See Hall, "Personal Recollections" Part III.

26. Qtd. in Strang, *Famous Actresses*, 189.

27. Hall, "Personal Recollections," Part III.

28. Augustin and Joseph Daly Correspondence, 10 vols., 4 and 6 September 1873.

29. Morris, *Life*, 338.

30. Unidentified review of *The Sphinx*, 21 September 1874, qtd. in Wilson, *A History*, 293.

31. Joseph Francis Daly, *Life of Augustin Daly*, 110.

32. Augustin Daly, *Horizon: An Original Drama of Contemporaneous Society and*

of American Frontier Perils, in *Plays by Augustin Daly*, edited by Don Wilmeth and Rosemary Cullen.

33. Joseph Francis Daly, *Life of Augustin Daly*, 154.

34. Morris, *Life*, 319.

35. See Marvin L. Felheim, "The Career of Augustin Daly," 516–523.

36. Joseph Francis Daly, *Life of Augustin Daly*, 153–154.

37. This refers to the case of *Lumley v. Wagner* (1852), in which the English Court of Equity held that although opera singer Johanna Wagner could not be ordered to perform her contract, she would be enjoined from singing at any competing music hall for the term of the contract. See VanderVelde, "Gendered Origins," 775.

38. "Agreement made the 13th day of February 1873 between Augustin Daly, party of the first part, and Miss Fanny Davenport, party of the second part," in Augustin Daly Personality File.

39. See the Daly's Theatre contract of 1889, reprinted in Barry B. Witham, ed., *Theatre in the United States: A Documentary History*, vol. 1, *1750–1915*, 183.

40. 19 October 1873, Daly Correspondence.

41. Joseph Francis Daly, *Life of Augustin Daly*, 166.

42. VanderVelde, "Gendered Origins," 807.

43. Felheim, "Career," 518.

44. Freedman qtd. in VanderVelde, "Gendered Origins," 810.

45. Ibid., 809.

46. Ibid., 834 and n. 309.

47. Ibid., 776.

48. Ibid., 804.

49. 15 September 1874, Daly Correspondence.

50. Joseph Francis Daly, *Life of Augustin Daly*, 166; Letter from Augustin Daly to Fanny Davenport, 16 May 1874, in Augustin Daly Personality File.

51. 12 September 1874, Daly Correspondence.

52. Letter from Augustin to Joseph, 12 September 1874, Daly Correspondence. Daly pledged to pay for Hall's share of the partnership over five years.

53. Letter dated 22 October 1878, qtd. in Joseph Francis Daly, *Life of Augustin Daly*, 281.

54. Qtd. in Review of *Our First Families*, *New York Herald*, 22 September 1880, p. 10.

55. *Needles and Pins*, adapted from Julius Rosen's *Starke Mittel*, ran from 9 November 1880 to 15 January 1881. See Michalak, "Management," 156.

56. W. Graham Robertson, *Life Was Worth Living*, 231–232.

57. Qtd. in Marvin L. Felheim, *The Theatre of Augustin Daly: An Account of the Late Nineteenth Century American Stage*, 42.

58. William Winter, *Ada Rehan: A Study*, 14–16.

59. Augustin Daly, *Woffington: A Tribute to the Actress and the Woman*.

60. See Felheim, *Theatre*, 40–44.

61. Cornelia Otis Skinner, *Family Circle*, 80–81.

62. Letter from Joseph to Augustin, 10 September 1874, Daly Correspondence.

63. Aileen A. Hendricks-Wenck, "Ada Rehan: American Actress (1857–1916)," 130.

64. Lathrop, "An American School," 268.

65. Otis Skinner, *Footlights*, 145–147.

66. *The Graphic*, 13 September 1885, n. pag., Daly's Theatre Scrapbooks, vol. 16.

67. *New York Dramatic Times*, 18 January 1886, n. pag., *Buffalo Advertiser*, 18 January 1886, n. pag., Daly's Theatre Scrapbooks, vol. 16.

68. Cornelia Otis Skinner, *Family Circle*, 80–83.

69. Russett, *Sexual Science*, 50–55.

70. See Michalak, "Management," 157–159, and Wilmeth and Cullen, eds., *Plays by Augustin Daly*, 35.

71. See, for example, *Love on Crutches* (1884), from the German of Stobitzer, in ibid.; and *The Lottery of Love* (1888), from the French of Bisson and Mars, Typescript promptbook. Similar tropes can be found in Daly's other adaptations for the Big Four, like *The Last Word* (1890), from the German of Franz von Schoenthan, on microfilm at the New York Public Library—42nd Street, and *Nancy and Company* (1886), from the German of Julius Rosen, Typescript promptbook.

72. *New York Herald*, 25 January 1891, p. 10.

73. See, for example, Welch, "Augustin Daly," 492; and William Winter, *The Wallet of Time*, vol. 2, 264.

74. Wilmeth and Cullen, Introduction to *Plays by Augustin Daly*, 21. Michalak, "Management," 242, suggests that though Daly had done much in his career to dismantle lines of business, he in effect reinstituted them by codifying the Big Four's role specializations.

75. Michalak, "Management," 253–254.

76. The moniker is from London's *The Bat*, 1 June 1886, p. 210, Daly's Theatre Scrapbooks, p. 17.

77. Edward Augustus Dithmar, *John Drew*, 63–64.

78. "Amusements: Augustin Daly's New Theatre," *New York Times*, 20 July 1879, p. 5. For the theatre's seating capacity, see the link for Daly's Theatre at "Pictorial Diagrams of New York Theaters—1883," Davis Crossfield Associates Archive, http://www.daviscrossfield.com/, accessed on 27 March 2006. Estimates of monetary value in today's dollars used throughout this study were calculated by using the commodity price index available at John J. McCusker, "Comparing the Purchasing Power of Money in the United States (or Colonies) from 1665 to 2005," Economic History Services, 2006, http://eh.net/hmit/ppowerusd, accessed in March 2006. McCusker cautions that economic historians continue to debate whether and how relative monetary value should be calculated across time. Different indices yield very different

results as Samuel H. Williamson demonstrates on another page on the Economic History Services site, "What is the Relative Value? Five Ways to Compare the Worth of a United States Dollar, 1790–2004." Like other available indices, the commodity price index does not take into account all the variables that can determine cost in a given historical moment. But it is the most widely used measure of relative monetary values and thus provides a reasonable benchmark of comparison.

79. Robertson, *Life*, 231–232.

80. Interview with Aileen Hendricks-Wenck, San Francisco, 7 August 1995. In writing her dissertation and now a biography of Rehan, she has undertaken an exhaustive study of Rehan's extant letters, which are housed primarily at the Folger Shakespeare Library and the University of Pennsylvania Library.

81. Letter from Rehan to Winter, 7 August 1899, Folger Shakespeare Library, qtd. in Hendricks-Wenck, "Ada Rehan," 320–321.

82. This incident is recorded in James Kotsilibas-Davis, *Great Times Good Times*, 188.

83. Sylvia Golden, "The Romance of Ada Rehan: Goddess of Daly's in the Rich Days of Our Victorian Theatre," *Theatre Magazine*, January 1931, pp. 21, 22, 64.

84. *New York Sun*, 21 February 1886, Daly's Theatre Scrapbooks, vol. 16.

85. *New York Dramatic News*, 3 April 1886, Daly's Theatre Scrapbooks, vol. 16.

86. *The Telegram*, New York, 8 October 1885, in Daly's Theatre Scrapbooks, vol. 16.

87. John Drew, *My Years on the Stage*, 106.

88. Golden, "Romance," 64.

89. See John W. Frick, *New York's First Theatrical Center: The Rialto at Union Square*, 6; Bruce A. McConachie, *Melodramatic Formations: American Theatre and Society, 1820–1870*, 251.

90. *Chicago Evening Mail*, 9 July 1887, Daly's Theatre Scrapbooks, vol. 18.

91. *Chicago Times*, 25 June 1885, Daly's Theatre Scrapbooks, vol. 15.

92. *Philadelphia Republican*, 23 August 1885, Daly's Theatre Scrapbooks, vol. 15.

93. Richard Butsch, "Bowery B'hoys and Matinee Ladies: The Re-Gendering of Nineteenth-Century American Theatre Audiences," *American Quarterly* 46 (1994): 374–405; rpt. in Butsch, *The Making of American Audiences*.

94. Bederman, *Manliness*, 17.

95. T. J. Jackson Lears, *No Place of Grace: Antimodernism and the Transformation of American Culture, 1880–1920*, 103–104.

96. Tori Haring-Smith, *From Farce to Metadrama: A Stage History of "Taming of the Shrew," 1594–1983*, 54.

97. Ibid., 60–61.

98. Lynda E. Boose, "Scolding Brides and Bridling Scolds: Taming the Woman's Unruly Member," *Shakespeare Quarterly* 42 (Summer 1991): 179–213.

99. Qtd. in Haring-Smith, *From Farce*, 71.

100. Cornelia Otis Skinner, *Family Circle*, 91–92.

101. Robertson, *Life*, 216.

102. Augustin Daly, *Taming of the Shrew, A Comedy by William Shakespeare, as Arranged by Augustin Daly*, 50.

103. "Ada Rehan's View of Katharine," unmarked clipping reprinting Preface to *Taming of the Shrew*, adapted by Augustin Daly, 1901 ed. Ada Rehan Personality File.

104. Felheim, "Career," 378.

105. Haring-Smith, *From Farce*, 66.

106. Augustin Daly, *Taming*, 73.

107. Felheim, "Career," 384–385.

108. "Ada Rehan's View of Katharine," Ada Rehan Personality File.

109. A copy of this volume can be found in the *Taming of the Shrew* Broadway Show Folder. See also Charles H. Shattuck, *Shakespeare on the American Stage*, vol. 2: *From Booth and Barrett to Sothern and Marlowe*, 67.

110. Haring-Smith, *From Farce*, 67.

111. This picture was part of "A Portfolio of Players" Daly had made to celebrate his company. See Joseph Francis Daly, *Life of Augustin Daly*, 449.

112. George C. D. Odell reminisced about evenings at Daly's: "And do you remember the Chinese Boy in Oriental dress who, in the later years of the theatre, used to hand you your programme, as you went up the richly carpeted steps." Odell, *Annals of the New York Stage*, vol. 11, p. 13.

113. "Justice a Dear Thing," *Chicago Herald*, 20 September 1892, n. pag., Daly's Theatre Scrapbooks, vol. 29.

114. Martha Banta, *Imaging American Women: Idea and Ideals in Cultural History, 1876–1918*, xxviii.

115. Joy S. Kasson, *Marble Queens and Captives: Women in Nineteenth-Century American Sculpture*.

116. See Lois Banner, *American Beauty*, 167; and John G. Cawelti, "America on Display: The World's Fairs of 1876, 1893, 1933," in *The Age of Industrialism in America*, edited by Frederic Cople Jaher, 340–341.

117. Banta, *Imaging*, 1–2; Henry C. Pitz, introduction to *The Gibson Girl and Her America: The Best Drawings*, selected by Vincent Gillon, Jr., vii–ix.

118. Howard Chandler Christy, *The American Girl as Seen and Portrayed by Howard Chandler Christy*, 69–70.

119. Rehan to Winter, 1 July 1899, qtd. in Shattuck, *Shakespeare*, 57.

120. Otis Skinner, *Footlights*, 269–272.

3 · BIRDS OF A FEATHER

1. The Theatrical Syndicate was legally formed as a partnership on 31 August 1896. In addition to Frohman, the Syndicate consisted of Al Hayman, Marc Klaw, Abraham Lincoln Erlanger, Samuel Nixon, and Fred Zimmerman. Because all

owned some theatres and controlled bookings for many others in various regions of the country, they could consolidate their enterprises and create a vast national booking chain. Of the six members, Frohman was by far the major producer of plays and provided most of the productions the Syndicate booked into the theatres across the United States over which it could exercise control. See Alfred L. Bernheim, *The Business of the Theatre: An Economic History of the American Theatre, 1750–1932*, 46–60; and Frick, "A Changing Theatre: New York and Beyond," in *Cambridge History of American Theatre*, vol. 2, *1870–1945*, edited by Don B. Wilmeth and Christopher Bigsby, 210–218.

2. See Gail Bederman, *Manliness and Civilization: A Cultural History of Gender and Race in the United States, 1880–1917*, 31–32; and Nicholas von Hoogstraten, *Lost Broadway Theatres*, 22–27.

3. Alan Dale, "The King of Theatres and His 42 Play Houses," *New York Journal*, Sunday, 12 June 1898, in Robinson-Locke Collection of Theatrical Scrapbooks, vol. 1, #221, p. 2.

4. Isaac F. Marcosson and Daniel Frohman, *Charles Frohman: Manager and Man*, 252.

5. Barnard Hewitt, *Theatre U.S.A., 1668 to 1957*, 257.

6. Samuel E. Moffett, "Charles Frohman," *Cosmopolitan* 33 (July 1902): 293.

7. William de Wagstaffe, "Coining Admiration Worth Half a Million a Year," *The Theatre Magazine*, December 1913, pp. 190–192.

8. See Eileen Karen Kuehnl, "Maude Adams, an American Idol: True Womanhood Triumphant in the Late-Nineteenth and Early-Twentieth Century Theatre," 198.

9. Gustav Kobbe, *Famous Actresses and Their Homes*, 26–27.

10. Marcosson and Frohman, *Charles Frohman*, 314.

11. David Gray, "Maude Adams: A Public Influence," *Hampton's Magazine*, June 1911, p. 737.

12. See Matthew Frye Jacobson, *Whiteness of a Different Color: European Immigrants and the Alchemy of Race*, 39–90.

13. See George Chauncey, *Gay New York: Gender, Urban Culture, and the Making of the Gay Male World 1890–1940*, 14–15, 100–101.

14. As has been well documented, the term "sexual inversion" was coined in medical publications of the late nineteenth century, beginning with the German Dr. K. F. O. Westphal's phrase "Die conträre Sexualempfindung," or "contrary sexual feeling," which appeared in 1869. An 1871 review of Westphal's essay in the London *Journal of Mental Science* translated the German into English as "inverted sexual proclivity." In 1897, Havelock Ellis first used "sexual inversion" in a publicly printed English work, *Sexual Inversion*, later reprinted as Part II of *Studies in the Psychology of Sex*. For further documentation of this coinage, see Jonathan Ned Katz, *The Invention of Heterosexuality*, 54–55.

15. Chauncey, *Gay New York*, 60–61.

16. Ibid., 39–44.

17. Ibid., 112.

18. Ibid., 14–15.

19. Richard von Krafft-Ebing, *Psychopathia Sexualis with Especial Reference to the Antipathic Sexual Instinct*, translated by F. J. Rebman, 334. Originally published in 1886.

20. See Lisa Duggan, "The Trials of Alice Mitchell: Sensationalism, Sexology, and the Lesbian Subject in Turn-of-the-Century America," *Signs* (Summer 1993): 791–814; and Carroll Smith-Rosenberg, "The New Woman as Androgyne," in *Disorderly Conduct*, 273.

21. Elizabeth Reitz Mullenix, *Wearing the Breeches: Gender on the Antebellum Stage*, 299. Duggan, "The Trials," 800–801, points out that the publicity surrounding the Mitchell-Ward case occasioned the printing of similar stories, some of which involved theatrical women.

22. Havelock Ellis claimed to dismiss the idea of a male soul inside the female invert's body and pointed out that cross-dressing did not necessarily indicate sexual inversion. Yet he nevertheless asserted that in the "actively inverted woman" resides "a more or less distinct trace of masculinity." He also noted "the very pronounced tendency among sexually inverted women to adopt male attire when practicable." See Ellis, "Sexual Inversion in Women," *Alienist and Neurologist* 16 (1895): 148, 155–156.

23. See Smith-Rosenberg, "The New Woman as Androgyne," in *Disorderly Conduct*, 279–281, for more discussion of the antifeminist influence of Ellis's ideas.

24. Cynthia Eagle Russett, *Sexual Science: The Victorian Construction of Womanhood*, especially chapter 2, "Up and Down the Phyletic Ladder," 47–77.

25. Ibid., 92–100.

26. Marcosson and Frohman, *Charles Frohman*, 127. Those traditions were, above all, to maintain respectability and draw high-class audiences. Organizationally, however, the stock company, while comprising a steady ensemble, was no longer organized primarily on the old repertory model. Rather, the long run was the desired aim, and plays were kept running as long as they drew audiences. Only on tour did the company play a repertoire, one in which it presented each of the previous winter season's plays for a week. See Harry Edward Stiver Jr., "Charles Frohman and the Empire Theatre Stock Company," 83.

27. Unmarked newspaper clipping in "Dillingham, Charles," Robinson-Locke Collection of Dramatic Scrapbooks, series 3, vol. 428, p. 91.

28. Marcosson and Frohman, *Charles Frohman*, 154.

29. Ibid., 156.

30. See "Frohman—as London Sees Him," *The Theatre* II (February 1910): viii; George Henry Payne, "Charles Frohman—An Enigma," *Metropolitan*, July 1910, n. pag., in "Frohman, Charles," Robinson-Locke Collection of Dramatic Scrapbooks,"

vol. 1, #221, p. 72; Photo by Underwood and Underwood, "Charles Frohman, Probably the Least Photographed Man of His Prominence in America," *New York Times*, 19 April 1914, in "Frohman, Charles," ibid., vol. 1, #222, p. 9.

31. Manuscript of Dillingham's unpublished memoirs, in the Charles Dillingham Papers, unpublished memoirs, Box 32, p. 68.

32. Untitled newspaper clipping, 12 May 1905, in "Dillingham, Charles," Robinson-Locke Collection of Dramatic Scrapbooks, series 3, vol. 428, p. 92.

33. Untitled clipping marked "New York Press," 16 August 1896, "Frohman, Charles," ibid., vol. 1, #221, p. 2.

34. See Dillingham's unpublished memoirs, in Charles Dillingham Papers, unpublished memoirs, Box 32, pp. 26–29. Also, see untitled newspaper clipping, "Dillingham, Charles," Robinson-Locke Collection of Dramatic Scrapbooks, series 3, vol. 428, p. 109.

35. See Dillingham's unpublished memoirs, in Charles Dillingham Papers, unpublished memoirs, Box 32, p. 28.

36. Untitled newspaper clipping, "Dillingham, Charles," Robinson-Locke Collection of Dramatic Scrapbooks, series 3, vol. 428, p. 91.

37. "Dillingham's Commission to Inquire into Grand Opera," *New York Telegraph*, 7 January 1909, in "Dillingham, Charles," ibid., series 3, vol. 428, p. 99. Maxine Elliott subsequently signed a five-year contract for Dillingham to manage her. See p. 86 of the same scrapbook in the Robinson-Locke Collection.

38. Alf Hayman (1865–1921) was the younger brother of Frohman's Syndicate partner, Al Hayman (1847–1917).

39. Charles Frohman Letter-Press Copy Books, vol. for 1906–1907, pp. 369, 378.

40. Ibid., vol. for 3/12/09 to 5/31/10, p. 56.

41. See Dillingham's unpublished memoirs, in Charles Dillingham Papers, unpublished memoirs, Box 32, p. 68.

42. See unmarked magazine article in the Robinson-Locke Collection of Dramatic Scrapbooks, vol. 1, #222, p. 143. Without naming Dillingham, James M. Barrie is quoted on Frohman's practice of sending a surrogate to the doctor, in Phyllis Robbins, *Maude Adams: An Intimate Portrait*, 174–175.

43. See, for example, the clipping entitled "Frohman's Health Restored," from a New Jersey paper, in the Robinson-Locke Collection of Dramatic Scrapbooks, vol. 1, #221, p. 75.

44. Untitled newspaper clipping, *New York Telegraph*, 1908, in "Dillingham, Charles," ibid., series 3, vol. 428, p. 97.

45. Erlanger was one of Frohman's business partners in the Theatrical Syndicate. Dillingham's unpublished memoirs, in Charles Dillingham Papers, unpublished memoirs, Box 32, p. 65. The repertory company was one Frohman funded at the Duke of York's Theatre in 1910. It staged plays by George Bernard Shaw, John Galsworthy, Harley Granville-Barker, Arthur Wing Pinero, and Elizabeth Barker. On

Frohman's London repertory company, see Thomas Postlewait, "The London Stage, 1895–1918," *The Cambridge History of British Theatre*, vol. 3, *Since 1895*, edited by Baz Kershaw, 48–49.

46. See Robert A. Schanke, "Alla Nazimova: 'The Witch of Makeup,'" in *Passing Performances: Queer Readings of Leading Players in American Theater History*, edited by Robert A. Schanke and Kim Marra, 129–150.

47. "C.B. Dillingham and Eileen Kearney Wed," *New York World*, 7 May 1913, in Robinson-Locke Collection of Dramatic Scrapbooks, series 3, vol. 428, p. 106.

48. Letter to Dillingham dated 28 October 1914 on Jacob S. Hirsh Insurance letterhead. In Charles Dillingham Papers, Box 16, Correspondence, 1914–1916, H–K.

49. Dillingham's unpublished memoirs, in Charles Dillingham Papers, unpublished memoirs, Box 32, p. 10a.

50. Letter on Lee Shubert's personal stationary dated 10 May 1915, New York, in ibid., Box 30 (Unsorted Letters, Stage Managers' Reports).

51. Letter dated 12 May 1915 from Alf Hayman on Charles Frohman letterhead, in ibid., Box 16 (Correspondence 1914–1916, H–K).

52. Hopkins wrote these memoirs in the 1970s. They are quoted in William J. Mann, *Behind the Screen: How Gays and Lesbians Shaped Hollywood, 1910–1969*, 30.

53. Marcosson and Frohman, *Charles Frohman*, 253.

54. Ibid., 423.

55. Elisabeth Marbury, *My Crystal Ball*, 95.

56. Marcosson and Frohman, *Charles Frohman*, 150; Jane S. Smith, *Elsie De Wolfe: A Life in the High Style*, 70.

57. See, for example, Bram Dijkstra, *Idols of Perversity: Fantasies of Feminine Evil in Fin-de-Siècle Culture*, 380–401.

58. Chauncey, *Gay New York*, 50.

59. Wilde quoted in Gary Schmidgall, *The Stranger Wilde: Interpreting Oscar*, 181.

60. See, for example, Neil Miller, *Out of Our Past: Gay and Lesbian History from 1869 to the Present*, 50.

61. Eaton was among those who traced Adams's roots back to the Quincy Adamses. See Walter Prichard Eaton, "Maude Adams Comes Back with a Host of Memories," "Clippings, Articles" File, Box 13, Maude Adams Collection. Maude Adams later became a lifetime member of the Massachusetts Society of Mayflower Descendants. See Robbins, *Maude Adams*, p. 112. More recent genealogical research linking her to John Howland and explaining her Mormon family background can be found in Armond Fields, *Maude Adams: Idol of American Theatre*, 1872–1953, 3–5.

62. These events are chronicled in the first installment of Adams's autobiographical series of articles titled "The One I Knew Least of All," published in the *Ladies' Home Journal*, March 1926, pp. 3–5, 206, and in Robbins, *Maude Adams*, 8–20.

63. Adams, "The One I Knew Least of All," p. 4.

64. The Salt Lake Collegiate Institute, now the nondenominational Westminster College, was founded with this mission of conversion in 1875. See http://en.wikipedia .org/wiki/Westminster_College,_Salt_Lake_City, accessed on 22 January 2006. According to Fields, Adams found this proselytizing disturbing and did not convert to Presbyterianism. See Fields, *Maude Adams*, 56.

65. "The Jewish 'Yentile' Governor of Utah," chapter 102 of Chapters in Jewish History, American Jewish Historical Society, http://www.ajhs.org/publications/ chapters/chapter.cfm?documentID=292, accessed on 23 January 2006.

66. Marcosson and Frohman, *Charles Frohman*, 207.

67. For more on Fitch and the impact of his relationship with Wilde on his career, see Kim Marra, "Clyde Fitch's Too Wilde Love," in *Staging Desire: Queer Readings of American Theater History*, edited by Kim Marra and Robert A. Schanke, 23–54.

68. Robbins, *Maude Adams*, 32.

69. Singling out this scene, critics praised Adams for maintaining an image of feminine delicacy and purity even while handling potentially degenerate material. See, for example, Acton Davies, *Maude Adams*, 5, in which he gathered his reflections about her while he was drama critic for the *New York Evening Sun*; and "Two Actors Named John," *New York Sun*, 4 October, 1892, p. 3.

70. Stiver, "Charles Frohman," 89.

71. On Fitch's college career as a female impersonator and director of campus theatricals and the praise professional actresses later accorded him for helping them play their characters, see Kim Marra, "Clyde Fitch: Transvestite *Metteur-en-Scène* of the Feminine," *New England Theatre Journal* 3 (1992): 15–38.

72. Marbury, *My Crystal Ball*, 82–83.

73. For more on Marbury and de Wolfe's relationship and their social circle, see Kim Marra, "A Lesbian Marriage of Cultural Consequence: Elisabeth Marbury and Elsie De Wolfe, 1886–1933," in *Passing Performances*, 104–128.

74. See, for example, Stacy Wolf, *A Problem Like Maria: Gender and Sexuality in the American Musical*, 64; and Marjorie Garber, *Vice-Versa: Bisexuality and the Eroticism of Everyday Life*, 165–185. Bruce Hanson, *The Peter Pan Chronicles*, 17–29, discusses Barrie's inability to consummate his marriage as well as his attraction to young boys.

75. Marbury, *My Crystal Ball*, 132.

76. "Maude Adams as Babbie, But the New Make-Believe Gypsy Is Not the Eerie Babbie We Used to Know So Well," *New York Times*, 28 September 1897, p. 6.

77. Edward A. Dithmar, "At the Play and with the Players," *New York Times*, 14 January 1900, p. 16.

78. Review of "The Little Minister," *New York Tribune*, 28 September 1897, p. 6. See also review of *Quality Street*, *New York Tribune*, 12 November 1901, n. pag., qtd. in Robbins, *Maude Adams*, 66.

79. Dithmar, "At the Play and with the Players."

80. Walter Prichard Eaton, "Personality and the Player," *Collier's*, 22 October 1910, p. 17. See also Eaton, "The Vexed Question of Personality," in *Plays and Players*, 388–389.

81. Reviews of Rehan's and Marlowe's performances quoted in Garff B. Wilson, *A History of American Acting*, 148–151.

82. "Maude Adams Comes Forward at the Head of a Company," *New York Sun*, 28 September 1897, p. 3. See also Fields, *Maude Adams*, 89.

83. Lewis C. Strang, *Famous Actresses of the Day in America*, 55–56.

84. J. Ranken Towse, "The Drama: L'Aiglon," *The Critic*, December 1900, p. 545.

85. Kuehnl, "Maude Adams," 247–248. See also two essays by Carroll Smith-Rosenberg in *Disorderly Conduct*: "Puberty to Menopause: The Cycle of Femininity in Nineteenth-Century America," especially pp. 183–184 emphasizing how the extent to which a woman's "sexual organization" dictated her emotions and behavior had no parallel in the male; and "The Hysterical Woman: Sex Roles and Role Conflict," pp. 205–207.

86. "When Two Popular Stars Were Younger," *Boston Sunday Herald*, 22 July 1906, in Phyllis Robbins Scrapbooks, vol. 2, Maude Adams Collection.

87. Leading theatre critics advanced this theory. See, for example, Alan Dale, "Why Women Are Greater Actors Than Men," *Cosmopolitan*, September 1906, pp. 521–522; and Walter Prichard Eaton, "The New Ethel Barrymore," *American Magazine*, September 1911, pp. 632, 640.

88. "Theatrical Gossip," *New York Times*, 8 October 1867, p. 7.

89. For the fiftieth anniversary of the Empire Theatre on 25 January 1943, the Players bestowed a bronze plaque on the building with Adams's name at the top because, as Harry Forwood, publicist for the event, telegraphed President Wood of Stephens College, where Adams was then teaching, "Hers is the one name that outshines all others in fifty years of Empire history." Qtd. in Robbins, *Maude Adams*, 281–282. Financial gains from *The Little Minister*, which launched Adams to that exalted position, are enumerated in Fields, *Maude Adams*, 129.

90. Douglas Gilbert, "The Legend of Maude Adams: Charles Frohman Began It When He Placed a Cloak of Mystery About His New-Found Star," *New York Telegram*, 17 May 1930, n. pag.

91. Marcosson and Frohman, *Charles Frohman*, 294–295.

92. Herbert M. Wells, "Recollections of Maude Adams," clipping in Maude Adams Personality File, n.d., n. pag.

93. Untitled newspaper clipping, Phyllis Robbins Scrapbooks, vol. 2, p. 19, Maude Adams Collection.

94. Harley Erdman, *Staging the Jew: The Performance of an American Ethnicity, 1880–1920*, 94–95.

95. In the summer of 1901, Adams spent two months at the Augustinian Convent in Tours, France. In March 1915 she rested at the Cenacle of St. Regis in New York.

The latter organization reportedly told Adams's secretary (Boynton) that a religious house would not ordinarily take in an actress, but upon learning that the actress in question was the unblemished Lady Babbie and Peter Pan, the sanctuary admitted her. See Robbins, *Maude Adams*, 82.

96. See, for example, Acton Davies, "Maude Adams," clipping in Phyllis Robbins Scrapbooks, vol. 3, p. 29, Maude Adams Collection; Ada Patterson, "The Real Maude Adams," ibid., vol. 1, p. 75.

97. See, for example, "A Time of Years," Adams's obituary in *Time Magazine*, 27 July 1953, and "Maude Adams Dies; Star of 'Peter Pan,'" *Hudson Dispatch*, n.d.; both in "Clippings, Articles" File, Box 13, Maude Adams Collection.

98. "Maude Adams, At Last: Plays Her Real Self; An Exclusive Interview with the Actress," *Kansas City Star*, 28 November 1937, n. pag., Maude Adams Collection Clipping File.

99. Maude Adams, "Miss Adams Says It Was Like This," *Boston Transcript*, 10 June 1939, n. pag., Maude Adams Personality File.

100. Tracy C. Davis, "Maude Adams," *American National Biography*, vol. 1, p. 116.

101. Robbins, *Maude Adams*, 35. Robbins does not specify the date of the burning, but she refers to all of Adams's "accumulated correspondence," which suggests that the conflagration occurred later in her career. It may have taken place either in 1910, when Adams put her farm up for sale but then decided to keep and improve it, or in 1921, when she donated her farm to the Cenacle. The first attempt to sell the farm is documented in Fields, *Maude Adams*, 265.

102. Adams, "The One I Knew Least of All," *Ladies' Home Journal*, March 1926, pp. 3–5, 206; April 1926, pp. 9, 213; May 1926, pp. 14–15, 150, 152, 155; June 1926, pp. 22–23, 161–162; July 1926, pp. 21, 70, 73–74; October 1926, pp. 23, 249, 259.

103. Ibid., March 1926, p. 3.

104. Robbins, *Maude Adams*, 35.

105. See newspaper clippings tracking her travels in Phyllis Robbins Scrapbooks, vol. 2, pp. 60–65, Maude Adams Collection.

106. Gottschalk's account of this carriage ride as well as chatty letters Adams sent to Fitch at his hotel to arrange social plans are quoted in *Clyde Fitch and His Letters*, edited by Virginia Gerson and Montrose J. Moses, 216–224.

107. Robbins, *Maude Adams*, 76.

108. Phyllis Robbins Scrapbooks, vol. 2, p. 65, Maude Adams Collection.

109. Robbins, *Maude Adams*, 35–36.

110. Correspondence to Nan Hodgkins with Reference to Maude Adams, Maude Adams Collection. Access to the Hodgkins correspondence was restricted until 1993. In a letter to Mrs. Fordham dated 8 October 1955, Hodgkins explains that she fell out of touch with Adams in the 1930s because she started to go blind and did not want to burden the actress with her problems.

111. Letter from Miss Louise M. Hitchcock to Nan Hodgkins, 3 January 1953, and Letter to Nan Hodgkins from "Pip" in Albany, New York, 15 May 1956; both in "Correspondence to Nan Hodgkins," Maude Adams Collection.

112. See Robbins, *Maude Adams*, 166–171.

113. Ibid., 290. The *Oxford English Dictionary* gives numerous examples from the 1920s to the 1950s of the use of "queer" as both an adjective and a noun to apply to homosexuals. In 1950 Senator Joseph McCarthy, in a statement quoted in the *New York Times* ("McCarthy Labels Marshall 'Unfit,'" 21 April, p. 3) declaring George Marshall unfit to have served as secretary of state, used the phrase "Communists and queers." In 1953 Adams could not have been ignorant of the double meaning of the word "queer" to mean both odd and homosexual. Given that she was being playful in a private conversation with one of her closest friends with whom she had long shared a common lifestyle, her use of the double entendre seems quite deliberate.

114. "Miss Adams Buried with Simple Rites," *New York Times*, 21 July 1953, n. pag., Maude Adams Clipping File.

115. A photograph of the tombstone shows the two names engraved together. The photo can be seen at "Bid Time Return," http://www.geocities.com/bidtimereturnmp/ma.html, accessed on 10 September 2005.

116. Fields, *Maude Adams*, 107.

117. "Maude Adams Buys House," 9 May 1900, untitled newspaper clipping, Phyllis Robbins Scrapbooks, vol. 1, p. 101, Maude Adams Collection.

118. See, for example, letter to Frohman from Alf Hayman, 11 June 1909, Charles Frohman Letter-Press Copy Books, Charles Frohman Papers, vol. for 12 March 1909–31 May 1910, p. 259.

119. "Miss Adams Says No: Denies Reported Marriage to Her Manager, Charles Frohman," untitled newspaper clipping, Phyllis Robbins Scrapbooks, vol. 1, p. 23, Maude Adams Collection.

120. "Mystery in Maude Adams' Return to Stage after Years in Seclusion," *New York Evening Graphic Magazine*, Saturday, 14 June 1930, Maude Adams Personality File.

121. "Maude Adams Dies, Star of Peter Pan," *Hudson Dispatch*, n.d., Maude Adams Clipping File.

4. THROUGH FAIRY AND FOWL

1. Untitled newspaper clipping marked "Paris, May 19 [1900]," Phyllis Robbins Scrapbooks, vol. I, p. 101, Maude Adams Collection.

2. Adams also played Viola in *Twelfth Night* at Harvard's Sanders Theatre, 3–4 June 1908, and Rosalind in *As You Like It* at the University of California's Greek Theatre, 6 June 1910. While furthering Frohman and Adams's high cultural aspirations, these productions were not on the same scale as the Broadway shows, nor did

they garner as much coverage. See Robbins, *Maude Adams: An Intimate Portrait*, 295–296.

3. Walter Prichard Eaton, "Rhyme and Unreason," in *The American Stage of Today*, 81; "Miss Maude Adams to Play Title Role in 'Chantecler,'" untitled newspaper clipping, "Articles, Clippings," Box 13, Maude Adams Collection. For the French premiere, the role of Chantecler ultimately went not to Bernhardt but to male actor Sacha Guitry. See also unnamed Boston newspaper clipping, Phyllis Robbins Scrapbook, vol. IV, p. 69, Maude Adams Collection.

4. Elizabeth Reitz Mullenix, *Wearing the Breeches: Gender on the Antebellum Stage*, 231–301.

5. See Richard von Krafft-Ebing, *Psychopathia Sexualis with Especial Reference to the Antipathic Sexual Instinct*, translated by F. J. Rebman, 334. See also Havelock Ellis, "Sexual Inversion in Women," *Alienist and Neurologist* 16 (1895): 156; and Havelock Ellis and John Addington Symonds, *Sexual Inversion*, 197–201.

6. Mullenix, *Wearing the Breeches*, 299–300.

7. Tina Gianoulis, "Sarah Bernhardt," in *glbtq: An Encyclopedia of Gay, Lesbian, Bisexual, Transgender, and Queer Culture* [on-line], edited by Claude J. Summers, www.glbtq.com/arts/bernhardt_t_s.html, last updated August 28, 2003, accessed April 20, 2004.

8. See the Bernhardt caricatures reproduced in Patricia Marks, *Sarah Bernhardt's First American Theatrical Tour, 1880–1881*, 30, 36, 41, 92. See also Gail Marshall, *Actresses on the Victorian Stage: Feminine Performance and the Galatea Myth*, 115–122.

9. Lisa Duggan, "The Trials of Alice Mitchell: Sensationalism, Sexology, and the Lesbian Subject in Turn-of-the-Century America," *Signs* (Summer 1993): 795.

10. Harley Erdman, *Staging the Jew: The Performance of an American Ethnicity, 1860–1920*, 48–50; and Richard Ellmann, *Oscar Wilde*, 371.

11. For more on anti-Semitism and the Syndicate, see Erdman, *Staging the Jew*, 93–95; and Mark Hodin, "The Disavowal of Ethnicity: Legitimate Theatre and the Social Construction of Literary Value in Turn-of-the-Century America," *Theatre Journal* 52 (2000): 218–219.

12. Eileen Karen Kuehnl, "Maude Adams, An American Idol: True Womanhood Triumphant in the Late-Nineteenth and Early-Twentieth-Century Theatre," 62. See also Acton Davies, *Maude Adams*, 93.

13. Mullenix, *Wearing the Breeches*, 129.

14. Internet Broadway Database, http://www.ibdb.com/production.asp?id=5414, accessed 4/20/04. Bernhardt played the title role in all of these but *Cyrano*, in which she played Roxane opposite Benoit-Constant Coquelin.

15. See, for example, J. Ranken Towse's review in the *Evening Post*, 17 November 1900, quoted in Kuehnl, "Maude Adams," 170.

16. See Lewis C. Strang, *Famous Actresses of the Day in America*, 72; and "A Theatrical Occasion: Maude Adams' Appearance in Edmond Rostand's Drama," *New York Sun*, 23 October 1900, p. 7.

17. See Amy Leslie, *Some Players: Personal Sketches*, 370–371; Kuehnl, "Maude Adams," 251.

18. See, for example, news clipping dated 15 September 1900, in Phyllis Robbins Scrapbooks, vol. I, n. pag., Maude Adams Collection.

19. See, for example, the scene in Act I when the Duke is supposed to be receiving a history lesson from his Austrian tutor but defiantly recites the politically suppressed glories of his father instead. Edmond Rostand, *L'Aiglon: A Play in Six Acts*, translated by Louis N. Parker, 66–69.

20. Ibid., 60.

21. Ibid., 183.

22. Ibid., 53.

23. Various dictionaries available on the Web track the symbolism of these colors. For example, http://outwilmington.com/symbology.htm notes that the poet Sappho wrote verses describing herself and her lover wearing tiaras of violets and that violets were worn in sixteenth-century England by men and women who did not plan to marry. http://www.gustavus.edu/oncampus/orgs/queers/main/dictionary_full.html#1 says that lavender was a color associated with gay men since ancient Greece, where the Greek word for lavender also meant a gay man. Associations with green have been traced back to the Byzantine Empire, where Procopius's *Secret History of Justinian* claims that the emperor recklessly persecuted homosexuals, starting first with members of a rival political faction known as the greens. More immediately, green was associated with Oscar Wilde and the green carnation. See, for example, Richard Ellman, *Oscar Wilde*, 365. Red ties were commonly worn by same-sex-desiring men at the turn of the century to signal their preferences. See George Chauncey, *Gay New York: Gender, Urban Culture, and the Making of the Gay Male World, 1890–1940*, 3.

24. Rostand, *L'Aiglon*, 197–198.

25. Ibid., 174–175.

26. Ibid., 179. The *Oxford English Dictionary* affirms the sexual use of the verb "come" as early as the seventeenth century. See sense 17, "To experience sexual orgasm. Also with *off. slang.* a1650 *Walking in Meadow Green* in *Bp. Percy's Loose Songs* (1868) Then off he came, & blusht for shame soe soone that he had endit. 1714 *Cabinet of Love*, Just as we *came*, I cried, 'I faint! I die!' c1888–94 *My Secret Life* III. 143 'Shove on,' said she, 'I was just coming.'"

27. Rostand, *L'Aiglon*, 199.

28. Ibid., 224.

29. Acton Davies, "Maude Adams," clipping in Phyllis Robbins Scrapbooks, vol. III, p. 29, Maude Adams Collection. See also Adelaide Samson, "Maude Adams—A Charming Personality: A Word Picture of the Clever Young Actress who Created

'Lady Babbie' and 'L'Aiglon,' by One Who Knows Her," Maude Adams Personality File; Walter Prichard Eaton, "Maude Adams Comes Back with a Host of Memories," "Clippings, Articles" File Box 13, Maude Adams Collection; and Ada Patterson, "The Real Maude Adams," Phyllis Robbins Scrapbooks, vol. II, p. 73, ibid.

30. "Maude Adams (Original Peter Pan) Is Dead at 80," *New York Herald Tribune*, 19 July 1953, "Clippings, Articles," Box 13, Maude Adams Collection.

31. William de Wagstaffe, "Coining Admiration Worth Half a Million a Year," *The Theatre Magazine* (December 1913): 191.

32. See, for example, "'Quality Street' Again," *New York Sun*, 7 January 1908, p. 7; and DeWolfe Hopper and Wesley Stout, *Once a Clown*, 108.

33. "Maude Adams in *L'Aiglon*: The Actress Scores a Great Success at the Baltimore production of Rostand's Work," *Boston Herald*, 16 October 1900, in Phyllis Robbins Scrapbooks, vol. I, p. 105, Maude Adams Collection.

34. "Maude Adams as the Stricken Eaglet," New York, 23 October 1900, Phyllis Robbins Scrapbooks, vol. I, p. 113, Maude Adams Collection.

35. Untitled newspaper clippings, Phyllis Robbins Scrapbooks, vol. II, pp. 5–9, Maude Adams Collection.

36. W.D.J., "The Little Lady: An Appreciation of Maude Adams," *Burr McIntosh Monthly*, June 1908, n. pag., in Adams Personality File.

37. The Hattons, "Mr. Frohman Renews His Interest in Us," *Chicago Herald*, 22 November 1914, sec. 4, p. 4.

38. See Carroll Smith-Rosenberg, *Disorderly Conduct: Visions of Gender in Victorian America*, 53–76, 245–296.

39. Havelock Ellis, "Sexual Inversion in Women," *Alienist and Neurologist* 16 (1895): 145–146.

40. For Robbins's account of the early development of her friendship with Adams, see the former's *Maude Adams: An Intimate Portrait*, 3–7, 58–64, 84–85.

41. Ibid., 112.

42. Ibid., 220–221.

43. See "Correspondence: Maude Adams and Others to Laura Kennedy," for example, Kennedy's notes dated 12 December 1937, in the Maude Adams Collection.

44. See Lillian Faderman, *Surpassing the Love of Men: Romantic Friendship and Love between Women from the Renaissance to the Present*, 156.

45. Ibid., 238, 314. Carroll Smith-Rosenberg parses this transition with statistics about college women of the same demographic as comprised Adams's fan base. From 1889 to 1908, 55% of Bryn Mawr women did not marry, and 62% went to graduate school. In the next decade, 1910–1918, as warnings against female sex perversion increased, 65% of Bryn Mawr women married, and the number seeking graduate training declined to 42%. See Smith-Rosenberg, "New Woman as Androgyne," 269–281.

46. Ellis, "Sexual Inversion," 146–157. This distinction is highlighted in Smith-Rosenberg, "New Woman," 276.

47. Untitled newspaper clippings dated 8–9 June 1901, Phyllis Robbins Scrapbooks, vol. II, p. 21, Maude Adams Collection.

48. *Romeo and Juliet* opened 8 May 1899 at Frohman's Empire Theatre starring William Faversham as Romeo opposite Adams's Juliet. For a summary of the mixed reviews of this production, see Kuehnl, "Maude Adams," 47–55.

49. Chauncey, *Gay New York*, 67.

50. Ibid., 106–107.

51. Ibid., 301–302.

52. Ibid., 68, 191.

53. Untitled newspaper clipping dated January 1901 in Phyllis Robbins Scrapbook, vol. II, p. 13, Maude Adams Collection.

54. See, for example, George Cruikshank's 1819 caricature, "The Dandies *Coat of Arms*," in Ellen Moers, *The Dandy: Brummell to Beerbohm*, op. p. 33.

55. Untitled newspaper clipping, January 1901, Phyllis Robbins Scrapbook, vol. II, p. 13, Maude Adams Collection.

56. Rostand, *L'Aiglon*, 49. Faderman, *Surpassing*, 155, cites medical doctor Allan McLane Hamilton, who wrote in 1896 that he attributed the new knowledge regarding lesbianism especially to Gautier's novel, which was first published in English in the United States in 1890.

57. Rostand, *L'Aiglon*, 60. Byron's separation from his wife, Annabella Milbanke, in 1812–1813 created an international scandal as speculation about the cause of their marital troubles abounded and his former paramour, Lady Caroline Lamb, spread rumors about his homosexual and incestuous activities throughout London. For more on Byron's bisexual liaisons and motifs in his work, see Louis Crompton, "Byron, George Gordon, Lord," in *The Gay and Lesbian Literary Heritage*, edited by Claude J. Summers, 128.

58. Rostand, *L'Aiglon*, 116–121.

59. Untitled newspaper clippings about *L'Aiglon* in New York and Boston October 1900–January 1901, Phyllis Robbins Scrapbooks, vol. I, pp. 107–117, Maude Adams Collection.

60. Kuehnl, "Maude Adams," 348, argues that the purpose of these alternating roles was to recuperate Adams into True Womanhood.

61. Chauncey, *Gay New York*, 60–61.

62. Quoted in Gary Schmidgall, *The Stranger Wilde: Interpreting Oscar*, 154.

63. Clyde Fitch, *The Knighting of the Twins and Ten Other Tales*, with drawings by Virginia Gerson, 251. Another story in the volume, "An Unchronicled Miracle," written in Chester, England, in May 1889, is dedicated to Walter Pater, a mentor shared by Fitch and Wilde.

64. Bruce K. Hanson, *The Peter Pan Chronicles: The Nearly One Hundred Year History of "The Boy Who Wouldn't Grow Up,"* 18.

65. See Elaine Showalter, "Syphilis, Sexuality, and the Fiction of the Fin-de-siècle," in *Sex, Politics, and Science in the Nineteenth-Century Novel*, edited by Ruth Bernard Yeazell, 88–115. For more on the evidence and impact of syphilis on Wilde's career, see Ellman, *Oscar Wilde*, 92; and Melissa Knox, *Oscar Wilde: A Long and Lovely Suicide*, 42–45. The Beardsley drawings are reproduced in Oscar Wilde, *Salome: A Tragedy in One Act: Translated from the French of Oscar Wilde by Lord Alfred Douglas: Pictured by Aubrey Beardsley*, 1894, reprint, New York: Dover, 1967. For more on Fitch and syphiliphobia, see Kim Marra, "Clyde Fitch's Too Wilde Love," in *Staging Desire: Queer Readings of American Theater History*, edited by Kim Marra and Robert A. Schanke, 23–54.

66. "Miss Maude Adams as Peter Pan," untitled newspaper clipping, *Peter Pan* Broadway Show Folder, Theatre Collection.

67. Qtd. in Robbins, *Maude Adams*, 93.

68. See Maude Adams, "The One I Knew Least of All," *Ladies Home Journal*, March 1926, p. 4.

69. For example, an untitled 1905 newspaper clipping discusses Peter as a matinee idol, Phyllis Robbins Scrapbook, vol. III, p. 87, Maude Adams Collection.

70. Fields, *Maude Adams*, 190. Twain qtd. in Robbins, *Maude Adams*, 90–92.

71. Walter Prichard Eaton, "Rhyme and Unreason," in *The American Stage of Today*, 81.

72. Miguel Zamacois, *The Jesters: A Simple Story in Four Acts of Verse Adapted from the French of Miguel Zamacois by John N. Raphael*, 76–77. Reviews attest that this is the version used for the Frohman-Adams production.

73. Ibid., 128.

74. Ibid., 45–48.

75. Ibid., 82.

76. Ibid., 133.

77. See, for example, Faderman, *Surpassing*, 297–308.

78. Zamacois, *The Jesters*, 168–169.

79. Kuehnl, "Maude Adams," 93. *The Jesters* opened 13 January 1908 at the Empire Theatre, Marcosson and Frohman, *Charles Frohman*, 430.

80. Review of *The Jesters*, *The Theatre*, February 1908, n. pag.

81. "Joan of Arc's Beatification at Harvard," *Current Literature*, August 1909, 198.

82. Edward Harold Crosby, "Miss Adams an Ideal Joan," untitled newspaper, 23 June 1909, Phyllis Robbins Scrapbook, vol. IV, p. 43, Maude Adams Collection.

83. At the National Horse Show in Madison Square Garden, which set the equestrian standard for high society, women did not ride astride until 1915. See the National Horse Show website, http://www.nhs.org/news/pressreleasesarchives .php?f=nationalhorseshowret.html, accessed 18 May 2004. Extolling Adams's "essential femininity," one commentator took pains to point out that she had never

ridden astride before preparing for this role. See "The Real Maude Adams: Barrie's Idea of Her Shown in Part in Maggie Wylie," untitled newspaper clipping, Phyllis Robbins Scrapbook, vol. IV, p. 63, Maude Adams Collection.

84. See Anna Alice Chapin, "Joan of Arc at Harvard," *Metropolitan Magazine*, August 1909, pp. 522–524; Charles Frohman Letter-Press Copy Books, Charles Frohman Papers, vol. for 3/12/1909–5/31/1910, pp. 159–160, 188, 273.

85. Annie Adams Kiskadden and Verne Hardin Porter, "The Life Story of Maude Adams and Her Mother," *Green Book Magazine*, November 1914, p. 812.

86. Chapin, "Joan of Arc," 516.

87. Samuel E. Moffett, "Charles Frohman," in *Cosmopolitan* 33 (July 1902): 293. On the Shuberts' abuses, see Foster Hirsch, *The Boys from Syracuse*, 108–109.

88. See several clippings in the Charles Frohman Personality File: "A Busy Day with Charles Frohman," *The Theatre Magazine*; "Charles Frohman—'The Man Who Never Broke His Word,'" based on reflections by Alf Hayman; John D. Williams, "C.F."; and Montrose J. Moses, "Charles Frohman," *The Bellman*, 29 May 1915, p. 86. See also untitled magazine article on Frohman, Robinson-Locke Collection of Dramatic Scrapbooks, vol. 1, #222, p. 147, and Letter from Frohman to J. M. Barrie, 10 December 1913, Charles Frohman Letter-Press Copy Book, 18 November 1901–31 January 1902.

89. Kiskadden and Porter, "The Life Story," November 1914, p. 820. See also Helen Ormsbee, "Michael, Who Flew Out the Window," *Herald Tribune*, Sunday, 12 October 1941, in "Clippings, Articles," File Box 13, Maude Adams Collection, in which Audrey Ridgwell shares her memories of playing Michael with Adams in *Peter Pan*. See also Fields, *Maude Adams*, 189.

90. See the floor plan of this railroad car theatre in Phyllis Robbins Scrapbook, vol. III, p. 92, Maude Adams Collection.

91. Chapin, "Joan of Arc," 517–519. For a more recent detailed account of the effort this huge, complex production entailed for Adams and her staff, see Yvonne Shafer, "Maude Adams as Joan of Arc at the Harvard Stadium," *Journal of American Theatre and Drama* 11 (Fall 1999): 30–45.

92. Chapin, "Joan of Arc," 516–518.

93. "Maude Adams in a Rehearsal of 'Joan of Arc' at the Stadium," untitled newspaper clipping, in "Clippings, Articles," File Box 13, Maude Adams Collection.

94. David Gray, "Maude Adams: A Public Influence," *Hampton's Magazine*, June 1911, p. 725.

95. Edward Harold Crosby, "Miss Adams an Ideal Joan," untitled newspaper, 23 June 1909, Phyllis Robbins Scrapbook, vol. IV, p. 45, Maude Adams Collection.

96. Daniel Frohman and Isaac F. Marcosson, "The Life of Charles Frohman," n. d., pp. 905–909, in "Clippings, Articles," File Box 13, ibid. On the Germanic Museum donation, see Fields, *Maude Adams*, 222.

97. Edward Congdon Cavanaugh, "Maude Adams at the Stadium," untitled magazine article, in "Clippings, Articles," File Box 13, Maude Adams Collection.

98. "Joan of Arc's Beatification at Harvard," *Current Literature*, August 1909, 196.

99. Robbins, *Maude Adams*, 133.

100. Letter to Frohman from Alf Hayman, 14 June 1909, Charles Frohman Letter-Press Copy Book, 3/12/1909–5/31/1910, p. 263. Hayman quotes Frohman's cable and responds to it.

101. "Great Crowds See Production of 'Joan of Arc' at the Stadium," untitled newspaper clipping, Maude Adams Collection; and "15,500 to See Maude Adams," untitled newspaper clipping, 11 June 1909, Phyllis Robbins Scrapbook, vol. IV, p. 25, ibid.

102. Letters to Frohman from Alf Hayman, 7, 24, 30 June, and 6 July 1909, Charles Frohman Letter-Press Copy Book, 3/12/1909–5/31/1910, pp. 248, 277, 293, 301.

103. "Maude Adams Starts Trek of Old Adorers to Newark," untitled newspaper clipping, Maude Adams Personality File. See also Marcosson and Frohman, *Charles Frohman*, 179.

104. Ibid., 179–180.

105. Edmond Rostand, *Chantecler: A Play in Four Acts*, paraphrased by Louis N. Parker, Ts promptbook (1911), Act II, pp. 23–24. All subsequent parenthetical citations also refer to this version.

106. Quoted in *Chantecler Told in Words and Pictures—Charles Frohman Presents Maude Adams*.

107. Adams quoted in Marcosson and Frohman, *Charles Frohman*, 180.

108. Robbins, *Maude Adams*, 93.

109. "Miss Adams to Play Title Role in 'Chantecler,'" clipping from [Boston?] *Herald*, n. pag., "Articles, Clippings," Box 13, Maude Adams Collection.

110. Kiskadden, "The Life Story," p. 818.

111. For accounts of Frohman's humor, see, for example: "Miss Adams Says It Was Like This," transcript of commencement speech in untitled newspaper clipping, Maude Adams Personality File; Marcosson and Frohman, *Charles Frohman*, 154–156; John D. Williams, "C.F.," *Century Magazine*, December 1915, 173–188; untitled newspaper clipping, section subtitled "Mixing Jest with Life," Robinson-Locke Collection of Dramatic Scrapbooks, vol. 1, # 222, p. 143; Charles Dillingham, unpublished memoirs, pp. 19–23, Charles Dillingham Papers, Box 32.

112. Charles Brookfield and James M. Glover, *The Poet and the Puppets*, adapted for the American production by Frohman author Clyde Fitch, opened at the Garden Theatre, which was one of the theatres into which Frohman booked productions and which he briefly assigned Dillingham to manage, on 8 April 1893, during the New York run of *Lady Windermere's Fan*.

113. "Cock," *Oxford English Dictionary* (1933), vol. 2, p. 566, sense 20. Earliest use in 1730 by Bailey, then used in 1737 by Rabelais (tr.). Under sense 20, the *OED* says, "In origin, perhaps intimately connected with sense 12: 'A spout or short pipe serving as a channel for passing liquids through, and having an appliance for regulating or stopping the flow; a tap.'" Earliest use in sense 12 was in 1481.

114. Marcosson and Frohman, *Charles Frohman*, 180.

115. Ibid., 181. I am indebted to Marlis Schweitzer for sending me pictures of the Chantecler hats from the *New York Times*, 20 March 1910, pt. 1, p. 7, and ads for Chantecler combs in the *Dry Goods Economist*, 2 April 1910, p. 107. While the combs were quite subtle, with pictures of birds engraved on the handle, the hats gave the impression of a whole rooster with his legs tucked under him plopped atop one's head.

116. Marcosson and Frohman, *Charles Frohman*, 181.

117. Review of *Chantecler*, *New York Herald*, 24 January 1911, p. 7; Marcosson and Frohman, *Charles Frohman*, 181; and "Maude Adams Presents 'Chantecler' in New York," untitled newspaper clipping, Phyllis Robbins Scrapbook, vol. IV, p. 71, Maude Adams Collection.

118. "Frohman to Have Canine Stock Company—His Success at the Kennel Club Exhibition Stirs Him to Seek Additional Laurels," untitled newspaper clipping, 14 February 1904, Robinson-Locke Collection of Dramatic Scrapbooks, vol. 1, #221, p. 8.

119. Higdon, "Modernism," 494.

120. Meyer, "Maude Adams," *New York Times*, 6 December 1931, sec. 8, p. 2X.

121. The range of negative criticism is covered in Kuehnl, "Maude Adams," 343–348.

5. A PRIESTLY ACTING PEDAGOGY

1. Production details gleaned from Salmi Morse, *The Passion: A Miracle Play in Ten Acts*.

2. Claire Sponsler, *Ritual Imports: Performing Medieval Drama in America*, 134.

3. William Winter, *The Life of David Belasco*, vol. 1, 118. Belasco admiringly recalled Maguire in his autobiography "My Life's Story," September 1914, p. 348.

4. Sponsler, *Ritual Imports*, 138–139, records that the show ran for ten performances between 3 March and 11 March. Maguire temporarily closed it so some of the actors could participate in a three-week run of *The Miner's Daughter*, starring Rose Eytinge at the Baldwin. *The Passion* reopened at the Grand Opera House on 15 April, Easter Tuesday, when the actors were arrested. They were released in time to resume performing the following night, but the run only lasted for a few more performances. Winter, *Life*, quotes the following notice in the *Alta California* dated 22 April: "Grand Opera House.— The management has the honor to announce that in deference to public opinion 'The Passion' will no longer be presented" (vol. 1, 118).

5. See Belasco's serialized autobiography, "My Life's Story," in *Hearst's Magazine*, November 1914, p. 610.

6. Winter, *Life*, vol. 1, 116.

7. Sponsler, *Ritual Imports*, 134, notes that rather than admit he was born of Jewish descent in Germany, Morse claimed to be an Englishman from Norwich. The choice seems telling, given Norwich's history of persecuting Jews for making blood sacrifices of Christian youth.

8. Winter, *Life*, vol. 1, 116.

9. Ibid., 119; Morse, *The Passion*, 9.

10. Sponsler, *Ritual Imports*, 138.

11. Qtd. in Craig Timberlake, *The Bishop of Broadway: The Life and Work of David Belasco*, 76. In the 1870s, after waves of immigration following the Gold Rush, Jews comprised 7–8% of the population of San Francisco, a higher percentage than in any city outside of New York. See Ava F. Kahn, "Joining the Rush," in *California Jews*, edited by Ava F. Kahn and Marc Dollinger, 30.

12. Magda Frances West, "Belasco's Views on Love, Women, and the Play of Tomorrow," *Green Book Magazine* 13 (October 1912): 580–581.

13. Belasco, "My Life's Story," November 1914, p. 610.

14. Ibid., November 1914, p. 611.

15. Timberlake, *Bishop of Broadway*, 19.

16. Belasco, "My Life's Story," March 1914, pp. 302–306.

17. Timberlake, *Bishop of Broadway*, 13–16.

18. Belasco, "My Life's Story," April 1914, pp. 488–489.

19. Wendell Phillips Dodge, "David Belasco," *Strand Magazine*, n.d., p. 649, David Belasco Personality File.

20. For a chronology of Belasco's acting career, see Winter, *Life*, vol. 2, 475–493.

21. Belasco, "My Life's Story," June 1914, pp. 771–772.

22. Timberlake, *Bishop of Broadway*, 46–54.

23. Belasco married Cecilia Loverich on 26 August 1873 in a ceremony performed by a rabbi in San Francisco. They were married fifty-two years until Cecilia died in 1926, five years before her husband's death. See Ibid., 38–40.

24. Dodge, "David Belasco," *Strand Magazine*, n.d., p. 660, David Belasco Personality File.

25. H. A. Harris, "David Belasco—The Man and His Work," *Cosmopolitan* 47 (November 1909): 757.

26. Morse, *The Passion*, 63. Sponsler, *Ritual Imports*, 137, reports that, in an attempt to appease critics, Maguire and Morse decided to omit the scenes of the Crucifixion and Resurrection before the play opened to the public, although they remained in the printed version approved by Joseph S. Alemany, the archbishop of California, and Belasco and others in the company would have read and likely worked on those scenes for at least part of the rehearsal period.

27. On Morse's peripatetic career prior to *The Passion*, see Sponsler, *Ritual Imports*, 134–135.

28. Belasco, "My Life's Story," May 1914, p. 644; and July 1914, 42.

29. Ada Patterson, "David Belasco in a Writer's Recollections: One Who Interviewed Him Many Times Quotes Bits that Linger in Memory," newspaper clipping, 24 May 1933, David Belasco Personality File.

30. Belasco, "My Life's Story," July 1914, pp. 42–43.

31. Ibid., July 1915, p. 71.

32. Montrose J. Moses, "Six Decades of Belasco Stage Magic," *New York Times*, Sunday, 27 October 1929, n. pag.; and Belasco, "'What I Am Trying to Do': A School for Actors and a Better Theatre for the Public," *The World's Work*, July 1912, p. 299.

33. Belasco, "My Life's Story," May 1914, pp. 643–44; and July 1914, p. 46.

34. Winter, *Life*, vol. 2, p. 28.

35. *Books from the Library of the Late David Belasco*; and *Books Chiefly from the Library of the Late David Belasco*.

36. Timberlake, *Bishop of Broadway*, 400–401.

37. The list is still extant and resides in the Thomas Albert Curry Sr. Papers, Ax315/Box 1.

38. Tracy C. Davis, "The Actress in Victorian Pornography," *Theatre Journal* 41 (October 1989): 294–315; and Davis, *Actresses as Working Women: Their Social Identity in Victorian Culture*, 105–136.

39. See Herbert Asbury, *The Barbary Coast: An Informal History of the San Francisco Underworld*; Susan Lee Johnson, "'My Own Private Life': Toward a History of Desire in Gold Rush California," in *Rooted in Barbarous Soil: People, Culture, and Community in Gold Rush California*, edited by Kevin Starr and Richard J. Orsi, 316–346; and Timothy J. Gilfoyle, *City of Eros: New York City, Prostitution, and the Commercialization of Sex, 1790–1920*, Part 3 "Comstock's New York, 1871–1920."

40. On pornography as a source of knowledge about sexuality, see, for example, the Preface to *Registrum Librorum Eroticorum*, compiled by Rolf S. Reade, ix–x; Jay A. Gertzman, *Bookleggers and Smuthounds: The Trade in Erotica, 1920–1940*, 73; and Ronald J. Berger, Patricia Searles, and Charles E. Cottle, *Feminism and Pornography*, 77–78.

41. Quoted in David Belasco, "Women and the Stage," *Ladies' Home Journal*, November 1920, p. 12.

42. For some collectors, the association of pornographic novels' insides with those of the whore went to the extreme of having the books custom bound in human flesh, and specifically in the skin of a woman's breast with the nipple embossed like a medallion on the front cover. See Norman D. Wiener, "On Bibliomania," *Psychoanalytic Quarterly* 35 (1966): 221.

43. Carroll Smith-Rosenberg and Charles Rosenberg, "The Female Animal: Medical and Biological Views of Woman and Her Role in Nineteenth-Century America," *Journal of American History* 60 (September 1973): 334–335.

44. According to his autobiography, Belasco, in his late teens in San Francisco,

found work at a cigar factory (Winter, *Life*, vol. 1, p. 17, says it was also a store) whose proprietor, learning of the young man's love of books, sent him to work at a bookstore run by the proprietor's brother ("My Life's Story," May 1914, p. 643). On the connection between cigar stores and the erotica trade in the nineteenth century, see John D'Emilio and Estelle B. Freedman, *Intimate Matters: A History of Sexuality in America*, 138. On the practice of writing synopses for circulars to entice customers to purchase rare books, such as "gallantiana" and other exotica, see Gertzman, *Bookleggers*, 4, 61. Belasco also writes of being a frequent visitor at White's cigar shop on Bush and Kearney Streets, claiming that "while White sculpted, I read Shakespeare to him" ("My Life's Story," August 1914, p. 196).

45. C. J. Scheiner, *Essential Guide to Erotic Literature*, 2 vols.

46. This portion of the list includes classics of the Roman Empire (Ovid's *Ars Amatoria*, Martial's *Epigrams*, and the *Golden Ass* of Apuleius); standards of Restoration and Georgian Britain (*Ten Pleasures of Marriage*, attributed to Aphra Behn; John Cleland's *The Memoirs of Fanny Hill*; and *The Merry Muses* of Robert Burns); works written or set in imperial France (*The Dialogues of Luisa Sigea* by Nicolas Chorier; Voltaire's *Princess of Babylon*; *Madame de Stael*, by Abel Stevens; *Stendhal on Love*; and *Orange Blossoms: The Story of a Beautiful Marchioness under the Second Empire*, by Ernest Feydeau); novels of the nineteenth century Parisian demimonde (*Sapho* by Alphonse Daudet; *Mademoiselle Giraud, My Wife*, by Adolphe Belot; and *Monsieur Venus* by Rachilde); Victorian standards (*The Lustful Turk*, by Emily Barlow [pseudonym]; *The Merry Order of St. Bridget*, by Margaret Anson [pseudonym]; *The Mysteries of Verbena House*, by George Augustus Sala); classical Indian guides to the arts of love (the *Kama Sutra*); and early sociological and scientific works on human sexual behavior published in the United States (*Bundling*, by H. R. Stiles; and *Psychopathia Sexualis*, by Krafft-Ebing).

47. Interview with Dr. C. J. Scheiner in New York City, by Mary Ellen Kelly, 13 July 1997, pp. 12, 21. Ts. in author's collection.

48. See Ava F. Kahn and Glenna Matthews, "120 Years of Women's Activism," and Kahn, "Joining the Rush," in *California Jews*, edited by Ava F. Kahn and Marc Dollinger, 143, 34.

49. Joseph Keppler immigrated to the United States at age thirty in 1868. He worked on *Leslie's Illustrated* in New York and then, in 1876, started *Puck*, first in German, then in an English edition beginning in 1877. See Harley Erdman, *Staging the Jew: The Performance of an American Ethnicity, 1860–1920*, 66–70, for an analysis of the Manhattan Beach episode and this cartoon. On Keppler's career, see John J. Appel, "Jews in American Caricature," *American History* (1981): 110–115.

50. For more on stereotypes of male Jews as effeminate, physically and emotionally incontinent, and skilled in the arts of music and mimicry, see Sander Gilman, *Freud, Race, and Gender*, 39. See also Gilman, *The Jew's Body*, 122–124; and *Modernity*,

Culture, and "the Jew," co-edited by Bryan Cheyette and Laura Marcus, especially their Introduction, 1–9, 14, and essays by Ritchie Robertson, "Historicizing Weininger: The Nineteenth-Century German Image of the Feminized Jew," 23–39, and Jean Radford, "The Woman and the Jew: Sex and Modernity," 91–104.

51. Belasco, "My Life's Story," November 1914, p. 612.

52. Qtd. in Timberlake, *Bishop of Broadway*, 112.

53. Winter, *Life*, vol. 1, 269.

54. Timberlake, *Bishop of Broadway*, 108–143.

55. Claude L. Shaver, "The Delsarte System of Expression as Seen through the Notes of Steele MacKaye," 55–56, qtd. in James H. McTeague, *Before Stanislavsky: American Professional Acting Schools and Acting Theory, 1875–1925*, p. 11.

56. MacKaye, qtd. in ibid., 7–9.

57. Genevieve Stebbins, *The Delsarte System of Expression*, 2nd ed., 7.

58. Philip G. Hubert, "New York's Lyceum for Actors," *Lippincott's* 35 (May 1885): 483–488.

59. Mary Gleason, Letter to the Editor of the *New York Mirror*, 28 May 1887, 3.

60. The account of faculty members and their hours of instruction was provided in a Letter to the Editor of the *New York Dramatic Mirror*, 4 June 1887, p. 10, by the school's director, Franklin Sargent.

61. McTeague, *Before Stanislavsky*, 70.

62. For more on MacKaye's schema and "circumincession," see ibid., 8, 13.

63. See, for example, *The Lustful Turk, The Merry Order of St. Bridget, The Dialogues of Luisa Sigea*, and *Ten Pleasures of Marriage*. Steven Marcus and H. Montgomery Hyde, leading historians of pornography, attribute the high incidence of anticlerical motifs to resentment over the church's humanly impossible dogmas of abstinence. Church censorship of books, in particular, rankled producers and consumers of pornography because religious authorities claimed they had to confiscate, examine, and hoard the material in order to record its sinfulness. Gaining access to what they denied their flocks, priests abrogated unto themselves a privileged relationship to forbidden knowledge from whose corruption they claimed immunity because of their vows of celibacy. As Hyde reports in his *History of Pornography* (1966), 153, the Catholic Church solidified its reputation as the archetypal censor during the Counter-Reformation, when it issued its *Index Librorum Prohibitorum*. The two major English-language bibliographers of pornography sardonically invoked the church's organ in titling their works. Herbert Spencer Ashbee (a.k.a. Pisanus Fraxi) issued his bibliography in three volumes, *Index librorum prohibitorum* (1877), *Centuria librorum absconditorum* (1879), and *Catena librorum tacendorum* (1885). Rolf S. Reade updated Ashbee's work in cataloguing the British Library's Private Case with his two-volume *Registrum Librorum Eroticorum* (1936). More than three hundred pages of Ashbee's seminal compendium are devoted to listings of pornographic books having to do with religion. See Steven Marcus, *The Other*

Victorians: A Study of Sexuality and Pornography in Mid-Nineteenth-Century England (1964), 61. Indeed, pornography may be a primary source for the possibly fictional existence of Belasco's childhood mentor, Father McGuire, or at least for the ways Belasco reconstructed him in memory, and in his own self-fashioning.

64. In pornography, the signal proof of male prowess is the transformation of the reluctant virgin into the willing and hungry whore, which accounts for what Hyde calls "the mania for defloration" that characterizes the genre. See Hyde, *History of Pornography*, 147.

65. Linda Williams, *Hard Core: Power, Pleasure, and the "Frenzy of the Visible,"* 50.

66. David Belasco, "How I Develop a Star," *New Idea Woman's Magazine*, October 1909, p. 54.

67. Stebbins, *The Delsarte System of Expression*, 6th ed., 455–456.

68. Ibid., 1st ed., (1885), 11, qtd. in McTeague, *Before Stanislavsky*, 35.

69. See entry on Steele MacKaye in Gerald Bordman, *Oxford Companion to American Theatre*, 450.

70. Stebbins, *Delsarte System* (1885), 83–85, qtd. in McTeague, *Before Stanislavsky*, 37.

71. Ibid., 13–14.

72. Ibid., 84.

73. Hubert, "New York's Lyceum," 487–488.

74. Ibid., 488.

75. Ibid., 488.

76. Taylor Susan Lake, "American Delsartism and the Bodily Discourse of Respectable Womanliness," 2002, 100.

77. Statue posing, in which participants often appeared to be nude or only partially clad, originally gained acceptance in respectable museum theatres of the 1840s under the aura of high art, but the practice had quickly degenerated into more overtly sexual model artist shows and tawdry lower-class displays. See Dudden, *Women in the American Theatre*, 116–118. Stebbins resuscitated the social standing of statue posing with her high-minded rhetoric.

78. Stebbins, *Delsarte System*, 2nd ed., 71. A photograph of the Gladiator statue can be found in Elsie M. Wilbor, comp., *Delsarte Recitation Book*, 4th ed., 40–41.

79. Stebbins, *Delsarte System*, 2nd ed., 82–83.

80. Ibid., 2nd. ed., 28.

81. Rachel M. Maines, *The Technology of Orgasm: "Hysteria," the Vibrator, and Women's Sexual Satisfaction.*

82. See ibid., 1–10.

83. George M. Baker, *Forty Minutes with a Crank, or the Seldarte Craze.*

84. Marcus, *The Other Victorians*, 21–23, records that the chief English colloquialism in the Victorian period for orgasm was "to spend."

85. See, for example, Wilhelmina Swanston, Letter to the Editor, 31 May 1887, in the *New York Mirror*, 4 June 1887, p. 10; and Mary Gleason, Letter to the Editor, 23 May 1887, in the *New York Mirror*, 28 May 1887, p. 3.

86. Baker, *Forty Minutes*, 10.

87. Ibid., 5.

88. Ibid., 6.

89. See Maines, *Technology of Orgasm*, 8, 12, 23.

90. Baker, *Forty Minutes*, 9.

91. Catalogue qtd. in McTeague, *Before Stanislovsky*, 83.

92. In Belasco's collection, *The Dialogues of Luisa Sigea*, by Nicolas Chorier, contains a paradigmatic example of a priest who enjoys ordering one of the heroines to strip naked and whipping her to expiate the sin of premarital sex. A variation on the motif can be found in *The Mysteries of Verbena House*, by George Augustus Sala, where the pubescent girls in a fashionable school in Brighton, England, are punished for teaching each other how to frig. The accused are whipped by a school mistress in a special bed chamber, the Red Room, where the resident priest secretes himself in a closet in order to watch.

93. Maines, *Technology of Orgasm*, 1–10.

94. See, for example, "How I Develop a Star," *New Idea Woman's Magazine*, October 1909; "Why I Believe in the Little Things and How They Have Made Successes of My Plays," *Ladies' Home Journal*, September 1911, pp. 15, 73; "The Great Opportunity of the Woman Dramatist," *Good Housekeeping Magazine*, November 1911, pp. 627–632; "The Truth about the Theater: How I Made Mrs. Carter into an Actress and How I Rehearsed Caruso to Be an American," *Ladies' Home Journal*, November 1917, pp. 19, 108; and "Women and the Stage," ibid., November 1920, pp. 12, 13, 108, 110. Belasco's expertise as a trainer of actresses was also highlighted by Acton Davies in "David Belasco, Star-Maker," *Good Housekeeping Magazine*, November 1911, 624–626.

95. In 1875, Lewes's text was published in Leipzig by Bernhard Tauchnitz and in New York by Brentano's. On its influence upon leading actors of the day, see Joseph R. Roach, *The Player's Passion: Studies in the Science of Acting*, 193. On Belasco's admiration of and association with these actors, see Winter, *Life*, vol. 1, 93–95, 132, 155, 168, 172, 316–317, 340–344, and vol. 2, 49, 154.

96. Belasco, "The Art of Acting," *Appleton's Booklover's Magazine* 6 (November 1905): 538–540. With the exception of one paragraph and a few transitional sentences, the entire article is lifted verbatim from Lewes's *On Actors and the Art of Acting*, pp. 13, 30, 33, 99–107. Belasco was forced to explain himself in the *New York Times* ("Plagiarism Charge All Mistake, Says Belasco," 23 November 1905, p. 6). In a tale told with as much melodrama as some of his plays, he claimed he was so busy that when a cub reporter desperate to sell an article pressed him for an interview on his methods, he succumbed to his "usual desire to help someone to make a few dollars,"

chatted with him, and told the fellow just to write it up and he would sign it. He alleged that the reporter evoked more of his pity by returning with his wife and bringing him six or seven pieces dealing with a range of topics, including "The Art of Make-Up," "How an Amateur Guy Becomes a Professional," and "How to Go on the Stage Though Not Beautiful," as well as "The Art of Acting." Very preoccupied, Belasco said he just flipped through them cursorily and signed them, accepting the responsibility for being "the champion hayseed" but shifting the blame for the plagiarism onto the reporter. When contacted for questioning, the reporter refused to confirm or deny Belasco's version of events. Belasco also pointed to another layer of villainy in the rival producers, members of the Theatrical Syndicate, who were using the incident to discredit him by bringing the plagiarized article to the attention of the newspapers.

97. Belasco, "About Acting," pp. 11, 93, 94, 97, 98. The article is laced with paraphrases of Lewes's thoughts on acting. Belasco also analyzes some of the same historical examples Lewes does. See Brentano's 1875 edition of Lewes, *On Actors*, 19, 22–23, 108, 111–113, 117.

98. Belasco, "About Acting," 94. For more on Lewes and Diderot, see Roach, *The Player's Passion*, 184–192.

99. Belasco, "About Acting," 97.

100. Belasco qtd. in the *New York Journal*, 8 December 1901, qtd. in Timberlake, *Bishop of Broadway*, 353.

101. The epistolary conceit is an attempt to authenticate the contents as being the true confessions of women, regardless of the sex of the novel's author. *The Memoirs of Fanny Hill* is attributed to John Cleland and *The Lustful Turk* to Emily Barlow, who is the novel's letter-writing heroine and a pseudonym for an anonymous author. See Kendrick, *Secret Museum*, 311.

102. In the books in Belasco's collection, lesbian scenes of initiation can be found in, for example, *The Memoirs of Fanny Hill*, when Fanny is primed for defloration by professional lesbian seductress Phoebe Ayres. Older girls initiate younger ones in a girls' school in *The Mysteries of Verbena House* and a nunnery in *The Merry Order of St. Bridget*. In *The Dialogues of Luisa Sigea*, Tullia first graphically explains the workings of the clitoris and inner reproductive organs during sexual intercourse to the virginal Ottavia, who appreciatively responds: "Thou describest the thing so well that methinks I behold in person all that is concealed in my innermost bowels, as if it were placed before my eyes" (p. 32). Literally taking the reader inside the female body, the two then proceed to look up each other's "sheaths" and assess how they might accommodate their respective husbands. Further graphic sharing of their sexual experiences with men follows Ottavia's wedding night. The book ends with a somewhat ominous, if titillating, picture of the two women practicing on each other the knowledge they have exchanged. They are having sex, missionary style, with the one on top usurping the man's role by wearing a dildo. Given his claims to knowing women's secret passions, it is not

surprising that Sappho became the female poet Belasco most admired, as he stated in "Acting, Belasco Says, Is a Woman's Art First of All," *Rochester New York Democrat and Chronicle*, 19 September 1909, n. pag. He would later acquire a bust of Sappho for his studio. See the *New York Mirror*, 21 December 1909, clipping the Robinson-Locke Collection of Theatrical Scrapbooks, vol 50. After his death, two volumes of her poetry were offered for sale from his collection: *The Songs of Sappho* and *Sappho Revocata*. Both are listed in the Academy Book Shop sale catalogue, *Books Chiefly from the Library of the Late David Belasco*, p. 21.

103. In the second of the two long letters that comprise the novel, Fanny embarks on a "new stage of my profession" in which her proprietress advises her to "pass for a maid," that is, to feign maidenhood. (See *Fanny Hill*, pp. 141 ff.) Having mastered these arts of deception makes Fanny a highly discerning and authoritative judge of genuineness in others, as she bears witness to a colleague, Louisa's, act of copulation, pinpointing the moment when "she was presently driven out of the power of using any art, and indeed, what art must not give way, when nature, corresponding with her assailant, invaded in the heart of her capital and carried by storm, lay at the mercy of the proud conqueror, who had made his entry triumphantly and completely" (p. 263).

104. Timberlake, *Bishop of Broadway*, 348.

105. Qtd. in "How Belasco Creates Dramatic Stars." *Current Literature* 42 (April 1907): 435.

6. DRILLING HER IN THE EMOTIONAL PARTS

1. See Daniel J. Pick, *Svengali's Web: The Alien Enchanter in Modern Culture*, for a full exegesis of the Svengali character. Pick introduces Svengali's eastern European Jewish origins on p. 4.

2. George du Maurier, *Trilby*, 13.

3. Ibid, 36.

4. Ibid, 212.

5. See, for example, Wendell Phillips Dodge, "David Belasco," *Strand Magazine*, n.d., p. 655, David Belasco Personality File; and Jane Dransfield, "Behind the Scenes with Belasco: How America's Leading Theatre Manager Has Solved the Secret of Successful Production," *Theatre Magazine* 35 (April 1922): 228.

6. Mrs. Leslie Carter, "Portrait of a Lady with Red Hair," *Liberty Magazine*, 15 January 1927, p. 14.

7. Caroline Louise Dudley and Leslie Carter were married in Dayton on 26 May 1880. See Charles Harold Harper, "Mrs. Leslie Carter: Her Life and Acting Career," 10.

8. Mrs. Leslie Carter, "Portrait," 15 January 1927, pp. 16–17.

9. *Carter v. Carter*, Transcript, 27 May 1889, p. 1262, qtd. in Harper, "Mrs. Leslie Carter," 16. In 1880, the French franc, which remained relatively stable until World

War I, was worth about twenty cents. See "Statue of Liberty Fund Raising, 1875–1885," 13 June 2005, http://www.endex.com/gf/buildings/libert/libertyfacts/LibertyConstruction/CasinoTheater/CasinoTheater.htm, accessed on 30 March 2006. Accordingly, four thousand francs would equal about eight hundred dollars in 1885, more than sixteen thousand dollars today.

10. Harper, "Mrs. Leslie Carter," 16.

11. *New York Times* editorial, 4 May 1889, qtd. in Craig Timberlake, *The Bishop of Broadway: The Life and Work of David Belasco*, 139.

12. *Carter v. Carter*, pp. 2293–2294, qtd. in Harper, "Mrs. Leslie Carter," 25.

13. Delos Avery, "Presenting Mrs. Leslie Carter in a Stirring Drama: 'Lexington's Redheadedest Beauty,'" *Chicago Sunday Tribune*, n.d., Mrs. Leslie Carter Clipping File.

14. Craig Timberlake, *Bishop of Broadway*, 139.

15. See Ellen Carol DuBois and Linda Gordon, "Seeking Ecstasy on the Battlefield: Danger and Pleasure in Nineteenth-Century Feminist Sexual Thought," in *Pleasure and Danger: Exploring Female Sexuality*, edited by Carol S. Vance, 34.

16. Mrs. Leslie Carter, "Portrait," 22 January 1927, p. 14.

17. Ibid., p. 14.

18. Ibid., p. 15.

19. David Belasco, *The Theatre through Its Stage Door*, 14–15.

20. Mrs. Leslie Carter, "Portrait," 29 January 1927, p. 35.

21. Qtd. in Timberlake, *Bishop of Broadway*, 149–150.

22. H. A. Harris, "David Belasco—The Man and His Work," *Cosmopolitan* 47 (November 1909): 760.

23. David Belasco, "About Acting," *Saturday Evening Post*, 24 September 1921, p. 11.

24. See Rachel M. Maines, *The Technology of Orgasm: "Hysteria," the Vibrator, and Women's Sexual Satisfaction*, esp. 1–42.

25. According to Maines, it was a common belief for centuries that horseback riding and carriage riding benefited hysterics. She cites the physician Charles Meigs, who recommended in 1854 that women enhance their "pelvic determination" of blood by "galloping on horseback, which powerfully develops it." Qtd. in ibid., 89.

26. See Timothy Gilfoyle, "Policing of Sexuality," in *Inventing Times Square: Commerce and Culture at the Crossroads of the World*, edited by William R. Taylor, 297–314.

27. Mrs. Leslie Carter, "What My Career Means to Me," n. d., n. pag., in Mrs. Leslie Carter Clipping File.

28. Belasco, *The Theatre*, 96.

29. Belasco qtd. in Craig Clinton, "Training the Actor: Belasco and Mrs. Carter," *Nineteenth Century Theatre and Film* 29 (June 2002): 69. Clinton cites Belasco, "How I Develop a Star," *New Idea Woman's Magazine*, October 1909, but the

statement, made in 1895, comes instead from another source he also cites in this article: Belasco, "How To Make an Actress," 22 December 1895, David Belasco Clipping File, Harvard Theatre Collection.

30. "The New Society Actress Mrs. Carter Explains Her Plans, Ambitions, and Prospects: The Heroine of the Notorious Chicago Divorce Case Getting Ready to Appear in Public—Her Likeness to Mrs. Potter, Her Dog, and Her Boy," n.p., Sunday, 23 March 1890, in Mrs. Leslie Carter Scrapbook.

31. Belasco, *The Theatre*, 97.

32. Mrs. Leslie Carter, "Portrait," 29 January 1927, p. 24.

33. Belasco, *The Theatre*, 97.

34. Ibid., p. 97.

35. "Wallack's Theatre—First Appearance of Miss Heron," *New York Herald*, 23 January 1857, n.p.

36. Belasco, *The Theatre*, 98–99.

37. Mrs. Leslie Carter, "Portrait," 22 January 1927, p. 15.

38. Letter from Belasco to Daniel Frohman qtd. in Timberlake, *Bishop of Broadway*, 143.

39. Mrs. Leslie Carter, "What My Career Means to Me," n.d., n.p., in Mrs. Leslie Carter Clipping File.

40. Mrs. Leslie Carter, "Portrait," 29 January 1927, p. 27.

41. "Only a Big Mouth," *San Francisco Examiner*, 15 November 1890, n.p., in Robinson-Locke Collection of Dramatic Scrapbooks, series 1, vol. 1, p. 54.

42. Harper, "Mrs. Leslie Carter," 51. Thomas A. Curry Sr.'s account of *The Ugly Duckling* tour emphasizes the extent to which Belasco was relying on Fairbank's credit in order to keep the play going in spite of losing money on ticket sales. See Thomas Curry, "Presenting David Belasco," Unpublished Ts, c. 1926, in Folder: "Articles on Belasco" 1, in Ax 315, Box #1: Thomas A. Curry Sr. Papers.

43. Mrs. Leslie Carter, "Portrait," 29 January 1927, p. 31.

44. Harper, "Mrs. Leslie Carter," 55. For an account of the play, set in the Spanish Pyrenees, see "Miss Helyett," *The Illustrated American*, 28 November 1891, in Mrs. Leslie Carter Scrapbook in the Players Collection.

45. "Mrs Carter Runs the Show," *New York Dramatic Mirror*, 16 January 1892, in Mrs. Leslie Carter Scrapbook in the Players Collection.

46. The play was *The Girl I Left Behind Me* (1893), co-authored with Franklin Fyles.

47. Belasco, *The Theatre*, 100.

48. David Belasco, "His Adventures in Life as Related to John J. Wallace," *New York American*, 13 December 1925, p. 3.

49. Mrs. Leslie Carter, "Portrait," 29 January 1927, p. 35.

50. Dialogue recorded as Mrs. Carter told it to William Winter, qtd. in his *Life of David Belasco*, vol. 1, 392.

51. Mrs. Leslie Carter, "Portrait," 22 January 1927, p. 15. In their respective life stories, Mrs. Carter and Belasco tend to collapse the two periods of training, before and after *The Ugly Duckling* and *Miss Helyett*, into one. Working from a detailed chronology based on newspaper sources, I have tried to sort out which of their statements apply to which of these two periods. Because some of the same training methods were used in both, some of their comments may be fairly applied to each.

52. "David Belasco and Mrs. Carter," miscellaneous clipping, Mrs. Leslie Carter Personality File.

53. Mrs. Leslie Carter, "Portrait," 29 January 1927, p. 27.

54. Exercise recalled by Mrs. Carter in the *New York Sun*, March 1904, n.p., qtd. in Harper, "Mrs. Leslie Carter," 39.

55. Mrs. Leslie Carter, "The Secret of Success on the Stage," *Broadway Magazine*, February 1902, n. pag., qtd. in Young, *Famous Actors and Actresses on the American Stage*, vol. 1, 166.

56. Belasco qtd. in an interview for the *New York Sun*, Sunday, 31 January 1904, n.p., David Belasco Papers, Series X Scrapbooks, microfilm reel 11.

57. Mrs. Leslie Carter, "The Secret," qtd. in Young, *Famous Actors and Actresses*, vol. 1, p. 166.

58. Delos Avery, "Presenting Mrs. Leslie Carter in a Stirring Drama: 'Lexington's Redheadedest Beauty,'" *Chicago Sunday Tribune*, n.d., Mrs. Leslie Carter Clipping File.

59. "Mrs. Leslie Carter's Story," *New York Herald*, 21 July 1902, n.p., Robinson-Locke Collection of Dramatic Scrapbooks, series 1, vol. 1, p. 103.

60. See Thomas Curry, "Presenting David Belasco," unpublished Ts, c. 1926, in Folder: "Articles on Belasco" 1, in Ax 315, Box 1, Thomas A. Curry Sr. Papers. Curry Sr. discusses Mrs. Carter's training as background in "I. Lenore Ulric in Lulu Belle," p. 15.

61. He may have begun this practice at the New York School for Acting, where there was a piano in the classroom. See James H. McTeague, *Before Stanislavsky: American Professional Acting Schools and Acting Theory, 1875–1925*, 81. Belasco striking the keys to define the pitch for Mrs. Carter is part of one of their training scenes in the film, *The Lady with Red Hair*.

62. Mrs. Carter qtd. in an interview by Elisabeth R. Thomas for the *Morning Telegraph*, 2 October 1921, n.p., "Mrs. Leslie Carter," Robinson-Locke Collection of Dramatic Scrapbooks, series 2, vol. 26, p. 92.

63. Jane Dransfield, "Behind the Scenes with Belasco: How America's Leading Theatre Manager Has Solved the Secret of Successful Production," *Theatre Magazine* 35 (April 1922): 230.

64. See, for example, Belasco, "My Life's Story," *Hearst's Magazine*, March 1914, pp. 301–302.

65. The poem was originally published in a Detroit newspaper in 1867. This text is taken from Rose Hartwick Thorpe, *Ringing Ballads, Including Curfew Must Not Ring Tonight*, 21.

66. Ibid., 22.

67. David Belasco, "Why I Believe in the Little Things, and How They Have Made Successes of My Plays," *Ladies' Home Journal*, September 1911, p. 15.

68. William Winter, *Life of David Belasco*, vol. 1, 11.

69. Belasco, "Why I Believe," 15.

70. Belasco, "My Life's Story," July 1915, p. 71.

71. Winter, *Life*, vol. 1, 392.

72. Mrs. Leslie Carter, "Portrait," 29 January 1927, p. 32.

73. "Maryland," *New Encyclopaedia Britannica*, 903.

74. Winter, *Life*, vol. 2, 28.

75. From the stage directions in the play text in *The Heart of Maryland and Other Plays*, by David Belasco, 232.

76. Timberlake, *Bishop of Broadway*, 163.

77. Mrs. Leslie Carter, "Portrait," 29 January 1927, p. 35.

78. Winter, *Life*, vol. 1, 436–437.

79. Harper, "Mrs. Leslie Carter," 67–70.

80. Mrs. Leslie Carter, "Portrait," 29 January 1927, pp. 35–36.

81. Qtd. in Winter, *Life*, vol. 1, p. 437.

82. Mrs. Leslie Carter, "Portrait," 29 January 1927, p. 36.

83. Qtd. in Timberlake, *Bishop of Broadway*, 163.

84. Mrs. Leslie Carter, "Portrait," 29 January 1927, p. 36.

85. See the detailed chronology provided by William Winter at the end of his *Life*, vol. 2, pp. 509–512. For an account of the play's earnings, see Harper, "Mrs. Leslie Carter: Her Life and Acting Career," 80.

86. "Hollis Street Theatre: 'The Heart of Maryland,'" n.d., in Mrs. Leslie Carter Scrapbook.

87. Belasco, *The Heart of Maryland*, 235–236.

88. Timberlake, *Bishop of Broadway*, 164.

89. George Jean Nathan, "The Physical Demands of the Stage," *Outing Magazine*, April 1909, American Periodical Series Online, http://proquest.umi.com, accessed 15 January 2004.

90. Program is in *The Heart of Maryland* Broadway Show Folder.

91. Female trapeze performers were also depicted on *carte de visite* photographs that allowed for private erotic consumption and fueled the pornotopic dynamic wherein sexual fantasies were projected onto public performers. See Laurence

Senelick, "Eroticism in Early Theatrical Photography," *Theatre History Studies* 11 (1991): 1–49.

92. H. Montgomery Hyde, *A History of Pornography*, 11–12.

93. Recalling this legendary scene more than fifty years later, Bennett Cerf remarked, "Since Mrs. Carter projected in the manner of Marilyn Monroe, her daring act on the flying trapeze brought down the house." Column entitled "The Cerf-board," n.d., in Belasco Personality File.

94. Qtd. in Timberlake, *Bishop of Broadway*, 149.

95. From a series of articles on "Tempted London," *British Weekly*, 10 February 1888, p. 278, qtd. in Tracy C. Davis, "The Actress in Victorian Pornography," *Theatre Journal*, 41 (October 1989): 295.

96. Untitled article by Margaret M. Lukes, *Waterbury Republican*, 1 January 1928, Mrs. Leslie Carter Clipping File.

97. Howard Whitman, "Mrs. Leslie Carter's Famed Red Hair—'Twas Only a Wig," n.d., Mrs. Leslie Carter Clipping File.

98. See Maines, *The Technology of Orgasm*, 8, 12, 23. This association is discussed in more detail in the previous chapter.

99. Mrs. Leslie Carter, "Portrait," 29 January 1927, p. 31.

100. Timberlake, *Bishop of Broadway*, 160.

101. Qtd. in ibid., 169–170.

102. Ibid., p. 170.

103. "Dragged Her by the Hair," *New York Times*, 5 June 1896, p. 10.

104. Timberlake, *Bishop of Broadway*, 190.

105. Ibid., 185.

106. For analysis of the material and ideological conditions surrounding "fallen" women in the period, see, for example, Ellen Carol DuBois and Linda Gordon, "Seeking Ecstasy on the Battlefield: Danger and Pleasure in Nineteenth-Century Feminist Sexual Thought," in *Pleasure and Danger: Exploring Female Sexuality*, edited by Carole S. Vance, 34; Carol S. Vance, "Pleasure and Danger: Toward a Politics of Sexuality," ibid., 3; and Andrea Dworkin, *Pornography: Men Possessing Women*, 152–153.

107. "The Stage: Mrs. Leslie Carter's Pluck," *Munsey's Magazine*, February 1897, n.p., in Mrs. Leslie Carter Scrapbook.

108. "Lights and Shadows," *San Francisco Daily Report*, 26 September 1897, p. 9, qtd. in Harper, "Mrs. Leslie Carter," 75.

109. Program in *Heart of Maryland* Broadway Show Folder.

110. "Lights and Shadows," *San Francisco Daily Report*, 26 September 1897, p. 9, qtd. in Harper, "Mrs. Leslie Carter," 75.

111. Photo in *Heart of Maryland* Broadway Show Folder.

112. Timberlake, *Bishop of Broadway*, 166.

113. Belasco qtd. in untitled clipping from *New York World*, 10 October 1914, David Belasco Papers, Series X Scrapbooks, Microfilm Reel 11.

114. Belasco, *The Theatre*, 99–100.

115. Belasco, "His Adventures in Life as Related to John J. Wallace," *New York American*, 13 December 1925, p. 3.

116. Belasco qtd. in George Brinton Beal, "Cupid Wins Another Round from Belasco—But Will Dean of American Theatre Ruin Another Career?" *Boston Sunday Post*, 10 May 1931, p. 2.

117. Thomas A. Curry Sr., "Outline and Preliminary Notes submitted to editor for proposed articles on Belasco," unpublished Ts. in folder: "Articles on Belasco" 2, in Ax 315, Box 1, Thomas A. Curry Sr. Papers.

118. Mrs. Leslie Carter, "Portrait," 22 January 1927, p. 15.

119. Wendell Phillips Dodge, "David Belasco," *Strand Magazine*, n.d., p. 652, in Belasco Personality File.

120. See Katie N. Johnson, "*Zaza*: That 'Obtruding Harlot' of the Stage," *Theatre Journal* 54 (May 2002): 223–243, for an astute analysis of the cultural work of this play in the Progressive Era.

121. Pierre Berton and Charles Simon, "'Zaza'; A Comedy Drama in Five Acts, Adapted from the French of Berton and Simon by David Belasco," Typescript [1898].

122. Gilfoyle, "Policing of Sexuality," 302.

123. Wendell Phillips Dodge, "David Belasco," *Strand Magazine*, n.d., pp. 652–653, Belasco Personality File.

124. "Mrs. Carter's Physical Endurance," Mrs. Leslie Carter Scrapbook n.d., n.p.

125. See Maines, *The Technology of Orgasm*, 9; and Steven Marcus, *The Other Victorians: A Study of Sexuality and Pornography in Mid-Nineteenth-Century England*, 31–32.

126. Mrs. Leslie Carter, "Portrait," 12 February 1927, 49.

127. Harper, "Mrs. Leslie Carter," 106–107.

128. David Belasco, "Mrs. Leslie Carter as Zaza: With a History of Her Stage Career and the Successful Production of the Play: Illustrated with Half-tone Engravings of the Principal Scenes in Which Mrs. Carter Appears," pp. 14–15. In *Zaza* Broadway Show Folder.

129. Mrs. Leslie Carter, "What My Career Means to Me," n.d., n.p., in Mrs. Leslie Carter Clipping File.

130. Mrs. Leslie Carter, "Portrait," 29 January 1927, p. 27.

131. To obtain the play, Belasco had to negotiate with Charles Dillingham and Charles Frohman, who owned the American rights to the French original by Pierre Berton and Charles Simon and retained a 50% interest in the production. See Charles Dillingham Papers, unpublished memoirs, Box 32, p. 79.

132. Dodge, "David Belasco," *Strand Magazine*, n.d., 652, David Belasco Personality File.

7. IMPERIAL EXPIATIONS

1. Wendell Phillips Dodge, "David Belasco," *Strand Magazine*, n.d., p. 659, Belasco Personality File.

2. David Belasco, "My Best Play, How I Wrote It and Why," *Green Book Album* 5 (February 1911): 436.

3. Edward Said, *Orientalism*, 20–21.

4. See Harley Erdman, *Staging the Jew: The Performance of an American Ethnicity, 1860–1920*, 108–113, for a detailed examination of Jewish representation in *The Auctioneer*.

5. Thomas A. Curry Sr., "Presenting David Belasco," Part I, unpublished typescript in Folder "Articles on Belasco" 1, in Ax 315, Box 1, Thomas A. Curry Sr. Papers.

6. Craig Timberlake, *The Bishop of Broadway: The Life and Work of David Belasco*, 202. Timberlake also notes (p. 304) that following her most successful "picturesque" vehicles, *The Darling of the Gods* (1902) and *The Girl of the Golden West* (1905), Bates failed with the greater emotional demands of *The Fighting Hope* (1908), which critics contended would have more befitted Mrs. Carter.

7. Mrs. Leslie Carter, "Portrait of a Lady with Red Hair," *Liberty Magazine*, 19 February 1927, p. 57.

8. Ibid., p. 57.

9. John L. Ford, *Mrs. Leslie Carter in David Belasco's* Du Barry, *with Portraits of Mrs. Carter by John Cecil Clay, Together with Portrait of David Belasco and Numerous Engravings of Photographs and Sketches in Black and White*, 9–13. Volume in *Du Barry* Broadway Show Folder.

10. Mrs. Leslie Carter, "Portrait," *Liberty Magazine*, 19 February 1927, p. 59.

11. Ibid., 19 February 1927, p. 60.

12. David Belasco, "My Best Play," *Green Book Album* 5 (February 1911): 434–438.

13. *Books from the Library of the Late David Belasco*, Sale Number 3935, New York City, Sold by Order of Mrs. Morris Gest, Unrestricted Public Sale December 15 and 16 at 2:15 p.m., American Art Association Anderson Galleries, Inc. Catalogue in the personal collection of Mary Ellen Kelly, New York, New York.

14. See Rolfe S. Reade, comp. *Registrum Librorum Eroticorum*, vol. 1, p. 95, #1275, and p. 200, #2679. According to Professor Downing Thomas, a specialist in eighteenth-century French literature at the University of Iowa, the title *Louis XV. Intime et Les Petites Maitresses* trades on meanings very specific to the period that do not translate well into English. He offers an admittedly unsatisfactory possibility, "The Intimate Louis XV and the *Petites Maitresses*," with the explanation that *Maitresses* means mistresses; *petite maitresse*, however, is a female version of the *petit*

maitre, who is not a dandy, but a man at court who affectedly considers himself important, acts decisively but also freely (too freely) and impetuously and self-centeredly. E-mail correspondence with the author, 27 March 2006.

15. Mrs. Leslie Carter, "Portrait," *Liberty Magazine*, 19 February 1927, p. 59–60.

16. David Belasco, "My Life's Story," *Hearst's Magazine*, July 1915, p. 71.

17. Quote is from the original program note to which Belasco, in an admitted instance of forgery, falsely appended the name of Guy de Maupassant. The note is reprinted with *Du Barry* in *Six Plays by David Belasco*, 40. On the forgery, see Timberlake, *Bishop of Broadway*, 401.

18. Mrs. Leslie Carter, "Portrait," *Liberty Magazine*, 19 February 1927, pp. 60–61.

19. Ibid., 19 February 1927, p. 61.

20. Ibid., 26 February 1927, p. 59.

21. Ibid., 19 February 1927, p. 61.

22. See, for example, William Leach, *Land of Desire: Merchants, Power, and the Rise of a New American Culture*, especially pp. 3–12, 191–224.

23. Belasco, *Du Barry*, in *Six Plays*, 53–54.

24. Ibid., 63.

25. Ford, *Mrs. Leslie Carter*, 44.

26. Belasco, *Du Barry*, in *Six Plays*, 66.

27. Ibid., 71.

28. Ibid., 71–73.

29. Ibid., 81.

30. Ford, *Mrs. Leslie Carter*, 14.

31. Ibid., 20–21.

32. Ibid., 17.

33. Ibid., 46.

34. Mrs. Leslie Carter, "Portrait," *Liberty Magazine*, 26 February 1927, p. 62.

35. John L. Ford, *The Story of Du Barry*, 125–126.

36. Ford, *Mrs. Leslie Carter*, 45.

37. Belasco, *Du Barry*, in *Six Plays*, 85.

38. Ibid., 93.

39. Ibid., 97.

40. H. A. Harris, "David Belasco—The Man and His Work," *Cosmopolitan* 47 (November 1909): 755.

41. Mrs. Leslie Carter, "Portrait," *Liberty Magazine*, 19 February 1927, p. 61.

42. Belasco, *Du Barry*, in *Six Plays*, 124.

43. Ford, *Mrs. Leslie Carter*, 25.

44. Mrs. Leslie Carter, "Portrait," *Liberty Magazine*, 19 February 1927, p. 60.

45. Ford, *Mrs. Leslie Carter*, 31.

46. Belasco, *Du Barry*, in *Six Plays*, 139.

47. Ford, *Mrs. Leslie Carter*, 59.

48. Qtd. in Timberlake, *Bishop of Broadway*, 215.

49. Mrs. Leslie Carter, "Portrait," *Liberty Magazine*, 19 February 1927, p. 61.

50. Ford, *Mrs. Leslie Carter*, 22.

51. Timberlake, *Bishop of Broadway*, 209.

52. William Winter, *The Life of David Belasco*, vol. 2, 50. The lease was secured a week later, on 14 January 1902.

53. Loving-cup engraving quoted in ibid., vol. 2, 47.

54. David Belasco, "My Life's Story," *Hearst's Magazine*, July 1915, p. 71; Winter, *Life*, vol. 2, 70.

55. Charles Harold Harper, "Mrs. Leslie Carter: Her Life and Acting Career," 127.

56. Timberlake, *Bishop of Broadway*, 216–218; Winter, *Life*, vol. 2, 49–51.

57. I am indebted to Barbara Grossman, who shared with me her unpublished chapter, "The New Victory Theatre: Catalyst for Change on Forty-Second Street," which brought to my attention a number of sources on the Republic Theatre. See, for example, the *New York Times*, 23 September 1900, p. 7.

58. See Nicholas van Hoogstraten, *Lost Broadway Theatres*, 46–48.

59. Winter, *Life*, vol. 2, 53–54.

60. "Belasco's Plans for Republic Now Complete," unidentified newspaper clipping, 19 April 1902, Robinson-Locke Collection, vol. 49.

61. *Du Barry* program, 17 November 1902, in *Du Barry* Broadway Show Folder.

62. Report in *Morning Telegraph* following 31 May 1902 closing of *Du Barry*'s first season, cited in Harper, "Mrs. Leslie Carter," 125.

63. "Belasco's Plans for Republic Now Complete," unidentified newspaper clipping, 19 April 1902, Robinson-Locke Collection, vol. 49.

64. Belasco's speech is quoted in Winter, *Life*, vol. 2, 61.

65. Mrs. Leslie Carter, "Portrait," *Liberty Magazine*, 26 February 1927, 63; Timberlake, *Bishop of Broadway*, 217.

66. "Belasco Theatre Opens," *New York Times*, 30 September 1902, 9.

67. Mrs. Leslie Carter, "Portrait," *Liberty Magazine*, 26 February 1927, 63.

68. Winter, *Life*, vol. 2, 59.

69. Timberlake, *Bishop of Broadway*, 46.

70. Curry, "Presenting David Belasco," II, p. 8, in Folder "Articles on Belasco," Ax 315, Box 1, Thomas Albert Curry Sr. Papers. See also Ada Patterson, "David Belasco, the Man," *Green Book Album* 7 (May 1912): 965. The Stuyvesant building was completed in 1907, but the rooms for Belasco's studio suite that housed his collections were not added until 1909. For a listing of items in the Belasco Napoleonic Collection, see *The Collection of the Late David Belasco*, Lots 625–637, 1011–1084.

71. Jane Dransfield, "Behind the Scenes with David Belasco: How America's Leading Theatre Manager Has Solved the Secret of Successful Production," *Theatre Magazine* 35 (April 1922): 228.

72. Magda Frances West, "Belasco's Views on Love, Women, and the Play of Tomorrow," *Green Book Magazine*, October 1912, pp. 586–587.

73. Belasco's workaholic schedule is well documented. Except for the few hours he reputedly went home to sleep between the end of performances and rehearsals, which often went past midnight, and resumption of theatrical business by 9 o'clock the next morning, he apparently spent little regular time with his family. His wife is a nearly invisible figure in the biographical record. In *Bishop of Broadway*, Timberlake writes that "during the fifty-two years of their marriage Mrs. Belasco often found herself playing second fiddle to Belasco's mistress, the theater" (39–40), and that "much of the time she lived apart from her husband, although they were not divorced" (386). The only mention of his taking significant time off to attend to family matters was when his younger daughter became fatally ill in the spring and summer of 1911 and he took her to Asheville, North Carolina, and Colorado Springs for treatment (316). Thomas A. Curry's papers contain discussion of how Belasco had to fend off the many would-be-the-next Mrs. Carters who tried to throw themselves at him. See Curry, "Outline" and "Presenting David Belasco," II, in Folder "Articles on Belasco" 1, in Ax 315, Box 1, Thomas Albert Curry Sr. Papers.

74. Ford, *The Story of Du Barry*, 12.

75. Ibid., 17.

76. "Belasco's Plans for Republic Now Complete."

77. Ada Patterson, "David Belasco, The Man," *Green Book Album* 7 (May 1912): 964.

78. "The Belasco Theatre," *New York Dramatic Mirror*, 27 September 1902, 15, and Timberlake, *Bishop of Broadway*, 218. A visit to the recently restored New Victory Theatre (formerly the Republic) in the summer of 2003 confirmed these decorative details.

79. Dransfield, "Behind the Scenes," 228; David Warfield, "David Belasco," *Green Book Album* 1 (February 1909): 365.

80. The incident, which occurred on 16 November 1903, is described in Charles Dillingham's unpublished memoirs, p. 98, in Charles Dillingham Papers, Box 32.

81. See Timberlake, *Bishop of Broadway*, 227.

82. Belasco expressed his views of Frohman's jealousy in a letter to his boyhood friend Peter Robertson at the *San Francisco Chronicle*, quoted in ibid., 246–247. His feelings of being "crushed" by the Syndicate were repeatedly referenced in the legal battles that ensued from the rivalry, the cases of *Brooks v. Belasco* and *Belasco v. Klaw and Erlanger*, beginning 6 April 1905. See ibid., 257.

83. For a recent invocation of Napoleon's legacy as a plunderer and collector, see G. Y. Dryansky, "Tales of the Raj: The Paris Apartment of Jean-Luc Gauziere Exemplifies the French Obsession with Treasures that Tell a Story," *House and Garden* (May 2000): 150–155.

84. See G. Legman's Introduction to Patrick Kearney, *The Private Case: An Anno-tated Bibliography of the Private Case Erotica Collection in the British (Museum) Library*, 21–22; Walter Kendrick, The *Secret Museum: Pornography in Modern Culture*, 70, 100–105; and H. Montgomery Hyde, *A History of Pornography*, 181.

85. Belasco's holdings of objects are catalogued in *The Collection of the Late David Belasco*. As noted in chapter 5, many of his rare and pornographic books were sold privately. Catalogues are extant for two public sales of his books, each dispersing thousands of volumes: *Books from the Library of the Late David Belasco* and *Books Chiefly from the Library of the Late David Belasco: Including Americana, First Editions, Art, Literature, Fine Bindings, Etc.* I am indebted to Mary Ellen Kelly of New York City for making copies of these book catalogues available to me. For a description of Belasco's studio in his second theatre, see Louis V. De Foe, "Where Belasco Works: The Unique Studio and the Art Museum of America's Most Picturesque Playwright and Manager," *Munsey's Magazine*, September 1910, pp. 803–810.

86. Susan Stewart, *On Longing: Narratives of the Miniature, the Gigantic, the Souvenir, the Collection*, xi–xii.

87. Jean Baudrillard, *The System of Objects*, translated by James Benedict, 8.

88. Stewart, *On Longing*, 148.

89. Numerous volumes are catalogued under the heading "Books About Books" in *Books Chiefly from the Library of the Late David Belasco*, 7–8.

90. Objects in these categories are itemized in the post-mortem sale catalogue, *The Collection of the Late David Belasco*. See also "Belasco Estate Put at $1,249,144," untitled newspaper clipping, May 1933, David Belasco Personality File.

91. Montrose J. Moses in *Six Plays by David Belasco*, 34.

92. See Kendrick, *Secret Museum*, 31. Belasco may have been inspired by classical accounts, such as Cassius Dio's *History of Rome*, Book 67, which tells of how the Emperor Domitian would conduct games at night and pit dwarves and women against each other.

93. Belasco, *Adrea* in *Six Plays*, 247.

94. Ritchie Robertson, "Historicizing Weininger," 33.

95. *The Collection of the Late David Belasco* lists fifty-nine lots of mainly European, but including some Indonesian, arms and armor from the sixteenth to the nineteenth centuries. In working out the business for the play, he drew anachronistically from these as well as Roman armors, including non-Roman features such as visors that raised and lowered.

96. Photographs of the production in the *Adrea* Broadway Show Folder document this pose.

97. See Timberlake, *Bishop of Broadway*, 233–234.

98. Mrs. Leslie Carter, "Portrait," *Liberty Magazine*, 5 March 1927, 62.

99. According to the official numbers reproduced in Craig Timberlake's chronology of Belasco's New York productions, *Adrea* opened at the Belasco (Republic) 11

January 1905 for an initial run of 123 performances and had one revival of 23 performances beginning 20 September 1905 for a total of 146. *Du Barry's* initial run of 165 performances was followed by revivals of 63 performances beginning 29 September 1902, 16 performances beginning 23 November 1903, and 16 performances beginning 16 October 1905, for a New York total of 260 performances. See Timberlake, *Bishop of Broadway*, 452–453.

100. Quotes from the character descriptions in the unpaginated front matter of David Belasco, "Repka Stroon."

101. Qtd. in Timberlake, *Bishop of Broadway*, 294.

102. The only other explicitly Jewish productions Belasco mounted came much later in his career and were vehicles chiefly for male actors: *The Wandering Jew* (1921) and *The Merchant of Venice* (1922), which did not risk the same level of feminized emotional and sexual exteriorizations.

EPILOGUE

1. *Le Fantôme de l'Opéra* was published in French in 1910. It was published in English first in serial form and then as the complete novel in 1911.

2. For more on *Phantom* and *Trilby*, see Jerrold E. Hogle, *The Undergrounds of the Phantom of the Opera: Sublimation and the Gothic in Leroux's Novel and Its Progeny*, 22–24.

3. I am indebted to Mary Ellen Kelly of New York City for first suggesting to me the connections between Belasco and *The Phantom of the Opera*.

4. Puccini was inspired to write the opera *Madama Butterfly* when he saw the one-act play *Madame Butterfly* by Belasco and John Luther Long in 1900. The opera premiered at La Scala in 1904. *La Fanciulla del West* is based on Belasco's Western melodrama, *The Girl of the Golden West* (1905). Belasco himself directed the opera's 1910 premiere at the Metropolitan Opera featuring Enrico Caruso and Emmy Destin.

5. See Hogle, *Undergrounds*, 12–24, for a detailed elaboration of the racial and gender ambiguities inscribed in Leroux's *Phantom*.

6. In another connection between theatrical impresarios and the Phantom, the actor Claude Rains played Belasco in the 1940 film based on Mrs. Leslie Carter's autobiography, "Portrait of a Lady with Red Hair," and then played the role of the Opera Ghost in the 1943 film version of *The Phantom of the Opera*.

7. *Phantom of the Opera* opened at New York's Majestic Theatre on 26 January 1988. On 9 January 2006, the show logged performance number 7,486, surpassing the former record holder, *Cats*. See Jesse McKinley, "'Phantom' Breaks Record with 7,486th Show," *New York Times*, 10 January 2006, section B, page 3, column 1.

8. Daly's Theatre at Broadway and Thirtieth Street was demolished in 1920 and Frohman's Empire at Broadway and Fortieth Street in 1953. See William C. Young, *Documents of American Theater History*, vol 1, *Famous American Playhouses, 1716–1899*, 210, 232.

9. See Margaret Knapp, "Introductory Essay" to "Part II: Entertainment and Culture," in *Inventing Times Square: Commerce and Culture at the Crossroads of the World*, edited by William R. Taylor, 120–132, for an overview of the theatre district's history. I am grateful to Barbara W. Grossman for sharing with me her unpublished essay, "The New Victory Theater: Catalyst for Change on Forty-Second Street," which analyzes the work of 42DP. See also Paul Goldberger, "An Old Jewel of 42d Street Reopens, Seeking to Dazzle Families," *New York Times*, 11 December 1995, pp. A1, C18.

10. The legend of Belasco's ghost has circulated throughout the decades since his death and is now perpetuated through such popular Web sites as City Search, http://newyork.citysearch.com/profile/11349770?cslink=roundup_location_ noncust&ulink=roundup__roundupentity1-8_2__0_profile__1, and Theatre Mania, http://www.theatermania.com/content/theater.cfm/int_show_id/103139, both accessed on 13 September 2004. Nick Paumgarten evoked Belasco's reputation as a "legendary hound" along with old stories of two ghosts haunting the Belasco Theatre—the impresario's and that of a showgirl who died falling down a backstage elevator shaft—in the "Talk of the Town" section of the *New Yorker* under "Relics: A Broadway Haunt," 3 July 2006, pp. 24–25.

11. Frank Rich, "Naked Capitalists," *New York Times Magazine*, 20 May 2001, 52.

BIBLIOGRAPHY

GENERAL SOURCES

Alstyne, Richard Van. *The Rising American Empire*. New York: Norton, 1974.

Appel, John J. "Jews in American Caricature, 1820–1914." *Jewish American History* 71 (1981): 103–133.

Applebaum, Stanley, ed. *The New York Stage: Famous Productions in Photographs: 1883–1939*. New York: Dover, 1976.

Auster, Albert. *Actresses and Suffragists: Women in the American Theater, 1890–1920*. New York: Praeger, 1984.

Bank, Rosemarie K. "Actor Training at the Mid-Point in Nineteenth-Century American Repertory." *Theatre History Studies* 8 (1988): 157–162.

———. "A Reconsideration of the Death of the Nineteenth-Century American Repertory Companies and the Rise of the Combination." *Essays in Theatre* 5 (November 1986): 61–75.

———. *Theatre Culture in America, 1825–1860*. Cambridge, UK: Cambridge University Press, 1997.

Banner, Lois. *American Beauty*. New York: Knopf, 1983.

Banta, Martha. *Imaging American Women: Idea and Ideals in Cultural History, 1876–1918*. New York: Columbia University Press, 1987.

Baudrillard, Jean. *The System of Objects*. Translated by James Benedict. London: Verso, 1996.

Bederman, Gail. *Manliness and Civilization: A Cultural History of Gender and Race in the United States, 1880–1917*. Chicago: University of Chicago Press, 1996.

Beer, Thomas. *The Mauve Decade: American Life at the End of the Nineteenth Century*. New York: Vintage, 1960.

Bernheim, Alfred L. *The Business of the Theatre: An Economic History of the American Theatre, 1750–1932*. New York: Benjamin Blom, 1932.

Bok, Edward. "The Young Girl at the Matinee." *Ladies Home Journal*, June 1903, pp. 16–17.

Brodkin, Karen. *How Jews Became White Folks and What That Says about Race in America*. New Brunswick, NJ: Rutgers University Press, 1994.

Brown, Gillian. *Domestic Individualism: Imagining Self in Nineteenth-Century America*. Berkeley: University of California Press, 1990.

Butsch, Richard. "Bowery B'hoys and Matinee Ladies: The Re-Gendering of Nineteenth-Century American Theatre Audiences." *American Quarterly* 46 (1994): 374–405.

———. *The Making of American Audiences: From Stage to Television, 1750–1990.* Cambridge, UK: Cambridge University Press, 2000.

Cawelti, John G. "America on Display: The World's Fairs of 1876, 1893, 1933." In *The Age of Industrialism in America*, edited by Frederic Cople Jaher, 317–363. New York: Free Press, 1968.

"Charles Dana Gibson." http://www.gibson-girls.com (accessed 10 July 2004).

Chernow, Ron. *Titan: The Life of John D. Rockefeller.* New York: Random House, 1998.

Cheyette, Bryan, and Laura Marcus, eds. *Modernity, Culture, and "the Jew."* Stanford, CA: Stanford University Press, 1998.

Christy, Howard Chandler. *The American Girl as Seen and Portrayed by Howard Chandler Christy.* 1906. Reprint, New York: Da Capo, 1976.

Coad, Oral Sumner, and Edwin Mims Jr. *The American Stage.* New York: United States Publishers Association, 1929.

Dale, Alan. "Why Women Are Greater Actors Than Men." *Cosmopolitan*, September 1906, pp. 521–522.

Davidson, Cathy N., and Jessamyn Hatcher, eds. *No More Separate Spheres!: A Next Wave American Studies Reader.* Durham, NC: Duke University Press, 2002.

Davis, Peter A. "From Stock to Combination: The Panic of 1873 and Its Effects on the American Theatre Industry." *Theatre History Studies* 8 (1988): 1–9.

Davis, Tracy C. *Actresses as Working Women: Their Social Identity in Victorian Culture.* London and New York: Routledge, 1991.

———. "Fiske, Minnie Maddern." *American National Biography*, vol. 8, 35–36. New York: Oxford University Press, 1999.

De Beauvoir, Simone. *The Second Sex.* New York: Bantam Books, 1961.

D'Emilio, John. "Capitalism and Gay Identity." In *Powers of Desire: The Politics of Sexuality*, edited by Ann Snitow, Christine Stansell, and Sharon Thompson, 100–113. New York: Monthly Review Press, 1983.

D'Emilio, John, and Estelle B. Freedman. *Intimate Matters: A History of Sexuality in America.* 2nd ed. Chicago: University of Chicago Press, 1997.

Dijkstra, Bram. *Idols of Perversity: Fantasies of Feminine Evil in Fin-de-Siècle Culture.* Oxford: Oxford University Press, 1986.

Dinnerstein, Leonard. *Anti-Semitism in America.* New York: Oxford University Press, 1994.

Du Maurier, George. *Trilby.* 1894. With an Introduction by Elaine Showalter. Notes by Dennis Denisoff. Oxford and New York: Oxford University Press, 1998.

DuBois, Ellen Carol, and Linda Gordon. "Seeking Ecstasy on the Battlefield: Danger and Pleasure in Nineteenth-Century Feminist Sexual Thought." In *Pleasure and Danger: Exploring Female Sexuality*, edited by Carol S. Vance, 31–49. Boston: Routledge and Kegan Paul, 1984.

Dudden, Faye E. *Women in the American Theatre: Actresses and Audiences, 1790–1870*. New Haven, CT: Yale University Press, 1994.

Engle, Ron, and Tice L. Miller, eds. *The American Stage: Social and Economic Issues from the Colonial Period to the Present*. Cambridge, UK: Cambridge University Press, 1993.

Erdman, Harley. *Staging the Jew: The Performance of an American Ethnicity, 1860–1920*. New Brunswick, NJ: Rutgers University Press, 1997.

Faderman, Lillian. *Surpassing the Love of Men: Romantic Friendship and Love between Women from the Renaissance to the Present*. London: Women's Press, 1985.

Fox, Richard Wrightman. "The Discipline of Amusement." In *Inventing Times Square: Commerce and Culture at the Crossroads of the World*, edited by William R. Taylor, 83–98. Baltimore, MD: Johns Hopkins University Press, 1991.

Frick, John. "A Changing Theatre: New York and Beyond." In *The Cambridge History of American Theatre*, vol. 2, *1870–1945*, edited by Don B. Wilmeth and Christopher Bigsby. 196–232. New York: Cambridge University Press, 1999.

Frick, John W. *New York's First Theatrical Center: The Rialto at Union Square*. Ann Arbor, MI: UMI, 1985.

———, and Stephen M. Vallillo, eds. *Theatrical Directors: A Biographical Dictionary*. Westport, CT: Greenwood, 1994.

Gabler, Neal. *An Empire of Their Own: How the Jews Invented Hollywood*. New York: Crown, 1988.

Gerould, Daniel C., ed. *American Melodrama*. New York: PAJ, 1983.

Gibson, Charles Dana. *The Gibson Book: A Collection of the Published Works of Charles Dana Gibson*. 2 vols. New York: R. H. Russell, 1906.

———, and Edmund Vincent Gillon. *The Gibson Girl and Her America: The Best Drawings*. New York: Dover Publications, 1969.

Gilfoyle, Timothy J. *City of Eros: New York City, Prostitution, and the Commercialization of Sex, 1790–1920*. New York: Norton, 1992.

———. "Policing of Sexuality." In *Inventing Times Square: Commerce and Culture at the Crossroads of the World*, edited by William R. Taylor, 297–314. Baltimore, MD: Johns Hopkins University Press, 1991.

Gilman, Sander. *Freud, Race, and Gender*. Princeton, NJ: Princeton University Press, 1993.

———. *The Jew's Body*. New York: Routledge, 1991.

Goldberger, Paul. "An Old Jewel of 42d Street Reopens, Seeking to Dazzle Families." *New York Times*, 11 December 1995, pp. A1, C18.

Grant, Ulysses S. "The New Administration." *New York Times*, 5 March 1869, p. 6.

Green, Jonathon. *Cassell's Dictionary of Slang*. 1st paperback ed. London: Cassell and Co., 2000.

Halttunen, Karen. *Confidence Men and Painted Women: A Study of Middle-Class Culture in America, 1830–1870*. New Haven, CT: Yale University Press, 1982.

Henderson, Mary C. *The City and the Theatre: New York Playhouses from Bowling Green to Times Square*. Clifton, NJ: J. T. White, 1973.

Hewitt, Barnard. *Theatre U.S.A., 1668 to 1957*. New York: McGraw-Hill, 1959.

Higdon, David Leon. "Modernism." In *The Gay and Lesbian Literary Heritage*, edited by Claude J. Summers. New York: Holt, 1995.

Higham, John. "The Reorientation of American Culture in the 1890s." In *Writing American History: Essays on Modern Scholarship*, 73–102. Bloomington: Indiana University Press, 1970.

Hirsch, Foster. *The Boys from Syracuse: The Shuberts' Theatrical Empire*. Carbondale and Edwardsville: Southern Illinois University Press, 1998.

Hodin, Mark. "The Disavowal of Ethnicity: Legitimate Theatre and the Social Construction of Literary Value in Turn-of-the-Century America." *Theatre Journal* 52 (2000): 211–226.

Hogle, Jerrold E. *The Undergrounds of the Phantom of the Opera: Sublimation and the Gothic in Leroux's Novel and Its Progeny*. New York: Palgrave, 2002.

Hoogstraten, Nicholas von. *Lost Broadway Theatres*. New York: Princeton Architectural Press, 1991.

"Jackson Park's The Republic." http://www.hydepark.org/parks/jpac/jprepublic .htm (accessed 10 July 2004).

Jacobson, Matthew Frye. *Whiteness of a Different Color: European Immigrants and the Alchemy of Race*. Cambridge, MA: Harvard University Press, 1998.

Jaher, Frederic Cople, ed. *The Age of Industrialism in America*. New York: Free Press, 1968.

Jennings, Francis. *The Invasion of America: Indians, Colonialism, and the Cant of Conquest*. Chapel Hill: University of North Carolina Press, 1975.

Johnson, Claudia D. *American Actress: Perspective on the Nineteenth Century*. Chicago: Nelson Hall, 1984.

Kaplan, Amy. *The Anarchy of Empire in the Making of U.S. Culture*. Cambridge, MA: Harvard University Press, 2002.

Kasson, John F. *Rudeness and Civility: Manners in Nineteenth-Century Urban America*. New York: Hill and Wang, 1990.

Kasson, Joy S. *Marble Queens and Captives: Women in Nineteenth-Century American Sculpture*. New Haven, CT: Yale University Press, 1990.

Katz, Jonathan Ned. *The Invention of Heterosexuality*. New York: Plume, 1996.

Kauffmann, Stanley. "Two Vulgar Geniuses: Augustin Daly and David Belasco." *Yale Review* 76 (Summer 1987): 496–513.

Kitsch, Carolyn. *The Girl on the Magazine Cover: The Origins of Visual Stereotypes in American Mass Media*. Chapel Hill: University of North Carolina Press, 2001.

Kittay, Eva Feder. "Woman as Metaphor." *Hypatia* 3, no. 2 (1988): 63–87.

Knapp, Margaret. "'Presented with Appreciation': Minnie Maddern Fiske as Producer and Director." *Journal of American Drama and Theatre* 1 (Fall 1989): 55–72.

Kolodny, Annette. *The Lay of the Land: Metaphor as Experience and History in American Life and Letters*. Chapel Hill, NC: University of North Carolina Press, 1975.

Leach, William. *Land of Desire: Merchants, Power, and the Rise of a New American Culture*. New York: Pantheon, 1993.

Lears, T. J. Jackson. *No Place of Grace: Antimodernism and the Transformation of American Culture, 1880–1920*. New York: Pantheon, 1981.

Leiter, Samuel L. *From Belasco to Brook: Representative Directors of the English-Speaking Stage*. New York: Greenwood, 1991.

Leroux, Gaston. *The Phantom of the Opera*. 1911. Reprint, New York: Harper Collins, 1987.

Levine, Lawrence W. *Highbrow/Lowbrow: The Emergence of Cultural Hierarchy in America*. Cambridge, MA: Harvard University Press, 1988.

Lloyd Webber, Andrew. *The Phantom of the Opera*. Lyrics by Charles Hart. Additional lyrics by Richard Stilgoe. Book by Richard Stilgoe and Andrew Lloyd Webber. Original London Cast Recording. London: EMI Studios, 1987.

Londre, Felicia Hardison, and Daniel Watermeier. *The History of North American Theatre*. New York: Continuum, 1999.

Marshall, Gail. *Actresses on the Victorian Stage: Feminine Performance and the Galatea Myth*. Cambridge, UK: Cambridge University Press, 1998.

Mason, Jeffrey D., and J. Ellen Gainor, eds. *Performing America: Cultural Nationalism in American Theater*. Ann Arbor: University of Michigan Press, 1999.

Mayo, Louise A. *The Ambivalent Image: Nineteenth-Century America's Perception of the Jew*. London: Associated University Press, 1988.

McArthur, Benjamin. *Actors and American Culture, 1880–1920*. Iowa City: University of Iowa Press, 2000.

McConachie, Bruce A. *Melodramatic Formations: American Theatre and Society, 1820–1870*. Iowa City: University of Iowa Press, 1993.

McCusker, John J. "Purchasing Power of Money in the United States (or Colonies) from 1665 to 2005." Economic History Services, 2006, http://eh.net/hmit/ppowerusd (accessed in March 2006).

McDermott, Douglas. "Structure and Management in the American Theatre from the Beginning to 1870." In *The Cambridge History of the American Theatre*, vol. 1, *Beginnings to 1870*, edited by Don B. Wilmeth and Christopher Bigsby 182–215. Cambridge, UK: Cambridge University Press, 1998.

McTeague, James H. *Before Stanislavsky: American Professional Acting Schools and Acting Theory, 1875–1925*. Metuchen, NJ: Scarecrow Press, 1993.

Moers, Ellen. *The Dandy: Brummell to Beerbohm*. New York: Viking, 1960.

Moses, Montrose J., and John Mason Brown, eds. *The American Theatre as Seen by Its Critics, 1752–1934*. New York: Norton, 1934.

Muccigrosso, Robert. *Celebrating the New World: Chicago's Columbian Exposition of 1893*. Chicago: Ivan R. Dee, 1993.

Mullenix, Elizabeth Reitz. *Wearing the Breeches: Gender on the Antebellum Stage*. New York: St. Martin's Press, 2000.

Nathan, George Jean. "The Physical Demands of the Stage." *Outing Magazine*, April 1909, vol. 54, no. 1, p. 49–60.

Nelson, Dana D. *National Manhood: Capitalist Citizenship and the Imagined Fraternity of White Men*. Durham, NC: Duke University Press, 1998.

Nemerov, Alex. "Doing 'Old America': The Image of the American West, 1880–1920." In *The West as America: Reinterpreting Images of the Frontier*, edited by William H. Treuttner, 285–343. Washington, DC: Smithsonian Institution Press, 1991.

Norton, Anne. *Alternative Americas: A Reading of Antebellum Political Culture*. Chicago: University of Chicago Press, 1986.

"Notable Sculpture at the World's Columbian Exposition," http://users.vnet.net/schulman/Columbian/sculpture.html (accessed 10 July 2004).

Odell, George C. D. *Annals of the New York Stage*. 15 vols. New York: Columbia University Press, 1927–1949.

Ohmann, Richard. *Selling Culture: Magazines, Markets, and Class at the Turn of the Century*. New York: Verso, 1996.

Patterson, Martha H. *Beyond the Gibson Girl: Reimagining the American New Woman, 1895–1915*. Urbana and Chicago: University of Illinois Press, 2005.

Peiss, Kathy Lee, Christina Simmons, and Robert A. Padgug. *Passion and Power: Sexuality in History*. Philadelphia: Temple University Press, 1989.

Pendennis. "Clyde Fitch Conducting a Rehearsal—His Knowledge of Women." *New York Times*, 1 October 1906, part 3, p. 6.

Pick, Daniel J. "Powers of Suggestion: Svengali and the *Fin-de-Siècle*." In *Modernity, Culture, and "the Jew,"* edited by Bryan Cheyette and Laura Marcus, 105–125. Stanford, CA: Stanford University Press, 1998.

———. *Svengali's Web: The Alien Enchanter in Modern Culture*. New Haven, CT: Yale University Press, 2000.

"Pictorial Diagrams of New York Theaters—1883." Davis Crossfield Associates Archive, http://www.daviscrossfield.com (accessed 15 March 2006).

Poggi, Jack. *Theater in America: The Impact of Economic Forces, 1870–1967*. Ithaca, NY: Cornell University Press, 1968.

Porter, Charlotte. "Boston Discovers Miss Nance O'Neil." *The Critic*, June 1904, 525–530.

Postlewait, Thomas. "The Hieroglyphic Stage: American Theatre and Society, Post–Civil War to 1945." In *The Cambridge History of American Theatre*, vol. 2, *1870–1945*, edited by Don B. Wilmeth and Christopher Bigsby, 107–195. Cambridge, UK, and New York: Cambridge University Press, 1999.

———. "The London Stage, 1895–1918." In *The Cambridge History of British Theatre*, vol. 3, *Since 1895*, edited by Baz Kershaw, 34–59. Cambridge, UK, and New York: Cambridge University Press, 2004.

Potter, Paul M. *Trilby*. 1895. In *Jack Sheppard* [and other plays], edited by George Taylor. Oxford and New York: Oxford University Press, 1996.

Pugh, David. *Sons of Liberty: The Masculine Mind in Nineteenth-Century America*. Westport, CT: Greenwood, 1983.

Rich, Frank. "Naked Capitalists." *New York Times Magazine*, 20 May 2001, pp. 50–56, 80–82, 92.

Roach, Joseph R. *The Player's Passion: Studies in the Science of Acting*. Newark, NJ: University of Delaware Press, 1984.

Rotundo, Anthony. *American Manhood: Transformations in Masculinity from the Revolution to the Modern Era*. New York: Basic Books, 1993.

Russett, Cynthia Eagle. *Sexual Science: The Victorian Construction of Womanhood*. Cambridge, MA: Harvard University Press, 1989.

Said, Edward. *Orientalism*. New York: Vintage Books, 1979.

Schaal, David George. "Rehearsal-Direction Practices and Actor-Director Relationships in the American Theatre from the Hallams to Actor's Equity." PhD diss., University of Illinois-Urbana, 1956.

Senelick, Laurence. "Eroticism in Early Theatrical Photography." *Theatre History Studies* 11 (1991): 1–49.

Slotkin, Richard. *The Fatal Environment: The Myth of the Frontier in the Age of Industrialization, 1800–1890*. Middletown, CT: Wesleyan University Press, 1986.

Smith, Henry Nash. *Virgin Land: The American West as Symbol and Myth*. Cambridge, MA: Harvard University Press, 1950.

Smith-Rosenberg, Carroll. *Disorderly Conduct: Visions of Gender in Victorian America*. New York: Oxford University Press, 1985.

———, and Charles Rosenberg. "The Female Animal: Medical and Biological Views of Woman and Her Role in Nineteenth-Century America." *Journal of American History* 60 (1973): 332–356.

Snitow, Ann, Christine Stansell, and Sharon Thompson, eds. *Powers of Desire: The Politics of Sexuality*. New York: Monthly Review Press, 1983.

"Statue of Liberty Fund Raising, 1875–1885," 13 June 2005, http://www.endex.com/
gf/buildings/liberty/libertyfacts/LibertyConstruction/CasinoTheater/
CasinoTheater.htm (accessed on 30 March 2006).

Steele, Valerie. *The Corset: A Cultural History*. New Haven, CT: Yale University
Press, 2001.

Strang, Lewis C. *Famous Actresses of the Day in America*. Boston: L. C. Page, 1902.

Susman, Warren. *Culture as History: The Transformation of American Society in
the Twentieth Century*. New York: Pantheon, 1989.

Szuberla, Guy. "Ladies, Gentlemen, Flirts, Mashers, Snoozers, and the Breaking of
Etiquette's Code." *Prospects* 15 (1990): 169–196.

Taylor, George, ed. *Trilby and Other Plays*. Oxford: Oxford University Press, 1996.

Taylor, William R., ed. *Inventing Times Square: Commerce and Culture at the
Crossroads of the World*. Baltimore and London: Johns Hopkins University
Press, 1991.

Tichi, Cecilia. *Embodiment of a Nation: Human Form in American Places*.
Cambridge, MA: Harvard University Press, 2001.

Trachtenberg, Alan. *The Incorporation of America: Culture and Society in the
Gilded Age*. New York: Hill and Wang, 1982.

Turner, Frederick Jackson. *The Turner Thesis: Concerning the Role of the Frontier
in American History*. Edited by George Rogers Taylor. 3rd ed. Lexington, MA:
Heath, 1972.

Vance, Carol S. "Pleasure and Danger: Toward a Politics of Sexuality." In *Pleasure
and Danger: Exploring Female Sexuality*, edited by Carol S. Vance. Boston:
Routledge and Kegan Paul, 1984.

Warrack, John, and Ewan West. *The Oxford Dictionary of Opera*. Oxford and New
York: Oxford University Press, 1992.

Wiebe, Robert. *The Search for Order, 1877–1920*. New York: Hill and Wang, 1967.

Williamson, Samuel H. "What Is the Relative Value?" Economic History Services,
http://eh.net/hmit/compare (accessed 14 December 2005).

Wilmeth, Don B., and Christopher Bigsby, eds. *The Cambridge History of
American Theatre*, vol. 2, *1870–1945*. Cambridge, UK, and New York:
Cambridge University Press, 1999.

Wilson, Garff B. *A History of American Acting*. 1966. Reprint, Wesport, CT:
Greenwood, 1980.

Winter, William *Vagrant Memories, Being Further Recollections of Other Days*. New
York: George H. Duran, 1915.

———. *The Wallet of Time*. Vol. 2. New York: Moffet, Yard, 1913.

Witham, Barry B., ed. *Theatre in the United States: A Documentary History*, vol. 1,
1750–1915. Cambridge, UK: Cambridge University Press, 1996.

Wood, William. *Personal Recollections of the Stage, Embracing Notices of Actors, Authors, and Auditors, during a Period of Forty Years*. Philadelphia: Henry Carey Baird, 1855.

Young, William C. *Documents of American Theater History*. Vol. 1, *Famous American Playhouses, 1716–1899*. Chicago: American Library Association, 1973.

———. *Famous Actors and Actresses on the American Stage*. 2 vols. New York: R. R. Bowker, 1975.

AUGUSTIN DALY AND ADA REHAN

Archival Sources

Ada Rehan Papers. Folger Shakespeare Library.

Ada Rehan Papers. University of Pennsylvania Library.

Ada Rehan Personality File. Theatre Collection, Museum of the City of New York.

Ada Rehan Scrapbooks in the Robinson-Locke Collection, vols. 497–498. Billy Rose Theatre Collection, New York Public Library for the Performing Arts, Lincoln Center.

Adah Isaacs Menken Correspondence. Harvard Theatre Collection.

Augustin Daly Personality File. Theatre Collection, Museum of the City of New York.

Augustin and Joseph Daly Correspondence, 10 vols. Billy Rose Theatre Collection, New York Public Library for the Performing Arts, Lincoln Center.

Daly's Theatre Papers. Rare Book Department, Butler Library, Columbia University.

Daly's Theatre Scrapbooks. New York Public Library for the Performing Arts, Lincoln Center.

Nineteenth-Century Actors Photographs. Special Collections, University of Washington Libraries.

Taming of the Shrew Broadway Show Folder. Theatre Collection, Museum of the City of New York.

Theodore Leavitt Collection. Special Collections, University of Illinois Champaign-Urbana Libray.

Other Primary Sources

"Amusements: Augustin Daly's New Theatre." *New York Times*, 20 July 1879, p. 5.

Austin, W. W., and Matthew White Jr. "A Famous American Manager." *Munsey's Magazine*, August 1899, 736–744.

Bunner, H. C., et al. *A Portfolio of Players: With a Packet of Notes Thereon*. New York: J. W. Bouton, 1888.

Daly, Augustin. *Citizen*. 24 August, 1867, p. 8.

———. *Courier*. 17 March 1861, p. 5.

———. "The Last Word." From the German of Franz von Schoenthan. Typescript on Microfilm. New York Public Library—42nd St.

———. *Leah, the Forsaken*. 1862. London and New York: Samuel French, 1872.

———. "The Lottery of Love." From the French of Bisson and Mars. Typescript promptbook. Billy Rose Theatre Collection, New York Public Library for the Performing Arts, Lincoln Center.

———. "Minor Theatrical Matters." *New York Times*, 18 July 1867.

———. "Nancy and Company." From the German of Julius Rosen. Typescript promptbook. Billy Rose Theatre Collection, New York Public Library for the Performing Arts, Lincoln Center.

———. "Obituary of Avonia Jones." *New York Times*, 7 October 1867, p. 4.

———. *Plays by Augustin Daly: A Flash of Lightning, Horizon, Love on Crutches*. Edited by Don B. Wilmeth and Rosemary Cullen. Cambridge, UK, London, and New York: Cambridge University Press, 1984.

———. Review of *Leaves from an Actor's Notebook*, by George Vandenhoff. *Courier*. 12 February 1860, 5.

———. Review of *Love's Sacrifice*. *New York Times*, 7 May 1868, p. 4.

———. *Taming of the Shrew, A Comedy by William Shakespeare, as Arranged by Augustin Daly*. New York: privately printed for Daly, 1887.

———. *Under the Gaslight*. In *American Melodrama*, edited by Daniel C. Gerould. New York: Performing Arts Journal Publications, 1983.

———. *Woffington: A Tribute to the Actress and the Woman*. Troy, NY: n.p., 1888.

Daly, Joseph Francis. *The Life of Augustin Daly*. New York: Macmillan, 1917.

Dithmar, Edward Augustus. *John Drew*. New York: Stokes, 1900.

Drew, John. *My Years on the Stage*. New York: Dutton, 1922.

Duncan, Isadora. *My Life*. New York: Boni and Liveright, 1927.

Eytinge, Rose. *Memories of Rose Eytinge*. New York: Stokes, 1905.

Gilbert, Anne Hartley (Mrs. G. H.). *Stage Reminiscences of Mrs. Gilbert*. New York: Scribner's, 1901.

Golden, Sylvia. "The Romance of Ada Rehan: Goddess of Daly's in the Rich Days of Our Victorian Theatre." *Theatre Magazine*, January 1931, pp. 21, 22, 64.

Hall, Margaret. "Personal Recollections of Augustin Daly." *The Theatre*, June–September 1905, 74–78, 88–91, 150–153, 213–215.

Lathrop, George Parson. "An American School of Dramatic Art: The Inside Working of the Theatre." *Century Magazine* 56, new series 34 (June 1898): 265–275

Morris, Clara. *Life on the Stage*. New York: McClure, Phillips, 1901.

———. *Stage Confidences: Talks about Players and Play Acting*. Boston: Lathrop, 1902.

"Outbreak of Virtuous Indignation—Letter from Lola Montez." *New York Daily Times*, 16 July 1852, p. 3.

Ranous, Dora Knowlton. *Diary of a Daly Debutante, Being Passages from the Journal of a Member of Augustin Daly's Famous Company of Players*. New York, 1910.

Review of Avonia Jones in *Medea*. "Drury Lane Theatre." *London Times*, 6 November 1861, p. 10, col. A.

Review of *Camille*. *New York Daily Tribune*, 23 January 1857, p. 5.

Robertson, W. Graham. *Life Was Worth Living*. New York: Harper, 1931.

Skinner, Cornelia Otis. *Family Circle*. Boston: Houghton Mifflin, 1948.

Skinner, Otis. *Footlights and Spotlights: Recollections of My Life on the Stage*. New York: Blue Ribbon Books, 1924.

"Wallack's Theatre—First Appearance of Miss Heron." *New York Herald*, 23 January 1857, n.p.

Welch, Deshler. "Augustin Daly, Dramatic Dictator." *Booklover's Magazine*, April 1904, pp. 491–504.

Winter, William. *Ada Rehan: A Study*. New York: privately printed for Augustin Daly, 1891–1898.

Secondary Sources

Asermely, Albert A. "Daly's Initial Decade in the American Theatre, 1860–1869." PhD diss., City University of New York, 1973.

Boose, Lynda E. "Scolding Brides and Bridling Scolds: Taming the Woman's Unruly Member." *Shakespeare Quarterly* 42 (Summer 1991): 179–213.

Felheim, Marvin. "The Career of Augustin Daly." PhD diss., Harvard University, 1948.

———. *The Theatre of Augustin Daly: An Account of the Late Nineteenth Century American Stage*. 1956. Reprint, New York: Greenwood, 1969.

Haring-Smith, Tori. *From Farce to Metadrama: A Stage History of "Taming of the Shrew," 1594–1983*. Westport, CT: Greenwood, 1985.

Hendricks-Wenck, Aileen A. "Ada Rehan: American Actress (1857–1916)." PhD diss., Louisiana State University and Agricultural and Mechanical College, 1988.

———. Interview with Hendricks-Wenck. San Francisco, California, 7 August 1995.

Kotsilibas-Davis, James. *Great Times Good Times*. New York: Doubleday, 1977.

Lesser, Allen. *Enchanting Rebel: The Secret Life of Adah Isaacs Menken*. New York: Beechhurst, 1947.

Marra, Kim. "Taming America as Actress: Augustin Daly, Ada Rehan, and the Discourse of Imperial Frontier Conquest." In *Performing America: Cultural Nationalism in American Theater*, edited by Jeffrey D. Mason and J. Ellen Gainor, 52–72. Ann Arbor: University of Michigan Press, 1999.

Michalak, Marion Victor. "The Management of Augustin Daly's Stock Company, 1869–1899." PhD diss., Indiana University, 1961.

Sentilles, Renée M. *Performing Menken: Adah Isaacs Menken and the Birth of American Celebrity*. Cambridge, UK: Cambridge University Press, 2003.

Shafer, Yvonne. "Count Johannes and the Nineteenth-Century American Audience." *Journal of American Drama and Theatre* 3 (Fall 1991): 51–64.

Shattuck, Charles. *Shakespeare on the American Stage*. Vol. 2, *From Booth and Barrett to Sothern and Marlowe*. Washington: Folger Shakespeare Library. London and Toronto: Associated University Presses, 1987.

Strangman, Dennis. *Lamplough Name Index*, http://home.vicnet.net.au/~adhs/LetterJ.html (accessed 20 July 2005).

Towse, J. Ranken. "Augustin Daly's Company and Ada Rehan." In *The American Theatre as Seen by Its Critics*, edited by Montrose J. Moses and John Mason Brown, 114–118. New York: Norton, 1934.

VanderVelde, Lea S. "The Gendered Origins of the *Lumley* Doctrine: Binding Men's Consciences and Women's Fidelity." *Yale Law Journal* 101 (January 1992): 828–832.

CHARLES FROHMAN AND MAUDE ADAMS

Archival Sources

Chantecler Broadway Show Folder. Theatre Collection, Museum of the City of New York.

Charles Dillingham Papers. Humanities-Manuscripts and Archives, Manuscript Division, New York Public Library.

Charles Frohman Letter-Press Copy Books. Charles Frohman Papers, Humanities-Manuscripts and Archives, New York Public Library.

Charles Frohman Personality File. Theatre Collection, Museum of the City of New York.

L'Aiglon Broadway Show Folder. Theatre Collection, Museum of the City of New York.

Maude Adams Collection. Harvard Theatre Collection, Houghton Library.

Maude Adams Personality File. Theatre Collection, Museum of the City of New York.

Peter Pan Broadway Show Folder. Theatre Collection, Museum of the City of New York.

Philip H. Ward Collection. Rare Book and Manuscript Library, University of Pennsylvania.

Robinson-Locke Collection of Dramatic Scrapbooks. Billy Rose Theatre Collection, New York Public Library for the Performing Arts, Lincoln Center.

Other Primary Sources

Adams, Maude. "The One I Knew Least of All," *Ladies Home Journal*, March 1926, pp. 3–5, 206; April 1926, pp. 9, 213; May 1926, pp. 14–15, 150, 152, 155; June

1926, pp. 22–23, 161–162; July 1926, pp. 21, 70, 73–74; October 1926, pp. 23, 249, 259.

Barrie, J. M. (James Matthew). *The Admirable Crichton, Peter Pan, When Wendy Grew Up, What Every Woman Knows, Mary Rose*. Edited by Peter Hollindale. New York: Oxford University Press, 1995.

———. *The Little Minister*. New York: Burt, 1902, 1910.

Brookfield, Charles, and James M. Glover. *The Poet and the Puppets*. 1892. Reprint, *The Decadent Consciousness: A Hidden Archive of Late Victorian Literature*, edited by Ian Fletcher and John Stokes, vol. 35. New York: Garland, 1975.

Chantecler Told in Words and Pictures—Charles Frohman Presents Maude Adams. New York: Charles Frohman, Empire Theatre, 1911.

Chapin, Anna Alice. "Joan of Arc at Harvard." *Metropolitan Magazine*, August 1909, pp. 516–526.

Dale, Alan. "The King of Theatres and His 42 Play Houses." *New York Journal*, Sunday, 12 June 1898, in Robinson-Locke Collection of Theatrical Scrapbooks, vol. 1, #221, p. 2..

Davies, Acton. *Maude Adams*. New York: Frederick A. Stokes, 1901.

Dithmar, E. A. Review of *The Little Minister*. "At the Play and with the Players." *New York Times*, 14 January 1900, p. 16.

Eaton, Walter Prichard. "The New Ethel Barrymore." *American Magazine*, September 1911, pp. 631–640.

———. "Personality and the Player." *Collier's*, 22 October 1910, p. 17.

———. "Playing the Piper." In *Plays and Players: Leaves from a Critic's Scrapbook*. Cincinnati: Stewart and Kidd, 1916.

———. "Rhyme and Unreason." In *The American Stage of Today*. Boston: Small, Maynard, 1908.

———. "The Vexed Question of Personality." In *Plays and Players, Leaves from a Critic's Scrapbook*. Cincinnati: Stewart and Kidd, 1916.

Ellis, Havelock. "Sexual Inversion in Women." *Alienist and Neurologist* 16 (1895): 141–158.

———, and John Addington Symonds. *Sexual Inversion*. London: Wilson and Macmillan, 1897.

Fitch, Clyde. *Beau Brummell* [1891]. In *Plays by Clyde Fitch*, vol 1, edited by Montrose J. Moses and Virginia Gerson. Boston: Little, Brown, 1920.

———. *The Knighting of the Twins and Ten Other Tales*. Drawings by Virginia Gerson. Boston: Roberts Brothers, 1891.

"Frohman—as London Sees Him." *The Theatre*, February 1910, p. viii.

Gerson, Virginia, and Montrose J. Moses, eds. *Clyde Fitch and His Letters*. Boston: Little, Brown, 1924.

Gilbert, Douglas. "The Legend of Maude Adams: Charles Frohman Began It When He Placed a Cloak of Mystery about His New-Found Star." *New York Telegram*, 17 May 1930, n.p.

Gray, David. "Maude Adams: A Public Influence." *Hampton's Magazine*, June 1911, pp. 725–737.

Hattons, The. "Mr. Frohman Renews His Interest in Us." *Chicago Herald*, 22 November 1914, sec. 4, p. 4.

Hichens, Robert Smythe. *The Green Carnation*. London: W. Heinemann, 1894.

Hopper, DeWolfe, and Wesley Stout. *Once a Clown*. Boston: Little, Brown, 1927.

"Joan of Arc's Beatification at Harvard." *Current Literature*, August 1909, pp. 196–199.

Kiskadden, Annie Adams, and Verne Hardin Porter. "The Life Story of Maude Adams and Her Mother." *Green Book Magazine*, June 1914, pp. 884–900; July 1914, pp. 4–20; August 1914, pp. 196–212; September 1914, pp. 389–403; October 1914, pp. 596–610; November 1914, pp. 808–822.

Kobbe, Gustav. *Famous Actresses and Their Homes*. Boston: Little, Brown, 1905.

Krafft-Ebing, Richard von. *Psychopathia Sexualis with Especial Reference to the Antipathic Sexual Instinct*. Translated by F. J. Rebman. Brooklyn: Physicians and Surgeons Book Co., 1908.

Leslie, Amy. *Some Players: Personal Sketches*. New York: Herbert S. Stone, 1899.

Marbury, Elisabeth. *My Crystal Ball*. London: Hurst and Blackett, 1924.

Marcosson, Isaac F., and Daniel Frohman. *Charles Frohman: Manager and Man*. New York: Harper, 1916.

"Maude Adams as Babbie, But the New Make-Believe Gypsy Is Not the Eerie Babbie We Used to Know So Well." *New York Times*, 28 September 1897, p. 6.

"Maude Adams Comes Forward at the Head of a Company." *New York Sun*, 28 September 1897, p. 3.

Maude Adams in L'Aiglon: A Pictorial Souvenir Published with the Authorization of Mr. Charles Frohman. New York: R. H. Russell, 1900.

Maude Adams in the Little Minister: Edition-de-luxe Souvenir Published by Arrangement with Mr. Charles Frohman, with drawings by C. Allan Gilbert. New York: R. H. Russell, 1899.

Meyer, Ouida R. "Maude Adams: A Sentimental Memory." *New York Times*, 6 December 1931, sec. 8, p. 2X.

Moffett, Samuel E. "Charles Frohman." *Cosmopolitan*, 33 (July 1902): 293.

Moses, Montrose J. "Charles Frohman." In *The American Theatre as Seen by Its Critics*, edited by Montrose J. Moses and John Mason Brown, 214–218. New York: Norton, 1934.

"'Quality Street' Again." *New York Sun*, 7 January 1908, p. 7.

Review of *Chantecler*. *New York Herald*, 24 January 1911, p. 7.

Review of *The Jesters*. *The Theatre*, February 1908, n.p.

Review of *The Little Minister*. *New York Tribune*, 28 September 1897, p. 6.

Rostand, Edmond. *Chantecler: A Play in Four Acts*. Paraphrased by Louis N. Parker. Produced at the Knickerbocker Theatre, 23 January 1911. Typescript. Billy Rose Theatre Collection, New York Public Library for the Performing Arts, Lincoln Center.

———. *L' Aiglon: A Play in Six Acts*. Translated by Louis N. Parker. New York: R. H. Russell, 1900.

Schiller, Friedrich von. *The Maid of Orleans: Friedrich von Schiller's Romantic Tragedy*. Adapted from the German by George Sylvester Viereck for Maude Adams. N.p.: George Sylvester Viereck, 1909.

"A Theatrical Occasion: Maude Adams' Appearance in Edmond Rostand's Drama." *New York Sun*, 23 October 1900, p. 7.

Towse, J. Ranken. "The Drama: L'Aiglon." *The Critic*, December 1900, p. 545.

"Two Actors Named John." *New York Sun*, 4 October 1892, p. 3.

Wagstaffe, William de. "Coining Admiration Worth Half a Million a Year." *The Theatre Magazine*, December 1913, 190–192.

Wilde, Oscar. *The Happy Prince and Other Tales*. 1888. New York: Brentano's, 1920.

———. *The Picture of Dorian Gray*. 1891. Reprint, New York: Dover, 1993.

———. *Salome: A Tragedy in One Act; Translated from the French of Oscar Wilde by Lord Alfred Douglas; Pictured by Aubrey Beardsley*. 1894. Reprint, New York: Dover, 1967.

Williams, John D. "C. F." *Century Magazine*, December 1915, pp. 173–188.

Zamacois, Miguel. *The Jesters, a Simple Story in Four Acts of Verse Adapted from the French of Miguel Zamacois by John N. Raphael*. New York: Brentano's, 1908.

Secondary Sources

"Bid Time Return: A Somewhere in Time Website: Maude Adams, 1872–1953," http://www.geocities.com/bidtimereturnmp/ma.html (accessed 10 September 2005).

Chauncey, George. *Gay New York: Gender, Urban Culture, and the Making of the Gay Male World, 1890–1940*. New York: Basic, 1994.

Crompton, Louis. "Byron, George Gordon, Lord." In *The Gay and Lesbian Literary Heritage*, edited by Claude J. Summers. New York: Holt, 1995.

"Cyrano de Bergerac," http://www.ibdb.com/production.asp?id=5414, Internet Broadway Database (accessed 20 April 2004).

Davis, Tracy C. "Maude Adams." In *American National Biography*, vol. 1, 115–116. New York: Oxford University Press, 1999.

Duggan, Lisa. "The Trials of Alice Mitchell: Sensationalism, Sexology, and the Lesbian Subject in Turn-of-the-Century America." *Signs* (Summer 1993): 791–814.

Ellmann, Richard. *Oscar Wilde*. New York: Vintage, 1988.

Fields, Armond. *Maude Adams: Idol of American Theatre, 1872–1953*. Jefferson, NC, and London: McFarland, 2004.

Garber, Marjorie. *Vice-Versa: Bisexuality and the Eroticism of Everyday Life*. New York: Simon and Schuster, 1995.

Gianoulis, Tina. "Sarah Bernhardt." In *glbtq: An Encyclopedia of Gay, Lesbian, Bisexual, Transgender, and Queer Culture*, edited by Claude J. Summers. http://www.glbtq.com (accessed 2 July 2005).

Hanson, Bruce. *The Peter Pan Chronicles: The Nearly One Hundred Year History of "the Boy Who Wouldn't Grow Up."* New York: Birch Lane Press, 1993.

Higdon, David Leon. "Modernism." In *The Gay and Lesbian Literary Heritage*, edited by Claude J. Summers. New York: Holt, 1995.

"The Jewish 'Yentile' Governor of Utah." Chapter 102 of Chapters in Jewish History, American Jewish Historical Society, http://www.ajhs.org/publications/chapters/chapter.cfm?documentID=292 (accessed 23 January 2006).

Knox, Melissa. *Oscar Wilde: A Long and Lovely Suicide*. New Haven, CT: Yale University Press, 1994.

Kuehnl, Eileen Karen. "Maude Adams, an American Idol: True Womanhood Triumphant in the Late-Nineteenth and Early-Twentieth-Century Theatre." PhD diss., University of Wisconsin-Madison, 1984.

Landro, Vincent. "Media Mania: The Demonizing of the Theatrical Syndicate." *Journal of American Drama and Theatre* 13 (Spring 2001): 23–50.

"LGBTQ Symbology 101," http://outwilmington.com/symbology.htm (accessed 20 April 2004).

Mann, William J. *Behind the Screen: How Gays and Lesbians Shaped Hollywood, 1910–1969*. New York: Viking, 2001.

Marks, Patricia. *Sarah Bernhardt's First American Theatrical Tour, 1880–1881*. Jefferson, NC: McFarland, 2003.

Marra, Kim. "Clyde Fitch: Transvestite *Metteur-en-Scène* of the Feminine." *New England Theatre Journal* 3 (1992): 15–38.

———. "Clyde Fitch's Too Wilde Love." In *Staging Desire: Queer Readings of American Theater History*, edited by Kim Marra and Robert A. Schanke, 23–54. Ann Arbor: University of Michigan Press, 2002.

———. "A Lesbian Marriage of Cultural Consequence: Elisabeth Marbury and Elsie De Wolfe, 1886–1933." In *Passing Performances: Queer Readings of Leading Players in American Theater History*, edited by Robert A. Schanke and Kim Marra, 104–128. Ann Arbor: University of Michigan Press, 1998.

Miller, Neil. *Out of Our Past: Gay and Lesbian History from 1869 to the Present*. New York: Vintage, 1995.

"National Horse Show," http://www.nhs.org/news/pressreleasearchives.php?f=nationalhorsehowret.html (accessed 18 May 2004).

"Queers and Allies Dictionary," http://www.gustavus.edu/oncampus/orgs/queers/
    main/dictionary_full.html#1 (accessed 1 May 2004).
Robbins, Phyllis. *Maude Adams: An Intimate Portrait*. New York: Putnam, 1956.
———. *The Young Maude Adams*. Francestown, NH: M. Jones, 1959.
"Salt Lake Collegiate Institute," http://en.wikipedia.org/wiki/Westminster
    _College,_Salt_Lake_City (accessed 22 January 2006).
Schanke, Robert A. "Alla Nazimova: 'The Witch of Makeup.'" In *Passing
    Performances: Queer Readings of Leading Players in American Theater History*,
    edited by Robert A. Schanke and Kim Marra, 129–150. Ann Arbor: University of
    Michigan Press, 1998.
Schmidgall, Gary. *The Stranger Wilde: Interpreting Oscar*. New York: Dutton,
    1994.
Shafer, Yvonne. "Maude Adams as Joan of Arc at the Harvard Stadium." *Journal of
    American Drama and Theatre* 11 (Fall 1999): 30–45.
Showalter, Elaine. "Syphilis, Sexuality, and the Fiction of the Fin-de-Siècle." In
    Sex, Politics, and Science in the Nineteenth-Century Novel, edited by Ruth
    Bernard Yeazell, 88–115. Baltimore: Johns Hopkins University Press, 1990.
Smith, Jane S. *Elsie De Wolfe: A Life in the High Style*. New York: Atheneum, 1982.
Stiver, Harry Edward, Jr. "Charles Frohman and the Empire Theatre Stock
    Company." PhD diss., University of Illinois, Champaign-Urbana, 1960.
Wolf, Stacy. *A Problem Like Maria: Gender and Sexuality in the American Musical*.
    Ann Arbor: University of Michigan Press, 2002.

DAVID BELASCO AND MRS. LESLIE CARTER

Archival Sources
Adrea Broadway Show Folder. Theatre Collection, Museum of the City of New
    York.
Byron Collection. Museum of the City of New York.
Charles Dillingham Papers. Humanities-Manuscripts and Archives, Manuscript
    Division, New York Public Library.
David Belasco Papers. Series X Scrapbooks. New York Public Library for the
    Performing Arts, Lincoln Center.
David Belasco Personality File. Theatre Collection, Museum of the City of New
    York.
Du Barry Broadway Show Folder. Theatre Collection, Museum of the City of New
    York.
The Heart of Maryland Broadway Show Folder. Theatre Collection, Museum of
    the City of New York.
Kinsey Institute for Research in Sex, Gender, and Reproduction. Bloomington,
    Indiana.

Mrs. Leslie Carter Clipping File. Billy Rose Theatre Collection. New York Public Library for the Performing Arts, Lincoln Center.

Mrs. Leslie Carter Personality File. Theatre Collection, Museum of the City of New York.

Mrs. Leslie Carter Scrapbook in the Players Collection. New York Public Library for the Performing Arts, Lincoln Center.

Personal Collection of Belasco Materials. Mary Ellen Kelly. New York, NY.

Robinson-Locke Collection of Dramatic Scrapbooks. Billy Rose Theatre Collection, New York Public Library for the Performing Arts, Lincoln Center.

Thomas Albert Curry Sr. Papers, Special Collections and University Archives, University of Oregon Libraries, Eugene, Oregon.

Under Two Flags Broadway Show Folder. Theatre Collection, Museum of the City of New York.

"X" Collection of Rare Books, Special Collections Department, University of Iowa Libraries.

Zaza Broadway Show Folder. Theatre Collection, Museum of the City of New York.

Other Primary Sources

Baker, George M. *Forty Minutes with a Crank, or the Seldarte Craze*. Boston: Walter H. Baker, Theatrical Publishers, 1889.

Beal, George Brinton. "Cupid Wins Another Round from Belasco—But Will Dean of American Theatre Ruin Another Career?" *Boston Sunday Post*, 10 May 1931, p. 2.

Belasco, David. "About Acting." *Saturday Evening Post*, 24 September 1921, pp. 11, 93, 94, 97, 98.

———. "Acting, Belasco Says, Is a Woman's Art First of All." *Rochester Democrat and Chronicle*, 19 September 1909, Mrs. Leslie Carter Scrapbook in the Players Collection, New York Public Library for the Performing Arts, Lincoln Center.

———. "The Art of Acting." *Appleton's Booklover's Magazine*, November 1905, 538–540.

———. "The Great Opportunity of the Woman Dramatist." *Good Housekeeping Magazine*, November 1911, pp. 627–632.

———. *The Heart of Maryland and Other Plays*. Princeton, NJ: Princeton University Press, 1941.

———. "His Adventures in Life as Related to John J. Wallace." *New York American*, 13 December 1925. See sec. L11, pp. 3, 6.

———. "How I Develop a Star." *New Idea Woman's Magazine*, October 1909, pp. 4, 54.

———. *Mrs. Leslie Carter as Zaza: With a History of Her Stage Career and the Successful Production of the Play: Illustrated with Half-Tone Engravings of the*

Principal Scenes in which Mrs. Carter Appears. New York: n.p., 1899. *Zaza* Broadway Show Folder. Theatre Collection, Museum of the City of New York.

———. "My Best Play, How I Wrote It and Why." *Green Book Album* 5 (February 1911): 434–438.

———. "My Life's Story." *Hearst's Magazine*, March 1914, pp. 296–306; April 1914, pp. 481–489; May 1914, pp. 641–652; June 1914, pp. 767–769; July 1914, pp. 42–54; August, 1914, pp. 187–200; September 1914, pp. 344–353; October 1914, pp. 454–465; November 1914, pp. 601–615; December 1914, pp. 784–797; January 1915, pp. 41–53; February 1915, pp. 154–168; March 1915, pp. 286–287, 319–321; April 1915, pp. 353–354; May 1915, pp. 422–423, 456; June 1915, pp. 500–501, 545; July 1915, pp. 22–23, 70–72; August 1915, pp. 106–107, 156–158; September 1915, pp. 178–179, 226–227; October 1915, pp. 248–249, 296–297; November 1915, pp. 326–327, 370–371; December 1915, pp. 397–399, 434–435.

———. "Repka Stroon: A Play in Four Acts." Typescript. 1905. Billy Rose Theatre Collection, New York Public Library for the Performing Arts, Lincoln Center.

———. *Six Plays: Madame Butterfly, Du Barry, the Darling of the Gods, Adrea, the Girl of the Golden West, the Return of Peter Grimm.* Boston: Little, Brown, 1928.

———. *The Theatre through Its Stage Door.* New York: Harper, 1919.

———. "The Truth about the Theater: How I Made Mrs. Carter into an Actress and How I Rehearsed Caruso to Be an American." *Ladies' Home Journal*, November 1917, pp. 19, 108.

———. "'What I Am Trying to Do': A School for Actors and a Better Theatre for the Public." *The World's Work*, July 1912, pp. 291–299.

———. "Why I Believe in the Little Things, and How They Have Made Successes of My Plays." *Ladies' Home Journal*, September 1911, pp. 15, 73.

———. "Women and the Stage." *Ladies' Home Journal*, November 1920, pp. 12, 13, 108, 110.

———, and Richard Walton Tully. "The Rose of the Rancho." Typescript. 1906. Billy Rose Theatre Collection, New York Public Library for the Performing Arts, Lincoln Center.

"The Belasco Theatre." *New York Dramatic Mirror*, 27 September 1902, p. 15.

"Belasco Theatre Opens: Large Audience Shows Appreciation of Beautiful Playhouse. Enthusiastic Greeting to Mrs. Carter in 'Du Barry'—Manager-Playwright Makes a Speech." *New York Times*, 30 September 1902, p. 9.

"Belasco's Plan for Republic Now Complete." Unidentified newspaper clipping, 19 April 1902, Robinson-Locke Collection of Dramatic Scrapbooks, vol. 49, Billy Rose Theatre Collection, New York Public Library for the Performing Arts, Lincoln Center.

Berton, Pierre, and Charles Simon. "'Zaza'; A Comedy Drama in Five Acts, Adapted from the French of Berton and Simon by David Belasco." Typescript

1898. Billy Rose Theatre Collection, New York Public Library for the
Performing Arts, Lincoln Center.

*Books Chiefly from the Library of the Late David Belasco: Including Americana,
First Editions, Art, Literature, Fine Bindings, etc.* New York: Academy Book
Shop, 1932.

Books from the Library of the Late David Belasco. New York: American Art
Association, 1931.

Carter, Mrs. Leslie. "Portrait of a Lady with Red Hair." *Liberty Magazine*, 15
January 1927, pp. 14–18, 21; 22 January 1927, pp. 11–15; 29 January 1927, pp. 24,
27, 31–32, 35–36; 5 February 1927, pp. 45–54; 12 February 1927, pp. 47–55; 19
February 1927, pp. 55–61; 26 February 1927, pp. 59–66; 5 March 1927, pp. 55,
57–58, 61–67; 12 March 1927, pp. 57–62; 19 March 1927, pp. 83–90.

The Collection of the Late David Belasco. New York: American Art Association,
Anderson Galleries, 1931.

Davies, Acton. "David Belasco, Star-Maker." *Good Housekeeping Magazine*,
November 1911, pp. 624–626.

De Foe, Louis V. "Where David Belasco Works: The Unique Studio and the Art
Museum of America's Most Picturesque Playwright and Manager." *Munsey's
Magazine*, September 1910, pp. 803–810.

De Mille, Henry Churchill, David Belasco, Charles Barnard, and Robert Hamilton
Ball. *The Plays of Henry C. De Mille, Written in Collaboration with David
Belasco.* Princeton, NJ: Princeton University Press, 1941.

Dodge, Wendell Phillips. "David Belasco." *Strand Magazine*, n.d., pp. 648–660.
David Belasco Personality File. Theatre Collection, Museum of the City of New
York.

"Dragged Her by the Hair: Mr. Belasco Tells More about the Training of Mrs.
Carter." *New York Times*, 5 June 1896, p. 9.

Dransfield, Jane. "Behind the Scenes with Belasco: How America's Leading
Theatre Manager Has Solved the Secret of Successful Production." *Theatre
Magazine*, April 1922, pp. 228–230, 260.

Ford, John L. *Mrs. Leslie Carter in David Belasco's Du Barry, with Portraits of Mrs.
Carter by John Cecil Clay, Together with Portrait of David Belasco and
Numerous Engravings of Photographs and Sketches in Black and White.* New
York: Frederick A. Stokes, 1902.

———. *The Story of Du Barry.* New York: Frederick Stokes, 1902.

Gleason, Mary. Letter to the Editor. *New York Mirror*, 28 May 1887, p. 3.

Harris, H. A. "David Belasco—The Man and His Work." *Cosmopolitan*, November
1909, pp. 755–764.

"How Belasco Creates Dramatic Stars." *Current Literature* 42 (April 1907):
434–438.

Hubert, Philip G. "New York's Lyceum for Actors." *Lippincott's* 35 (May 1885): 483–488.

The Lady with Red Hair. 1940. Film. Directed by Curtis Bernhardt. Warner Brothers.

Lanston, Aubrey. "A Rehearsal under Belasco." *Theatre Magazine*, February 1905, pp. 42–43.

Lewes, George Henry. *On Actors and the Art of Acting*. New York: Brentano's, 1875.

MacArthur, Charles, and Edward Sheldon. *Lulu Belle: A Play in Four Acts*. 1926. In *The Stage Works of Charles MacArthur*, edited by Arthur Dorlag and John Irvine, 11–75. Tallahassee: Florida State University, 1974.

Morse, Salmi. *The Passion: A Miracle Play in Ten Acts*. San Francisco: Edward Bosqui, 1879.

Moses, Montrose J. "Six Decades of Belasco Stage Magic." *New York Times*, Sunday, 27 October 1929, n.p.

Nathan, George Jean. "The Physical Demands of the Stage." *Outing Magazine*, April 1909, vol. 54, no. 1, p. 49.

Patterson, Ada. "David Belasco, the Man." *Green Book Album* 7 (May 1912): 961–966.

Potter, Paul M. "Under Two Flags: A Drama in Five Acts and Nine Tableaux Founded on Ouida's Novel." 1901. Typescript. *Under Two Flags* Show Folder. Theatre Collection, Museum of the City of New York.

Reade, Rolf S., comp. *Registrum Librorum Eroticorum*. London: privately printed, 1936.

Sappho, Erinna, Ovid, Marion Mills Miller, and David M. Robinson. *The Songs of Sappho, including the Recent Egyptian Discoveries: The Poems of Erinna, Greek Poems about Sappho, Ovid's Epistle of Sappho to Phaon*. New York: Frank-Maurice, 1925.

———, and J. M. Edmonds. *Sappho Revocata: Being an Emended Text with an English Translation*. London: P. Davies, 1928.

Sargent, Franklin. Letter to the Editor. *New York Dramatic Mirror*, 4 June 1887, p. 10.

Scarborough, George. "The Heart of Wetona." 1916. Typescript. Billy Rose Theatre Collection, New York Public Library for the Performing Arts, Lincoln Center.

Scarborough, George, and David Belasco. "The Son-Daughter: A Play of New China in Three Acts." 1919. Typescript. Billy Rose Theatre Collection, New York Public Library for the Performing Arts, Lincoln Center.

Skolsky, Sidney. "Meet the Governor." *Theatre Magazine*, October 1929, p. 22.

Snow, Mary Lydia Hastings. *Mechanical Vibration and Its Therapeutic Application*. New York: Scientific Authors, 1904.

Stebbins, Genevieve. *The Delsarte System of Expression*. New York: Edgar S. Werner, 1885.

——. *The Delsarte System of Expression*. 2nd ed. New York: Edgar S. Werner, 1887.

——. *The Delsarte System of Expression*. 6th ed. New York: Edgar S. Werner, 1902.

Swanston, Wilhelmina. Letter to the Editor. *New York Dramatic Mirror*, 4 June 1887, p. 10.

"The Theatre Republic," *New York Times*, 23 September 1900, p. 17.

Thorpe, Rose Hartwick. *Ringing Ballads, Including Curfew Must Not Ring Tonight*. Boston: D. Lothrop, 1887.

"Wallack's Theatre—First Appearance of Miss Heron." *New York Herald*, 23 January 1857, n.p.

Walter, Eugene. *The Easiest Way*. 1908. In *Chief Contemporary Dramatists*, edited by Thomas Herbert Dickinson, vol. 2, 167–227. Boston: Houghton Mifflin, 1921.

Warfield, David. "David Belasco." *Green Book Album*, February 1909, p. 365.

West, Magda Frances. "Belasco's Views on Love, Women, and the Play of Tomorrow." *Green Book Magazine*, October 1912, pp. 477–590.

Wilbor, Elsie M., ed. *Delsarte Recitation Book*. 4th ed. New York: Edgar S. Werner, 1905.

Secondary Sources

Asbury, Herbert. *The Barbary Coast: An Informal History of the San Francisco Underworld*. New York: Knopf, 1933.

Ball, Robert Hamilton, ed. *The Plays of Henry C. De Mille, Written in Collaboration with David Belasco*. Princeton, NJ: Princeton University Press, 1941.

Berger, Ronald J., Patricia Searles, and Charles E. Cottle. *Feminism and Pornography*. New York: Praeger, 1991.

Bordman, Gerald. "Mackaye, [James Morrison] Steele (1842–94)." In *Oxford Companion to American Theatre*, 450–451. New York and Oxford: Oxford University Press, 1984.

Clinton, Craig. "Mrs. Leslie Carter: 'The Bernhardt of America' and the 'Producer of Spectacular Plays.'" *Journal of American Drama and Theatre* 15 (Winter 2003): 1–13.

——. "Training the Actor: Belasco and Mrs. Carter." *Nineteenth Century Theatre and Film* 29 (June 2002): 66–79.

Davis, Tracy C. "The Actress in Victorian Pornography." *Theatre Journal* 41 (October 1989): 294–315.

Dryansky, G. Y. "Tales of the Raj: The Paris Apartment of Jean-Luc Gauziere Exemplifies the French Obsession with Treasures That Tell a Story." *House and Garden*, May 2000, pp. 150–155.

Dworkin, Andrea. *Pornography: Men Possessing Women*. New York: Perigree/Putnam, 1981.

Gertzman, Jay A. *Bookleggers and Smuthounds: The Trade in Erotica, 1920–1940*. Philadelphia: University of Pennsylvania Press, 1999.

Grossman, Barbara. "The New Victory Theatre: Catalyst for Change on Forty-Second Street." Unpublished essay.

Harper, Charles Harold. "Mrs. Leslie Carter: Her Life and Acting Career." PhD diss., University of Nebraska-Lincoln, 1978.

Hyde, H. Montgomery. *A History of Pornography*. New York: Farrar, Strauss, Giroux, 1966.

Johnson, Katie N. "*Zaza*: That 'Obtruding Harlot' of the Stage." *Theatre Journal* 54, no. 2 (May 2002): 223–243.

Johnson, Susan Lee. "'My Own Private Life': Toward a History of Desire in Gold Rush California." In *Rooted in Barbarous Soil: People, Culture, and Community in Gold Rush California*, edited by Kevin Starr and Richard J. Orsi, 316–346. Berkeley: University of California Press, 2000.

Kahn, Ava Fran, and Marc Dollinger, eds. *California Jews*. Hanover, NH, and London: University Presses of New England, 2003.

Kearney, Patrick. *The Private Case: An Annotated Bibliography of the Private Case Erotica Collection in the British (Museum) Library*. London: Jay Landesman, 1981.

Kendrick, Walter. *The Secret Museum: Pornography in Modern Culture*. Berkeley: University of California Press, 1987.

Lake, Taylor Susan. "American Delsartism and the Bodily Discourse of Respectable Womanliness." PhD diss., University of Iowa, 2002.

Maines, Rachel M. *The Technology of Orgasm: "Hysteria," the Vibrator, and Women's Sexual Satisfaction*. Baltimore: Johns Hopkins University Press, 1999.

Marcus, Steven. *The Other Victorians: A Study of Sexuality and Pornography in Mid-Nineteenth-Century England*. New York: Basic Books, 1964.

Marker, Lise-Lone. *David Belasco: Naturalism in the American Theatre*. Princeton, NJ: Princeton University Press, 1975.

Meserve, Walter. "David Belasco." In *Dictionary of Literary Biography*, vol. 7, *Twentieth-century American Dramatists*, edited by John MacNicholas, 90–100. Detroit, MI: Gale Research, 1981.

Paumgarten, Nick. "Relics: A Broadway Haunt," Talk of the Town column, *New Yorker*, 3 July 2006, pp. 24–25.

Robertson, Ritchie. "Historicizing Weininger: The Nineteenth-Century German Image of the Feminized Jew." In *Modernity, Culture, and "the Jew,"* edited by

Bryan Cheyette and Laura Marcus, 23–29. Stanford, CA: Stanford University Press, 1998.

Scheiner, Clifford J. *Essential Guide to Erotic Literature*. 2 vols. Ware: Wordsworth Classics, 1996.

———. Interview by Mary Ellen Kelly. 13 July 1997. Transcript in author's Collection.

Sponsler, Claire. *Ritual Imports: Performing Medieval Drama in America*. Ithaca, NY, and London: Cornell University Press, 2004.

Stewart, Susan. *On Longing: Narratives of the Miniature, the Gigantic, the Souvenir, the Collection*. Durham, NC: Duke University Press, 1993.

Timberlake, Craig. *The Bishop of Broadway: The Life and Work of David Belasco*. New York: Library Publishers, 1954.

Wiener, Norman D. "On Bibliomania." *Psychoanalytic Quarterly* 35 (1966): 217–232.

Williams, Linda. *Hard Core: Power, Pleasure, and the "Frenzy of the Visible."* Berkeley: University of California Press, 1989.

Winter, William. *The Life of David Belasco*. 2 vols. New York: Moffat and Yard, 1918.

Books in Belasco's Pornography Collection

From the list of titles in the Thomas Albert Curry Sr. Papers. Special Collections and University Archives, University of Oregon Libraries. Some books are listed here in more recent editions.

Anson, Margaret [pseud.]. *The Merry Order of St. Bridget: Personal Recollections of the Use of the Rod*. York, UK: printed for the author's friends, 1857.

Apuleius. *The Golden Ass*. Translated by William Adlington. London: D. Nutt, 1893.

D'Aurevilly, Barbey. *Weird Women*. London: Lutetian Bibliophiles' Society, 1900.

Barlow, Emily [pseud.]. *The Lustful Turk: The Historic Account of Two Young and Beautiful English Girls Trapped in an Algerian Harem*. Atlanta, GA: Pendulum Books, 1967.

Bauer, Bernhard A. *Woman and Love*. 2 vols. Translated by Eden Paul and Cedar Paul. New York: Boni and Liveright, 1927.

Beaumont, Edouard de. *The Sword and Womankind*. London: Society of British Bibliophiles, 1900.

Behn, Aphra. *The Ten Pleasures of Marriage and the Confession of the New Married Couple*. Reprinted with an Introduction by John Harvey and the Original Twenty Plates and Two Engraved Titles Re-Engraved. London: privately printed for the Navarre Society, 1922.

Belot, Adolphe. *Mademoiselle Giraud, My Wife*. London: privately printed for the Trade, n.d.

Black, Alexander. *Modern Daughters*. New York: Scribner's, 1899.

Bloch, Iwan. *The Sexual Life of Our Time*. Translated from the German by Eden Paul. New York: Rebman, 1908.

Burns, Robert. *The Merry Muses: A Choice Collection of Favourite Songs Gathered from Many Sources: Not for Maids, Ministers, or Striplings*. [London?]: privately printed, 1827.

Burton, Richard Francis. *The Kama Sutra of Vatsayana, Translated from the Sanskrit, in Seven Parts, with Preface, Introduction, and Concluding Remarks*. Reprinted by Cosmopoli for the Kama Shastra Society of London and Benares, and for private circulation only, 1883.

Caldwell, Erskine. *Poor Fool*. Illustrations by Alexander Couard. New York: Rariora Press, 1930.

Casanova, Giacomo. *The Memoirs of Jacques Casanova De Seingalt*. London: privately printed for the Navarre Society, 1922.

Chorier, Nicolas. *The Dialogues of Luisa Sigea*. Paris: Isidore Liseux, 1890.

Cleland, John. *Memoirs of Fanny Hill*. A Genuine Reprint of the Rare Edition of 1749. Cosmopoli: privately printed, 1889.

Colville, William F. *Philosophy and Psychology of Human Relations*. Davenport, IA: Psychological Publishing, 1914.

Le convent en rue. New York: Erotica Biblion Society, 1899.

Crawley, Ernest. *The Mystic Rose*. London: Methuen, 1927.

Cruise of the New Decameron. 1907. Boston: privately issued for C. Nile Dix and his friends, 1920.

Daudet, Alphonse. *Sappho*. New York: Street and Smith, 1907.

Devereaux, Charles. *Venus in India*. Paris: Carrington, 1898.

Dreiser, Theodore. *Gallery of Women*. 2 vols. New York: Liveright, 1929.

Ellis, Havelock. *Marriage Today and Tomorrow*. San Francisco: Westgate, 1929.

——. *Studies in the Psychology of Sex*. 3 vols. Philadelphia: Davis, 1903.

Feydeau, Ernest. *Orange Blossoms: The Story of a Beautiful Marchioness under the Second Empire* [c. 1880]. Paris: Privately Printed, 1903.

Flaubert, Gustave. *The First Temptation of St. Anthony*. Translated by Rene Francis. New York: Brentano's, 1915.

Fontaine, Jean de la. *Tales and Novels of J. de la Fontaine*. London: Society of English Bibliophiles, 1896.

Forel, Auguste Henri. *The Sexual Question*. New York: Rebman, 1908.

Fornaro, Carlo de. *The Arabian Droll Stories*. New York: Lotus Society, 1929.

Gourmont, Remy de. *Natural Philosophy of Love*. Translated by Ezra Pound. London: Casanova Society, 1926.

Green Girls. N.p.: Fuckwell, 1900.

Haggard, Andrew C. P. *Madame de Staël, Her Trials and Triumphs*. New York: G. H. Doran, 1922.

Hecht, Ben, and Maxwell Bodenheim. *Cutie: A Warm Mama*. Chicago: privately
   printed, 1924.
Hermann, John. *What Happens*. Paris: Contact, 1926.
Krafft-Ebing, Richard von. *Psychopathia Sexualis*. Philadelphia: Davis, 1893.
Kuprin, Alex. *Yama (The Pit), A Novel*. Translated from the Russian. New York:
   privately printed, 1922.
La Maziere, Pierre. *The Brothel*. New York: private printing, 1930.
Lawrence, D. H. *Pornography and Obscenity*. London: Faber, 1929.
———. *Sun*. Unexpurgated Version. N.p.: privately printed, 1929.
Loti, Pierre. *A Spahi's Love Story*. Illustrated by Gaston Trilleau. Paris: Charles
   Carrington, 1907.
Louys, Pierre. *The Collected Tales of Pierre Louys*. Illustrated by John Austen.
   Chicago: Argus, 1930.
———. *Leda*. Translated by M. S. Buck. New York: privately printed, 1920.
———. *Les aventures du roi Pausole*. Paris: E. Fasquelle, 1901.
———. *Satyrs and Women*. New York: Covici, 1930.
———. *The Twilight of the Nymphs*. New York: Pierre Louys Society, 1927.
———. *Woman and Puppet: A Spanish Romance*. Translated and adapted by G. F.
   Monkshood [pseud. William James Clarke]. New York: Brentano's, 1908.
Lubbock, John. *The Pleasures of Life*. London: Macmillan, 1899.
Lucas, Netley. *Ladies of the Underworld*. New York: J. H. Sears, 1927.
Lys, Claudia de. *How the World Weds*. New York: Martin, 1929.
Machen, Arthur. *The Shining Pyramid*. Chicago: Covici-McGee, 1923.
Martial. *Epigrams*. Translated by Walter C. A. Ker. 2 vols. New York: Putnam's,
   1919.
Morant, Georges Soulie de. *Eastern Shame Girl*. Translated and illustrated by
   Marcel Avond. New York: privately printed, 1929.
The Mystic Rose from the Garden of the King. Translated by Fairfax Cartwright.
   London: privately printed, 1898.
The Old Man Young Again. Translated from the Arabic by an English Bohemian.
   Paris: C. Carrington, 1898.
Ovid. *The Love Books of Ovid*. London: J. Lane, 1925.
Perceau, Louis. *Douze sonnets lascifs: Pour accompagner la suite s'aquarelles
   intitulée* Les Delassements d'Eros. N.p., 1925.
Proal, Louis. *Passion and Criminality in France*. Paris: C. Carrington, 1901.
Rachilde. *Monsieur Venus*. Brussels: Auguste Brancart, 1884.
Roscaud, Count. *Human Gorillas: A Study of Rape with Violence*. Paris:
   C. Carrington, 1901.
Royer, Louis Charles. *Au pays des hommes nus*. Paris: Les Editions de France, 1929.
Sade, Marquis de. *Dialogue between a Priest and a Dying Man*. c. 1780. Chicago:
   Covici, 1927.

Sala, George Augustus. *The Mysteries of Verbena House; or, Miss Bellasis Birched for Thieving.* London: privately printed, 1882.

Sale, Antoine de la. *The Fifteen Joys of Marriage.* New York: E. P. Dutton, 1926.

Serviez, Jacques Roergas de. *The Roman Empresses.* Translated by Bysse Molesworth. 1752. New York: American Anthropological Society, 1925.

Silvestre, Armand. *Le Nu au salon.* Paris: E. Bernard, 1880.

Steckel, William. *Frigidity in Woman, in Relation to Her Love Life.* 2 vols. Introduced by Emil A. Gutheil. Authorized English Version by James S. van Teslaar. New York: Grove Press, 1926.

Stendhal. *Stendhal on Love.* With Preface to the edition of 1842. New York: Brentano's, 1916.

Stiles, Henry Reed. *Bundling, Its Origins, Progress, and Decline in America.* Albany, NY: Joel Munsell, 1869.

Stopes, Marie Charlotte Carmichael. *Sex and the Young.* New York: Putnam's, 1926.

The Strange Confessions of Monsieur Mountcairn. New York: Samuel Roth (private), 1928.

Summers, Montague. *The Vampire in Europe.* London: Paulk, Trench, Trubner, 1929.

Symonds, John Addington. *Studies in Sexual Inversion.* 1928. New York: Bell, 1984.

Tips to Maidens. London and New York: Erotica Biblion Society, 1901.

Vincent, Arthur. *Twelve Bad Women.* London: Unwin, 1897.

Voltaire. *The Princess of Babylon.* London: Bladon, 1768.

The Way of a Virgin. Compiled by L. and C. Brovan. London: Brovan Society, 1922.

INDEX

pornography: and actresses, 154–156, 161–162, 168, 171, 173–175, 179, 298n103; appeal of, 154, 295n64, 297n101, 297–298n102, 302–303n91; and collecting, 153–156, 248–250, 292n42; and foot fetishism, 229–233, 239; and recent consumption, 259–260. *See also* Belasco

"Portrait of a Lady with Red Hair" (Mrs. Leslie Carter), 209

Potter, Cora, 236

Potter, Paul M., 177, 189

Pray, Malvina, 5

Price, E. D., 191

prostitution, 4, 5, 7, 79, 96, 107, 119, 150, 152, 154–156, 162, 174, 182, 211, 220–221, 223–238, 241, 255, 298n103, 303n106

Puccini, Giacomo, 258, 311n4

Puck. See Keppler, Joseph

Pygmalion (Shaw), 186

Pygmalion and Galatea (Gilbert), 150

Quality Street (Barrie), 121

queer, 284n23; and green, 110–111, 120, 140; and red, 110–111, 120; as term, 77, 102, 282n113; and violet, 110, 117, 120–121

race: and cultural hierarchy, 13, 15–16, 51–52, 68, 81, 97–98, 130, 179, 182, 184, 211, 214, 216–220, 222, 229, 232, 235, 244, 249–255, 258–259; and ethnicity, 76–77; and sexual/gender differentiation, 51–52, 71, 80, 156–158. *See also* Irish identity; Jewish identity; whiteness

Rains, Claude, 210, 310n6

Ranous, Dora Knowlton, 34, 35, 36

realism, 53; as goal of acting training, 161–163, 167–175, 179, 183, 199,

202–203, 206–208, 236–237. *See also* Catholicism; scenery and decor

recapitulation theory, 51–52, 80–81

Rehan, Ada: and American Girl, 67–70; and animal nature, 50, 55, 61, 62; as athlete, 50, 62; and Daly, 32, 48–71; earnings, 56; and female fans, 57–60; as grande-maitresse, 50, 67; and Irish Catholic identity, 49–50, 56–57, 71; and John Drew, 48, 52–55, 61, 62–66; as Katharine in *Taming of the Shrew*, 32, 60–65; as model for statue of Justice, 67–70, 97; as Spirit of Comedy, 48, 49; star appeal, 50, 52–53, 57–59, 62, 64, 66–71; as Trilby, 48–49, 56, 70–71

"Repka Stroon" (Belasco), 250, 253, 254

respectability: as social value, 7, 11, 14, 17, 29, 47, 59, 118, 128, 160, 202

Rich, Frank, 260

Richepin, Jean, 220, 221

Ring Cycle (Wagner), 250

Rip Van Winkle (Boucicault), 150

Ristori, Adelaide, 14

Robbins, Phyllis, 100, 102, 116–118, 131, 133

Robertson, W. Graham, 48, 50, 62, 71

Rockefeller, John D., 244

Rockefeller, Mrs. John D., 135

Romeo and Juliet (Shakespeare), 119

Roosevelt, Theodore, 135, 218, 253

Rose of the Rancho, The (Tully and Belasco), 255

Rostand, Edmond, 106, 132–133, 135

Sade, Marquis de, 248

Said, Edward, 217

Salome (character), 90, 92, 94, 108, 130, 141, 145, 151–152, 211, 250, 252

Salome (Wilde), 107, 123

STUDIES IN THEATRE HISTORY AND CULTURE